The Reporter Who Knew Too Much

The Reporter Who Knew Too Much

*Harrison Salisbury and
the* New York Times

Donald E. Davis and Eugene P. Trani

ROWMAN & LITTLEFIELD PUBLISHERS, INC.
Lanham • Boulder • New York • Toronto • Plymouth, UK

4|23|13
ww
#45-

Published by Rowman & Littlefield Publishers, Inc.
A wholly owned subsidiary of The Rowman & Littlefield Publishing Group, Inc.
4501 Forbes Boulevard, Suite 200, Lanham, Maryland 20706
www.rowman.com

10 Thornbury Road, Plymouth PL6 7PY, United Kingdom

British Library Cataloguing in Publication Information Available

Library of Congress Cataloging-in-Publication Data

Davis, Donald E., 1936–
The reporter who knew too much : Harrison Salisbury and The New York Times / Donald E. Davis and Eugene P. Trani.
p. cm.
Includes bibliographical references and index.
ISBN 978-1-4422-1949-6 (cloth : alk. paper)—ISBN 978-1-4422-1951-9 (electronic)
1. Salisbury, Harrison E. (Harrison Evans), 1908-1993. 2. Journalists—United States—Biography. 3. Foreign correspondents—United States—Biography. 4. New York times. I. Trani, Eugene P. II. Title.
PN4874.S266D38 2012
070.92—dc23 [B]
2012026756

The paper used in this publication meets the minimum requirements of American National Standard for Information Sciences Permanence of Paper for Printed Library Materials, ANSI/NISO Z39.48-1992.

Printed in the United States of America

For our mentor, Professor Robert H. Ferrell—
teacher, scholar, role model.

Contents

Chapter One

Journeyman Journalist

Condolences flooded Charlotte Salisbury's mailbox after her husband's death on July 5, 1993, at the age of eighty-four. They had first met in 1955, but it was not until 1964 when she was fifty that they married—a second for him and a third for her. He referred to her as his "love" and "comrade." She called him "Harry" and had always realized that Harrison was important to American reporting and needed space. David Levine's whimsical pen-and-ink sketch of Harrison for the *New York Review of Books* in 1967 was a good sign that Harrison was no ordinary journalist.[1] Levine pictured him as lean and mustachioed, with fingers outstretched to his Remington Standard typewriter. Homages to the writer portrayed him as a mighty journalist of the daily news, an editor of the *New York Times*, a winner of Pulitzer Prizes, a founder of the op-ed page, a Russia and China expert, and an author of twenty-nine books.

Charlotte, Harrison's wife of almost thirty years, contrasted Levine's caricature with her favorite picture of him, the one she kept on her end table, the one with a soft smile and warmly glowing eyes. That was her Harry, the one she remembered best.[2] Nevertheless, she soon came to realize his fans wanted to cherish a giant. Not only had America lost a titan of journalism, she thought, but it also mourned a literary lion.[3]

Colleagues and contemporaries were exuberant in their praises and saddened by a heartfelt loss. *New York Times* columnist Russell Baker summed up Harrison's lifetime of reporting: "The work was so important that a grown man could be proud of doing it well." Harrison's protégé, David Halberstam, thought of Harrison and Charlotte as "role models" and referred to him as an "American original." Halberstam's friend and fellow journalist David Remnick wrote, "I am so terribly sorry that Harrison is gone. I can only tell you that as a journalist and as a man he was a great hero to me, an absolute example of what it was, and is, to report honestly, to write honestly, and to live honestly." Hedrick Smith, like Remnick part of the generation after Harrison on the Moscow beat, told Charlotte, "He was always going to the heart of the matter, whether in Hanoi or Moscow or Birmingham or 43rd Street." Arthur O. Sulzberger Jr., publisher of the *New York Times*, summed up everyone's thoughts: "I would often subject my actions or decisions to a simple test: 'What would Harrison think?'"[4]

Salisbury's friends echoed the journalists' tributes. Helen Frankenthaler, the American abstract expressionist painter, said of him, "What an elegant and hearty man he was!" She continued, "His generosity of spirit, his humor, his patience[; he] was never too busy to pause for consideration." John V. Lindsay, former mayor of New York City, echoed others in expressing the "terrible shock" of Harrison's passing. The diplomat George F. Kennan wrote Charlotte, "I think you know how much both his life and his work meant to me. His contribution to America's understanding of Russia and China was unique." Former President Richard Nixon told Charlotte that Harrison was a "fine reporter, a fair critic, a good friend and always a gentleman." Gwendolyn Brooks, America's poet laureate, concluded her condolences with an original poem, "Goodbye to Harrison Salisbury, Who Introduced Me to Russia":

A colon is tense.
A semi-colon relaxes a little.
Such facts he knew.
He knew also how to enjoy, how to nourish, when and how to review, how to edit and tally.
And finally he was a skilled hand at the wheel of coordination.
The world will miss the quick-stepping body that served itself and the world, wisely.
The world will miss the supporting spirit, the furioso, the andantes.
Bravo.[5]

Eric Pace's obituary in the *New York Times*, July 7, 1993, outlined the arc of Salisbury's career. Pace cited his leading assignments in Chicago, Washington, DC, New York City, London, and Moscow. Squeezed among these were Birmingham, Alabama—with its resulting libel suit—his editorship of national news coverage at the *Times* during Kennedy's assassination; Hanoi; the Balkans; and, then, China and its orbit. Pace quoted Turner Catledge, former *New York Times* editor: "Mr. Salisbury was versatile, a 'journalistic one-man band.'"[6] The *Times* op-ed page was the start of its kind, and Harrison was its first full-time editor.

Two collections of testimonials appeared, one in the *Proceedings of the American Philosophical Society* and the other in the *Nieman Reports* of Harvard University. John B. Oakes, once editor of the *New York Times* editorial page, wrote that Harrison was much more than a celebrated journalist, historian, political analyst, editor, author, or correspondent: "Salisbury had become by the time of his death widely recognized as one of America's most versatile men of letters." Yet, he continued, Harrison was always a reporter. "One morning in late December of 1966, readers of the *Times* were startled to see on the front page a dispatch, bylined Harrison Salisbury and datelined Hanoi." He had personally experienced B-52 bombings from a makeshift shelter in the capital. As president of the American Academy, the Institute of Arts and Letters, and the Authors' League, he had focused his attentions on freedom of thought and the press. At age eighty, he was in Beijing working on a TV documentary when the bloody massacre at Tiananmen Square took place beneath his window. Result: *Tiananmen Diary: Thirteen Days in June*, published soon after the riots. Age barely slowed his output. His book *The New Emperors* came out in 1992, and his last essays in 1993, under the title *Heroes of My Time*.[7]

Playwright Arthur Miller wrote of Harrison that he had a particular sense for finding the "power nerve of an event," by which he meant, "the spine of power relations which the event cuts across." Miller agreed with Oakes: "Fundamentally, he was a reporter down to the end, but one with an awesome moral courage. He really knew no favorites when it came to telling the facts." Of Harrison's books, Miller cited at least two of lasting permanence: *The New Emperors* about Mao Zedong and *The 900 Days* on the Nazi siege of Leningrad. Miller ended this tribute to his friend by writing, "above all perhaps, Harrison Salisbury was a necessary writer. He had the constitution of a camel, the will of a military commander, and the sensuous soul of a poet."[8]

Thomas Whitney, translator, journalist, and closest friend, told of first meeting Harrison in 1949 at the Hotel Metropole in Moscow. In July 1953, he related, Harrison was ready to break the story on the "strange and threatening events leading up to the death of Stalin and its rapidly developing aftermath." In 1955, the resulting articles won him his first Pulitzer for international reporting. That was just one of many great scoops, according to Whitney. He got wind of Khrushchev's secret speech from a telephone conversation at the *Times* newsroom in 1956. By 1957, he had run a series on the Soviet Union's satellites in Eastern Europe and the great Russia-China rift. That effort won for him a second, shared Pulitzer as part of the *Times* foreign journalists' team.

In *Nieman Reports*, David Halberstam recounted throwing a birthday party for Harrison even though Harry was in China and working on his book *The Long March*. When the guests assembled to honor the absentee journalist, Carol Sulzberger, wife of Arthur Ochs "Punch" Sulzberger, chairman of the *New York Times*, remarked, "There's no one here but people who have caused trouble for the *New York Times*." Clifton Daniel, former managing editor of the *New York Times*, remembered his friend as "one of the great newspapermen of the 20th century." His personal history was the history of the twentieth century. This was especially true, Daniel continued, for his two great fields of expertise—Russia and China. In 1966, Daniel suggested that Harrison circle China, perhaps even helping to get a visa to go there, since the Chinese were not issuing them to American reporters. After circling, he was invited to Hanoi for the biggest scoop of his life: his articles on the U.S. bombing campaign. "Harrison," Daniel noted, "had blown the lid off again, and LBJ and Company were furious." Those articles caused a general firestorm. There were even, *Times* war correspondent Gloria Emerson wrote, "men in the newsroom who did not want to shake his hand." That kind of political animosity cost him another Pulitzer Prize in 1967.

Arthur Miller once observed, "He had a way of emitting cold in the presence of bullshit, and real heat when truth was spoken." Roger Wilkins termed Salisbury's protégés at the *Times* "Harrison's Revolutionaries." Vladimir Pozner, Russian TV personality and reporter, labeled him the quintessential American, and irreplaceable. Once the great Russian writer Alexander Solzhenitsyn caught him putting a clean-side-up page of typing paper into his Remington Standard, and he asked Harrison what he was doing now: "HES was brisk. 'I have delivered the manuscript for that book,' he said, 'I am starting the new one.' But you must be a horse!" Solzhenitsyn quipped.

Clifton Daniel wrote that Harrison worked furiously to the end, and a review of his last book, *Heroes of My Time*, was due out that next Sunday after his death: "Last July 5, he quietly ended his career and his life with his head on his wife's shoulder as she was driving them home from a happy holiday weekend. He was 84 years old."[9] He had died of a heart attack. A Harvard friend, Ross Terrill, jotted in his diary,

> Harrison Salisbury is dead. His was such a rich life, you could almost say a complete life. On virtually everything he was interested in, he had the chance, and seized the chance, to write about something. So the world has a rather complete record of Harrison Salisbury's experiences and thoughts. It must have made him very happy.
>
> I knew him only for a short span; still that was over twenty years. I enjoyed his company. His mind was questing, he always had a new project (or two) underway, he was full of questions for me about China. He combined vision, practicality, and energy in a rare way.[10]

♦♦ 1 ♦♦

Harrison Evans Salisbury always remained that kid from 107 Royalston Avenue, Minneapolis, Minnesota. No distance, time, or achievements erased his ties to his roots. "It was home [and] hardly a day of my life was to pass without my thinking about it. In strange cities I put myself to sleepwalking through the rooms at 107."[11]

He was born at 107 Royalston, the house his grandfather built, on November 14, 1908, and he spent much of his early life there, learning old-fashioned values from his family. During flights of nostalgia, recorded in memoir and letters, he recalled vivid moments like colorful panels of a renaissance fresco. His mother, Georgiana, calling him home from play, "Bunny! Bunny! Time to come in. You'll catch your death of cold." As an old man, he remembered his children's regiment standing guard before Tsar Nicholas II's Winter Palace. He looked out from under his gray felt Budënny helmet with its red star, wore a great Red Army coat and high Cossack boots, and carried a Berdan rifle. He was too young to hear Lenin proclaim, "All power to the Soviets!" Only later did he peruse John Reed's *Ten Days That Shook the World*, where he encountered the Red Guards' storming of the Winter Palace.[12] When this fourth grader came in from a Minneapolis snowstorm, Petrograd vanished, and he was home again. He leaned his roughly carved two-by-four rifle beside the kitchen door and sat at the dining room table for a plate of pork and beans. He wistfully recalled, "I've looked back a hundred times at that nine-year-old youngster, particularly during my long years in Russia, wondering whether, in fact, I was 'just playing.'"[13]

The once-fashionable Oak Lake Addition of the 1880s had, by 1918, turned from stuffy Victorianism into something of a Jewish ghetto. In February 1918, Harrison's best friend was Reuben "Rub" Rosen. His father, Nathan, regaled the boys with stories of his escape from tsarist Russia, from pogroms, from military service, from Black Hundreds reactionaries and Stolypin neckties. Nathan had turned up in London, then Winnipeg, and now Minneapolis. The boys sat around a samovar and sipped tea through a lump of sugar. Nathan told them how Tsar Nicholas II and then Prime Minister Alexander Kerensky of the Provisional Government were finished and how the Bolshevik's Vladimir Lenin and Leon Trotsky were changing the world by revolution. Bunny added these names to his era's favorites—Floyd Gibbons of the *Chicago Tribune*, General John "Blackjack" Pershing, Lord H. H. Kitchener, British nurse and martyr Edith Cavell, and mayor of Minneapolis Colonel George E. Leach.[14]

As he shared in Rosen's Russian adventures and the turbulence of wartime Minneapolis, so also he devoured his grandfather's library by age thirteen. It was a nineteenth-century treasure trove of everything from English novelist Charles Dickens to American poet John Greenleaf Whittier. Through his father, Percy, he became a Theodore Roosevelt Bull-Mooser against Yellow Dog Woodrow Wilson. With his aunt Sue Salisbury's Red Cross letters from Paris, he learned about the horrors of World War I. Governor J. A. A. Burnquist whipped Minnesota into a pro-war frenzy. Christmas always illustrated Minnesota's financial stagnation, because Percy had the habit of acting the part of Santa for his family by buying radios, freezers, bikes, and the like. They were all charged against his life insurance because salaries at the factory had been cut and cut and cut again. [15] But the real world had cut short his father's college education in the financial panic of 1893. He dropped into the bag business for the great flour mills, where he and his family remained. Percy's personal philosophy, he told his son, was "If a thing is worth doing, it is worth doing well." With the grain boom bursting in 1920, Minnesota's and the Salisbury's economic depression began. [16]

Georgiana championed his education, got him into summer school, and tried to enroll him into the *keder*, a Jewish school, but the rabbi objected. Ethnicity was an important aspect of 107 Royalston for it bordered on the Russian-Jewish quarter at Sixth Avenue and Royalston. "Here," he wrote, "everyone spoke Yiddish and I was a goy." His friends and playmates in grammar school were of Russian-Jewish origin. Poor as they were, Harrison would later come to believe they were Russia's greatest gift to America: "Russia's tragedy, America's fortune." In school, he got good grades, but on the streets it was all wits and fists. Beyond the schoolyard, there was Liberty Theater and the fantasy film world of Buster Keaton and Harold Lloyd.

In 1922, at the age of fourteen, Harrison accompanied Georgiana and his only sister, Jan, to the East Coast. Percy could not leave his job, so he put his son in charge with some caring words: "You are to look out for your mother and Janet, as you are the man of the party. Always be a gentleman and never foolhardy in taking chances in having an accident." In these sealed orders, to be opened only after the journey began, Percy reminded Harry of his Boy Scout principles, adding, make a good impression, be polite and please, thank others, do things without being told; remember this as an unusual opportunity in "seeing a little of the world." [17] They traveled to Washington, DC, and up to New York City.

Georgiana did not share Percy's caution. She was one for risk and adventure, a family trait. Her brother Scott Ford Evans rushed to the Klondike in 1900. He made enough money to join and run a Baltimore company, but he skimmed the till. In the middle of seeking his million, he died of a heart attack. Her other brother, Wesley, took to drink and deserted his wife and daughters, finally shooting himself in a New Orleans flophouse.

Georgiana herself dreamed of becoming a writer, reading all the English novels. She was subject to violent hysterics and daydreams—one of which was that her son must become an author or journalist. Aunt Sue Salisbury came closest to being a writer. After all, she was the friend of the novelist Dorothy Canfield Fisher. Sue edited a children's magazine and always encouraged her nephew. Harrison got into the habit of writing and soon was typing seventy words per minute. This skill served him well the rest of his life, as he admitted having terrible handwriting and spelling. Even so, he graduated two years ahead of his class at North High School, where he had helped edit its annual, *The Polaris*, and participated in its Philatelic Society. Salisbury entered the University of Minnesota at sixteen. He always blamed his comparatively young age for his reticence around girls, who only wanted to date older boys. [18]

He majored in journalism, became a cub reporter for the campus *Minnesota Daily*, and ended up its editor. The *New York World* was his bible and the Muckrakers his gods—H. L. Mencken, Upton Sinclair, and Frank Norris. He nourished himself on a diet of the *New Yorker*, *Vanity Fair*, and *American Mercury*. His passions were the novels of Fitzgerald and Hemingway. "I and my friends became Hemingway, that is, monosyllabic, repetitive, cynical: the Lost Generation." Then, of course, there was his college English teacher, Dr. Anna von Helmholtz Phelan, who taught him how to write. Here he also learned how to survive. He had to if he wanted to remain in her seminar. He spent two years in the Phelan Circle and acquired a literary taste. Toward the end, Harrison worked his way from a faded Algonquin style to his own voice. The university was all meat and potatoes, all facts and figures. It was neither Socrates' Athens nor Robert Hutchins' University of Chicago, places stressing excellence, brilliance, individual initiative. Nevertheless, the University of Minnesota was home to Oscar Firkins, the best critic of American theater, who became a mentor to the young man. "What he had," as Harrison put it, "was taste, knowledge, love, style, humor, analysis and devotion to the theater—the whole theater from the Greeks to Broadway. . . . No one taught me more. And to rebel. Never to accept banality. That was the main thing." [19]

In the spring of 1927, Harrison dropped out of school to earn enough cash to return, while helping support his family. Leslie Harkness, editor of the *Minneapolis Journal*, told him, "You'll get a better education on the *Journal* than at the university." Harrison remarked that in a way he was right. Harrison had hired on at the *Journal* because of a story he had scooped: the St. Paul airport had been flooded, out of service, and the problem concealed. That story was his first of many scoops, and it became a front-page, banner headline. At only eighteen, he started on his lifelong career, beginning at only fifteen dollars a week. Cheap wages meant older men moved on and cubs advanced. Starting with obituaries and traffic accidents, he progressed to bigger stories such as tornadoes, bank robberies, and interviews with the mayor and governor. Salisbury received a strong letter of recommendation from Harkness when he returned to school after putting in two summer vacations with the *Journal* : "he has proven himself careful, accurate and efficient [therefore] consider him one of the best men that has ever come to the *Journal* without previous newspaper training. His ability to learn quickly and profit by every experience placed him on a par with men of much more experience within a short time."[20]

Harrison returned to the University of Minnesota in the autumn of 1929 and edited its college newspaper, the *Minnesota Daily.* He was a member of the Gray Friar Honorary Senior Society, journalism's Sigma Delta Chi, and the *Gopher Yearbook.* Exposés were the order of the day. That got Harrison and the *Daily* into trouble. He led a crusade against a new university rule forbidding smoking in the library's vestibule. The penalty was a year's suspension. He flouted the rule and paid the price. That stunt made front-page copy at the *New York Times*, in a story that quoted Dean E. E. Nicholson, who charged Salisbury with a deliberate, public defiance of the regulations. Oscar Firkins believed the penalty disproportionate to the act, and he continued to invite Salisbury to student gatherings at his home. Afterward, Harrison called the United Press (UP) office in neighboring St. Paul and was hired there.[21] Aunt Sue considered his smoking incident fortunate. If he got to New York, he would not be unknown.[22]

When he returned to the university, Salisbury had his first love affair with a girl named Jean. He drove her around in his Packard, embraced her passionately, even getting his hands on her breasts. When he pulled away, she asked why. "I must be a man," he said. "To this day," he later admitted, "I don't know what I meant." She decided to go to the University of Texas to study with Dr. Hermann Muller, a geneticist who won a Nobel Prize in 1946. Harrison kept writing her that fall of 1929. He wondered whether she was "out celebrating a Texas team's victory or sitting with the Mullers chatting about the latest in the entomological world or just what."[23] In the end, Jean married a man named Wilson. "Your marriage created a real sensation up here, as you can guess. . . . I congratulate you, no less than he."[24] Salisbury had suffered a passionate encounter and rejection.

Salisbury, amid love and career, found his United Press bosses tight with the company's money but lavish with its praises. UP identified him as HES, his initials, a nickname that stuck. Year one of the Great Depression, 1930, was tough. As he put it, there were no help agencies, no welfare, no relief, no social security, no unemployment insurance, no federal works programs. These absences formed the core of his first UP story, which he wired. "KA-BOOM," he recalled. New York called within the hour, responding to a message received from the *Minneapolis Journal* : "Either the UP would kill that story and fire its author or the *Journal* would cancel the service." Salisbury's St. Paul boss, Hillier Krieghbaum, was astonished at the *Journal* 's reaction, and so was Chicago's UP office. His job was saved, but the *Journal* kept muttering, "that goddamn radical kid from the university." The big bosses in New York said, "O.K.," but kept his name off the wire until the flap cooled. Hundreds of the same lessons lay ahead for Salisbury: "Shut up! Don't rock the boat! Keep those unpleasant truths to yourself! The truth, I was ultimately to learn, is the most dangerous thing. There are no ends to which men of power will go to put out its eyes."[25]

From Minneapolis, UP sent HES to Chicago in 1931, just after he had finally graduated from the university in 1930 after the year's suspension. HES referred to Chicago as the big time or the best test. "I knew on that night train to Chicago that I would carry 107 within me like a cave to crawl in when lonely or distant or fearful." His fantasy was that he was going to take Chicago by storm from his cheap room at the Berkshire Hotel, "a kind of glorified whorehouse or cheap theatrical hotel for $6.37 a week, sharing a room with my fellow inmate of the Chicago UP."[26] From the Berkshire, he wrote an unsigned dispatch about an amateur bootlegger being blown to pieces by his concoction.[27] Chicago was immersed in Prohibition-style gang wars and Al Capone. Harrison sat two feet from the mobster for twelve days, covering Capone's income tax evasion trial for UP at the old Federal Building. Capone tried to bribe and intimidate his jurors. He had headed Chicago's "Outfit," dealing in bootlegging, illegal gambling, prostitution, and gangland's 1929 Saint Valentine's Day Massacre. His conviction left Harrison stunned. After a long trial, Capone got off with only eleven years and heavy fines for tax evasion.[28] HES realized Prohibition was a "cozy conspiracy, everyone in it for the bucks, everyone in on the payoff—the gangs, the government, the police, the businessmen, the banks, the quiet and respectable interests that owned those fine old breweries where the beer was brewed."

Robert T. Loughran, a police reporter who never wrote anything, now signed all of Salisbury's leads, but he ordered a rewrite for everyone else. It was the Chicago of Big Bill Thompson, where a half-million people were out of work. According to Salisbury, President Herbert Hoover did not have a clue about what to do. On weekends, Harrison would visit his mother's niece and her fascist husband, Dapper Dan. Sometimes he would go to the suburb of Libertyville and see a distant cousin and her husband who, in their seventies, were reduced to nothing: "the state, the government, society did not feel any responsibility for what happened to Emma and George Faulkes."[29] Salisbury was lucky. He had a job.

By March 1933, Franklin D. Roosevelt was president, and a possible assassin's target. Loughran promised Harrison a big scoop: Mayor Anton Cermak was due to be bumped off along with the president. This was going to be, Loughran boasted, "one helluva big story, the biggest goddamn story you'll ever get your asses into." Only the banks kept going south, taking people's money and the American dream with them. Cleveland and Detroit followed Chicago down the Great Depression's tubes, with Salisbury there to cover the story. For days, he huddled at the Detroit ticker tape and then from Miami came news of an assassination attempt on FDR and the wounding of Cermak. The promised scoop had switched from Chicago to Miami. HES, UP's scoop artist, was foiled. Whatever the double cross, there was never a word of warning out of him. He never lifted a finger to prevent a possible crime. He just wanted to get the Cermak scoop and run.[30]

Into his rough-and-tumble world, a little leprechaun stepped in: "an Irish minx, with dancing eyes, a smile to melt a miser's heart." Except she was Hungarian, not Irish. His friend Julian Bentley asked HES to take her off his hands. Harrison recounted, "The moment that tiny woman danced into the room, I knew she was meant for me." Seven months later, on April 1, 1933, at 11 a.m., he married Mary Jane Hollis at the county clerk's office, fourth floor, Chicago City Hall. After a wedding breakfast, he showed up for work at 1 p.m. for Saturday's twelve-hour shift. They took an apartment at number 8 Walton Place, next door to the home of Jane Addams, the famous social worker. Mary had come up to Chicago from the Illinois coalfields. It was a Depression-era marriage that presented HES with a dilemma: "I loved Mary but I knew by now that my Irish lassie was not all spice and sparkle. She had a fiend of a temper and spent money like Saturday night in a mining camp." He brushed all this aside though a cold voice rebuked him "for leading an immature young woman onto a trail that could easily end badly." It would, finally, spell tragedy. It was, he admitted, "a savage wrecking of lives which need not have been."[31]

In later years, Harrison reflected on his first marriage: he was too young, too innocent, too backward when it came to girls. Mary's parents had died when she was ten, and she had grown up in the care of a neighbor. His hasty romance was egged on by his parents' stern disapproval, especially Georgiana's. Mary had come to Chicago, returned home to Evansville, and reappeared in Chicago. "I felt terribly responsible and sorry for this little girl and so, depression or not, job or not, we went down to the Municipal Bldg on Saturday and got married." He had defied his family. Though it was a big love, within three weeks, "I was certain, especially inside of me, that it was a mistake. That we would have one hell of a time making it. And that if so I would have to carry a great burden of understanding and changing my own way of life and philosophy to make it go." Family opposition made him determined to prove himself. There was nothing wrong with Mary, nor had she represented herself to be something she was not. He simply would not recognize his "inability to talk to this girl whom I married or ever really to be in the same world with her." She came to have the same feelings toward him.[32]

♦♦ 2 ♦♦

When the Chicago World's Fair of 1933 opened, HES pounded out a story about it on his Remington. It scored. His career with United Press skyrocketed. At twenty-five, he was a UP star covering the fair. Harrison followed this hit with stories on the fair's pavilions; on fan dancing burlesque queen Sally Rand, the fair's sex symbol; on Commodore Balbo's flight over the fair grounds; on Commander Settle's balloon rides for the kiddies. He was finally writing under his own name, not under Loughran's byline. Harrison's vaunting ambition paid off, and the United Press sent him to Washington to cover President Roosevelt's New Deal.

It was a huge promotion. The Salisburys invited their friends to join them. They judged Washington to be a fine old southern city, full of fine old Kentucky colonels. Friends could come down and visit, they wrote, join with the New Deal, if they could get by those colonels, have a drink, and report on FDR's budding communism. If any advice were needed, their friends could "call on the Salisburys—they know all the latest dope." It seemed a happy honeymoon for the Salisburys as well as FDR. The swift current of Roose-veltian politics carried Salisbury's career along. He and Mary Jane invited more friends to Washington. "This is," they laughed, "a very sleepy sort of place. We have all been taking long naps hoping that when we woke up we would find that Congress had gotten tired of it all and gone home, but today somebody sneezed and it woke us up and darned if Congress wasn't still all here and that was what gave me the idea of a letter. Christ you have to do something to pass the time away." They delighted in Washingtonian humor and intrigue. "Frankie is thru—and what we say, is what the neighbors say and they have it from a certain party mighty close to the top—I wouldn't want to say how close, that's how close it is."[33] HES joined journalist Heywood Broun's newspaper union, which soured his UP boss Hugh Baillie. His salary and promotions were frozen. He was assigned few good UP stories for four years. In one, however, he made the most of it.

That story was a social analysis similar to the one that had upset the *Minneapolis Journal.* Harrison traveled to Louisiana to cover the aftermath of the 1935 assassination of Senator Huey Long in Baton Rouge. Long had become a national sensation. As Salisbury put it to his friends before the tragic event occurred, "FDR better start tooting his horn or Huey will have all the play. Huey is a smart feller—that is right out of the FEED BOX, too. Down here in Washn, D.C. you hear plenty of stuff, see and lots of it is too red hot to put in a letter. They ain't much that gets past the Washn, D.C. boys, believe me."[34] Huey Long, former governor of Louisiana and now senator, had launched his share-the-wealth society in 1934. In radio broadcasts, he promoted a simple formula of every man a king: confiscate big fortunes, levy steep progressive income taxes, distribute revenues to each family of five thousand dollars, guarantee minimum annual incomes of twenty-five hundred dollars, promise shorter working hours, improve veterans' benefits, give educational subsidies to the young and pensions to the old. Long admonished FDR to keep his word and boldly told audiences, "It is not Roosevelt or ruin, it is Roosevelt's ruin!"[35] Long's meteoric rise was cut short by his murder in September 1935.

Salisbury flew to Long's funeral, taking a week down south to discover what had made the catfish Mussolini tick. "I talked to the Louisiana newspapermen, I began to get a few things straight. The vitriol and paranoia hadn't been on one side." Huey had spent millions on roads and bridges. That freed the rural poor to leave their homes and enter America's growing urban life. First as governor, then as senator, Long stole from the rich and gave to the poor.[36]

UP's Huey Long assignment demonstrated Salisbury's style and analytical prowess. It was a terse twelve-page piece featuring a flowing narrative of the reporter's journey to Baton Rouge and side trips to Alexandria and New Orleans. Salisbury girded it with explosive exposés of Louisiana's bitter poverty and the slain leader's attempts to ameliorate it.

His flight to Baton Rouge began at midnight in a Curtis Condor, refueling every hour along the way. As the meandering trip progressed through rain and fog, the Condor stopped in Richmond, Raleigh, Charlotte, Spartansburg, Atlanta, Montgomery, and Mobile before touching down in New Orleans. The radioman on the Curtis mentioned that Long, shot on the eighth, had died at 4:10 a.m. on September 10, 1935, uttering his last words, "God, don't let me die! I have so much to do!"[37] Salisbury took a small Wendell-Williams plane from there to Baton Rouge. Along the way, a fellow journalist filled him in on Long's life. The landscape below seemed all bogs and fields of red clay, so eroded that it looked terraced from the air.

He landed at the Baton Rouge airport, another of Long's monuments. Everyone there was either violently for or against Long. The cabbie made excuses for Long's assassin, Dr. Carl Austin Weiss, who had immediately been riddled by the blazing guns of Long's bodyguards. "This fellow," Salisbury remarked, "says he went to school with Weiss, that inside story is that Long made dirty remarks about Weiss' wife and that Weiss wouldn't stand for it; that bodyguards took [his] gun away from him, threw him to [the] floor and opened up on him." Salisbury took a tour of Huey's statehouse, built for ten million dollars by the same firm that constructed the Empire State Building. Huey had not trusted local contractors to get it right—all limestone on the outside, all marble on the inside. Huey's legislature had just passed his last thirty-seven laws when the kingfish was murdered in the hall of his own statehouse.

A local UP man, Coogan by name, told HES of Huey's final night and showed him the spot where the shooting took place. Coogan related that he had given Huey a copy of the *New York Daily News* picturing Long leading a cheering Louisiana State University football crowd. Huey paraded around with it, saying, "I guess that shows we're getting some recognition." Then he walked into the corridor from the legislature's chambers. Shots rang out. Coogan pointed to bloodstains on the floor. Salisbury described the scene: "The wall was chipped in four or five places. This was where the bullets of the bodyguards glanced off as they pumped them into Weiss, slumping on the corridor floor." The melodramatic atmosphere was "like a music comedy only there were too many signs of seriousness to get a hearty laugh out of it." The senator's embalmed body was brought to the statehouse on Wednesday afternoon, up the forty-eight steps to the rotunda. HES had a look: "After I saw the body, I didn't blame whoever it was that complained. He was powdered and rouged like a chorus girl, but maybe that's the way they always do it." Flowers overflowed the rotunda. Multitudes passed Huey's coffin single file. All Wednesday night workers dug his grave in the muggy heat of the front yard of the statehouse. It was a hot and crowded funeral day.

A drunk passed the capitol's pressroom, Salisbury wrote, cussing out newspapers and journalists. That was the Long attitude, according to Salisbury. "They hated the papers, especially the *New Orleans Times-Picayune* and they didn't give them any house. The papers, on the other hand, probably were responsible as much as anything for Huey's rankest dictatorial tactics. They falsified, distorted and manufactured news." Harrison accused the local papers of being directly responsible for Huey's murder. They inflamed people. He alleged, "Ultimately out of all the people in Louisiana they were certain to so work on the sensibilities of at least one individual that he would eventually try to kill Huey as they had demanded time and time again." That, in Salisbury's estimation, was the "only reasonable explanation of why this obscure, quiet, home-loving and studious doctor finally went up to the statehouse one day with a gun in his pocket and took it out and shot Huey— willing to give his own life in return." However one felt, HES admonished in his report, that was not the way to fight and, if you did, you had no complaint if the other side "throws all principle to the winds in meeting the attack."

Salisbury took a side trip to Alexandria and New Orleans, "because it gave me for the first time, a glimpse of what was behind Huey Long, what sort of country produced him and why he could not help having been the type of demogog [*sic*] he was." The drive revealed Huey's concrete highways and bridges running past the "heartbreaking little shacks and cabins, rough, never painted, one-room and a shed." Kids crawled on dirt floors. There were no fences, no telephone wires, no signs, nothing but Huey's highways and bridges beside swamps and cabins. People never had a dollar from one year to the next ten. They never had anything, never had a chance of having anything. Huey came, gave them roads, brought them the notion something was wrong, handed them a way out. Why should only a handful of millionaire sugar barons and cotton kings thrive? Huey's roads offered a future free of travel tariffs—tariffs that previously blocked rivers, bayous, byways like artificial mountains. If you were rich, you did not like the state's bonded indebtedness, jumping from tens to hundreds of millions. Salisbury had developed his Midwestern populist sympathy for Huey into a powerful indictment of the laissez-faire system that had brought on the Great Depression. Maybe, just maybe, Huey was right.

On Sunday, Salisbury went to New Orleans for dry martinis, for shrimp Arnauld, for southern-style coffee, for petit and brandy, for a cigar, for a tour of the French Quarter and cathedral. Then he was off to nightclubs, to jazz bands, to floorshows. He was up all night and caught the morning plane to DC—a fast Douglas with only a stop in Atlanta.[38]

Baton Rouge taught Salisbury that beneath the headlines another, more profound story hides. He wrote on the plane and filed the story soon after he landed. It was a hit and ran in papers nationwide.

His first son, Michael, was born on March 16, 1939, and Georgiana came to help Mary Jane. The two women, never accepting each other, fought like proverbial cats and dogs. HES ducked out of the house and onto his DC beat. In addition to his UP work, he freelanced for magazines under various aliases, earning three times his frozen UP salary by writing for such slicks as *Periscope*, *Coronet*, and *Ken*. *Ken* was too hot: "It was violently anti-Hitler, violently anti-appeasement, violently against hypocrisy not only in Europe (where this was safe enough) but in the good old U.S.A." It was too radical, too red. Ads disappeared from *Ken* and its sister magazines, *Esquire* and *Apparel Arts*. Owner David Smart wanted to drop *Ken*. His partner Arnold Gingrich held out. Both wanted HES in Chicago as editor. The risk to his own career was too great, though he agreed with Smart's assessment: "Hitler is going to bring on World War II and Chamberlain and Daladier do not have the will to halt him." *Ken*'s crash was another lesson for Salisbury: "the truth is no defense; the truth is dangerous; it upsets apple carts."[39]

Salisbury was just turning thirty-one when World War II started. Things had settled down for him at UP. His feud was over. Mike was six months old. HES had arrived as an important UP asset, though he still freelanced. He knew DC, especially the Senate, and, increasingly, he learned about the State Department.

The German dictator's attack on Poland in 1939 changed Salisbury's life. He was transferred to New York to deal with all cables and wireless reports from London, Paris, Berlin, and Moscow. He wrote on the war's early months, the phony war, and Germany's attack on France. Salisbury located his family in a Mamaroneck home, which he bought from historian Henry Steele Commager. While spending a lovely day barbecuing on June 21,

1941, Harrison predicted to Bernie Geis, editor of *Coronet*, that Hitler would attack the USSR that weekend. Bernie did not believe it. It was 10:30 a.m. and Harrison said the Germans were already crossing the Soviet border. The phone rang. Bernie said, "That's probably it." "It is!" HES shot back.[40]

Stalin also failed to anticipate the German invasion in a massive intelligence gaffe. Increasingly immersed in foreign affairs, by February 1942 Salisbury was determined to become a war correspondent. UP filed his credentials with the U.S. government for overseas work. At the same time, his marriage was falling apart. Perhaps because of that, by December 1942 he was ready to accept a position in London as bureau chief for UP. Maybe a reprieve would help. After a routine custodial detention, the U.S. government allowed him to leave.[41]

The curtain raised on a new act in the life of the boy from 107 Royalston. The drama thrust him into a dazzling career as a foreign correspondent. It also brought him star-crossed loves. As the footlights began shining on a band of journalistic brothers—Harrison E. Salisbury, Edward R. Murrow, and Walter Cronkite—HES paid little attention to the increasing shadows cast over his own personal life. Nevertheless, his craft had improved from cub reporter, to mass circulation reporter of a world's fair, to politics in the nation's capital. Most importantly, he had probed beneath the surface of events to understand social and economic forces, as in the assassination of Senator Long. He was ready to try his hand as the head of UP's London office in the midst of a great war.

Chapter Two

Foreign Correspondent

Number 107 Royalston Avenue, Minneapolis, and 1917: they stuck in Salisbury's fondest memories. The steep, winding road from there to Chicago, to Washington, to New York joined him to a demanding employer and a testy wife. However, London offered him an escape from domestic concerns and a wartime challenge from United Press.

Number 30 Bouverie Street, London, and 1943: they remained among his happiest recollections of a foreign correspondent's life—and of his love for an American nurse he called Ellen. UP would later transfer Harrison to Algiers, to Cairo, to Teheran, and to Moscow. It was the making of a foreign correspondent's career.

Salisbury managed UP's London bureau, where he and his sixty employees reported on everything from German bombings to blackouts, from aristocratic bigwigs to British chippies. He rose at seven, took breakfast while reading the papers, and arrived at the News of the World Building by nine. Correspondence, messages, filings, and interviews awaited him. Success depended on glad-handing his way to reliable government contacts. He pursued Labourite luminaries and Conservative ministers. He chased newspaper moguls. He danced with the Mayfair crowd, took tea at Connaught's, dined at the Savoy, and sipped cocktails at the embassies. London was the epicenter of Allied planning for war in Europe. And there was Salisbury, cultivating two critical sources about this from his barnstorming: American Ambassador John Winant and USSR Ambassador Ivan Maisky.

Winant, New Hampshire's formerly republican governor, was FDR's choice to replace Joseph Kennedy in London. Salisbury and Winant discussed French and Polish problems, military strategy, and the question of opening a second front in France. It was FDR's friend Lend-Lease Administrator Averell Harriman, who really conducted the important American interests and was close to Prime Minister Winston Churchill. Other correspondents, sensing this, chose Harriman and formed an elite, which Salisbury disparaged—Edward R. Murrow, Geoffrey Parsons Jr., Helen Kirkpatrick, and Peter Daniell.[1]

Ambassador Maisky, an old Bolshevik, became Salisbury's foundation of success in London. "When I went to London in 1943, Freddy Kuh set me up with Maisky and I have known him ever since."[2] Kuh, a seasoned diplomatic correspondent for the *Chicago Sun*, took Salisbury under his tutelage. He maintained that Maisky knew more about the war than anyone else did. Salisbury first interviewed the ambassador in May 1943. "He had been serving in his post for fourteen years," Salisbury reflected, "and there was not much he didn't know." What Maisky did not say was important, and Salisbury came prepared to catch the ambassador's drift. There was, Maisky noted, the Russian victory at Stalingrad, and he speculated about the overdue opening of an Allied second front in France to relieve German pressure on the USSR. Maisky liked relating Churchill's story about oversized American divisions of fifty thousand soldiers. He laughed at their miscellaneous laundresses, milk sterilizers, hairdressers, tailors, cobblers, and whatnot. With those extras, Maisky added, there was "no use reckoning on a Second Front in Northern France in the spring of 1943."[3] Harrison caught Maisky's drift and saw him every fortnight, until Stalin recalled him in August.[4]

By July, Salisbury's discussions with Winant and Maisky ranged over international politics. England, they thought, would falter after the war. Britain's economy would only slowly revive, especially in competition with the United States. The British had liquidated their foreign assets in fighting the war. Though Churchill was a holy wonder, his formula meant England would be a junior partner to America. "No one," except Winant and Maisky, so Salisbury believed, "could face the fact that the United States had become *the* world power and was taking England's markets and production away."[5] Britain would be Hollandized, that is, reduced in status. Those Labourites who opposed American foreign policy and Churchill favored maintaining the French in Africa and working for a closer relationship with Russia rather than America. "Now, I think," Salisbury wrote in his journal, "the Conservative Party in England, which seems to have a virtual monopoly on the clever shrewd brains in English politics, realizes most of these points—though some of them be rather sensed than admitted—the way you sense you are getting old but don't admit it to yourself. And I think these people are doing whatever to avert that fate which may be inevitable."[6]

Rebuilding, even with streamlined socialist leadership, was insufficient, according to Salisbury. He believed postwar political realignments were inevitable. Churchill's reelection after the war seemed certain. France was critical for Britain's future as a shield and ally, a bulwark against a resurgent Germany aligned with Soviet Russia. A red France would bring Soviet Russia to Calais; red Europe would then stretch from Abbeville to Omsk. A democratic France, bound to England, kept "Britain's council seat at the head of the table." Salisbury concluded that, so far, neither British nor American policy toward France had succeeded. Further, there was little or no discussion about postwar Germany beyond cutting it to bits. He termed that "naïve or incredibly idealistic." This added up to "a hell of a lot of trouble settling the world's affairs when peace is declared."[7] Salisbury learned his Maisky lessons well.

By September 1943, Salisbury caught the attention of the *London Times*, though it misprinted his name as "Sandburg." Likewise, Ed Murrow of CBS became "Morrow" and Bob Bunnelle of the Associated Press ended as "Dunnelle." Harrison was "consorting with their Lordships." British media picked him as a representative of the American press. Salisbury sat at the head table, close to Lords Camrose, publisher of the *Daily Telegraph*, Rothermere of the *Daily Mail*, Kemsley of the *Daily Sketch*, and Astor of the *London Times*. Lord Burnham gave the toastmaster's speech. The media club promoted Anglo-American friendship. Camrose spoke to the great future of his paper. Young Rothermere seemed affable enough. Lord Astor was a "bit courtly and very English in manner." In addition, Harrison met American actor Clark Gable doing air force instructional films with studio director William Wyler. One evening he even dined with King Peter and Princess Alexandra of Yugoslavia. He heard Churchill speak at Guildhall. "It was very impressive."[8]

London, with all of its wartime intensity, remained for Salisbury a shining moment. "It was, of course, an incredibly confused period for me personally and the confusion continued, as you so well know, for years into the postwar life with sad and tragic results in every kind of direction. But the London days were gold, and they still are even when they were really nutty"—as he told "Ellen" years later.[9] He complained there were many "sharp edges [but] there weren't in London."[10] This improvement likely had to do with a certain woman.

He casually mentioned her as "Ellen." She was an American Red Cross nurse "of whom I was becoming very fond . . . "[11] He often traveled by bus with her to Petticoat Lane to check on street fairs at the East End before the Nazis flattened it.[12] He was drinking heavily and sleeping with many girls.[13] That spring Ellen marched by them to the center of Salisbury's life. They had breakfasts at South Audley and caught trains to High Wycombe. They frequently tramped across muddy fields, returning by moonlight to London. "How pleasant it would be," he thought, "to wander over England with Ellen, how easy I felt with her and she, I knew, with me. But I closed my mind to these because Ellen was the friend of a friend and this kind of thinking was not loyal."[14] He avoided her all summer, then relented in September and invited her to spend a day in the country. Harrison realized he should be cutting loose, not bringing more complications into his life, but "We fell in love that day. We spent the next weekend together in her flat in Weymouth Mews."[15] Fortunately for Salisbury, at almost that moment, his UP boss cabled him with orders to go to North Africa and reorganize UP's coverage there. Earl Johnson, he writes, "saved me by sending me into orbit." On October 23, 1943, he left love and London.[16]

Earl Johnson had intended to use Harrison to undermine UP chief Hugh Baillie's favorite, Virgil Pinkley, because of Pinkley's "inability—naiveté, rather, on the news side. This was a cause to which I attached myself with enormous enthusiasm."[17] They failed to budge Pinkley. Johnson salvaged Harrison's career from a battle with Pinkley by sending him off to North Africa. Harrison left Ellen perched at the Prestwick station, "looking back as long as I could at this woman with chestnut hair, red cheeks, pert nose, brown eyes and my heart in her hands, standing alone in her dark blue uniform."[18]

From Salisbury's Prestwick departure on October 23, 1943, until his accidental arrival in Astrakhan on the Caspian Sea, on January 13, 1944, he went to Algiers, then Cairo and Teheran, to cover the great wartime conferences of the Big Three. Cairo, he observed, mixed wealth and poverty—well-stocked stores alongside filth and disease. The Egyptians were not in the war and couldn't care less whether Britain or Germany won. He saw Churchill in an off-the-record press conference and made something of a hit covering Teheran. "My North African experience had been fleeting." In Algiers, General Dwight D. Eisenhower scolded him to "mind my conduct." Otherwise, it would be back to the states. "I was not taken by Eisenhower nor by his headquarters, ridden by cliques and rich with intrigue."[19] He heard from neither his wife, Mary Jane, nor his mistress, Ellen. He wrote his wife, "I got there on the button for the big break on the Teheran Conference and our play must have been something you could use for fireworks on the Fourth of July. Any rate, I never had such a sunburst of congrats, etc., in my life. So I guess that went off okay."[20]

Harrison reported on the Teheran Conference and FDR's proposal for a shuttle-bombing plan, where the Western allies would use bases in the USSR. Stalin considered it. FDR laid out a plan for a world organization, consisting of a world assembly, an executive committee, and a third component made up of what he called the Four Policemen—Russia, the United States, Britain, and China. Stalin had doubts and preferred two separate organizations—one for Europe and one for Asia. Salisbury noted Churchill presented Stalin with a sword from King George VI in celebration of the great Russian victory at Stalingrad.[21]

UP wanted Harrison back in Cairo, but because of a sudden vacancy in Moscow, UP temporarily sent him there. That temporary accident, with its string of adventures and misadventures, would result in his first book, *Russia on the Way*, and become the core of his subsequent career as a foreign correspondent and Russia expert.

◆◆ 1 ◆◆

The thrill of entering Russia took Salisbury's mind off trysts and Teheran. On January 13, 1944, he flew in a DC-3 over the Elburz Mountains into Russia, landing briefly in Baku and taking off for Astrakhan. Henry Shapiro, UP's ace correspondent in Moscow, was going on a lecture tour in the United States, and Salisbury had been assigned to replace him. He had a Russian visa but little else to prepare him—a few Russian phrases like "Ya tebya lublu" (I love you). He knew not a single Cyrillic letter. He later wrote, "But what I could not then comprehend was the real depth of my ignorance, not only about Stalin and Communist Russia, but about the eternal Russia that had existed long before the Romanovs and would persist long after the Soviets."[22] To his surprise, he would remain more permanent than temporary in Russia—from January 1944 to September 1945.

Within five days, he met newly appointed American Ambassador Averell Harriman and his daughter Kathy at their Spaso House residence. Then he was off to Katyn, accompanying a Soviet commission to investigate German accusations that the Russians had killed 4,500 Polish officers there in 1940. It was grim: bodies "neatly stacked like cordwood," each man executed with a bullet to the base of the skull, all still wearing their greatcoats and boots. Few believed the German account, but neither could the Russians then be proven guilty.[23]

Moscow's UP office, located in room 346 in the Metropole Hotel, was one floor above his own room 264. Shapiro's Russian wife, Ludmilla Nikitina, remained with him in Moscow, along with Salisbury's assistant Meyer Handler and UP courier Olga Khludova. Olga's family had been wealthy textile manufacturers, closely associated with art connoisseur Saava Morozov. "I was," Salisbury admits, "attracted to Olga the moment I saw her green eyes, *châtain* (the Russians use the French word for auburn) hair, freckled face and the lilt of her head." On Shrove Tuesday, February 22, 1944, Harrison was invited to a blini party, which Olga also attended. Another one of Harrison's misadventures began.

They spent a weekend at Zagorsk with the self-styled Anglo-American-Russian Walking Club.[24] The monks of Zagorsk had repaired and replaced whatever the commissars had removed for safekeeping from the advancing

German army in 1941. The Radonezh monastery's churches, "were wonderfully colored—pastel blue, yellows, etc., and make a thrilling sight against the snow." The Zagorsk toy factory was the industry's center, creating shapes for the rest of the country and from which people bought Zagorsk toys by the pound. On the train ride back to Moscow, an accordionist serenaded the walking club. Everyone was in good humor. "Olga and I were very close. I put my arm around her. She did not push it away."[25]

Harrison made his first trip to Leningrad on February 6, 1944. He wrote from there of the skeleton of the once great Kirov industrial works, what remained of the Peterhof Palace, and the pure barbarism of the invaders. The center of Krasnoye Selo, the former imperial residence, was flattened by the Germans, as was much of downtown Leningrad. Tikhvin railway station, retaken at great cost, had kept the ice bridge across Lake Ladoga open. Otherwise, Leningrad would have starved. Kronstadt naval fortress had remained a key to the city's defenses, and it was never taken. The city had to provide for and protect itself—in spite of Stalin—and the dictator never forgave that success. Salisbury interviewed Mayor Pyotr Popkov, who emphasized the city's heroism in the face of Nazi shellings and bombings. He stayed at the Astoria Hotel, where the plumbing failed and meals were curious combinations of GI rations, canned foods, and delicacies from Teheran. Salisbury roomed with Yale professor Jerome Davis, who had witnessed the 1917 revolution from the Astoria. Through all the evidence of carnage, Harrison confessed that he "fell in love with Leningrad. Part of it—maybe most of it—was the contrast with Moscow. But to me the people of Leningrad seemed to walk more proudly, to be brisker, intelligenter—superior in every physical and mental test—to the Russians I had seen in Moscow."[26] It was not, he maintained, a false impression. It was the Western world in Russia. Its survival left a Russia worth saving; the victory at Stalingrad rescued Russia. He wandered in and out of Leningrad "like a well-oiled newspaper correspondent at an embassy cocktail party."[27]

By Easter, April 9, 1944, he had completely settled in at Moscow's Metropole Hotel. It was back to the rounds of concerts, embassy parties, theater, and ballets. War movies were bad, but he could catch some Ginger Rogers and Fred Astair at the U.S. embassy. And, of course, there was the magnificent Moscow circus. Amid this whirl, a dangerous event broke his routine. UP's London office scooped a scandalous story, which turned out to be false. It almost cost Salisbury his Moscow job and the UP its status in Russia. He saved both.

Sam Hales, UP reporter in London, got the story on Sunday, February 13, 1944, from a Spanish diplomat. It went something like this: On November 30, 1943, at Churchill's sixty-ninth birthday party during the Teheran Conference, Marshal Semën K. Timoshenko allegedly made a noisy, drunken speech. Stalin, so the story ran, smashed a bottle of Champagne over the

Marshal's baldpate. The warrior collapsed. Hales transmitted it to UP's New York office, which put it over the national wires on February 14, without verification. It circulated on radio and to some five hundred newspapers. UP, belatedly smelling a skunk, killed it. On February 15, President Franklin D. Roosevelt called it a lie. FDR confirmed Timoshenko never attended the Teheran Conference.[28] The remainder of the story played out on two levels: public and private.

Publicly, on late Tuesday, February 22, 1944, Salisbury received a call to appear the next day at Narkomindel—the People's Commissariat for Foreign Affairs. An officer briskly escorted him to Deputy Commissar Vladimir G. Dekanozov's office. Dekanozov told him of the slanderous Timoshenko story, the first Harrison had heard of it. The commissar demanded a prompt UP public apology or else there would be no UP in Russia. Salisbury also considered the Timoshenko story bogus. He had handled Teheran communiqués for UP, and he knew of Timoshenko's absence at Teheran. Of course, he told Dekanozov, UP would do everything to limit the story's damage.[29]

UP President Hugh Baillie cabled apologies to Premier Stalin and Foreign Minister Molotov. They were dissatisfied and, through Dekanozov, demanded UP publicly apologize to its outlets. Salisbury secured Dekanozov's approval of a statement and cabled it to New York. That got on the national wires between 2:00 to 3:00 a.m. on the 24th, though not all papers printed it. The Timoshenko Affair left an ominous atmosphere in Moscow. Foreign correspondents in Russia became hostages to unflattering stories about the Soviet Union breaking anywhere else and carried by their outlets.[30]

As it turned out, that statement of apology was not good enough. Dekanozov called Salisbury back and said UP's version failed because it never called the Timoshenko story a lie. Dekanozov then handed Salisbury a new statement, "Denial by the United Press Agency," written by the Russians in what Salisbury labeled as TASS (the Telegraph Agency of the Soviet Union) style. It repeated that the story was false, acknowledged UP's apologies, and demanded steps taken by UP to preclude recurrences. Harrison then cabled to New York the new Soviet note, but no immediate response was forthcoming from UP. Once again, Salisbury was summoned to the Foreign Ministry. Molotov now received him and lectured Salisbury on Dekanozov's demands. Salisbury pointed out UP had done all that was requested. The latest note, in his opinion, would only puzzle and even antagonize readers, but UP would comply. Molotov retreated and suggested UP use its own language. UP stuck with the TASS language. In the future, Molotov inquired, could Russia use the U.S. courts to redress a grievance? Harrison said they were free to try. Each time Harrison had appeared at the Foreign Ministry, he noticed, there were notes on Dekanozov's and Molotov's desks written in red pencil. Only

Stalin used red. Over the weekend, UP carried the TASS-style note.[31] In reality, there was much more to this episode, as Salisbury's correspondence reveals.

Privately, on the day of his first appearance before Dekanozov, Wednesday, February 23, Salisbury sent a letter to Stalin with a verbatim copy of his cablegram to New York. The cablegram acknowledged, as Dekanozov had put it, the "disgraceful report of correspondent who permitted himself to report such libel and of an agency which published his report [and that it was] insulting for head of our government." Harrison had assured Dekanozov there was no malicious intent on UP's part, and he had no knowledge of the Spanish diplomat's motives. UP was "utterly [and] completely opposed [to] offending [the] head of government." UP would immediately institute an investigation and make a "public" apology. The Russian censor had translated Dekanozov's demands, but had left out the word "public" in the written statement. Salisbury pointed out the difference one word meant. "It changes it from a private to a public matter as it would have given further currency to [the] most unfortunate and fully inaccurate story [stop] would have added that if unipress has actually injured sovunion head as they report we naturally only too eager make all possible redress."[32]

In his cover letter to Stalin, Salisbury also stressed that, whatever the facts were, the UP was "utterly without malice or motive [but only wished] objectively to report the great achievements and outstanding news affecting the U.S.S.R., which is now our close and magnificent ally."[33] On the following day, he reported to Dekanozov Hugh Baillie's "sincere apologies and my assurance that appropriate measures are being taken to prevent recurrence of any such mistake from London or anywhere else."[34]

The Timoshenko flap seemed to have resolved itself by March 6, 1944. On that date, Salisbury informed Molotov that Dekanozov's new denial-apology had been transmitted to outlets receiving UP service. Salisbury privately summarized and analyzed the entire affair for Baillie. Ambassador Harriman, he noted, had recounted the event to the State Department. Harriman and British Ambassador Sir Archibald Clark-Kerr were frequently consulted. They agreed the affair gave the Russians a "crack back at the complaints they had from the British and Americans over the Russian press and, partly, it would appear, due to Stalin's personal resentment at the story." Russians, Harrison continued, hated to appear as barbarians or "people who pick their teeth with their knives. They have a terrible inferiority complex and this kind of thing outrages them." UP had reacted promptly by submitting a denial-apology as suggested and approved by Dekanozov. At first, that covered the matter. In fact, as Salisbury put it, "There is no doubt in my mind—or in Harriman's or Clark-Kerr's—that, after my second conference, Dekanozov thought we had put the matter to rest." He could not question what was said or thought because his own censor acted as Russian interpreter and referred Salisbury's cable back to Dekanozov before sending it. Dekanozov's points were accepted, and the UP routinely reported the apology.[35]

The next event, Salisbury continued, remained conjecture. Most likely, he thought, the matter passed up to Stalin, who probably looked at the censor's translation and said, "This stinks!" Back it went to Dekanozov with orders to get it right or else. Dekanozov found someone to draft a TASS-style denial and called Salisbury back to his office. Though Dekanozov squirmed, he had to recant by telling Salisbury the first apology failed.[36] Interference from the top only further muddied the episode.

Dekanozov requested an informal, frank discussion about Americans, their correspondents, and their differences with Russians. The whole experience left Salisbury "burning [because they] had taken a position which was embarrassing and ungracious—to put it mildly to us—but which from their own standpoint was bound only to react to their disadvantage." Salisbury believed the only thing the Russians could get out of the Dekanozov denial-apology text was what he called a "Bronx Cheer"—a situation made much worse for them than what Salisbury had first achieved. The Russians had climbed out on a limb, and they would not crawl back. "Therefore, if it suddenly only dawned on them that they were, they would have, under their code, to go on being damn fools because anything else would be a sign of weakness in their book."[37]

Salisbury had stalled by sending Dekanozov another letter, but it was only a ploy to keep the officials off balance and prevent being kicked out of Russia immediately. His summons to the Foreign Ministry on Saturday evening indicated this stalling had failed. He planned for the worst, especially when he was led past Dekanozov's office and instead to Molotov's. The commissar greeted him, correcting Salisbury's poor Russian. Molotov wanted to know why Salisbury and UP opposed publishing the denial Dekanozov submitted? Salisbury repeated the same reasoning he had given Dekanozov—the vice commissar's failure to tell Salisbury what he wanted. Molotov began to realize that he had "a hold of a hot one—which they couldn't let go because of the old man [Stalin] and sure enough he trotted out his suggestion that the Dekanozov text be abandoned and we write our own ticket." That, according to Salisbury, was no minor point: "that and the fact Molotov spent fifty minutes discussing the thing with me—is one hell of a put down for the Russians." That was as close as the Russians came to admitting being wrong. Harriman agreed, though puzzled at why Molotov saw Salisbury. Molotov must have believed it had become necessary because Dekanozov had botched it up and Stalin's concern made it necessary for Molotov to "get the one straight himself."[38]

Publishing Dekanozov's denial-apology text was just what the Russians deserved, as further fiddling of the TASS style by Salisbury would have opened the door to endless Russian criticism. They would have been back on the offensive. That is why Molotov suggested abandoning it. He understood it put them in the wrong. "But they couldn't be gracious enough to withdraw it. So they got a little of their own medicine and they had it coming." Harrison did not believe they would pick on UP again. The Russians did not like being scored against, but found UP smart, not panicky.

Dekanozov was now supposedly ill and unavailable, and the Russian Press Department became easier to deal with, especially Nikolai Palgunov, its head. Both Harriman and Clark-Kerr were helpful and even consulted Salisbury, which he considered worth all the jarring of his nerves.[39] Salisbury later came to realize that Stalin's anger over the story was not that it was a lie, as both Dekanozov and Molotov contended, but that it was too close to the truth of how Soviet generals behaved.[40]

◆◆ 2 ◆◆

Other news stories in Moscow were breaking quickly. For instance, Stalin and Molotov were hostile to the London Poles, the Polish government-in-exile, and the Soviets insisted on reconstructing the government-in-exile by removing those tainted with fascism and replacing them with figures friendly toward Moscow. As possible members of a new Polish government, Molotov suggested Dr. Oskar Lange, a Polish economist teaching at the University of Chicago, and Fr. Stanislaus Orlemanski, a Catholic priest of a parish in Springfield, Massachusetts. "It was [Harriman's] impression that the Russians would not insist on a total purge. Stanislaw Mikolajczyk, leader of the Polish Peasant Party, could pass muster [and] 'by eliminating the irreconcilably anti-Soviet members and bringing in at least one Polish leader from the United States, one now in Russia, and perhaps one from Poland.'"[41] That was when Stalin and Molotov invited Lange and Orlemanski to Moscow. They put each forward as potential candidates for a reconstructed Polish government.[42]

Salisbury inserted himself in the midst of this evolving story. Fr. Orlemanski had organized the Kosciusko League in America. The first impression of Salisbury's "boys," his fellow correspondents, was that the priest was "kind of a nut." Harrison figured Orlemanski had to have church approval to come to Moscow. That meant something. Other priests might be allowed into Russia. Fr. Leopold Braun was the only resident Catholic priest in Russia at the time; he had arrived with William C. Bullitt, America's first ambassador to Soviet Russia in 1933. The "boys" invited the two priests to dinner to discover Stalin's position on Poland. Orlemanski had written to Stalin about Polish freedom, and Stalin had invited him to Moscow. Russian newspapers sported large pictures of Fr. Orlemanski with Stalin and Molotov. The priest gave his story to Henry Cassidy of the Associated Press (AP), with the understanding that he should share it with the press corps. Cassidy hid it. Harrison wormed it out of him when the priest threatened to tell Molotov.

Fr. Orlemanski left Moscow to visit Polish soldiers on the front. When he returned, Harrison and Jim Fleming of CBS took him to dinner. They asked if the Russians were using him. Orlemanski denied that and insisted he knew how to deal with them. He would be seeing Stalin that night. He later told Salisbury that Stalin told him, "he didn't have to bother with Mr. Molotov that anytime he had anything to talk over to phone up to see Mr. Stalin and he would do it!" After Fr. Orlemanski's interview with Stalin and Molotov, he came away favorably impressed. Stalin, the good priest insisted, only wanted peace and quiet. Fr. Orlemanski's congregation and supporters in the United States were free to give aid to the Poles. Both Salisbury and Fleming believed this gullable priest to be "ignorant and naïve [and] didn't realize he was being used on each side—by the Vatican and by Stalin—[and they were] a little awe stricken and stunned by the unreality of the man and the role he appeared about to play." After seeing Stalin again, Fr. Orlemanski, at Salisbury's suggestion, wanted something in writing confirming his conversation with the Kremlin boss. Stalin had him write it out and send it over to the Kremlin for review. Orlemanski gave a copy to Salisbury while waiting for Stalin to reply. Meanwhile, Fr. Braun came over to Salisbury's place. They were convinced, and rightly so, that the priest had been used. The affair ended up as another Soviet propaganda ploy. Neither Orlemanski nor Lange were made candidates, but only used as trial balloons for a Soviet maneuver to force the reconstruction of the Polish government-in-exile. Harriman objected to them because they had almost no Polish following in the United States.[43]

Another story occurred in March 1944, when Salisbury realized something "unusual involving the American air forces and Russia was afoot." Air force personnel and a flying fortress arrived in Moscow. Rumors circulated. The United States gave the Russians one hundred flying fortresses. Bill Lawrence of the *New York Times* discovered they were for shuttle bombing: London-Poltava-London, beginning in May 1944. The "boys" were invited to Poltava in the Ukraine for the full story: American heavy bombers in Britain and Italy would fly strike missions deep in Nazi occupied territory and land at Poltava, refuel, and rearm before returning for a second attack run. Molotov and the Russian general staff cleared their travel, yet only five members of the press corps were invited. They demanded all or none. All went to the airport, as Salisbury wrote, "a united front for the first time in Moscow history." Instead of just five, all thirty were permitted, joined by

Ambassador Harriman and his daughter. On arriving, Russian and American military personnel were enthusiastic. Major General John R. Deane, head of America's military mission, was on hand. In Salisbury's opinion, "It was delightful. American and Russian soldiers side by side."

By June 2, 1944, the planes were due, following a bombing mission over Debrecin, Hungary. They arrived in formation with a roar, flying at one thousand feet, and landing on U.S. steel mats at three secret American bases in Soviet Russia at Poltava, Mirgorod, and Pyriatin. Major General Robert L. Walsh took command of shuttle bombing, accomplishing much in its "eighteen strong attacks on important strategic targets in Germany which would otherwise have been immune" but incurred a disaster on June 21–22, 1944. A German air raid on Poltava, following an American one over Germany, destroyed fifty forts as the Russian defenses failed.[44] The program collapsed and ended in September.

But the story that was the highlight of Salisbury's Russian adventures was covering Eric Johnston's 1944 interview with Stalin and his subsequent journey to Siberia and Central Asia. Johnston had come to Moscow by Stalin's special invitation as president of the U.S. Chamber of Commerce. Those who interviewed Stalin were few, and the UP's Eugene Lyons had been one of them. As Harrison put it, "The next best thing to having an interview with Stalin yourself is to get a firsthand report from someone who has talked to the Marshal. I made it a habit to cross-examine closely everyone I knew who talked to Stalin."[45] It was possible to learn much about Stalin from them. The best report Salisbury ever got was from Johnston. Johnston's interview lasted two and a half hours. At a news conference at Spaso House, Johnston told correspondents how well-informed Stalin was on U.S. industry, production figures, and the importance of this aid to the Red Army. Stalin, he related, smoked Ambassador Harriman's Chesterfields and wore his marshal's uniform with a single medal, Hero of Socialist Labor. He looked fit. Throughout, Stalin doodled with his red pencil but remained lethargic.[46]

In the verbatim report, Johnston noted that, as he was about to leave, he tried a last conversational gambit. He got a look at one of Stalin's doodles and, noticing it looked like a damsel in distress, said he hoped it was not "Miss America." That remark caught the dictator by surprise. He finally engaged in candid conversation. As they talked, Johnston became more aware of Stalin's appearance and personality. His hair was thinning, his teeth were bad, he had a double chin. Stalin often laughed uproariously. His constant refrain was, "If I live that long [or] If I'm still alive." Stalin suggested that America would have a bad depression after the war. Russia would have to buy plenty from the United States to keep Americans employed. He insisted Americans gather unemployment figures because Russia would have to purchase American goods to help U.S. employment. When Johnston queried why Stalin was so interested, he replied, "You've done us a favor and now we want to do you a favor." He wished to deal directly with businessmen. Would FDR, he asked, be reelected? Johnston, though a Republican, thought so, but Stalin disagreed. The Marshal joked that Johnston was the second Republican he had met, the first being former presidential candidate Wendell Willkie. Stalin, it seemed, had U.S. newspapers translated. They were opposed to FDR. Stalin hoped FDR would win, because Republicans would not give the USSR long-term credits.

Johnston asked about the need of Russia for consumer goods after the war. Stalin said that had to wait. He was anticipating two postwar five-year plans to help the Soviet economy recover from Nazi devastation. As to reconstruction, rebuilding the Donbas seemed impossible. It was better to create new plants for steel production. Stalin focused on catching up to the United States in heavy industry. Johnston wanted to know what Stalin would buy from the United States. He answered consumer goods such as shoes and woolens, and also the machinery used to make those items. Johnston suggested Russia needed the advice of U.S. distribution experts who ran America's chain stores, explaining to Stalin what coast-to-coast retailers were. Johnston asked about taking correspondents such as Salisbury on his Siberian–Central Asian tour. Stalin agreed. So did Molotov, who remarked that he always agreed with his boss. Salisbury, through Johnston's direct appeal to Stalin, would finally get beyond the Urals.[47] Few Americans ever had.

The June trip with Johnston, a "small, dapper man who bounced through life like a tennis ball," included such places as Sverdlovsk, Novosibirsk, Omsk, Tomsk, Alma-Ata, Tashkent, and Samarkand. That trip confirmed what Salisbury believed: Russia would have lost the war if it had not moved its industries east. Stalin would be remembered for creating this industrial powerhouse: "At dozens of points along the four-thousand mile sweep of the continent from the Urals to the Pacific huge industrial enterprises have sprung up." Komsomolsk-on-Amur was typical—a vast steel and coal complex on the Trans-Siberian Railway.[48] A trip to Siberia and Central Asia with Johnston provided Salisbury with a necessary breather from Moscow's intense work.

Johnston, like FDR, backed a postwar six-billion-dollar credit to rebuild Russia. It eventually failed due to Stalin's "derangement," or what Salisbury termed "the density of Stalin's suspiciousness." Harrison got back to Moscow on July 9, 1944, and arranged, with his UP bosses, to leave Russia, and Olga, in 1945. He now had a Russian story to tell the folks back home.

♦♦ 3 ♦♦

His lengthy return trip to the United States took him through to Teheran, then on to Calcutta, New Delhi, and Brisbane. He met with General Douglas MacArthur at Hollandia, and he went to Honolulu and chatted with Admiral Chester Nimitz. Finally, on September 23, 1945, he arrived in New York City. There he reunited with Mary Jane and his son, now six years old, whom he had not seen in over two years.

To his surprise, "Everyone wanted to know about Russia." This was the hot question. He had much to say, so much so that he took Mary Jane and Mike to St. Petersburg, Florida, got out his Remington Standard, and typed his first book, *Russia on the Way.* It is an important early essay in understanding the evolution of Salisbury's thinking about a topic—Russia—that consumed much of his life as well as his generation's. Few, if any, Americans had a concept of the destruction Russia had suffered: twenty million or more Russians died and another twenty-five million were left homeless. Many feared Russia.[49] Churchill's Iron Curtain speech of February 1946 egged them on. FDR's death in April 1945, whose funeral Salisbury covered, and Harry S. Truman's emergence as president complicated matters. His friend and fellow Moscow correspondent Dick Lauterbach's book, *These Are the Russians*, came out before his and stole the market.

Much was wrong with Salisbury's first try at writing a book anyway. Nevertheless, he later claimed it "good, solid, accurate, lots of details, fresh, and the writing is not too bad, if I may say so."[50] Yet he criticized it: "A lot of it isn't worth the paper I wrote it on." He did not foresee the depth of polarization. He "kissed off" Poland and the Balkans. He thought the Dardanelles and Azerbaijan meant little to the United States and more to the British. However, some things were right: that U.S.-USSR friction was most likely in the Far East; that the USSR showed little interest in Mao and was only concerned with its Far Eastern security by regaining its 1905 losses to Japan. The Kremlin was hard thinking, logical, precise, and analytical. Russia was in transition, making plans for peace. He took pride in the book's last paragraph, in which he predicted the United States and the USSR would not go to war with each other; otherwise, there would be no victor, no world.[51]

In his book, Salisbury mistakenly thought there were checks on Stalin's dictatorship: Russian public opinion, the Politburo, and the Secret Police (NKVD). Public opinion existed and, so Salisbury maintained, it guided Stalin. Salisbury then believed it was "a most important factor in Russia." If that were not so, then why did the Soviet government make "extraordinary efforts" to mobilize it and to report what people were thinking and saying? "What he [Stalin] can do and how he does it are constantly modified by Russian public opinion." His impression of the eight-man Politburo with its five alternates implied a collegial body with Stalin only occasionally overruling it. Rather, Salisbury emphasized Stalin's argumentive skill and leadership prestige in holding his colleagues in line. The junta, like its boss, thought pragmatically and saw the logic of things, which led them to the same conclusions as Stalin. Salisbury's view of the NKVD was that of both a protective shield for Stalin, a kind of FBI on the American model, and a guarantee of the security of the Soviet state. This notion led him to think, "The Kremlin makes policy, but the NKVD gives it a long, cold, hard look strictly from a security angle."[52] There Salisbury had it wrong: the tail did not wag the dog. Nor did it occur to Salisbury that the NKVD conducted aggressive spying. In reality, Russians feared its brutal punishment.

Salisbury correctly identified the greatest postwar concern of the USSR: security. To achieve this, Salisbury believed, the Communist Party followed two lines, major and minor. He defined the former as "collaboration with the United States and Britain toward the common ends of world peace and security."[53] But while "accepting Anglo-American-Soviet collaboration as her major policy, she did not close the door to other means of attaining her security minimums."[54] The secondary or reserve line meant creating a security zone in Eastern Europe and in the Far East. Even with this second possibility, Salisbury believed, "with patience, it was possible to work with Russia." Here, again, he was overly optimistic and forgiving, relying on Stalin's comment to General Eisenhower: "Russia and America must be joined in immutable friendship [and] Stalin has stated time and again his desire for collaboration with America."[55]

Finally, Salisbury believed Russia had achieved a stability approaching monolithic strength. He thought most Americans would believe Molotov would succeed Stalin, but Salisbury suspected the reality was that any of his associates in the Politburo might, though the most likely three were Andrei Zhdanov, Andrei Andreyev, or Georgii Malenkov. These three were members of both the party secretariat and its organizational bureau. Nowhere did he mention Lavrentia Beria or Nikita Khrushchev. He admitted, "no one can or will truly succeed Stalin." Russia would be ruled by a collective leadership because, "except Zhdanov, Malenkov and Andreyev, there is no one now on the horizon who combines enough power, prestige, and influence to challenge Stalin in filling the focal position of secretary-general of the party."[56]

Even though all of these possibilities, except for Malenkov, failed, Salisbury predicted a hot war with Russia would not happen. The notion of a cold war did not occur to him. He still had much to learn.

♦♦ 4 ♦♦

The four-year period following his return to America in 1945 turned out to be the most trying and tragic of Salisbury's life. Two stories emerged from this period: the first one—public—was of his physical and mental collapse and recuperation in a psychiatric ward. The second—private—filled in the details. Taken together, they are important for fully understanding his recovery on the road to becoming one of America's greatest journalists.

On Salisbury's return, he covered President Roosevelt's funeral at Hyde Park in early April 1945. Then he sought refuge in St. Petersburg, Florida, where his wife and son could play in the surf and sand while he drafted *Russia on the Way*. He had dashed out to San Francisco in late April to report on the opening of the United Nations and encountered the first dangerous deterioration in relations with Russia. His friend from Johnston's Siberian junket, Bill White, had also published a book, called *Report on the Russians*, and it presented some of the earliest signs of the Cold War. White told the seamy side of communism with "mean, ungracious, even vicious remarks," Harrison thought, "about the Russians." Since fellow reporters were mentioned, including Harrison, they were angry. Salisbury slammed back with a bitter letter to the *Saturday Review*, which had become a forum for *l'affaire* White. Bill, Harrison later admitted, was "swimming with the tide, but had gotten a little ahead of it."[57]

Salisbury continued with UP, but he also did freelance writing. His ultimate goal, however, was a job at the *New York Times*. Germany had surrendered in May, and the end of the war that fall meant postwar planning. As he put it, "I was working my head off."[58] He began cultivating his friends at the *Times*—Ted Bernstein, Manny Freedman, Lester Markel, Cy Sulzberger, and Bill Lawrence. Sulzberger was chief *Times* correspondent in Europe, and Lawrence ran the *Times* Washington bureau. Salisbury also kept up with Russians. At the United Nations opening in San Francisco, he spoke with Molotov and Andrei Gromyko. He accompanied Soviet writers Alex Simonov and Ilya Ehrenberg during their visit in the United States. He had become friends with Bernard Pares, then teaching at Columbia University and the greatest English specialist on Russia.[59] He also talked with the *New York Times* editors Edwin James and Turner Catledge. The *Times* had had no correspondent in Moscow ever since the Kremlin refused a reentry visa to Drew Middleton. Consequently, it had given up on Moscow and closed its office there. Salisbury turned down the editorship of the *Reporter* magazine and a position with *Time* magazine. Above all, he valued getting a job with the *New York Times* and told James, "If the *Times* wanted to send me to Moscow, I would try to help get a Soviet visa, although I could guarantee no result."[60] He did all of this despite writing a tough article on Russia for the

New York Times Sunday magazine section, "Russia Tightens the Iron Curtain on Ideas," published December 26, 1948. There was then taking place in Russia a "thought purge," with increasing censorship and xenophobia. That same day, the *Times* published a "Christmas Letter to Marshal Stalin." In it, James insisted the *Times* wanted to present the Soviet side, but could not do so without someone there to do it. It was, Harrison thought, a "screwball gambit."[61]

While professionally advancing, Salisbury's personal tragedy unfolded. His situation at the end of the war was complex. There was his ongoing problem with women. His relationship with his wife was as difficult as ever. Two ladies he felt especially close to were Ellen in London and Olga in Moscow. He had to leave Moscow and Olga, but during his time in Russia, he had not heard from Ellen. There must have been some letters, but "god knows what happened to them." He "really thought it was over between E and me." The situation in Moscow was tense enough, and, then, there was his dad's death in 1944.

He believed, "I was coming home to make a new start on my married life." But even that first night back in New York City, with his wife Mary Jane still visiting in Minneapolis, he pestered an old flame. When Mary Jane returned to New York, his sister, Janet, contended he told her that while coming home in a taxi with his wife and child, "I knew that it wasn't going to work; but anyone with any sense would have known that before getting into that taxi."

Meanwhile, back in London, Ellen had married a Royal Air Force pilot, but that marriage failed. She returned to New York in 1946. At that point, they took up again: "I just didn't know what in the hell to do because I was in love with her; and wanted to get out of my marriage but I was stuck with MJ and she was pregnant and it was all a bloody mess."[62]

Harrison could not quite remember when he had reconnected with Ellen, but he suspected that she had written him when she briefly returned to New York. When he covered the inaugural flight of American Airlines to London in October 1945, he met her, and they spent a day at the Savoy. By her return in 1946, Ellen had realized her mistaken marriage and had gotten a divorce. Of course, Harrison was very sympathetic. As he admitted, they wrote and wrote: "she cried on my shoulder and we fell in love all over again by mail [and finally] she turned up again in NYC." Things progressed.[63]

By August 1947, Harrison wrote his mother, "I have left Mary and WE ARE SEPARATED finally and for good." He believed his marriage would have broken up if he had not left for London. That would have been better than at present. He returned in 1945 to try "one more big pitch at making our marriage a go." Within six months, he knew the marriage had failed. To make matters worse, there was "this girl with whom I fell in love while in England, with whom I am in love now and whom I want to marry when, and

if MJ EVER AGREES to a divorce." Two years before, he realized they
would finally end up divorced, but he let it drift. It was "completely screwball to go ahead with another child, and yet for two reasons it might work:
the importance to Mary for a normal pregnancy and another preoccupation
[but he admitted that was all] specious reasoning." The pregnancy was difficult and tensions grew. His older son became affected by his parents' behavior. After his second son's birth, the older boy suffered. As he recouped,
Mary attempted suicide. The doctor asked Harrison to level with her, revealing all but the woman's name. Mary tried suicide again, but failed again, and
a trained nurse came as a live-in. Harrison's departure temporarily settled the
situation. His sister, Jan, stayed on for a while. Mary was adamantly against a
divorce. Harrison's finances crumbled, and he could do no writing in that
madhouse. Meanwhile, the third party, Ellen, was staying with his sister.
Ellen was a psychiatric nurse working at Bellevue. Harrison insisted he was
not unstable and that his decision to divorce Mary "was not arrived at without years of consideration and as much facing of realistic facts as I am
capable of."[64]

No matter how bad the crisis, he did care for his family's welfare. His
wife would explode at anytime into a ball of fire. If his mother could manage
it, he wished for her to come there. She would have to cope with his wife's
"blind, hysterical anger and jealousy alternating with good behavior and
rationality." She threatened to ruin him financially, though moderated with a
sense that she would be ruined also. He accused Mary Jane of being psychopathic. His son feared her anger.[65] Ellen was with Janet, perhaps not so good,
as he wanted to keep Ellen's identity and living arrangement secret from his
wife, who remained under a doctor's care. He wondered whether he should
tell Mary all the facts—or not—and run the risk of her suicide. Eventually,
she would have to be told.[66]

He delayed writing his mother again for three weeks and published some
articles, one on Andrei Vishinsky in the *New York Times* magazine section.[67]
Other published pieces might straighten out his finances. He also needed a
lawyer. He told his mother more about Ellen. She was thirty-two, of German
parentage, had a stepmother, had never known her real mother. Her father
was a wealthy insurance man. She had attended Long Island College, trained
for nursing at Columbia Presbyterian, become a psychiatric nurse, and was
now working at Bellevue Hospital in Manhattan.[68]

Sometime between October 1947 and February 1948, Harrison underwent
a physical and mental collapse so severe that it left him exhausted and dazed.
On March 31, the Payne Whitney Psychiatric Clinic on Manhattan's Upper
East Side admitted him on the advice of Ellen, with the approval of his
mother and sister and his own consent. He was not violent; he had collapsed
due to sheer psychological and physical exhaustion. Once there, he revealed
how a little medicine, a glass of milk, and a sandwich were what he needed to

get a full night's sleep: "I remember," he wrote, "looking at my watch at 9:30 and then waking up, thinking I'd had a brief nap—low and behold it was 6 a.m.—the best night's sleep I've had in lord knows when." At first, he shared a room with many other patients and slept on a cot. Afterward, he had his own room that, he joked, he shared only with himself—"a practical looking gent." He seemed to think the other patients there were "schizophrenic [or] gloomy depressed lads." Ellen had played an important role in convincing Harrison that he needed professional help. He admitted his need for rest. Harrison saw a pattern comparable to the others, who "did not have the good luck to have an Ellen, who was smart enough to see the symptoms and toss the ball to Dr. Brodsky at the right moment—plus myself, I must admit, in finally recognizing the evidence when it was properly presented." He had only wished that he had known enough himself to avoid what he called "the great rescue operation—but *nitchevo*." He had "closed down the worry department [and would] build myself up and we will have a very worth-while investment." By lunchtime of his second day, he had had the "first good meal I've eaten in ten days and feel generally on the mend."[69]

It was then that Salisbury identified Ellen to his mother by her real name: Eleanor Ungerland.[70] He had begun writing again and started paying attention to the news. "Do you realize that I have not been beyond its walls since March 31?"[71] He could phone his wife, and Eleanor was allowed to visit him, though he still fretted about Mary Jane and Eleanor meeting.[72] By June 29, 1948, things were going well. His doctors thought he was on the right road. They lifted most of his restrictions. He was eager to get started.[73]

On October 10, 1948, Salisbury was discharged, but he continued sessions with his doctors. He discovered then that his job with UP had been, as he put it, "kaput" since June, but he had not heard of it until early October—on the advice of his doctors. Baillie would not rehire him because "my crack up would simply be an incubus which could not be overcome." UP hoped that his doctors would tell him not to return to UP, but they refused, believing his job had nothing to do with his collapse. He would remain on the payroll, enjoy a year's sick leave, and UP would pay for the hospital stay. Salisbury regarded this as a fair settlement and started hunting for work while freelancing. He still believed that the *New York Times* was his best bet. Mary Jane would have to economize and, what is more, she agreed to see a lawyer about getting a divorce. "I will be getting out of here pronto now—both because I am cured and because the budget permits no lagging at P-W costs." Though UP's firing was a "stunner, [it did not] throw me off balance in any way—one more tribute to the fact that I am really fit and raring to go."[74]

Surprisingly, events moved swiftly, even though he reported to his mother and Jan that "the odds are strongly against anything developing" with the *New York Times* and the reopening of their Moscow bureau, with him as its chief.[75] On January 2, 1949, he made a formal visa application at the Russian embassy in Washington, DC. Although they were pleasant, the decision was in Moscow's hands, and he observed that the "Kremlin is not very friendly to the *Times*." Even if the visa did come through, it would, he thought, take months, and he remained pessimistic. He pressed his Washington friends about getting a job in DC, as he would be "tickled to death" to work again there, even preferring it to Moscow.[76] Then came the stunning news on the tenth: "I have word from the Russians that my visa will be issued as soon as I apply for it! This astonishing intelligence came through five days after I formally applied." He had no idea what it meant and never heard of things happening so quickly. It had also taken the *Times* by surprise—as if Stalin himself had thrown a lightning bolt. It meant getting Harrison's personal life in order—his lawyers, his divorce, Eleanor—eventually moving her to Moscow also.[77] He went again to Washington, picked up his visa and passport, conferred with various experts about Moscow. Mary Jane would learn about it by reading the *Times*—so he did not need to keep that a secret. The lawyers for both sides would have a conference.

The *Times* was "pleased and a little amazed about the visa—as I am, too."[78] That led to much speculation as to what it meant, or it may have just been an opportune moment and he was still persona non grata. Harrison knew he would do a good job. Now he had to make all arrangements to get there. As for Eleanor, if the divorce could be arranged, she could come later, and they would be married in Helsinki.[79] By January 27, 1949, Harrison thought he could get Eleanor into Russia "by some device," or maybe the Russians would save him the trouble "by tossing me out on my ear," which they could do. He could tell his mother and Jan he was "okay on the money end," and he had already booked passage of the SS *Gripsholm* for February.[80]

He left for Russia on February 18, 1949—and once again that Prestwick girl now looked on from a Hudson River dock as the *Gripsholm* slowly slid downstream—and he arrived via Helsinki and by train to Leningrad's Finland Station on March 7, 1949. By then he had overcome the saddest time of his life. He was beginning a new career, a new life—one that fulfilled a journalistic dream, one that would place him in the pantheon of America's greatest correspondents.

Chapter Three

Moscow Bureau Chief

Salisbury's little group entered Soviet Russia by train from Helsinki, including America's ambassador to Finland, Avra W. Warren, and his wife. They settled in Leningrad's Astoria Hotel, the very place Hitler had planned a banquet after conquering the city. They took in *Swan Lake* at the Mariinsky Theatre. Soviet authorities, contrary to Harrison's request to interview Mayor Pyotr Popkov, obliged them to board the next Red Arrow train for Moscow. Unknown to him, Popkov's arrest days earlier in the infamous Leningrad Affair preempted a story. "To mention Popkov's name in the Astoria was like asking about black spots on a man's face in a city of the plague." Harrison checked into Moscow's Metropole Hotel, room 393, the following day, March 8, 1949. He reopened the *New York Times* Moscow bureau in room 317.[1]

The USSR had refused the previous *Times* correspondent, Drew Middleton, a visa in mid-1947. Harrison now reorganized Middleton's old office and started his routine from scratch. At first, he seemed preoccupied with getting Eleanor to Moscow: "All that is lacking is you—which, of course, is the whole thing." They were practical from the start "in this most realistic of countries," but Harrison was optimistic about her travel plans.[2] It would take some "hard readjustment in my thinking." After all, things had changed drastically since 1945, so much so that "It is hard to convey the atmosphere of the foreign colony here." Typically, correspondents compared Moscow to Hitler's Berlin.[3] The "piddling difficulties" made him think, "I love you. I miss you and I want you with me."[4] He passed spare hours reading Russian classics, catching old Hollywood flicks at Spaso House, or partying at the U.S. embassy. He reconnected with old friends from 1944–1945, including

Ludmilla Shapiro, Henry's wife from UP, who read him the Russian papers and took him to the theater and ballet. Soviet art bulged with ideology, usually brave communist leaders catching American spies. All punch lines featured anti-American political jokes. He saw a slanted Russian rendition of *Uncle Tom's Cabin* at the Transport Workers' Theater.[5] Harrison had not expected a cozy Moscow tea party and blini. Eleanor's presence might "take most of the curse off."[6] He found Moscow darker, angrier, and more distrustful of Americans. He intended to show that in his *Times* articles.

Salisbury distracted himself from tensions in Moscow with frequent trips. He traveled to Yasnaya Polyana and the bygone world of Leo Tolstoy with his friends the Whitneys; Tom of the AP had married this lovely Russian *devushka* Juli. Harrison could write Eleanor about touring, but otherwise Russia was too depressing. Driving to Tolstoy's estate was like passing through a rich garden with peasant villages on either side of the road and sleepy provincial towns. Just beyond Tula resided the great Russian writer's home. It was easy to imagine taking a coach over from Tula only to find the Tolstoys off for a visit elsewhere. The caretaker was also a Tolstoy: "He knew everything Tolstoy had ever written and everything that had been said about him." The grounds and home were just as Tolstoy had left them—very homey, with paintings of the family by Ilya Repin, Russia's greatest painter, all about. A very old Remington typewriter caught Salisbury's eye. These were the rooms where Tolstoy wrote *War and Peace* and *Anna Karenina*. Photos of the famous who came there lined the walls.[7]

Another one of Salisbury's visits took him to Stalingrad, formerly Tsaritsyn, on the Volga River. Eleanor, he thought, might be interested. Two things impressed him: the tremendous devastation and the vast reconstruction task. Much had already been done in its ten-year plan. Survivors told him how Nazi bombardment had begun on August 23, 1942, and within a few weeks the invaders flattened Stalingrad's center. During Salisbury's October 1949 visit, President Harry Truman announced exploding a newer atomic bomb. That created much nasty language to be thrown back and forth. According to Harrison, Stalingraders wanted peace. When the initial flurry was over, "it is my conviction that this should be a considerable help toward getting somewhere with a realistic solution of some of our postwar problems."[8]

At the end of October, he was off again to Leningrad for another tour of his favorite Russian city; the city had more drama than any other in the world. It captured Russia's essence. Eleanor might like that. Reconstruction was happening full tilt, but even so, its shabbiness impressed him. He did standard touristy things by visiting the great architectural monuments. Harrison believed Leningrad was "still brisker, brighter, gayer, somehow more adult, more 'cultured,' as the Russians like to say, than Moscow." It lived on the glories of the past. He returned to Moscow just in time to experience the thirty-second anniversary of the Bolshevik Revolution on November 7. He went to the Bolshoi to see huge portraits of Lenin and Stalin and to hear Politburo member Georgii Malenkov speak. Malenkov's star, he reported, was on the rise. It was all very *kulturny*, with the ladies dressed to the nines. The next day, crack military units marched and civilians massed on Red Square with their banners. The Politburo mounted Lenin's tomb with Stalin at the head.[9]

Eleanor passed from Salisbury's life. Moscow seized his imagination. "Strand by strand, our relationship simply unraveled." Harrison returned home on leave from Moscow in May 1950 after fourteen months there. He divorced Mary Jane and dismissed Eleanor. "Ellen was going her own way. Somehow none of this mattered."[10] Her love had cast a spell over him. It lifted as their correspondence ebbed. He filled her diminishing space with news about Soviet Russia under its aging, psychopathic tyrant. That new space grew with his often-censored dispatches, with his often-uncensored letters. He analyzed and evaluated the heightened drama of Soviet life. Therein lay the poignancy of his stories: of anti-Americanism; of the Leningrad Affair; of cosmopolitanism; of Stalin-Mao negotiations; of Ambassador George F. Kennan; of the Doctors' Plot. By the time of the Nineteenth Party Congress in October 1952, Harrison had become America's foremost Soviet correspondent and a leading Russian expert. But ominous clouds were gathering over the Kremlin. Harrison would have a rendezvous with Soviet destiny.

For a breather, he again got to Zagorsk and returned to see the Bolshoi Ballet put on *The Fountain of Bakhchisarai*, based on Alexander Pushkin's tale. Mary Jane was holding up their divorce for childish reasons, and he needed a respite. Along with that annoyance, Russian newspapers continued to print bloody nonsense from which he could not make good story. He was anxious for a leave to settle matters at home—Mary Jane and Eleanor—but he did not want to disturb his position with the *Times*. He wondered just what went on in the minds of his editors. Did they like his work?[11]

The lawyers—his and his wife's—finally worked out a divorce agreement: $100 per week with custodial right to Mary Jane, pay for their children's medical and dental bills and college educations, but the parents' estates to remain free of each other.[12] In June 1950 he came home to settle his affairs. Harrison wrote his mother and sister from Reno, Nevada, where he spent six weeks getting the divorce finalized. He reported to his mother and sister, "Reswick phoned to say the divorce agreement was all settled and Mary was agreeing to appearance here (legal participation in this case) which—unless she reneges—will wrap-up the whole ball of wax very neatly and make the decree fully binding, etc." He continued, "I have heard nothing further from E. I think that is washed up. But lord only knows. I am afraid she has put herself in the hand of these wild birds and it makes me feel bad. But I don't know what can be done with it."[13] She had fallen in and out of love with her psychiatrist.[14] On his way back to Moscow in September 1950, Eleanor met him for one last time in Paris. They had a great week together, but "For one thing, we agreed that we certainly couldn't get married for the present and goodness knows whether we ever will. It depends entirely on Eleanor, and whether she can work out these problems of hers."[15] Then he was off to Moscow on the Orient Express. Eleanor never worked things out. Harrison did. Her growing personal problems had finally passed him by.

The return trip to Moscow in September 1950 on the Orient Express gave Harrison a chance to rethink his Moscow experience so far and consider how to report on the emerging Cold War. The outbreak of the Korean War on June 25, 1950, had made it seem likely for some observers that a Russian attack on Western Europe was imminent. Harrison's observations while trekking across Eastern Europe would refute that scenario and cause a firestorm at the *Times*. Just now, he wondered about himself and Russia since his arrival back in March 1949. He reflected on his previous year's experience as his train rolled across the plains and bogs of Poland.

Personally, he had gotten over Eleanor, improved his skills as a foreign correspondent, and made good progress mastering the Russian language. Back in the USSR, he found ordinary Russians feared a new war. They were busy reconstructing the homeland. Censorship remained harsh. Two correspondents had been expelled—Anna Louise Strong (*Moscow News*) and Robert Magidoff (Associated Press)—and charged by the government with spying. The anti-Semitic campaign against "homeless cosmopolitans," those undermining national roots and pride, remained relentless. American Embassy ex-staffer Annabelle Bucar married a Bolshoi tenor and wrote *The Truth about American Diplomats*, charging her former colleagues with espionage. Restrictions on foreign correspondents increased: limited travel, few interviews, restricted mixing with Soviets, censorship.[16]

All of Salisbury's articles, as well as those of other foreign journalists, had to be submitted to the Press Bureau for review before he could send them on to the *Times*. They were often rewritten and certain details excised. In a letter to Edwin L. James, managing editor of the *New York Times*, Harrison stressed that Soviet censorship killed all conclusions, all analysis, all speculation from his dispatches. The Press Bureau of the Foreign Ministry slanted his stories toward favoring the USSR. Misrepresenting the news fit Soviet propaganda. The *Times*, Harrison argued, needed to carry a warning "slug," reading "Passed by Soviet Censorship." Otherwise, the text of his censored dispatches deceived *Times* readers and adversely affected his reputation.

Harrison reread each dispatch and, compared with the original, found most mangled. OVIR (Office of Visas and Registration), under the MGB (Ministry of State Security) searched and opened mail, both incoming and outgoing. Only the diplomatic pouch was secure. He also complained to the *Times* European chief, Cy Sulzberger. Onerous censorship, he wrote Cy, did not prevent him from seeking interviews with top Soviet brass, artists, writers, and scientists. He begged the Foreign Ministry for trips around the country and visits to Soviet institutions. One Soviet bureaucrat told him big shots were busy or gone. Factories and institutions were moved or *remont*—closed for repairs.[17]

By April, after a month of study, Harrison was aware of no significant changes in government except for the disappearance of N. A. Voznesensky, the head of state planning and a member of the Politburo. He had dropped from sight—from the government, from the Politburo. Harrison speculated Voznesensky had sided against Eugene Varga, the economist who predicted capitalism's postwar reemergence. Varga had contended that revolutions in the West were unlikely. Wars among capitalist states were not inevitable. At first, the party hurled sharp criticism at Varga, but his predictions proved correct. After a self-criticism in 1949, the party rehabilitated him. Stalin's handpicked successor, Georgii Malenkov, doomed Voznesensky, Varga's critic and the late Leningrad chief Andrei Zhdanov's protégé. Malenkov and his ally Lavrentia Beria, head of the MGB or secret police, purged Zhdanov's people.[18] Unknown to Salisbury, the MGB arrested Voznesensky, tortured, and murdered him. Stalin asked Malenkov about Voznesensky. "Oh," said Malenkov, "he froze to death in the back of a prison truck."[19]

Salisbury tried to report on the "cosmopolitan" crusade. Fearing censors' cuts, he restricted his criticisms to letters for the diplomatic pouch, "Jewish writers have been singled out for very vicious attacks because of alleged pandering to Jewish religion and Zionism." The *Times*, wary of Soviet reprisals, still refused Harrison's suggested "slug." Manny Freedman, *Times* foreign editor, wrote him, "We think that the censorship, though very tough, follows a very consistent pattern, which indicates that our approach should be successful."[20] Even Soviet jokes, which Salisbury quoted directly from the Soviet humor magazine *Krokodil*, were cut. One joke read, "Alla: 'I think the dress material is good, but I don't like the pattern.' Natasha: 'Don't worry, that pattern will disappear after the first washing.'" Salisbury did report the announcement on Moscow radio of lifting the Berlin Blockade and the meeting of the Council of Foreign Ministers in Paris.[21] Otherwise, the news he could send home remained thin.

A pattern of correspondence emerged between Harrison and his longtime friend Cy Sulzberger. These were the letters sent through the diplomatic pouch, containing Harrison's uncensored messages. They were an extraordinary series of analysis and evaluation that could not appear in his dispatches or the open mail. He cloaked them in the secrecy of the pouch, far removed from the prying eyes of the secret police and the knives of the Soviet press department's censors. His earliest were sent in May 1949. Censorship had grown worse since Middleton had left, and dispatches took longer to clear. One of the most serious results, he told Cy, was that censors "effectively concealed the real extent and bitterness of the anti-American campaign into which every organ of Soviet propaganda had been mustered." The Soviet government taught its public to hate the word *American*. Propaganda had reached the same proportions as the Soviet's anti-Nazi campaign during the war. It accompanied Soviet jamming of Voice of America (VOA) and the British Broadcasting Corporation (BBC).[22]

In another May letter, Harrison concentrated on the forthcoming Council of Foreign Ministers Meeting set for Paris. He advanced two theories about the Russian approach: The first was a press for German unification, with four-power control of the Ruhr, while denouncing the Atlantic Pact (NATO). A second theory, more radical, suggested the Russians would accept all the Western policies on Germany with the aim of weakening support for NATO, in turn forcing an early retreat of U.S. forces from Europe. It would gain for the USSR propaganda value and strengthen the German Communist Party. American interest would dwindle. Any lessening of European tensions allowed Russia to redirect its interests to the Far East. Salisbury thought this alternative too radical. Russians worried about a U.S. attack, as was shown in their relief at the ending of the Berlin Blockade, an attempt by Stalin to cut the city's land communications off and the resulting Allied airlift to relieve Berlin by supplying it with necessities, and anger over Truman's failure to take seriously Stalin's offer for a summit.

Harrison illustrated Russian anger by writing about Anatoly Surov's play *The Mad Haberdasher*—a take on Truman as a Missouri Mussolini put in the White House by the Pendergast gang. He reported on the lessening of the "cosmopolitan" purge and the total disappearance of anything referring to Voznesensky and his associate A. Andreyev. That meant Malenkov was on the rise, and he was especially featured during Moscow's official May Day festivities. Conditions for reporting Malenkov's ascendancy could not be worse as shown by Salisbury's more than thirty individual requests to the Soviet Press Bureau that got no action. He told a friend that he had often seen Malenkov, but Stalin only twice—once on May Day and again at a session of the Supreme Soviet. "If anyone wants to know—he is looking very chipper. As far as I can tell he had changed hardly at all in the past five years."[23]

In June, Harrison wrote Cy on what he called the "Soviet peace offensive" and its moves to integrate Eastern European satellite economies with its own. Integration was part of the overall Russian postwar reconstruction and a counter to the Marshall Plan, the American program to aid Western Europe after the war. Also, the Russians ended the communist Greek insurrection as part of reducing Soviet commitments. The peace offensive provided Stalin with a breathing spell to drive Yugoslavia's independent-minded Marshal Josip Tito into the Western camp and out of the Comintern association. Stalin hoped to divide the world into black and white camps with no gray shades. Harrison stopped short of using the word *purge* for cleansing the ranks of the communist cadre in the USSR and its satellites. Instead, he described what he called a certain "weeding out." He noted the closing down of the Leningrad Affair, guessing that Malenkov had arrested and executed Voznesensky, Popkov, and A. Kuznetzov—all Zhdanov's former Leningrad colleagues. The international situation for a brief moment, he thought, had stepped back from direct confrontation, though the Paris Conference remained sterile. If only, he often mused, large numbers of Russians could come to the United States and, conversely, Americans to Russia—then understanding might be achieved because of the "very considerable differences which are rooted deep in culture and tradition [and] differing social philosophies."[24]

In June 1949, the new English and American ambassadors arrived in Moscow, Sir David Kelly and Admiral Alan G. Kirk. That was the good news. The bad news was that, at a *New Republic* magazine forum on the USSR in New York, participants believed Salisbury's dispatches suggested either he was taken in by Soviet propaganda or was trying to get in good with communist officials. Salisbury told Edwin James, "No one is more aware than myself that my dispatches do not and cannot give a balanced picture of conditions here." Salisbury thought *Times* stringer Harry Schwartz was pushing this idea, but Turner Catledge, assistant managing editor, said no.[25]

Undeterred, Harrison continued pursuing Soviet officials for their comments. He wrote Stalin for information: would the Soviet Union be willing to start large-scale trade with America? He sent a letter to Manny Freedman showing his originals and censored copies of his dispatches. Harrison's mutilated dispatches did not mention his opinion that Malenkov was heir apparent or his observation that Molotov and Andreyev were absent from former Comintern chief Georgii Dimitrov's funeral. Only certain old-line Politburo members had composed the honor guard: Stalin, Malenkov, Beria, K. Voroshilov, L. Kaganovich, A. Mikoyan, N. Shvernik, and N. Bulganin. Malenkov led the mourners to the Belorussky Railway Station, where they dispatched Dimitrov's body to his native Bulgaria.[26]

Salisbury suspected Stalin's growing suspicion of Molotov and his anger toward Molotov's wife, Polina, a Russian Jew, and with Jews in general. Stalin brooded about the "dangerous duplicity of Molotov." He demanded Molotov divorce Polina. Stalin dismissed her from the Communist Party and had her arrested on January 21, 1949, along with her sisters and brother. Polina went into Siberian exile and the others died in prison; she would eventually reemerge after Stalin's death. Stalin banished Molotov from the party's highest echelons and forbade him from signing documents. Molotov acknowledged his political incorrectness by abstaining from these actions.[27] He divorced his wife, saving her life and his. Harrison sensed changes with the notable rise of Malenkov and Molotov's increasing absence. Simultaneously, the Cold War got colder: "We have replaced Nazi Germany as their chief concern."[28]

Harrison argued that there could be Cold War "flare-ups [but] concentrated passion and hysteria are wearing thin." The Russian spy and security phobia rooted out Western contacts between scientists, intelligentsia, and ordinary folks. Such relations froze in the Cold War's great glacier. Harrison never ceased complaining about censorship, especially when he quoted material directly from the Soviet press on economics and the Five-Year Plan, which the censors deleted. Long-delayed dispatches, he speculated, went to the Kremlin for inspection.[29] Like personal contacts, information froze at the censor's doorstep. He terminated his on again, off again liaison with the Russian UP courier Olga Khludova, though he missed her borzoi. Their trysts had avoided Russian spies by some of the most ingenious methods since Harrison had returned to Moscow.[30] Harrison certainly did not fit the romanticized picture of a foreign correspondent in trench coat, surrounded by beautiful but mysterious Russian women.

That fall of 1949, Harrison's articles stressed Stalin's struggle with Marshal Tito of Yugoslavia. He went from friend and ally to "enemy and adversary of the Soviet Union." Russia nullified the alliance and denounced Tito with a "solemn warning." Russia hinted it might have to resort to more effective means, whatever that meant, though formal diplomatic relations continued. As Harrison put it, "The most important conclusion to be drawn from the 4th and 5th notes to Belgrade, those of Aug. 12th and Aug. 20th, is that the Soviet has decided most firmly that Tito must go." All that remained was how. Time was running out. In the face of Moscow's anger, Belgrade's reaction was "belligerent rejection." Harrison did not rule out direct military intervention, but he predicted the breaking of diplomatic relations and possible guerrilla operations.

What was deeply troubling for Salisbury during the Tito crisis was that the Ministry of Internal Affairs (MVD) had tampered with his incoming mail. The Foreign Ministry at first did not respond to such charges and then denied them. Harrison warned James, "We must expect in the future that a blind incoming censorship will be operating." Anything dealing with "sensitive topics" would simply disappear.[31]

Glavlit (Main Literary and Art Administration) delayed, killed, and mutilated his dispatches more often than usual during the Tito crisis. He believed even with the censorship his "dispatches have managed to convey the impression that the Russians mean business and are playing for keeps where Tito is concerned."[32] Nevertheless, the censor passed quotable phrases when referring to Tito as "enemy and adversary" or "state of war" or "a deserter of the very worst type."[33] Harrison commented to a friend that Ivan the Terrible would recognize a "good many things [as] nothing changes very rapidly here."[34] To another friend, he summarized Moscow in early September 1949 as preoccupied with Tito, the harvest, rebuilding, and American warmongering.[35]

Moscow tried to tie Tito to American intelligence agencies. Virulent anti-American propaganda continued, though evidence of it was cut from his dispatches to "conceal the full force of the anti-American propaganda which fills the stage, screen, papers and magazines." As he told James, "serving as an American correspondent in Moscow in these times is very much like living under siege behind the enemy lines. The idea is constantly hammered into the mind of the public that we are spies." Would a spy, Harrison thought, keep pestering Stalin with provocative questions: Would it be useful for him to meet with Truman? Should controls be put on atomic weapons? Could a new international agreement be made between the United States and the USSR?[36]

With the temporary closing of the Reuters News Service at the end of October and the departure of Joe Newman (*New York Herald Tribune*), Ed Stevens (*Christian Science Monitor*), and Don Dallas (Reuters), Harrison believed the "western press corps has literally fallen apart in the nine months or so that I have been here." That decreased the effectiveness of those who remained. Less pooling of information occurred. Reuters, for the time being, would get its Moscow news from a Soviet outlet in London.[37]

In early December 1949, the *New York Times* became concerned about Salisbury's safety as well as his possible expulsion. This worry arose because of a November report by Will Lissner, the *Times* in-house communist specialist. Sometimes the U.S. embassy carelessly put his letters into the open mail instead of including them in the diplomatic pouch. That was dangerous, as he added censored materials—those cut from his dispatches as well as his personal analysis and speculations. Some of this "boldness of my reporting and by the sharpness of my complaints" might be used by other *Times* correspondents and contributors such as freelancer Harry Schwartz. As Lissner warned in a memo of November 1, 1949, the "closest precautions" were required to protect Salisbury. A letter to Harrison from Manny Freedman had somehow slipped into the open mail, precipitating these worries. As Lissner put it, "we ask enough in asking Salisbury to try to do an honest job of reporting; we should not ask him to put himself at the mercy of careless idiots."[38]

Salisbury dismissed Lissner's worries. He wrote him about the conditions of working in Moscow, mentioning, "shadowing should not be conceived of as continuous [but also noting] at the same time, they must be ready to provide minute-by-minute information should the MVD desire it." Most Soviet surveillance, he thought, was "spot-checking."[39] Arthur Hayes Sulzberger, *Times* publisher, warned his staff to exercise extreme caution. When Lissner and the *Times* did not hear from Salisbury for several days, they wrote an obituary just in case. [40] Harrison again wrote Lissner, blithely suggesting that his relations with Soviet authorities were "at all times correct." As far as he was concerned, "I do not think there is a faintest possibility of any connection between expulsion of a correspondent and normal, diplomatically phrased representations such as I have made." [41]

He was referring to his "representations" to Andrei Gromyko in the Soviet foreign office in November: tell correspondents of news-breaking events before announcing them on Soviet radio, clear dispatches quickly, allow correspondents access to conferences, grant greater travel freedom. He hoped to get automatic reentry visas for correspondents before they left Russia. Harrison warned the commissar that shrinkage of the foreign correspondents' corps weakened the value of their news coverage. [42] No appeals helped.

Lissner's warnings pestered Salisbury. So did the *Times* caution and avoidance of the suggested "slug." Years later he found out from Gay Talese's book *The Kingdom and the Power* that Talese had heard Salisbury was the target of the MVD and might be arrested, shot, or killed. [43] And it was not until 1977 that he met MVD defector Yuri Nosenko, who had also worked for the CIA. He related to Harrison that in 1953, while heading the MVD's section for overseeing foreign correspondents, he had read a fat file on Salisbury. "He found that a proposal had been made 'to Stalin' that I be given a drug that would induce paralysis." The drug's effects might last eight months and require his departure from Moscow, if not his death. Though Stalin refused its use as too risky, Nosenko related, the agents suggested Salisbury's dispatches revealed much more than he had obtained from public sources. He got secrets, they thought, from high within the Kremlin itself. [44] At the time, Salisbury felt secure in his position.

Harrison still found "confidence and tranquility" in Moscow, living conditions were improving, and the world to Muscovites was looking "a good deal brighter" than in 1945. It was also the approach of Stalin's seventieth birthday on December 21, 1949. Salisbury used the occasion to send the dictator a congratulatory letter. He suggested it was a good time for a foreign press interview. It had been a long time and "your words would be read with the greatest interest, not only by the readers of *The New York Times* but by citizens of the whole world." [45] Harrison received no reply.

Mao Zedong arrived at the Yaroslavsky Railway Station on December 16, 1949, greeted by a dapper Molotov and Nikolai Bulganin, bedecked in his marshal's uniform. They took Mao directly to Stalin's Lipki *dacha*, where he remained isolated. It was not until January 2, 1950, that Stalin sent Molotov and Soviet economic expert and Politburo member Anastas I. Mikoyan to Mao to begin talks on a treaty.

Mao attended Stalin's birthday celebrations at the Bolshoi, where he greeted Stalin as "the teacher and friend of the Chinese people." Mao won a standing ovation. The "Committee for Preparations for Comrade Stalin's Birthday" spent 487,000 rubles on gifts, a "Stalin pack" to each of the attendees with grooming items. The head of Stalin's private secretariat, Lieutenant General N. Poskrebyshev's daughter, Natasha, presented Stalin with a bouquet of red roses. The exotic entourage, including Mao, then reassembled at the Kremlin's Georgievsky Hall for a banquet and concert. Hymns of praise followed in the Moscow papers.[46]

Chinese Foreign Commissar Zhou Enlai arrived on January 20, 1950, to join Mao in negotiating a treaty with the new foreign minister, Andrei Vishinsky. Stalin ordered the demoted Molotov to speak with Mao, whose Marxism he found wanting. Molotov referred to him as a "Chinese Pugachëv," that is, a peasant rebel but not a Marxist. Salisbury and his colleagues sought interviews with Mao or, at least, a statement. But Stalin cloaked everything Chinese in secrecy. Only a statement of Mao to TASS revealed that any new Sino-Soviet treaty would follow the 1945 treaty's example, although technical and financial aid would increase.[47]

The Soviet press ranked China the equal of the USSR and noted that Zhou Enlai had joined in treaty negotiations. Yet the Chinese embassy still denied the two Chinese leaders were even in Russia. That led Salisbury to confess, "I don't know any inside information on the visit of Mao and Zhou. No one here knows a damn thing about what is going on."[48] Yet Vishinsky denounced U.S. Secretary of State Dean Acheson for claiming the USSR had taken over four areas of China—Outer Mongolia, Manchuria, Inner Mongolia, and Sinkiang. Salisbury thanked Vishinsky for getting his statement to the foreign press before announcing it over the radio, thus giving the Moscow-based foreign correspondents a chance to file their dispatches first.[49] By February 7, 1950, Harrison commented, "Never in recent history has the head of a major foreign state paid a visit so prolonged as that of Mao Zedong to the Soviet Union." That long visit caused speculation: Would many of the 1945 agreements need revisions? The Sino-Soviet Treaty of Friendship, Alliance, and Mutual Assistance, finally signed on February 14, 1950, allowed Russia to hold Port Arthur and Dairen for thirty years. The territorial integrity of the three Northern provinces and Sinkiang and the independence of Outer Mongolia remained. The USSR extended a $300 million credit as well as the return of the Changchun railway and broader security terms with mutual aid in the event of aggression and consultation on important international issues.[50]

Mao, it was later reported, fussed over Stalin's reticence about the treaty. Supposedly, Stalin shouted, "To hell with that! We must go all the way." That depressed Mao. His Chinese interpreter, trying to calm the atmosphere, suggested inviting Stalin to Mao's residence. Mao hissed, "Don't invite him!" The rest of that evening went badly with neither leader speaking to the other. At a Metropole gala banquet on February 14, 1950, they signed the treaty. Only sporadic exchanges passed between the pope of international communism and his Asian cardinal.[51]

It was then that Stalin found an excuse to purge the Moscow Communist Party apparatus and bring Nikita Khrushchev from Kiev to Moscow. He needed Khrushchev to balance the growing power of Malenkov and Beria after Zhdanov's death and the purge of the Leningraders. To find a place for the Ukrainian leader, Stalin removed his Moscow party chief, G. M. Popov, and Popov's favorites. It began with a campaign of criticism and self-criticism, led off by Malenkov's Stalin anniversary article in which he attacked "Popov's pets"—factory managers, local Soviet officials, and assorted small fry. In the cultural area, Anatoly Sofronov, prizewinning author of such plays as *Moscow Character* and *Bekitov's Career*, was smeared as antipatriotic and cosmopolitan, even though he had previously won the 100,000 ruble Stalin prize. His fictional heroes now became villains. How, Salisbury asked, could *Literary Gazette* make such a 180-degree turn? "It was greedily published and highly praised by the sycophants last summer. Then, low and behold, the No. 1 play critic, Mr. Stalin, read the work and said it stank. So it was torn to ribbons in a series of critiques along with the lads who had praised and published it."[52]

By now, on the eve of Salisbury's return to America in May 1950 for a four-month leave, he had become a shrewd Kremlinologist. Salisbury recognized the ascent of Malenkov and liquidation of the Zhdanov clique. Malenkov was consolidating his influence while his opposition sought to counterbalance him. In that regard, it was reasonable to understand the transfer of Khrushchev from Kiev to take Popov's position as well as the mounting criticism of Andreyev: "Khrushchev's move into Moscow was designed to strengthen the anti-Malenkov forces, who probably represent as close to the 'old guard' faction as you can get inside the Politburo." Nevertheless, Salisbury was reluctant to suggest that Andreyev would be liquidated. Rather, he postulated something short of his being disgraced, say, that he would be removed from chair of the collectives, the system of Soviet communal agriculture. He had just been around too long and was too important—thirty years in the Central Committee and twenty-five years in the Politburo. Probably, he would "confess his sins and promise to be a good boy." That left Molotov as number two and Malenkov as number three, followed by Beria, Klement Voroshilov, Lazar Kaganovich, Mikoyan, Andreyev, Khrushchev, Bulganin, Aleksei Kosygin, and Nikolai Shvernik—in that order. "For my money that emphasis supports the theory that if Stalin dies Molotov will become the Premier and front man with Georgii [Malenkov] holding the reins and the very grey figure of Beria looming strongly in the background." The results of these moves were two Politburo groupings: Molotov's versus Malenkov's.[53]

About China, Salisbury viewed the Sino-Soviet Treaty as one-sided, financially cheap, and pro-Russian on territorial concessions or the use of Dairen. About Mao, Harrison believed, "he is not to be considered as a puppet or mere Russian agent." Even Harrison's Russian friends, he told Cy, knew nothing much of China, of the H-bomb, of Cold War debates in the United States, of Churchill's Fulton speech, of Politburo manipulations, or of dealings with Mao. "The blackout is complete."[54]

In early March 1950, Harrison had managed a brief trip to Odessa. Otherwise, life remained much the same in Moscow. "So far," he told Cy, "there are no ostensible indications of any particularly aggressive or threatening attitude on the part of the Russians."[55] He sent a few more letters off to Soviet big shots but received no replies. Harrison spent time securing a reentry visa, though it did not guarantee his readmittance. Konstantin Simonov at the foreign office's press department said OVIR of the MVD controlled visas. He saw no problem assuring readmittance and took up the matter with his chief, U. P. Frantzev. As Simonov put it, "he felt there would be no question of any difficulty in my case."[56] James, on the other hand, worried about Salisbury's ability to reenter the USSR. There were, he cautioned, no other foreign positions available at the *Times*. Their agreement, he reiterated, was for a minimum of two years in Moscow.[57] However, the *Times* would make an honest effort to place him somewhere. On May 20, 1950, Salisbury left Moscow for New York City with more savvy about Moscow's Byzantine ways and a competence in conversational Russian on his way to finalize his divorce in Nevada. By September 1950, he had solved his personal problems. Many of his friends expressed amazement at his ability to rebound and continue rebounding. Salisbury dismissed that as melodramatic exaggerations.[58]

Again, Salisbury arrived back in Moscow from Paris on September 12, 1950, with all these reflections from his train ride fresh in his mind. The long trek from Paris to Moscow—on the Orient Express, then the Kuriersky Express—had given him a clearer sense of his past year in Moscow, March 1949–June 1950. But his train ride from Paris had also offered him a fresh peek behind the Iron Curtain. Curiously, it was what he said he did not see that shocked his colleagues at the *Times*.

♦♦ 2 ♦♦

The Kuriersky Express took Harrison along the great invasion path once traveled by the armies of Napoleon, the Kaiser, and Hitler: through Baronov- ichi, Minsk, Orsha, Smolensk, Vyazma, and Mozhaisk. At Warsaw, the *Times* chief there, Ed Morrow, acted as his guide. At Brest, where the gauge and rail carriages changed to the wider Russian type, he explored this impor- tant junction. He saw no guns, no munitions, no rations, no flatcars carrying weapons, no troop concentrations. He had a scoop: no European war, though people were worried because of the Korean War. Moscow itself remained quiet, without shortages. In a series of dispatches, Harrison reported his behind–the–Iron Curtain observations. None of them received significant censorship, though their delay meant they were getting Kremlin attention.[59]

What did Harrison report that so electrified the *Times* newsroom? While still aboard the Kuriersky Express, he wrote a friend that he saw no hysteria in Europe, unlike America.[60] In Moscow, although he heard talk of the Korean War, there was nothing "an honest observer could possibly describe as a war scare or war hysteria." No Russian felt war with the United States was imminent. Food and clothing were ample. Queues were normal and Soviet propaganda about the same. On September 22, 1950, Harrison re- ceived a telegram from Catledge requesting more information: prices, earn- ings, purchases, defense budgets, military recruitment figures, citizen alerts, Soviet propaganda. "We," the telegram read, "upholding series pending re- ceipt above inserts and clarifications."[61] Unknown to Harrison, the *Times* business manager, General Julius Adler, and the Sunday editor, Lester Mar- kel, mounted an attack on the series, suggesting Harrison was a communist dupe. It was they who demanded the new data, most of which he provided, except for prices. As Harrison later put it, "most of [this] had little or nothing to do with my articles, inserts, elaborations, statistics, new facts galore." Catledge told Adler that Harrison "had sent all he could, with the exception of the prices." Prices never cleared the censor. Dissatisfied, Adler and Mar- kel demanded Salisbury's recall. *Times* publisher Arthur Hays Sulzberger had just returned from Europe and, as Harrison wrote, "put it bluntly to Markel: did he really want Salisbury fired?" Markel backed down.[62]

Harrison had written Catledge when it seemed his series would not be run: "you must feel that you have very compelling reasons for not publishing the dispatches." Again, Harrison defended his scoop and emphasized there was "no evidence of a step-up in Soviet military preparations in the last four months and a general lack of war paranoia in the Soviet public." Harrison was only interested in giving the *Times* the facts and not selling a Soviet bill of goods, regardless of whether or not party sympathizers seized on his dispatches as an indication of Russia's "desire for peace."[63] Catledge came clean: "I'd be less than frank with you if I didn't say your series did cause a great deal of discussion among the editors of the *Times*."[64] That was why, he confessed, they had asked for details.

A few more persons bothered Harrison. Irving Brown, an AFL-CIO union representative in Europe, pestered Markel. Further, General R. W. Grow, the U.S. embassy's military attaché, wrote the Pentagon of his belief that Salisbury's future series was a Soviet propaganda handout.

In the end, Manny Freedman revised and condensed the series, which finally was published with, at last, the warning "slug." Harrison had campaigned for that "slug" all along, which cautioned its readers, "As is the case with all news dispatches from Moscow, these articles were subject to Soviet censorship and were written with that fact in mind."[65] However, in Harrison's opinion, his soup had been spoiled "by some rather ignorant cooks." For a long time, he noticed a "touchiness" and a "lack of confidence" in him from his editors.[66] Whatever the touchiness on the editors' part or his feelings of being ignored, his third article in the series laid out his opinion clearly. There was no war scare, no military preparations, no hoarding, no panic, no price inflation. Rather, Soviet reconstruction rapidly continued, and "so far as research can determine, there has been no substantial changeover of the economy from its predominantly peacetime aspect to one of preparation for, or anticipation of, war."[67] Internal firestorm or not, Harrison made his point. He wrote a friend, "I thought the series went over quite well. It was certainly far from as complete a picture as I should have liked to present but considering all the difficulties of the present times one can't hope for perfection."[68]

This scoop was another example of the journalist reporting truth to power. Harrison often remarked that truth is no defense—it is dangerous, it upsets applecarts. The messenger "bringing the bad but true news was beheaded." Or, at the very least, his eyes gouged out.[69]

Arthur Hays Sulzberger wrote his nephew Cy Sulzberger about Harrison's series. The boss noted both James and Catledge were for publishing the series, but Charles Merz, head of the editorial page; Lester Markel, Sunday editor; and editorial writer Anne McCormick disapproved on the belief that Harrison's scoop was Soviet propaganda, the line against Salisbury most ardently pushed by General Adler. They made further efforts to get more data from Harrison. Soviet censors would not pass that information. That was the situation when the boss returned to New York. He believed that if the *Times* lacked confidence in Harrison, he should be fired. Otherwise, "it is unwise for us to determine whether or not to print what he sends, in the manner in which we were obviously doing with these articles in question." Salisbury admitted personally writing a onetime "slug," which he had been advocating for placement on all his dispatches. Henceforth, the *"Times* did occasionally express regret in its editorial for the 'distorted or incomplete report from Russia, through no fault of our correspondent.'" This helped to a degree. [70]

Arthur Hays Sulzberger visited the State Department and found that, though nothing was held against Salisbury, diplomats preferred his removal if he continued to submit such stories. They had liked Drew Middleton's finesse. Sulzberger recalled the "considerable discussion" accompanying Salisbury's appointment to Moscow and the belief by a few that there was something "fishy" about it. "I took the responsibility at that time of having him go forward, and did this with the endorsement of the News Department." Sulzberger was for keeping Salisbury there, but cautioned, "provided he in turn can develop a little more acumen in beating the censorship, and provided of course that he isn't merely playing, even innocently, the Russian game." In terms of the actual issue at hand, he took an ambiguous position. On the one hand, he personally believed Russia must be on a war footing. On the other hand, he relied on what Salisbury said, that he did not discern any sign of Russia's rearmament. That was, he concluded, important news, and he urged Cy Sulzberger to get to Moscow to confirm both Salisbury's views as well as whether the *Times* should keep him in the Russian capital. Arthur ended with this warning, "I wouldn't consider removing him at this moment at any rate, if only for the reason that I spoke to those boys in the State Department such a short while ago." [71]

Cy had also objected to the series, but on different grounds than the others. He wanted a single article instead of a series. Harrison would simply give impressions of Moscow on his return there after his four month leave in the states. The situation, Cy continued, had been mishandled in the *Times* newsroom. Cy remained confident in Salisbury, and he was anxious to look the scene over personally. "I think we should let the matter rest in abeyance until the fate of my Moscow trip has been decided by the boys in the Kremlin." The Kremlin boys, however, said no to Cy's visit, never, despite Salisbury's efforts on his behalf. [72]

That firestorm—Harrison termed it a Russian noise or *"shum"*—was as close as Salisbury ever came to being fired or recalled, though one eye had been temporarily put out. [73]

At this time, the Korean War had been dragging on since June 25, 1950. The United Nations had condemned the invasion of South Korea by North Korea on June 27. President Harry Truman had backed the UN's condemnation of the North's invasion of the South with American forces as a "police action." The military situation looked desperate until September when General Douglas MacArthur made a daring landing at Inchon and reversed the North Korean action temporarily, until a huge Chinese force entered the fray as UN forces approached the Yalu River. It was in these tense months that Salisbury's reporting from Moscow entered a very difficult stage because of intense Soviet anti-Americanism.

The thirty-third anniversary of the Bolshevik Revolution on November 7, 1950, passed on an icy autumn day when even the air show was grounded due to drizzle and fog. The foul weather kept Harrison griping about censorship. His review of one of Stalin's *Pravda* articles passed the censor's blade. Truman, that Stalin article ran, needed war, not peace. The Korean War had dealt a "shattering blow" to America's "strong policy." Truman, Stalin proclaimed, was fanning war hysteria.[74]

Manny Freedman, the *Times* foreign editor, criticized Salisbury's point about not seeing Russia on a war footing and drew a rebuttal from his Moscow bureau chief. Salisbury had complained that a high percentage of his stuff was going in the *Times* wastebasket. Freedman replied that space in the *Times* was at a premium and the competition for it was keen. He returned to the core issue that disturbed Salisbury's critics: "I will say, however, that lack of justification in some of your copy as it reaches us sometimes troubles us." Though the paper did not mind using explanatory brackets for a single dispatch, it feared doing so for a series. It would look like editing. The *Times* could, Freedman thought, assume that omissions were the censor's work, or qualify whenever it felt justified. Otherwise, it would eliminate questionable material.[75] Salisbury agreed. He remained firm on his line of interpretation. The Russians feared a general war and believed peace worked to their advantage. Capitalism would eventually destroy itself, though the Soviets were not averse to giving it a nudge. It allowed for improvisations. Korea was a miscalculation only intended as a hit-and-run operation by North Korea, so the Soviet version went, not aimed at producing a military counteraction by the United States. Yet the North Korean attack surprised Russians by its audacity, as did the success of General Douglas MacArthur's Inchon landing. The fatal U.S. mistake, according to Russians, was the United States' proceeding beyond the thirty-eighth parallel. At that point, according to Salisbury's analysis of Russian opinion, Americans lost their moral edge. Had they stopped there, the action would have been justified. Russians had a naïve faith in their government, probably due to its victory over the Nazis and a general improvement in their standard of living.[76]

Harrison continued his peace interpretation. Harry Schwartz, ex-stringer and now a regular correspondent for the *Times*, sided with Adler against Salisbury, pontificating from his cushy tenth-floor office in the *Times* building. Such critics could not deter Harrison, who did the hard on-the-spot reporting from Moscow. While in New York City, the *Times* specialists, editorial board, and bull pen could only guess at the Russian reality. They were, in his opinion, throwing a "large gob of smear" his way. The Russia that Harrison depicted "did not fit the popular image."[77] Although the Soviet press wrote of war hysteria in America and sharply criticized Truman-Acheson policies, it also eased the severe vigilance campaign against foreign reporters.

About P. Pospelov's speech suggesting Americans "have always been the No. 1 sons-of-bitches," that initiative had little chance of "reversing a long, deep and historic feeling of goodwill and admiration towards America." Ordinary Russians felt "bewilderment and incredulity" toward America, not hatred. Salisbury finished, "the danger and possibility of war is not in the forefront of the Muscovite mind and [if] it isn't in the forefront in Moscow you know how far back it must be out in the provinces."[78]

Harrison laid this same emphasis with Cy. He noted the Kremlin's policy of lowering prices and Stalin's emphasis that war was not inevitable. Instead, Stalin called on Western peoples to demand their governments change policies. Writing from Leningrad, Harrison related speaking with many persons. The idea of war was not uppermost in their minds, nor was Pospelov's vilification campaign. As Salisbury put it, *"they never had it so good here."* He slyly confessed to Sulzberger, "I actually feel considerable embarrassment in reporting the state of Russian public opinion because people in America seem to resent the fact that Moscow isn't all stirred up."[79]

The Soviet peace initiative further bothered Salisbury in reporting it. So much so that even Cy had to reassure him. He sent another letter to Cy, amplifying his Leningrad trip. Sergei Kirov and Andrei Zhdanov remained popular, but dead, heroes there. Stalin ran for the Soviet from a Leningrad district. In addition, Salisbury reemphasized that the dictator had brought Nikita Khrushchev to Moscow to strengthen Molotov and Voroshilov against the Malenkov group in the Politburo.[80] Leningrad remained "damned important." It had the best machine plants, the best electrical and precision instruments manufacturing. It was the home of the most brilliant intellectuals. Of course, Salisbury only then had a vague idea of the Leningrad Affair, and only a "cloudy impression that there had been a bloody purge of the Leningrad Party apparatus in 1949–50."[81] Finally, words of encouragement from the *Times* came. A letter from Brooks Atkinson, a previous Moscow bureau chief, complimented him on his "admirable work," which was unbiased and gave a rounded picture of life in the Soviet Union.[82] Cy wrote to tell him not to fear reporting on the "state of Russian public opinion as it seems to be." Be fair and accurate, he cautioned, within the limits of the censorship. The items of personal gossip from Harrison's conversations with ordinary Russians were particularly interesting to Cy.[83]

In March, the state budget passed, increasing funding for the armed forces by ninety-six billion rubles. That pleased Stalin, who looked good at the session of the Supreme Soviet. Harrison guessed that Stalin attended the funeral of his mother-in-law, Olga Alliluyeva. Harrison was interested in Khrushchev and the new initiative in agriculture: farm collectives were being amalgamated into huge *agrogorods* in an effort to industrialize agriculture and erase the divide between the peasants and proletariat.[84] In May 1951, Harrison finally got to spend three weeks in Soviet Georgia, where he interviewed people who had known Stalin as a young man. Both his articles on Georgia and Leningrad were criticized by *Times* readers, mainly because he portrayed life there as "not as black as seems to be generally supposed among the public."[85] Cy told him, "You must not worry about attacks against you published in our column of Letters to the Editor. Brother, I have had them by the yard."[86]

By the spring of 1951, Harrison had become close friends with Tom and Juli Whitney, and the three of them rented a *dacha* in Saltykovka, twenty miles from Moscow. The Whitneys, eventually with the addition of Ambassador George F. Kennan to their circle, altered Salisbury's life in Russia. Tom, a reporter for the AP, was a specialist on the Russian economy and fluent in Russian. His wife was a talented musician. Harrison took the *dacha*'s attic room. The village, once the infamous home of Countess Darya, a celebrated sadist, was now where workers in the State Planning Committee (Gosplan) were rewarded with *dachas*, often built by themselves. Neither the local peasants nor the Gosplan bureaucrats liked these foreigners, who made them uneasy. However uneasy the locals were, for Harrison it was an oasis of solitude from Moscow's maddening crowd, a retreat from the scoop's firestorm. It was here that Salisbury learned about eternal Russia while perfecting his Russian with the Whitneys and their special guests.[87]

Saltykovka had provided a respite from the criticisms of the *Times* bull pen, from endless letters to the editor criticizing his dispatches, seemingly mindless of Moscow's censorship, and from Moscow's cauldron of suspicion. "For Salisbury in Russia these were days of denial and loneliness, a time when he came to suspect that his every move was watched, his every story censored, when nearly every young Russian woman who caught his eye was later questioned by the secret police." Perhaps that picture of an American spy in trench coat, dark glasses, and fedora could not be escaped. He had tired of his censored pieces from Moscow running side by side with Harry Schwartz's articles written from the safety of his tenth-floor office in the *Times* building. Schwartz, reporters continually rumored, said that Salisbury was "taken in" by the Soviets or was "trying to get in good with them." The Salisbury-Schwartz relationship cooled and remained that way.[88]

In July 1951, the Soviets appeared ready to liquidate the Korean conflict. The USSR's UN delegate, Jacob Malik, proposed a truce on June 23, 1951, and talks began on July 10, 1951, at Kaesong. They were broken off on August 23, 1951, but restarted on November 27, 1951, at Panmunjom. Harrison also speculated that, finally, a Japanese peace treaty with the United States was in the offing. It was clear America had never intended to fight either China or Russia in the Far East. A Korean-type threat in Europe by

Russia would bring U.S. retaliation. In one of his periodic letters to Stalin, none of which was ever replied to, he asked the generalissimo whether there was a basis for peace in the Far East. He always inquired of Stalin about the possibility of an interview with the Western press.[89]

At the end of July 1951, after two years on the job and at the age of forty-two, Salisbury was growing weary of his Moscow assignment and thought, perhaps, it was not worth the effort of the *Times* after all. He wrote *Times* editor Edwin James that various diplomats questioned its value. James answered, "The *Times* feels that, on balance, Moscow must and should be covered, despite the disabilities and handicaps." Salisbury had agreed to serve two years, provided the strain was not too great. He wanted neither to be stuck nor get stale. He had never envisioned an indefinite stay, unless the *Times* "felt it to be worthwhile, and sufficiently worthwhile to justify some more or less consistent salary increases." If he were quasi-permanent, it would relieve the *Times* of finding another with the right qualifications or who could get a visa. Salisbury told James he was willing to work on this basis. It would solve the "chronic Moscow problem" for the *Times*.[90]

Continued censorship mutilations from the Soviets and total kills from the *Times* still depressed him. He hankered for some editorial note, especially since his Georgian copy had been censored by one-fourth. The *Times* had, he believed, laid itself open to justifiable criticism. He once again appealed to James and asked why he should bother to make fact-finding trips when his stories were so severely cut by either Moscow or New York or both. Curious-ly, copy on changes in Soviet foreign policy got through without a censor's scratch.[91]

What irritated Harrison so much was that letters to the editor harped on two points about his dispatches. Letter writers complained, first, that they were naïve and ill informed or, second, that he was either deliberately or unintentionally a mouthpiece for Soviet propaganda. Harrison believed there was an "organized campaign on the part of certain individuals to discredit the *Times* Moscow correspondent." Some of the letters picked on minor points: if Harrison called something a "Soviet spade," the censor turned it into a "god-damned red shovel." That was not good for the reputations of either the *Times* or Salisbury for "some to think that the *Times* correspondent in Moscow is a Red or a Pink or naïve or stupid." Once again, he insisted the *Times* put the "slug" above every dispatch of his. Moscow censorship was unique and required a unique policy.[92] It should be noted that the *Times* occasionally regretted in its editorials the censor's distortions, through no fault of its correspondent. That aided Harrison somewhat. It did not offset the problem enough. Also, Harrison disliked Schwartz's criticisms of Russia placed next to one of Harrison's censored pieces. Harrison came to believe, though thought it better not to accuse, that the "*Times* editors or owners did not wish to antagonize powerful Zionist groups in America by putting a censorship tag on their stories." After all, he thought, Jewish censorship in Jerusalem was as harsh as Moscow's.[93]

♦♦ 3 ♦♦

Ambassador Alan Kirk resigned and left Russia in early October, believing, according to Harrison's paraphrase, that instead of an improvement in relations, there had been a progressive deterioration. Partly it was because neither side recognized the vast historical, cultural, and social differences between them. The admiral was blunt: "Relations are worse than when I came—not better." Kirk gave a farewell interview to the press on October 5, 1951, and departed. Already that fall, George F. Kennan, who held a position at Princeton's Institute for Advanced Study, had received word from Secretary of State Dean Acheson that President Truman wanted to appoint him as ambassador. Though reluctant, he felt, as he later recalled, it was "a task for which my whole career had prepared me, if it had prepared me for anything at all."[94] That appointment was officially announced on December 27, 1951.

There had been talk in Moscow about Kennan's appointment. As Salisbury related to Cy, "I am both pleased and disturbed at the talk about Kennan. Pleased because there is no one whose judgment with regard to Russia I respect more highly but disturbed because I believe there is very little possibility of an *agreement* for him." It may have been such a rumor that inspired him to write Catledge: "I am quite willing, if it is the desire of the *Times*, to stay here for a considerable period of time, and particularly if it seems that war may be coming at any time in the relatively near future, I should want to stay on until the final moment."[95]

Scotty Reston at the *Times* Washington bureau had broken the Kennan story. Harrison wrote him saying Kennan's chances were not very bright. "I think this is highly unfortunate because I think Kennan's appointment here would be a wonderful first step toward extricating our Soviet policy from the state of sterile 'you're another' tactics into which it so often falls these days." If nothing else were accomplished, Kennan's "observations and analysis" brought back to Washington would carry the weight of his influence. Salisbury feared there had been what he called a growing gap between actual conditions in Russia and the Washington crowd's impressions of them. Russia made the same mistake about America.[96] As late as December 26, 1951, *Pravda* sharply attacked Kennan. On the next day, the Soviet government accepted him. Salisbury called that acceptance "one of the most encouraging developments in recent months." It came as a big surprise. It was the first time, according to Harrison, the U.S. embassy in Moscow would be "headed by a man who has specialized in precisely this field."[97]

News of Edwin James's death and his replacement as managing editor of the *Times* by Turner Catledge did not slow Harrison's work, and the transition was seamless. Maxim Litvinov passed away on December 31, 1951, announced by a brief remark in *Pravda*; Salisbury's dispatch of January 2, 1952, noted the former foreign affairs commissar's burial at the New Maiden cemetery and the irony of his death just before Kennan's arrival. For Harrison, as for Kennan, Litvinovs's death marked less the end of an era than a "fleeting intrusion of past and almost forgotten days into an alien present."[98]

The Kennan ambassadorship announcement of December 27, 1951, offered hope. Kennan, who had felt alienated by the increasing militancy of Truman's approach to the Soviets, had suggested that Truman find someone closer to him on both policy and friendship. Nevertheless, he was selected. His appointment went before the Senate in mid-February and was unanimously approved by mid-March. In early April, he went to Washington for consultations and instructions. As Kennan put it, "He [Truman] indicated that he shared my views as to the motives and principles of behavior of the Soviet leaders, and had never believed that they wanted another great war." However, as Kennan later remarked, Truman issued no instructions. Nor did Secretary of State Acheson. Kennan also spoke to Russia's ambassador to the United Nations, Andrei Malik, who seemed bitter and claimed American capitalists wanted war. On April 18, 1952, Kennan met again with Acheson and his top advisors. It was clear that Acheson wanted no German agreement with Stalin and no discussion with the Russians on any German matters. Everything was geared toward a new West German arrangement with a European Defense Community. This left Kennan, as he put it, discouraged. "So far as I could see, we were expecting to be able to gain our objectives both in the East and the West without making any concessions whatsoever to the views and interests of our adversaries."[99]

Kennan returned to Princeton a lonely man. He was taking, he believed, an impossible task, "of assiduously concealing from the world the fact that I could not win at all and taking upon myself the onus of whatever failures were involved." He arrived in Moscow on May 6, 1952, with "very mixed feelings." He could see the Kremlin walls from his office on the Mokhovaya, a mere two-minute walk away, but Stalin's lack of an invitation made it seem like light years away.[100]

For Salisbury, nothing much occurred in March and April. He did establish a cryptic message to be sent to the *Times* in the event of Stalin's death: "Freedman final expense account mailed today regards Salisbury Catledge regarding expense account please check with Freedman Salisbury." This message would be filed "L.C." If Stalin's death occurred the day before the message was filed, it would say, "Final expense account mailed yesterday." If Stalin's death was two days earlier, it would read appropriately, and so forth.[101]

Catledge soothed Salisbury's nerves about readers' complaints. The editorial board had the matter under discussion. Though nothing happened, Harrison reminded Arthur Hays Sulzberger that the entire U.S. press corps in Moscow amounted to only five Americans. There was Harrison and the four who were married to Russians—Eddy Gilmore and Tom Whitney of AP, Henry Shapiro of UP, and Andrew Steiger of Reuters. He considered them well equipped, professional, and not biased despite their Russian wives. Moscow was the only Iron Curtain city where American correspondents remained, since William Oates of AP had been arrested and put on trial in Prague. Psychologically, the situation was difficult; as former Ambassador Kirk put it, they lived in the "eye of the hurricane." That created a recurring fascination, frequently repeated: "under certain circumstances and conditions I am prepared and willing to stay on in Moscow for what we might call the 'duration of the cold war.'" It was made more difficult because of the negative reception of his dispatches in the states as well as those of the other four. New travel restrictions, even around Moscow, made travel to Saltykovka questionable. He told Cy he awaited Kennan's arrival with "great anticipation." He was anxious to correlate his views with Kennan's: "It should be damn helpful to me in figuring out potentialities of staying on here longer and it should be of equal value to the *Times* in weighing the situation."[102]

By February 1952, Salisbury complained that he had left the wrong impression with the *Times* office that he was fed up and wanted out of Moscow. To the contrary, he would consider his Moscow assignment as on a "permanent basis, or as permanent as such things can be regarded in these troubled times." Things began looking up in March and April 1952. The Salisbury-Whitney *dacha* was not in the restricted zone, so he had an escape. Further, his fate with the *Times* was practically decided: "I am to remain in Moscow indefinitely, with home leaves, of course."[103]

With Kennan's arrival pending, Salisbury threw himself into his work. He reported on Stalin's belief that a third world war was not in the offing, that heads of state should meet, and that German reunification should be reconsidered. Stalin was once quoted as saying that all outstanding problems were capable of settlement through negotiations and suggested a meeting of heads of state. Salisbury reported on the May Day demonstrations in Red Square and thought Stalin looked fit. With his free time, Salisbury spent more of it in the country and even planted a garden. Kennan arrived on May 6, 1952, at Vnukovo airdrome. He bore no special assignment and cautioned realism. Salisbury felt it good to have an ambassador after a six-month hiatus. As he reported, "Not only does he [Kennan] look with trained eyes, but he has the trained mind to interpret what goes on before his eyes."[104]

Immediately, Kennan noticed the changed atmosphere in Moscow. The foreign community was closely observed and guarded. "I knew myself to be the bearer of a species of plague. I dared not touch anyone, for fear of bringing to him infection and perdition." Malik had proposed Korean truce talks in June. They began on July 10, 1952, at Kaesong. After the battles at Blood and Heartbreak Ridges in August and September, the truce talks continued at Panmunjom, where a cease-fire line was agreed to in late November. Korea aggravated the already hostile Soviet press against America; there were hostile dramas in the theaters, hostile movies, and hostile placards. For relaxation, Kennan spent weekends at Saltykovka. Here, away from Moscow, he could sense the mood of ordinary Russians within "an atmosphere of health and simplicity and subdued hope."[105]

Kennan, of course, was the most special guest. He became Salisbury's guide, inspiration, and mentor. For Harrison, Kennan was an original thinker. According to Kennan, Stalin was willing to sacrifice East Germany in favor of an overall settlement with the United States, including German unification, to prevent any agreement tying West Germany to NATO. Rumors, Harrison thought, "matched the hysteria of Soviet policy (and confirmed Kennan's estimate that up against the stone wall of containment, the Russians would change stance and negotiate)." Washington was frozen against such a deal, and President Truman and Secretary of State Acheson ordered Kennan's silence. He sharply disagreed, but he had to accept it.

Salisbury thought Kennan was an optimist and romantic. Somehow he might find a "totally irregular and undiplomatic route that would put him in touch with the men of the Kremlin." Could it have been the Saltykovki trio? Probably not. Other possibilities were even slimmer. Yet Kennan's visits to the *dacha*, with his Soviet "caretakers" parked discreetly far away, were revelatory moments on things Russian, like something out of Chekhov or Turgenev. For a brief and golden instant, as Salisbury put it, he and the Whitneys with Kennan "sat under the pines of Saltykovka and argued about Stalin."[106]

With Kennan's family finally in Moscow, he came less often to the *dacha*. Salisbury reminisced about these lazy days. By now he knew Russian behavior and the ordinary lives of Russians. He trusted his language competency as well as his expertise as a Soviet specialist. He did not, as he put it, have Tom Whitney's economic knowledge, nor was he in a class with Kennan. He matched his judgment on the Soviet Union against any of the foreigners in Moscow. He was well ahead of the drive to create a corps of Soviet specialists in the United States.[107]

The Whitney *dacha* was, for Kennan, "as close as I ever came to breaking, in that strange summer, the barrier" separating him from the common Russian folk. Salisbury wrote about his talks with Kennan under the birches and pines and around the fireplace at the Saltykovka *dacha*: "I believe I am safe in saying that his ideas and mine about conditions in Russia coincide to a very remarkable degree. He is not optimistic, of course, but he is by no means pessimistic or defeatist."

In July the U.S. embassy was ordered to move its location for the first time since its establishment on July 5, 1934, at number 13 Mokhovaya Street.[108] By early August, Harrison could evaluate Kennan's first few months. The new ambassador was running affairs with an "iron hand" and was "completely frank and open in his relations with correspondents." Salisbury continued: "I see a good bit of him as he has taken a great liking to coming out to the dacha, which Tom Whitney and I share. So, as I say, I am no longer worried about any little nastiness which might make life here less pleasant." Kennan did not take an alarmist view of events, but the propaganda annoyed him. The impressions he had gained were mostly from strolling around Saltykovka.[109]

The foreign news business in New York was improving for Salisbury. Manny Freedman wrote him, "the welcome mat is always out for Moscow copy, particularly balanced stories that give the appearance of having passed the censorship without mutilation." Brooks Atkinson requested a thousand-word article from him on the Moscow Art Theater. A brightly shining, warm summer sun beat down on the Saltykovka foursome, while on the horizon thunderclouds formed.

Chapter Four

A Death in Moscow

Salisbury sensed vast atmospheric changes in the making during Moscow's Indian summer of 1952. Events quickened. Zhou Enlai came to broaden military and economic cooperation of the USSR with the People's Republic of China. Stalin announced on August 20, 1952, a Nineteenth Party Congress, the first since 1939, to meet on October 5, 1952. In a surprising change, it was announced that Georgii Malenkov would deliver the main report, a role Stalin always had held before. The Politburo and Orgburo would be replaced by a Presidium. Added to these, Harrison cataloged mounting numbers of charges and countercharges, "the whole miasma of terror that was to precede Stalin's death in March, 1953."[1] Who but George F. Kennan would think, "Russia was nearing a time for a change in policy," and that this was not a mystical hunch?[2] Moreover, who but Kennan would be among the first foreigners struck by Stalin's lightning?

◆◆ 1 ◆◆

At the end of July 1952, Harrison heard the drumroll of distant thunder in the oncoming Moscow storm. Stalin purged Lavrentia Beria's Georgian satrapy, though the MVD boss appeared at the party plenum, ousting his Georgian comrades.[3] Unknown to Salisbury, Khrushchev would later remember, "It seemed sometimes that Stalin was afraid of Beria and would have been glad to get rid of him but didn't know how to do it."[4] Kennan also sensed something was happening "behind the scenes." As he later wrote, "A curious deadness, caution, and feeling of uncertainty hung over the Russian capital that summer."[5]

Kennan had heard from Italian Ambassador Di Stefano that Stalin had abandoned hope for a settlement even though Russia had agreed to accept German unification. According to Salisbury, Kennan believed the U.S. position in Germany unassailable. Further, East Germany would be an unreliable Russian partner. Eventually, Russia would have to talk to the West. Kennan prepared to wait another seven or eight months for such conversations to begin with him.

Pietro Nenni, a left-wing Italian socialist, had visited Moscow to receive the Stalin Prize and had been granted a lengthy interview with Stalin, which he described in detail to Di Stefano. Someone in the State Department, receiving Kennan's "eyes only" dispatch about the interview, leaked Nenni's secrets to Joseph Alsop, *Washington Post* columnist. Kennan was embarrassed because "they matched the hysteria of Soviet policy (and confirmed Kennan's estimate that up against the stone wall of containment, the Russians would change stance and negotiate)."[6] The Italians had insisted on complete secrecy. Salisbury believed the State Department not only leaked Kennan's dispatch, but also, what was worse, "The report with its quotations of Stalin, etc., represents, in the main, deductions by Di Stefano with some additions by Kennan but not statements by either Nenni or Stalin."[7] Harrison emphasized this was the fourth leak and was not doing Kennan's position any good.

By late August, Salisbury was already speculating about the forthcoming Nineteenth Party Congress in his letters and dispatches. "The emphasis on Malenkov is very marked. Not only does he present the report which Stalin has delivered at each Congress since he consolidated his grip on the party but neither Molotov nor Beria are listed for a principal address." What that meant, should Stalin die, Salisbury emphasized, was "Malenkov . . . would assume the General Secretaryship of the Party and the real power that goes with it." A large Presidium replaced the Politburo and Orgburo, with the Party Secretariat absorbing much of their functions. It would be an "even more effective fulcrum of power." There Malenkov's predominance was clear. Molotov and Beria were absent from it. Though Harrison mentioned talk of a new "purge," he only thought so concerning "local cleanup drives." When he later republished this letter to Cy Sulzberger in his *Moscow Journal*, he added a postscript: "In reality, purges had been going on almost continuously since I reached the Soviet Union in 1949 and preparations for an even greater one were currently under way."[8]

Perhaps the only significant report Salisbury made in early September was on Kennan's departure, September 19, 1952, for consultations with American diplomats in London. He recorded that Kennan still believed containment was the "only effective policy which the United States can follow under the present circumstances." He planned to return on the eve of the Nineteenth Party Congress.[9] Kennan recounted a number of small incidents occurring just before his departure, such as the breach of the embassy's security by the supposed son of the minister of state security and the discovery of a listening device in Spaso House.[10] On the nineteenth, he landed at Tempelhof airport in Berlin, prepared for reporters' questions. Did the U.S. embassy, a young reporter from the Paris *Herald Tribune* wanted to know, have "many social contacts with Russians in Moscow?" Kennan was annoyed and was reminded of his five-month internment in 1941–1942 in Germany. Kennan let loose: "Well," he said, "I was interned here in Germany for several months during the last war. The treatment we receive in Moscow is just about like the treatment we internees received then, except that in Moscow we are at liberty to go out and walk the streets under guard."[11] He had forgotten to declare his remarks off the record. On September 26, Salisbury reported that *Pravda* had branded Kennan "an enemy of the Soviet Union, a slanderer under the mask of a diplomat and a violator of the elementary rules obligatory for a diplomat." Vishinsky declared him persona non grata on October 3, 1952, and refused to allow him to reenter the country. Salisbury called it a "great propaganda move on the opening of the Nineteenth Party Congress!"[12] There followed the sharpest propaganda attack yet on the United States by Malenkov at the Party Congress: America was preparing a new world war directed at Russia.[13]

Toward the end of October, Salisbury analyzed Kennan's ouster. It was, of course, a shock. Personally, Salisbury had loved the "adult and knowledgeable conversations" with Kennan as a "healthy corrective to some of the naiveté which permeates so much official thinking about Russia and to know that for once in a lifetime Washington was getting from its embassy a perceptive, intelligent, sensitive analysis." How the mishap occurred was still a mystery and puzzled Harrison. He knew once *Pravda* had the story, Kennan's "fate was in the fire." Harrison speculated that the eve of the party congress made it even more likely that Kennan would be expelled.[14] After only five months in Moscow as U.S. ambassador, Kennan was out.

As to the congress itself, a new five-year economic plan was announced, but, of special interest to Salisbury, Malenkov remarked that the USSR was no longer "a lone island encircled by capitalist lands." Capitalist encirclement was broken, and there was enough power in the socialist bloc to "live and develop regardless of what happens beyond the Elbe and across the Bering Straits."[15] Stalin was still firmly in control. Salisbury believed, if Stalin died, Malenkov would head the party and Molotov would be head of state. Beria's portrait had dropped a few notches, and he warned that no one should overlook Khrushchev.[16]

Stalin appeared only at the beginning and end of the party congress, which ran from October 5 to 14, 1952. Just before it opened, he issued his last theoretical work, *Economic Problems of Socialism in the USSR*. It declared the objectivity of economic laws, that imperialism drove capitalist states to war, and that communism was possible in Stalin's lifetime. Molotov and Mikoyan disagreed but remained silent. The Politburo was expanded to thirty-six members and converted to a Presidium; this unusually large size made them fear Stalin's boast, "You've grown old! I'll replace you all!"[17] On October 16, 1952, Stalin announced the membership of the Presidium with many new names. From its inner bureau he excluded the names of Molotov and Mikoyan, to the astonishment of the remaining magnates. "They're scared," Stalin explained, "by the overwhelming power they saw in America." Then he threateningly linked them to such formerly purged rightists as Aleksei Rykov and M. Frumkin. By Stalin's seventy-third birthday, December 21, 1952, they still showed up for dinner, though Stalin was indignant. It was clear Stalin wanted their physical destruction. But what would precipitate a purge? The answer came on January 13, 1953: a *Pravda* article announced the arrest of nine "doctor wreckers" who had preyed on the highest echelons of Soviet power, "at the direction of Jewish-American-British intelligence."[18]

Salisbury went on to mention the parallels between the "Doctors' Plot" and the terror of the 1930s: "there were charges of criminal plotting by some of the best-known Soviet physicians directed at some of the most famous figures in the Soviet Union." Sharp words were also directed against the failure of security agencies. Among the arrested doctors was Professor Vladimir Vinogradov, who had signed the death certificates of former Soviet Union President Mikhail Kalinin and Bulgarian leader Georgii Dimitrov.[19] Not only was there no let up on the Doctors' Plot, but it began to have a strongly anti-Semitic flavor.

Stalin had unleashed a "wave of hysterical anti-Semitism" by announcing the arrest of the doctors in *Pravda*: "Ignoble Spies and Killers under the Mask of Professor-Doctors," a phrase Stalin had coined. The doctors were tortured. Stalin ordered Polina Molotova out of Moscow. He demanded Beria get the doctors' confessions. Beria assured Stalin of the confessions. "Arrange it," Stalin told him. Semyon Ignatiev, their torturer, would be "shortened by a head" if he failed, Stalin shouted at Beria. Vishinsky announced severance of relations with Israel. Prominent Russian Jews began disappearing. Russian papers tried to draw a line between anti-Semitism and anti-Zionism.[20]

Suddenly, on March 4, 1953, Salisbury was able to get a dispatch through to the *Times* : "The government announced shortly before eight o'clock this morning that Generalissimo Stalin on Sunday night, March 1–2, suffered a [massive] brain hemorrhage with paralysis of the right hand and leg, loss of speech and of consciousness." Unknown to Salisbury was Stalin's horrible death agony, as he choked to death on his own saliva. His daughter Svetlana Alliluyeva recounted that at the last moment his eyes opened; his glance swept the room; he raised his arm; and he brought it down as if casting a curse.[21] Only by March 6, 1953, was Salisbury able to use his special code, indicating the tyrant's death the day before, though its transmission was delayed and not received in New York until over five hours after the bulletin on Stalin's death was announced on Soviet radio, just after 4:00 a.m. Harrison passed by Stalin's casket in the great funeral procession at the Hall of Columns, where hundreds of thousands came to view the dead tyrant.[22] Salisbury was in place to report on the stunning transformation in Moscow with the death of Stalin.

The whole truth of the final purge, the purge master's death, and Soviet Russia in the aftermath of its master's life awaited a series of articles by Harrison Salisbury in 1954. That effort would gain for Harrison his Pulitzer Prize.

♦♦ 2 ♦♦

On September 19, 1954, the first of a series of fourteen articles on Salisbury's years in Russia appeared in the *Times* under the title "Russia Re-Viewed"; the last ran on October 2, 1954. *Time* magazine, on October 4, 1954, summarized these articles as "a fresh, firsthand report," with Salisbury completely freed of the overbearing Russian censorship for the first time. *Time* highlighted these articles by underlining Salisbury's main themes: the new Russian leadership after Stalin's death brought a fresh change to Stalinism with more graceful tactics; in fact, the junta may have murdered Stalin and gotten rid of MVD chief Lavrentia Beria to save themselves from being purged; the Doctors' Plot may have been the first indication of the dying dictator's efforts to instigate another Great Terror; Beria almost succeeded in taking over; the Red Army and Marshal Zhukov supported the junta; the junta had set out to erase the memory of Stalin, increase consumer goods, and do away with night work in factories and government offices; though many were amnestied, the prison camps still existed; and, finally, Russia's successes in the arms race gave the junta, dominated by Georgii Malenkov and Nikita Khrushchev, a necessary measure of confidence in dealing with the United States—so much so that America may be suffering from an inability "to adjust realistically to Moscow's new look."[23]

Harrison had returned to New York City in September 1954 from an almost six-year stint in Moscow as the *New York Times* bureau chief. He traveled, lectured, and began the series on Russia for the *Times*. Arthur Hays

Sulzberger suggested the series title, helped edit each article, and promoted them. Not ideological, but descriptive and amazingly analytical, they were a realistic portrait of Russia immediately after Stalin's death. Harrison described them as a "firsthand and intimate glimpse of the new leaders, the new policies, the extent to which they were, and were not, breaking from their Stalinist roots." He had dragged his Remington portable to the famed Algonquin Hotel, where he started typing. Out of his room's windows, he saw the *Times* delivery van roll by with his huge photograph plastered to its side that first Sunday morning, September 19, 1954: "I was so excited," he later wrote, "I could hardly see straight. I'd made it!"[24]

It was obvious from the start that everything hinged around the biggest of big scoops: the death of Stalin. Harrison reported that seminal moment and its consequences. Events had reached fever pitch during Stalin's last days, with important persons like Andrei Andreev dropped from the Presidium and Aleksei Kosygin losing his candidate membership on the Central Committee. There was the movement and replacing of pictures on Red Square on November 6, 1952, before the November 7 celebrations of the Bolshevik Revolution, with Lavrentia Beria placed below that of Marshals Bulganin and Voroshilov. Then there was the uncovering of a plot in the Kiev trade network; a military tribunal was set up to investigate mostly Jews, and it handed out death sentences to those found guilty. All this occurred just on the eve of the Doctors' Plot, which broke in the papers on January 13, 1953. As Salisbury put it in his first interpretive journal letter of March 11, 1953, just days after Stalin's death, "Everywhere it was Malenkov, Malenkov, Malenkov. It was plain that he was the Party Big Shot."[25]

Salisbury had had premonitions. He made elaborate preparations to get any late-breaking story on Stalin out of Moscow by using codes and setting up direct telephone links to the London and Paris offices of the *New York Times*. All these intricate preparations failed when Stalin's death was finally announced. In the aftermath, Salisbury tirelessly wrote the new ruling elite requesting interviews, but to no avail.[26] Only when he arrived home in September 1954, after an exhaustive tour of the USSR, could he tell the full story.

Harrison never let an opportunity slip away. Writing freely, without censorship, he titled his first piece "Under New Management, Soviet Tactics Change." That title indicated his intention to take a fresh path in "re-viewing" Russia: "The death of Joseph Stalin has given Russia a new regime with a new way of doing business that has already achieved notable success at home and abroad." The ultimate goal of destroying capitalism and communizing the world remained. Nor had "sweetness and light" descended. The "world's greatest police state" remained, but that was neither new nor immediately important. Rather, "Russia has passed into the hands of a group of men who are displaying striking flexibility and adaptability in their handling of domestic and foreign problems."[27]

The new approach, Salisbury argued, meant facing Stalinism's unpleasantries and often breaking with its rigidity. "Graceful tactics" could be employed with confidence since Russia could back these up with atomic weaponry, jet aircraft, and science and industry matching America's. Harrison characterized the new look: subordinating ideology to commonsense reformism, especially big increases in consumer goods and services; ameliorating police abuses by placing civilians over police power; repairing agriculture through profit motives, while adding a fresh network of state farms, machinery, and personnel; creating a more rational and restrained foreign policy, including convening the Berlin and Geneva Conferences, settlements in Indochina and Korea, and defeating plans for a European defense community. Life in Soviet Russia, Salisbury admitted, had become more relaxed for foreigners, so much so that *Pravda* could complain of an "American Iron Curtain." Russia's new rulers were "not a group of little Stalins [but] a highly interesting and diverse group of men with individual and differing personalities, which they have been at some pains to exhibit to foreigners in recent months."[28]

This new collective leadership not only buried Stalin, but it removed his name almost completely from *Pravda* and resurrected Lenin's. Old Bolsheviks were rediscovered and presented medals. Half in jest, Salisbury mentioned other signs of the end of the Stalin era: canceling construction of a Red Square skyscraper; opening Red Square to the public; ending the Stalin prizes; making bicycles instead of Zil limousines; returning to a nine-to-six office schedule instead of Stalin's all-night regime; making Professor Trofin D. Lysenko, Stalin's misguided agricultural "genius," answer his critics instead of jailing them. Siberian exile had not been abandoned, although considerable numbers of prisoners were released. Nevertheless, an atmosphere of apathy and resignation continued.

Salisbury ended his first installment by noting, though conditions had ameliorated, "There was no sign, however, that the new regime has the slightest intention of abolishing the camps or the police system in general."[29] Likewise, censorship had eased, but not to the point of allowing criticism of the regime.

Harrison's second serial ran a provocative title: "Was Stalin Put to Death to Avert a Blood Purge?" It was, Salisbury began, "by no means impossible that Stalin was murdered on or about March 5, 1953, by the group of his close associates who now run Russia."[30] He admitted that there was no way to prove this. Many Muscovites believed it possible. After all, there was motive and incentive because of obvious signs of Stalin's dementia and the coming of another Great Terror, making that of the 1930s seem trivial—a new massacre of those closest to him. Stalin had appeared robust, but a ruptured artery in his brain on March 2, 1953, "must be recorded as one of the most fortuitous occurrences in history."[31] It saved the lives of thousands, including those who stood nearest him. To understand the atmosphere surrounding his last days, it was necessary for Salisbury to summarize some of the history of Stalin's epoch.

Salisbury reviewed the dictator's Georgian background, his suspicious nature, his Othello complex, and the sinister weapons, including mass torture and murder, by which he gained and maintained power. But the immediate story started with the Nineteenth Party Congress of October 1952. Everyone expected Stalin to name his successors. He did not. Stalin himself played the great role and issued a new economic gloss on Marx. He further reduced the roles of his two chief lieutenants—Georgii Malenkov and Nikita Khrushchev. He replaced the Politburo of twelve with a Presidium of twenty-five and eleven alternates. This move confused the succession. Likewise, he enlarged the secretariat and took over daily control from Malenkov. Stalin had deliberately shuffled the cards.

For the traditional November 7 celebration, the portraits of Beria, Malenkov, and Molotov were dropped and Klement Voroshilov's and Nikolai Bulganin's moved up. The sinister Beria, secret police chief (MVD), fell to sixth place instead of number four. In addition, only six months earlier, Stalin had purged Beria's satrapy in Georgia. In Kiev three top men were shot and others given long prison sentences for "counter-revolutionary wrecking." Most were of Jewish extraction. They had directly served Mikoyan and Khrushchev. Beria did not take part in the prosecution. Simultaneously, Ambassador George F. Kennan, the only foreigner who might have correctly interpreted these events, was barred from returning to Moscow. Others were made to apologize for economic mistakes—those under Malenkov and Lazar Kaganovich. All of this was followed by the most sinister event, announced on January 13, 1953: the Doctors' Plot.

Nine Kremlin doctors, six of them Jews, were arrested and charged with plotting against the lives of government and military leaders. These doctors were said to be connected with Zionist organizations and British-American intelligence. Soviet security organs were slack. It seemed apparent that a pattern was emerging: "a purge more deadly than that of the Thirties and a bloodbath more terrible than any of Ivan's, 350 years ago."[32] Two obvious targets were Beria and the Jews. Only Stalin stood behind laying another major purge. Nor was the intention to limit its focus. The germs of the new purge, Salisbury said, "raced through the Soviet body politic."[33]

Provincial newspapers revealed new arrests, with the heaviest toll in the Ukraine, Khrushchev's satrapy. Moreover, it turned from Jews to the party organization, in general, which had supposedly permitted scandals in trading organizations, the professions, and the arts and sciences. Khrushchev, Beria,

Mikoyan, and Malenkov headed these organizations. Most of all, it affected Molotov—his personnel in the Foreign Ministry, especially those closely connected with foreigners. The military seemed least implicated. They were often cast as victims and saviors of the country. Nevertheless, as in the thirties, they, too, might succumb. The rumor mill ratcheted up. Famous persons were said to have vanished. Everyone, especially those closest to Stalin, was threatened.

Was it possible, Salisbury asked, that those chiefly in harm's way took no action? "In any event," Salisbury continued, "it was apparent to all in Moscow in February 1953 that great and sinister events were in the making."[34] Salisbury tried to report the big news from Moscow with Aesopian language, but the censorship was too drastic. Only the dictator's death ended these events. Censorship began to ease. Harrison finished on this ominous note: "if Stalin died a natural death in March 1953, it was the luckiest thing that ever happened for every man who was close to him. And probably for Russia as well."[35]

Harrison's third article began with his sensational analysis of the seventy-eight hours after Stalin's death, when Beria held the fate of Russia in his hands, then let it slip through his fingers: "He was supreme. There was no one who could challenge him—not Malenkov, not Khrushchev, not Molotov, not the Army."[36] Why he failed to act, thus sealing his own doom, may never be known. It was "one of the great dramas of modern times."[37] Yet enough was known to trace Beria's removal and execution. While still in Moscow, Salisbury noted in his private correspondence that a "showdown over Beria's power was inevitable."[38] To understand that, Salisbury traced the real story of Stalin's death and not the emasculated one perpetrated by the censors.

After the brief official news of Stalin's cerebral hemorrhage on March 2, 1953, it was followed on March 6 by a notice that he had passed away the previous evening. Censorship clamped down. Links abroad were severed. Since no copy of Salisbury's would be passed, he had his driver make several tours of the city. At 5:00 a.m., the city's center was absolutely quiet. About an hour later, convoys of trucks converged there, each with special MVD detachments. They congregated on various city squares. By 7:30 a.m. the total censorship relaxed and thousands of troops and columns of tanks appeared, all bearing the red-and-blue insignia of the MVD. They cleared crowds from the city's center and formed an impenetrable iron band from March 6 to 9. No one left or entered. This iron collar's tentacles stretched to the city's outskirts. By March 8 thousands arrived from all over Russia to view Stalin's body. No one could get to the city's center—not even by metro. No trains could enter within the suburban radius. "Moscow was a city sealed off—not only on the inside, but from without as well."[39]

Harrison strolled from his room at the Metropole Hotel to Red Square. He found it deserted with only workers busy chiseling Stalin's name beside Lenin's on the mausoleum. The thought struck him: the MVD and Beria controlled Moscow. The leaders of the Kremlin were, in effect, Beria's prisoners. This powerful and ruthless man had accomplished a miracle. "Beria had with the smoothness of clockwork put Moscow into his grasp."[40] He had a chance at making himself master of Russia. Nor did he realize this, especially since he had been one of the targets of the Doctors' Plot. Perhaps he had overplayed his hand so badly because of this. He had not been prepared when his chance came. Beria did not understand the momentary extent of his power. Whatever the explanation, his speech at Stalin's bier sounded condescending and with the "undercurrent [that] could have flowed from his knowledge of his power."[41] He had shown the others, especially the army, the danger of his power: "There can be no shadow of a doubt that, from the moment Beria sealed off the Kremlin and Moscow with his troops, he signed his own death warrant."[42]

From this assessment flowed Salisbury's most daring insight—the one that caught everyone's attention and clinched his Pulitzer Prize for international reporting. Beria was, Salisbury estimated, both too big and too weak simultaneously. He was not powerful enough to rule. He was "too dangerous to any other ruler or rulers."[43] The measure of his weakness was that his end came so swiftly. As soon as the MVD left Moscow, the others could be rid of him. No liberal myth that he had revealed the Doctors' Plot or that he had advocated better treatment for the nationalities could undo the facts of his brutality. The person he appointed to expose the Doctors' Plot was executed along with him in December 1953. On December 22 a secret police court sentenced him to death. General P. F. Batitsky had Beria stripped, his hands manacled and hooked to the wall. The general stuffed a towel in Beria's mouth to stop his crying. Batitsky fired a single shot to Beria's forehead. All that demolished any hints of Beria's liberalism.[44]

The fourth article in Harrison's award-winning series came as a balm on troubled Russia. The USSR narrowly missed a more sinister figure than Stalin himself. The reluctant savior was, in Salisbury's interpretation, Marshal Georgii Zhukov. Therefore, he titled his next front-page piece "Army Playing a Major Role, with Zhukov Key Figure." Harrison pointed to the uncertainty of the army's role in the immediate aftermath of Stalin's death, and to its vital importance subsequently, especially the part played by Marshal Zhukov.

Much of this hinged on the fate of General Sergei Shtemenko, who was chief of the general staff until twelve days before Stalin's illness, when he was replaced around February 23 by Zhukov's friend, Vassily Sokolovsky. Shtemenko had been one of five officers named as an intended victim of the Kremlin doctors. The military had hardly been mentioned, and its favor solicited, in the run-up to the Doctors' Plot. Zhukov returned from obscurity in Odessa. He and five other officers composed part of the twelve-man honor guard at Stalin's bier. Zhukov was named minister of defense with Alexander Vasilevsky as his deputy. His and Marshal Konstantin Rokossovsky's popularity as World War II heroes was considerable. Zhukov's resurgence after Stalin's death raised questions.

Zhukov was waiting in the wings after the dismissal of Shtemenko. His significant shift occurred while General Vassily Chuikov was transferred from commander in chief in Germany to important work in the Defense Ministry. General Andrei Grechko, Khrushchev's protégé, took his place. Salisbury emphasized, "This was a very important move. It would appear to mark the first—but by no means the last—occasion in which the political forces represented by the Army and Mr. Khrushchev's Ukrainian and Moscow party organizations, standing side by side with Mr. Malenkov, gave the present ruling clique the power to deal with Mr. Beria."[45]

Beria retaliated by removing Leonid G. Melnikov, Ukrainian party chief, but it was a Pyrrhic victory against Khrushchev. Beria was out on July 10, 1953. Salisbury did not know the exact details of his removal, but he did realize the army had a vital role. Tanks were spotted at Beria's residence the day after his arrest. Salisbury speculated that a few army officers took him into custody in a conference room of the Kremlin. Simultaneously, Marshal Zhukov rose from candidate to full member of the party's Central Committee. "It was clear to everyone that the 'Zhukov group' was 100 per cent behind the Government if, in fact, it had not dictated the Government's action."[46]

The Transcaucasian command was transferred to a Zhukov protégé. Beria's MVD generals were arrested. The army supported a lessening of foreign commitments and an improving of Russia's consumer economy. It was Zhukov who pressed for "justice" in the Beria affair at the November 7 celebrations. In addition, Zhukov paid unusual compliments to General Ike Eisenhower and Field Marshal Viscount Montgomery while celebrating the May 1945 victory over Germany. As Salisbury put it, Zhukov was "drawing a long oar in the Soviet Government," and it might be time for the United States to play on that wartime goodwill.[47]

The fifth in the series, "Members of the Ruling Clique Are Depicted Close Up," appeared in late September. Following Muscovite practice, Harrison referred to the ruling clique as the "junta." It consisted of a triumvirate of Premier Georgii Malenkov, First Party Secretary Nikita Khrushchev, and Foreign Minister Vyacheslav Molotov, with the strong support of Marshal Zhukov's group and backed by a second string of Marshal Nikolai Bulganin, Lazar Kaganovich, and Anastas Mikoyan. Beria's elimination removed the MVD from directly participating in policy making. In fact, the MVD was taken over by Sergei Kruglov and his assistant, Colonel General Ivan Serov, both strictly old-style police professionals. The junta had, up to Harrison's writing, displayed itself as a unified group, but "rumors had started to circulate abroad concerning rivalry between Malenkov and Khrushchev."[48]

Everyone had been impressed at how well the junta worked together. If there were rivalries, foreign experts were betting on Malenkov. No members of the junta continued living in the Kremlin, which was being reopened to the public. Formerly moribund institutions such as the Central Committee were now functioning, meeting every three months in plenary session. Red Square reopened with 150,000 to 200,000 strolling about it daily. The new GUM department store and the Kremlin had become a town hall for Muscovites. Areas close by had been redecorated for the junta, especially in the "old stalls" and Arbat areas. Their *dachas* were west of Moscow, some twenty-five miles along the Moshzhaisk highway. For a month in late summer, they basked in the sunshine just south of Sochi along the Black Sea coast.

The junta traveled about, inspecting this and that. However, "There are many contrasts between Malenkov and Khrushchev."[49] The premier exuded "grace and charm" while the general secretary bulled along in contrast to Malenkov's refinement. Khrushchev was the "hearty type." He was a bluff, open, frank onetime miner who blurted out things the premier was too tactful to mention. Also, Malenkov toasted with white wine, but Khrushchev preferred vodka and many "*do adnas*," or "bottoms up." His rough language peppered the air with "*znachits*," or "it means." Salisbury reported that the members of the junta frequently interrupted one another. All paid respect to Molotov, who now initiated foreign policy instead of merely carrying it out. Minor junta members listened and said little. Zhukov was usually present but never far away. He gave the impression that "his affairs were in good hands and going well. As far as anyone in Moscow can tell, he has every reason for such confidence."[50]

In his sixth article, "Life of Soviet Common Man Is a Constant Struggle," published on September 24, 1954, Salisbury outlined the lives of three typical Russians. Admittedly, it was the hardest one in the series to write for it was almost impossible for foreigners to have any real Russian friends. Therefore, he invented Ivan, Dmitri, and Maria. Ivan was a thirty-nine-year-old carpenter, married, with a nine-year-old daughter and sons seven and five. He spent barely four years in school, served in World War II, and was severely wounded. Though he had a steady job in a factory's woodworking shop near Moscow, his wages were poor. He lived in a rural slum with his in-laws. His diet was potatoes, borscht, and black bread. Ivan could hardly read, criticized those around Stalin, was afraid of war, drank too much, and knew little of the United States. Dmitri, likewise, served in World War II, but graduated from a language institute, lived in the stylish Arbat, and planned to go to Germany to improve his language skills. He kept to literary matters, but wondered why the United States was so hostile. His wife also graduated from the same institute, and they had two children. Maria was a woman of sixty whose life had been ruined when her engineer husband had been purged in 1937. Her son died of war wounds in 1944. She was a nurse in a large Moscow factory and had few expenses. Harrison noted, "The new Government and the death of Stalin encourage her a little, but she is really afraid to hope too much, and besides, as she and some of her friends say, it is too late for hope. There is no one left for whom to hope."[51] It was a dreary picture that Salisbury drew of the lives of these ordinary Russian citizens.

Salisbury returned to an important policy topic in his seventh piece: "Chou [Zhou] Talks Back in Moscow to Communist Sponsors," dated September 25, 1954. The USSR faced in two directions—east and west. The junta had dramatically improved its relations with Britain and France. However, "Its relations with the United States have remained diplomatically correct, politically sterile and, practically, often recriminatory."[52] In the east, signs of strain continued, though not serious problems. Harrison used the word "detected" as it required "the combined talents of Sherlock Holmes, Ellery Queen and, possibly, Mr. Moto, to find out anything at all about the true state of Soviet-Chinese relations."[53] The secrecy of the matter indicated that it was not a smooth relationship. U.S. tensions were greater than were those in Europe.

Chinese premier Zhou Enlai had returned from the Geneva Conference of 1954 by way of Moscow. He had made pointed remarks while there. These indicated no subservience to Russia. Though polite to the junta, he chose to sit with lesser dignitaries. He ridiculed Mikoyan and Kaganovich for being unable to speak Chinese or English. Though Zhou knew Russian, he chose to speak in English. Salisbury commented, "Whether, in fact, a radical change in United States policy toward Communist China might allow the natural strains of the Russo-Chinese alliance that flow from inevitable basic national differences to become operative is an open question"[54]

The junta had moved to improve Indian and European relations. Trade had worked with Britain and France, especially on goods restricted by the United States. Germany remained a big obstacle in Europe. Any changes there would affect the rest of Eastern Europe. Anti-American propaganda continued with varying intensity. The junta saw a bipolar world of the United States and the USSR. As to ensuring peace with the United States, they said, "At least for a time." Harrison remarked, "In any such agreement, Russia's rulers, and only Russia's rulers, would know how fast the minutes were ticking off on the clock by which they were measuring the period they had in mind when they said, 'At least for a time.'"[55]

In the eighth piece, Harrison returned to one of the bitterest topics of Stalinism: "Amnesty Too Late for Many; Mme. Molotov Was Saved," which appeared on September 26, 1954. Harrison remembered the censorship had allowed him to report the death of Mikhail Borodin, the famous Comintern agent in China, on May 29, 1951, by only noting his death and nothing more. The fact that Borodin had died in an east Siberian prison camp at the age of sixty-seven had not been allowed by the censors. Had he survived Stalin's death, it seems clear he would have been amnestied. Large numbers had been released since April 1953. One of the first to be brought back from Siberia was Mme. Molotov, who had been arrested during the Doctors' Plot—she was most famous as the foreign minister's wife, former head of the cosmetics industry, and an alternate member of the Central Committee. Another well-known released prisoner was Marshal Aleksandr Novikov, former air marshal. And so it went.

Stalin had shown, Salisbury related, particular vindictiveness and secrecy toward those involved with his personal family life. For instance, did he take Rosa Kaganovich as his third wife? He displayed great sensitivity about his second wife, Nadezhda Allilyueva, who was believed to have committed suicide. Perhaps he had a guilty conscience. Lawyers were being sent out to Siberia to review and release many more. Salisbury concluded, "One thing seems certain. For the first time in many years, a certain interest of an inquiring investigatory nature is being shown in Moscow in the fate of millions sent away to labor and to die in the Far North, the Far East and Central Asia."[56]

Harrison continued this theme into his ninth installment, "The Prison Camps of Siberia." He began with his own eyewitness description of a camp near Yakutsk, near the Lena River—the camp where the once famous Soviet publicist Karl Radek perished as well as the well-known diplomat Gregorii Sokolnikov. "It was," he remarked, "probably the most extensive survey of this grim region by an American since the journey in the late Eighteen-Eighties of George Kennan, grand-uncle of George F. Kennan, former United States Ambassador to Moscow." Nothing much had changed. The capital of this MVD-land was Khabarovsk on the Amur River: "This correspondent, partly by chance and partly by management, happens to have traveled through more of this vast area of MVD-land than any other foreigner."[57]

MVD-land was a vast area with tentacles stretching outward—a huge empire within an empire. Impressions were in the beholder's eye, and situations in MVD-land varied. For example, ten years earlier former presidential nominee Wendell Willkie and Vice President Henry Wallace visited Yakutsk and were favorably impressed, just the opposite of Salisbury—even though improvements had been made. General Sergei Goglidze, MVD-land's boss, guided Wallace. Harrison called Goglidze "the biggest police boss in the world."[58] And Goglidze, Harrison was quick to point out, had been executed with his boss, Beria, in December 1953. Even though there had been a big reshuffling of chairs in the MVD, nothing had materially changed at MVD headquarters in Moscow or in Siberia, where all the major construction was still being carried out by prison labor. Mixed crews were increasingly used.

Further enlarging on the previous two articles on Siberia and prisons, Salisbury offered in this tenth installment "The Spets' System of Exile," or how the MVD forced "millions to live under restrictions in remote areas."[59] "Spets" meant a person living under "special residence conditions," that is, limited to a particular city or region. The word *spets* was stamped into that person's internal passport. They lived everywhere, but especially in Central Asia, Siberia, the Far North, and the Far East. They could only leave their restricted zones by special permission, but they were free to find their own residence and work. They were frequently oppressed minorities like Jews, Balts, and Caucasian tribesmen: "They are the millions of citizens of the Soviet Union who, somehow or other by their own actions or more likely by accident of geography, residence or nationality have fallen afoul of the Soviet authorities and been sent off to live in some distant and usually unpleasant locale."[60] Not much foreign attention had been paid to this "far more common and equally vicious phenomenon, with all kinds of variety." Whole nationalities had been transplanted—Volga Germans, Ukrainians, and Crimean Tatars, the former relocated in Samarkand, Tashkent, and Alma Ata.

As for the Tatars, they were sent north to an alien climate—the pattern being to keep them separated from Central Asian Moslems, or to put the Germans among Tadzhiks. No one was sent where life was easy or pleasant. Russians replaced Balts, who were sent east, away from the Baltic littoral. "Divide, and rule more safely, is obviously the copybook maxim of the secret police."[61] Many *spetsi* were only required to live one hundred kilometers from Moscow. Several large one-hundred-kilometer towns had grown up. Free Russians could roam about except in the north and east, where MVD rule was supreme. Spot checks of internal passports were often made. The new post-Stalin government had quit sending large numbers of *spetsi* into exile. Nevertheless, "so long as the whole notorious prison system is continued; so long as the MVD runs Siberia and the Far North; so long as these industrial jailers need hands for their mines, mills and farms—just so long will the Government have an incentive and an interest in discovering new causes that will enable it to uproot large masses of population from comfortably settled areas and ship them off to frontier regions in the East."[62] Soviet propaganda encouraged urban youth to move to the "Virgin Lands" to boost crop production, but primitive conditions caused bitterness. Such sacrifice, as Salisbury put it, was the kind "any loyal and patriotic worker should be ready to make in the hour of his country's need!"[63]

The eleventh piece, published on September 29, 1954, was titled "Anti-Semitism and Religion." The new regime sustained a "low tension campaign against the Russian Orthodox Church," but it strongly opposed recurrent anti-Semitism. Three major anti-Semitic campaigns had been carried out since 1941, along with the German extermination program during the war. A few synagogues remained in the largest cities. Jews continued playing an important role in the country's cultural and scientific life. Those imprisoned during the Doctors' Plot were released and restored. The benign policy came almost too late. There was little Jewish culture left to preserve or make any early revival possible. The press never mentioned Judaism. Rather, it was Russian Orthodoxy, Roman Catholicism, and Mohammedanism *Pravda* harped on. During the war, the government suggested that Jews were deserting Moscow. In July 1948 through 1949, Jews were labeled "cosmopolites"—which brought an end to Jewish communities and cultural life, especially in Minsk. Many families from Byelorussia and Odessa were sent east. A notable nonvictim was Ilya Ehrenburg, even though his novel *Storm* was denounced. When called by the writers' union to respond, he chose to quote a letter from one reader: "I have enjoyed your novel very much." It was signed J. Stalin. "That ended the attempt to purge Mr. Ehrenburg."[64] Salisbury remarked that anti-Semitism is so deep-rooted that few Russians were aware of it. Jokes were usually anti-Semitic, with a similar lampooning of other minorities. Anti-Semitic feeling aroused by the Doctors' Plot had spread like wildfire.

The attack on the Orthodox Church was quite different, especially after Stalin made peace with it in 1943. Since then, it had grown rapidly, so much so that even communists went to church, especially to the annual Easter service. More churches were being rehabilitated. *Izvestiia* published ecclesiastical items. Salisbury interpreted this as the government's efforts to pump a little morality into the population.

The twelfth subject of Salisbury's articles was Soviet weaponry: "Atomic Sites Are Deduced"—a closely guarded secret, he wrote, but in the United States they were widely known. Nor did he stumble on any revelations about this. He was able to make intelligent guesses. For instance, he figured there were sites east of the Angara River for hydrogen bombs, or by Novosibirsk on the Ob River, or within one hundred miles of Moscow. Testing areas were probably in Russia's deserts from the Aral to the Caspian Seas. A key research facility might be near Zvenigorod. He surmised that nuclear energy plants were probably in the Urals, where Russia's heavy industry was located. They were on the Angara and close to Lake Baikal. It was a logical pick because it was the source of tremendous hydroelectric power and in the heart of Eurasia, away from intercontinental bombers. Accompanying all of this was a news blackout on atomic scientists such as Peter Kapitza. Russia used metro additions for civil defense. The government had developed long-range jet bombers and radar systems. No foreign airlines were permitted in the USSR. Salisbury thought he saw the beginnings of a vast arms race between the United States and the USSR.[65]

The series wound down with the last two numbers, thirteen and fourteen. The former, titled "Crime Wave Goes Unchecked," ran on October 1, 1954, and the latter was "Censorship of News Is Erratic," October 2, 1954. With

Stalin's death, crime surged. The new rulers campaigned against alcoholism and introduced anticrime measures such as reestablishing the death penalty. The psychology of relaxed tensions after Stalin's death contributed to drinking and crime. Amnesty set free petty criminals. Anticrime measures were inadequate. Often bars were turned into ice cream parlors. Large-scale banditry was unusual, but commercial theft was common—embezzling, kickbacks, and bribery. People dipped into the till. Manufacturers faked their production figures, and goods were stolen from factories. These items were found in the "gray market."[66]

The last article was titled, "Censorship of the News Is Erratic." As Salisbury remarked, "The most important single fact about the censorship, however, is that it exists and that every line filed from Moscow must go through the censor's hands."[67] It varied from day to day in its severity. Only differences in the individual censor's taste seemed to explain why it was so erratic. With the easing of travel restrictions, censorship was somewhat lifted after Stalin's death.

Harrison's last few months in Russia had been filled with excursions to closed regions in which the only restrictions were those on the use of his camera: "Perhaps," he wrote, "[it] has been because he has gone armed with a camera and the Interior Ministry fears a camera like the devil fears holy water."[68] Often the film was rifled through and exposed. It was nothing unusual to be tailed by secret agents, sometimes twenty or more. Though he was rarely tailed in Moscow, in Siberia they swarmed around him. Even a steamboat ride down the Volga earned Salisbury a four-man escort.

Harrison's last two dispatches from Moscow had tested censorship: he wrote on forced labor and the prison system. They were severely censored. As Salisbury finally put it, "A progressive lightening of censorship has been observed since Stalin died." Even former restrictions were lifted such as reporting on retail prices and the quality of goods or economic production data and wages. Criticisms of Soviet foreign policy were still killed, and one had to be cautious about military matters. "However," Salisbury went on, "any mention of the Ministry of Interior is cut. Almost any mention of the police, or militia, as it is called in Moscow, is cut."[69] Being arrested for taking pictures was a serious hazard. One Canadian reporter set a record in Moscow by being arrested seven times in a single day. Taking a picture of a local market was a sure way of being arrested.

Finally, according to Salisbury, he had renewed two requests he had made almost six years earlier: take a trip to the Stalin auto works and to a collective farm. Both were granted. Referring to the granting of these requests, he ended his series on this note: "Maybe it's a trend."[70]

♦♦ 3 ♦♦

On May 2, 1955, Grayson Kirk, president of Columbia University and chair of the Pulitzer Prize committee, telegrammed Salisbury that the university trustees had awarded him the Pulitzer for his reporting of international affairs.[71] The following day, Kirk sent Harrison the Pulitzer certificate.[72] The Pulitzer committee's press release stated, "The perceptive and well-written Salisbury articles made a valuable contribution to American understanding of what is going on inside Russia. This was principally due to the writer's wide range of subject matter and depth of background plus a number of illuminating photographs which he took."[73]

Julius Ochs Adler, general manager of the *New York Times*, wrote Salisbury: "Warmest congratulations upon the well deserved Pulitzer Prize. You have been outstanding in the field of international reporting and I rejoice with your many friends that the Pulitzer Award Committee makes it unanimous."[74] Cass Canfield, editor at Harper, anxious to get a book from Harrison, wrote him on September 29, 1954, about these articles: "I have read a number of your pieces in the *Times* and want to tell you how much I liked them. To me they reveal more about Russia and how the people feel there than anything I have ever read." He continued, "Everyone I know is reading the pieces day by day and I can't remember when a newspaper serial has attracted so much interest and attention."[75] His friends at the *Times* chimed in. Arthur Krock, *New York Times* Washington bureau chief, wrote to Salisbury, "It was a one horse race insofar as your entry was concerned. This is rare in the history of the Prize for international reporting. I hope it adds to your pleasure."[76] Drew Middleton at the *Times* London office sent a telegram: "Delighted to hear about your getting the Pulitzer Prize [stop] It ought to compensate for all those years in the Metropole Hotel."[77] And so it went.

All was not sweetness and light. Joseph Clark, a fellow correspondent in Moscow and writer for the *Daily Worker*, complained, "Your recent series in the *New York Times* and syndicated nationally flatly contradicts the articles you wrote from Moscow." He continued, "I charge that this contradiction is a result of censorship by the editors and publishers of the *Times* or fear of such censorship in order to give the public an opportunity to judge the facts for themselves. I hereby challenge you to a public debate."[78] When Harrison declined debate, Clark wrote him again: "In Moscow you wrote that no segment of the Soviet population wants war. In New York you wrote that the Soviet leaders are murderers and slave drivers with whom obviously no agreement is possible." Unfortunately, according to Clark, the *Times* editors had concluded from Salisbury's articles that "we are dealing with a group of Kremlin rulers who are masters of Byzantine intrigue, geniuses at dissimulation and conspiracy, men who find it easy to pretend friendship and cordiality while plotting bloodshed." The *Times* editors, Clark insinuated, had arrived at this solely on the basis of Salisbury's evidence as presented in his fourteen articles. But the issue involved more than just consistency of reporting. It embraced the question of whether peace was possible with the USSR. Clark cited many of Salisbury's stories from Moscow, especially from 1950, which seemed to contradict the articles in the series.[79] Harrison replied that Soviet censorship had perverted his earlier pieces from 1950 to 1953 and that he would stand on the truth of the current series.[80]

A *Times* reader, Irma Otto, also wrote Harrison that he had betrayed his earlier dispatches from Moscow and asked, "Has that Harrison Salisbury sold his immortal soul to Satan?"[81] Harrison responded, "I do not feel that I have 'sold my immortal soul to Satan.'" There were differences from his earliest book, *Russia on the Way*, and the Russia he depicted in his fourteen articles. He put it this way: "For one thing, times have changed. For a second, I have seen a great deal more of Russia, and have seen the country in peacetime and lived through some of the great moments of their history." He meant that the 1946 book dealt with heroic Russia under Nazi siege and his current articles studied postwar Russia. He continued, "It may well be that you do not like the picture of the Russia which I paint in the series as well as the picture which I drew in the earlier book. Frankly, neither do I." Then Harrison speculated, "I would much rather that the mirror which I held up to Russia in the post-war years had reflected a more pleasant visage. Unfortunately, the Russia of the years in which I have been there has not been a very pleasant place to live in, either for the Russians or for foreigners like myself."[82]

From an anticommunist reader, Robert Anson, Harrison received the following: "I should like, without wasting your time, to express my admiration for your courage in collecting the information you have acquired, and your fearless expose of a terrible human state." He wrote further, "Whereas I am no friend of Senator McCarthy, I have been studying and combating Communists for a long time. Apparently with enough success to make them annoyed with me. How much more furious they must be about you!"[83] They were. A few years later, the Ministry of the Interior would refuse him a visa to return.

Another unexpected problem arose meanwhile with former vice president Henry Wallace. In Harrison's ninth article, dated September 27, 1954, he had criticized the naïveté of Henry Wallace when he had visited wartime Russia and toured the Siberian camps. Others had used this as a way of criticizing Wallace. As Salisbury put it, "there was nothing in what I wrote which was intended to reflect in the manner [a critic] assumes against you or Mr. Will-kie. I believe implicitly in your patriotism and high sense of duty." Harrison continued, "The point I wished to underline was the very real danger inherent in these quick trips to Russia, particularly by a prominent person like yourself. Hasty impressions of any country are dangerous and, as you well know, there are special dangers in connection with Russia."[84] Wallace was appreciative of Salisbury's letter.[85] As Wallace later told Salisbury, "My method of traveling enabled me to see some things you could not see and your method enabled you to see many things I could not see. I am sure that it will be worth while to compare notes."[86] There is no record they ever did meet.

By May 1955, Salisbury had his first Pulitzer, his fourteen articles had been syndicated nationwide, and handsome book contracts were in the offing. From his seemingly remote post in Moscow, he had catapulted to national prominence as America's preeminent spokesperson on Russia. For the next thirty-six years, Russia would remain one of the centers of his, and America's, attention.

It was only in the spring 1955 that Harrison again resumed permanent residence in New York City and began a fresh career as a regular *Times* correspondent. Naturally, the bull pen seated him on a side aisle of the *Times* staff and handed him some trial stories to cover. He realized that was typical. The first was on garbage collection in New York City. Not to be dismayed, he turned New York City's garbage into a problem of epic proportions. The city editors would think twice about Harrison's abilities. Once again, he was the journalist who knew too much, even about garbage. Even so, he could not escape from once in a while drawing an assignment behind the Iron Curtain, this time in Eastern Europe.

Chapter Five

Life in a Satellite

Harrison started for Eastern Europe in the fall of 1957 on something of a lark. His best writings often began that way. After all, he was just filling in from August through October for fellow *New York Times* foreign correspondent Elie Abel, who was taking a scheduled leave from his Belgrade post. It was foreign editor Manny Freedman's idea to send him to Yugoslavia. Salisbury had been banned from Moscow since 1954 because of his Pulitzer Prize–winning series on the aftermath of Stalin's death, so it was curiously interesting for him to stroll down the Terazlie of Belgrade and again smell communism and speak with Balkan party notables. One such was dissident Milovan Djilas's wife Stefica, as the publication of her husband's book *The New Class* found him again in jail. Another was Tito's buddy and biographer Vlado Dedijer. Just to further his East European lark, he decided on cracking into Yugoslavia's neighboring states.

He was granted permission to enter Albania, though it was closed to most foreigners. He made it there even though it was generally off-limits to American travelers by State Department decree. He left Belgrade for Tirana on August 21, 1957, even though Albania was unofficially at war with its neighbor and, supposedly, the target of CIA plots to put deposed King Zog back on the throne. Enver Hoxha and Mehemet Shehu, Albania's communist bosses, were too clever to allow that to happen.[1]

From Albania, he moved to Sofia and Bucharest. Bulgaria he termed a "rather tedious market-gardening communist country." He visited the Golden Sands resort, Bulgaria's new gambling casino. Bulgaria had no diplomatic relations with the United States and Romania just barely. He stayed at the once-glamorous Athénée Palace hotel and visited Ploesti. By now he had gotten to know the backwaters of communism—all different, but all shabby. Budapest, the Hungarian capital, was still dazed from its October 1956 revolution, and the American embassy had a token presence. In Prague, the Czech capital, he feasted on *keks garazh*, the nine-layered chocolate cake. He finally wound up in Warsaw, Poland, on October 5, 1957, where *New York Times* correspondent Sydney Gruson showed him around. The students were still in the streets shouting, "GES-TA-PO!" and throwing bricks at party chief Wladyslaw Gomulka's police.[2]

Salisbury left Eastern Europe for home on October 13, 1957. He was now conscious that all communist countries were not one shade of red but many hues, unlike the view of communist solidarity preached by Secretary of State John Foster Dulles and Senator Joe McCarthy. Only later would he discover that his many dispatches would move the Pulitzer Prize jury to pick him, then reconsider on his recommendation, and award the Pulitzer to the entire *New York Times* staff of foreign journalists.

These approximately fifty articles offer a unique insight into communism's diversity in 1957. "Now, out of Warsaw, out of Budapest, out of Tirana, I began to sketch for myself a broader horizon—the whole of the communist world from the Elbe to the Bering Strait. If I could score a hat trick in Eastern Europe, why not in Asia, China, Mongolia, Korea, Indochina?" The Iron Curtain was, he learned that summer of 1957, a "leaky tin roof" over a "lot of grubby little dictatorships." Salisbury's destiny, as he then saw it, was to "report on the inevitable collapse of the century's colossus." He would "pick the lock" of the Iron and Bamboo Curtains. That desire was the real importance of his Balkan summer.[3] His analysis and some of his predictions were incredibly accurate.

♦♦ 1 ♦♦

On the eve of his departure, in an article that appeared on July 28, 1957, Harrison noted that the number of Americans traveling behind the Iron Curtain was headed for a new record, about ten thousand, including those to the Soviet Union. Cold War restrictions to military and industrial sites existed, but usually they were a result of a lack of adequate accommodations. A bright spot was that Moscow expected thirty thousand foreign delegates to the Moscow Youth Festival. Groups of fifteen to thirty usually came into these Iron Curtain countries. International conferences drew in experts of one sort or another. Then there were the usual officious difficulties with state tourist agencies such as the Soviet Union's Intourist.[4] By August 3, 1957, Harrison was already reporting from Belgrade.

His first East European article, "Political Gains by Tito Implied," was published by the *Times* on August 4, 1957. It reviewed the communiqué of Yugoslav President Josip Broz Tito's meeting with Russia's General Secretary Nikita S. Khrushchev in Bucharest. The price for Russia's making up with Tito after Stalin's hostility was recognizing Belgrade's "special interest in Eastern Europe." Tito promised "greater unity within the Communist family of states." Neither side spelled out any details to these broad goals. However, there would be no revival of such international communist organizations as the Comintern or Cominform. Harrison pointed out that Soviet leaders Otto Kuusinen and Nikolai Ponomarev replaced Marshal Nikolai Bulganin's former role in Eastern European affairs. He speculated that dictator Enver Hoxha of Albania might be sacrificed and Bulgaria persuaded to adopt a more friendly tone toward Yugoslavia. On the ideological front, *coexistence* became the byword.[5] The Russians seemed to be accepting different routes to communism.

During the following few days, Harrison explained Marshal Bulganin's demotion. The previous June, three top Soviet leaders were deposed—Vyacheslav M. Molotov, Georgii M. Malenkov, and Lazar M. Kaganovich. It was believed that Bulganin had sided with them. Khrushchev replaced their Stalinist line of Russian dominance with friendly cooperation regardless of ideological differences. As Salisbury put it, "The new Khrushchev system appears to recognize the full independence of Belgrade and a substantial degree of independence for Poland (except in defense matters)."[6] The policy toward the other satellite states seemed more related to security. The old antagonistic stance toward Belgrade ended and "complete equality" began. Apparently, it was "Molotov and his friends who had sabotaged all the earlier attempts."[7]

By August 7, 1957, Salisbury called these changes in Soviet policy important. They provided for greater independence in the satellite states, even though Khrushchev was "still somewhat unclear precisely how this objective is to be achieved."[8] Except for Molotov and his friends, personnel changes in Eastern Europe were less important than changing policies. "Bulganin's star has dimmed rapidly since he made a wrong guess on the outcome of the recent leadership struggle in Moscow."[9]

Harrison reported that the Yugoslav party paper *Kommunist* wrote that an "abyss" still divided Moscow from Belgrade. Khrushchev complained that the "obstacles and rancors" remained. Tito demanded the full independence of all working-class organizations. It was, in Tito's estimation, the right of progressive movements to choose separate paths toward socialism. Salisbury remarked on this ideological dispute that "the Yugoslavs and Russians are so far apart as almost to be in different worlds."[10]

The following day, he noted that the latest accord was the third try to bridge differences over the last two years. Khrushchev was undercut by "less pliable colleagues" at home and in certain of the satellites. Miracles could not be achieved overnight, but only by establishing regimes that had popular support. Yugoslavia would continue increasing its friendship with the West, especially the United States, and President Tito would follow the "middle way" between the United States and the USSR. A cartoon accompanying this article showed Khrushchev returning to Moscow from an unsuccessful fishing trip—the fish jumping out of the water was labeled "Tito's independence."[11]

Even though talk of greater freedom filled the Yugoslav media, there was a snag. That snag was the publication in the West of communist dissident Milovan Djilas's book *The New Class: An Analysis of the Communist System*. Harrison labeled it an "explosive new commentary on Communist society." Djilas's thesis, accepted by many in Yugoslavia, was that "Communist bureaucracy constitutes a new class in the Marxist sense [by exploiting] the masses more viciously than the capitalists did."[12] At the time of publication, Djilas was serving a three-year prison sentence for criticizing Tito's policies in the foreign press, and he would be sentenced to another seven years because of the book. Yet Yugoslavs believed that worker self-management, peasant control of their plots, and lessening central authority met this menace.[13] The party organ *Borba* attacked him, probably to reassure the Russians. It called the Djilas book Goebbels-style propaganda, a "rude interference into our internal affairs as well as into the affairs of other Socialist counties."[14] The Yugoslav communist party feared the book could be used as a propaganda device directed against Eastern Europe by opposing coexistence and promoting fascism. Djilas, however, stressed the bureaucratic system could not be improved.[15]

On August 14, 1957, Harrison wrote his mother and sister: "I have some nice stories from here and some more coming up with pix which I have taken—which I always enjoy." He would be off in a few days for his next stop. Harrison was not sure where, probably Romania or Albania. "I enjoy the Serbs and the pleasant contrasts with Russia—a much more divergent, freer, more articulate and contrasty people than the Russians—with very great problems but solving lots of them and, right now, doing quite well." Though they understood his Russian, many refused to speak it: "There is lots of hatred of Russia here and lots of chauvinism, too, much of it directed with the union of the six kinds of south Slavs, especially the Croats and the Serbs against each other."[16] He could see the Yugoslavian break with Stalinist monotony manifested in its new office buildings, apartments, and other public structures. "Simplicity, airiness, pastel pinks, blues and yellows are the hallmark of the new Belgrade [architectural] school, sharply contrasting not only with the mixed baroque of Stalinist style, but with the heavy, dark constructions that were typical of the pre-war city."[17]

Harrison wrote another three pieces on Yugoslavia before departing for Tirana, Albania's capital. In the first, he suggested the so-called "abyss" or split between Yugoslavia and Russia would continue into the distant future. This was especially true in arts and letters. Whereas Moscow was just beginning a thaw, in Belgrade nonconformity ran wild. For example, James Joyce's *Ulysses* was just about to be published in Belgrade, but in Moscow Joyce was considered the most decadent of modern bourgeois writers. "Nothing is worse for the writer," Salisbury quoted Jacob Davico, the editor of *Delo*, "than shackles. That is what has ruined literature in the Soviet Union." A poet, the editor told Harrison, should publish what he pleases. When Harrison reminded him that Djilas was once a poet, the editor responded that Djilas was a bad poet. And he was no longer composing poetry. He was writing politics and should be so judged. Among Western poets, Ezra Pound and T. S. Eliot were most admired in Belgrade. Moscow still clung to Socialist Realism and there such poets were despised. Ernest Hemingway and William Faulkner led the list of most read novelists in Belgrade. American murder mysteries had a mass following, such writers as Earle Stanley Gardner and Mickey Spillane—what Moscow called opium for the masses. No one in Belgrade was prepared to indicate how such divergent views could be reconciled.[18]

The second article was a short and lighthearted piece on the vogue of American comic books appearing in Serbo-Croatian adaptations: Mickey Mouse, Donald Duck, Felix the Cat, Maggie and Jiggs, Flash Gordon, and Cowboy Jimmy. Harrison wryly noted, "There is no strip treatment of the life of Karl Marx or a translation of *Das Kapital* into ideograms."[19]

The third of Salisbury's Yugoslav articles, datelined Belgrade, August 19, and published August 20, covered the most startling aspect of Tito's innovations: private peasant enterprise. The *Times* headlined it "Yugoslav Crops to Set a Record." Harrison put it bluntly: "Yugoslavia's farm economy, based on free peasants privately producing on their own land has scored an enormous success." This success would hasten that trend in other satellite countries. They would turn away from the Soviet model of forced collectivization. In the end, the Yugoslavs' agrarian success would be a bigger political event than Djilas's book. Weather had helped as well as hybrid corn and fertilizers. The goal was to make Yugoslavia self-sufficient in foodstuffs. The general cooperative movement's success was an object lesson to Yugoslavia's neighbors.[20]

Salisbury did not take his eyes off the USSR while in Belgrade. He found time to write about Soviet politics. They were relevant to Yugoslavia. The first announced Marshal Vasily K. Bluecher's rehabilitation. He had been

executed in Stalin's purge of the Red Army in 1937. This caught Yugoslavian attention as a sign of moderation in Russia. It furthered the line Khrushchev introduced in his anti-Stalin "Secret Speech" of 1956. The Molotov
clique had previously blocked rehabilitation. Belgrade believed Marshal
Georgii K. Zhukov supported Khrushchev's efforts. Stalin had said Bluecher
was a German, but *Red Star* now announced that Bluecher was Russian.[21]

A second piece posted from Belgrade, while Harrison awaited visa clear-
ance for Albania, again called attention to the diminishing role of Marshal
Bulganin, his place taken by Russia's economic boss, Anastas I. Mikoyan.
What formerly was the "Bulganin-Khrushchev team" ended. Bulganin be-
longed to the "antiparty" group. Marshal Klement Y. Voroshilov and Dmitri
T. Sheplov were also mentioned as opposed to the party line. They "practiced
haughty scorn for the other Socialist [Communist] countries [and] rejected,"
according to *Pravda*, "the necessity for establishing contacts between the
Communist Party of the Soviet Union and the progressive parties abroad."[22]

The last major Belgrade byline, dated August 25, was a penetrating analysis of what Harrison called the "Fatal Flaw in the Soviet System." A cartoon
of Khrushchev followed by the shadow of a pleading Lenin accompanied it.
The fate of the Stalinist system seemed sealed. Europeans wondered what
would follow. Two events currently signaled Stalinism's collapse: the leadership crisis in Moscow, resulting in ousting the antiparty group, and the publication of Djilas's book, *The New Class*. Djilas was working on a patriotic
biography from his prison cell—a biography of nineteenth-century Montene-
grin hero Bishop Petar Njegos.[23] "Communism, as it developed under Stalin
in Russia," as Salisbury interpreted Djilas, "is not a genuine system of
government but merely a mechanism of rule. It has no formal structure for
transferring power peacefully and smoothly from one leader or group of
leaders to another. The only way a new ruler can arise is by a test of force."[24]
Djilas regarded the communist bureaucrats as the "worst class of all-time,
worse than the bourgeoisie whom they replaced or the feudal lords who
preceded the bourgeoisie."[25]

Harrison reduced communism to a system without government, without
justice, without laws. The man with the gun was boss. Regicide under the
tsars became purge under the commissars. Even Lenin recognized this. He
was unable to devise a substitute. The Soviet facade meant every little question had to go to Stalin, the "very pinnacle of power before being decided."
Lenin's democratic centralism was all centralism and no democracy. It prevented checks and balances. Like Lenin, Stalin was uninterested in any theory of government. Even so-called collective leadership in the post-Stalin era
was a verbal trapping. Georgii Malenkov's stepping down as party secretary
in February 1956 and the June 1957 test of strength against the antiparty
group were examples of winner take all. When police chief Lavrentia P.
Beria was arrested and later executed, Zhukov and the army provided

Khrushchev with strength. The stage was set, according to Harrison, for a showdown between Khrushchev and Zhukov. The Russians were tiring of this, demanding a better and easier life. Salisbury thought a basic question was being posed: "Can a modern technological state afford the fantastic price of a murderous struggle for power each time a transition in the leadership is required?" Would Russia be able to endure many more such contests?[26]

Salisbury summarized Yugoslavia: "population 17,500,000. Communism's crazy, mixed-up kid. Economy and politics blend totalitarianism and democratic methods. Slav. Warm historic relations with Russia. Now replaced by universal nationalistic antagonism that is unaffected by Marshal Tito's political rapprochement. Strongest and only independent Eastern European regime."[27]

On August 28, Salisbury sent the first American dispatch from Tirana, Albania, in ten years: his long interview with Albania's Premier Mehmet Shehu. He did another sequence of five articles on Albania for the *Times*, but the paper only later serialized them from September 9 through September 13. He left Albania on August 30, writing his family, "I emerged safe and sound from the Albanian venture, albeit a little the worse for wear. I do not recommend it as a summer vacation spot. Nor for the winter, either. I have seen some crummy parts of the world, especially in Siberia. But Albania has them beat for sheer nastyness." The *Times* would do a big series on the little nation. He had "not spared the horses." He was going to Bucharest next and then for a week in Sofia. He would include Hungary, if his visa came through, and then Poland and Czechoslovakia. "I have had all I really want of this part of the world. Frankly, I had it before I came over here. And my opinion has not changed. I rather enjoy Yugoslavia, because it is so screwball and pleasant. But even that has its very narrow limits."[28]

Harrison had scored a scoop by visiting Albania—*terra incognita*—and interviewing its Stalinist premier after a week's stay there. The premier bitterly denounced the United States in "cold war invective," while appealing for a renewal of American-Albanian relations. No American correspondent had been to Albania in the last ten years. The Eisenhower-Dulles regime, Shehu asserted, systematically attempted to subvert the Enver Hoxha regime. Though his responses to Harrison's previously submitted questions were in writing, he spoke good idiomatic English. Albania, he emphasized, was not a Soviet satellite. As if to underline that statement, he noted that only about half of Albania's agriculture was still collectivized. He praised Soviet aid in extravagant terms. He also wished for better relations with his Balkan neighbors. Albania, he insisted, was not a police state, but democratic. The standard of living, he admitted, was low but improving. They had wiped out illiteracy.[29]

Salisbury's five-article series made it clear—Stalinist Albania was only one side of its coin. The other side was Western negligence of Albania. It was a bitterly poor country, "harshly wounded by World War II, racked by 'cold war' hostilities." Its standard of living was the lowest in Europe. Albania wanted a normalization of relations both within and without the communist block. It seemed to Harrison that he had landed in another poor Soviet republic, perhaps in the Caucasus—dirty, poor, women workers paving the roads, soldiers parading. Stalin's statue looked down benignly from every town square. Albanians were proud Stalinists. They feared Yugoslavia; they feared war from without; they feared revolt from within. That was why the country looked like an armed camp. Sadly, Harrison wrote, shunned by the West, "Albania has eyes and ears only for Moscow." Thus it followed Stalinist dictates for industrialization and collectivization, however poorly suited to the mountainous region. Private farming and herding, he believed, would have improved the common lot faster. [30]

In the next two serials, Harrison expressed his belief that Albania never had emerged from World War II. It was still a backward nation under arms and with strict rationing. Even soap was restricted. It needed food imports to feed itself, massive Soviet aid, including fourteen Soviet-built installations—everything from a film studio to a hydroelectric dam, with sugar and cotton plants in between. From Harrison's tour of farmland, hand plows rather than tractors did the main work. As he put it, "The Russians have been far less generous in providing tractors than in setting up export manufacturing plants." Besides, he predicted that unless some rationalization of agriculture took place, "Albania is going to stay on ration cards for a longtime [*sic*] or the Soviet Union is going to have to help out more with food shipments." [31] Women and donkeys carried various burdens. Cars used wine as brake fluid. The ancient Romans had built the roads. Military units trudged over the mountains. The diplomatic colony consisted exclusively of bloc countries, and hotels were filled with Russian experts. One Albanian, who had lived in Cleveland before the war, told Harrison he no longer could even imagine the United States. [32]

The high point of Salisbury's visit to Albania was attending a stand-up banquet at the palace of the former King Zog, who was then a refugee in Cannes, France. One hall was reserved for top officials, another for second-raters, and a third for everyone else. The guests only danced the Albanian *prima* when initiated by Premier Shehu. After Shehu left, the music became more Western, and Albanian plum brandy, *raki*, flowed. It seemed the only vestiges of America were cowboy movies of Tom Mix with his trusty horse Tony, Albanian favorites. The hit song of the day was a mournful Indian tune, "The Vagabond," from a film of the same title. Albanians flocked to the film. It suited their temperament. One Albanian accosted Harrison, "I am surprised that you in America don't know this picture." As Salisbury put it,

"Clearly he felt that America was a land of considerable cultural backwardness."[33] Harrison inferred that Albania was more like Kazakhstan or Georgia, a carbon copy of the Stalinist way. It was a country racked by anti-Americanism and primitive xenophobia. Only once was Harrison asked about America. When he told of America's remarkable prosperity, the questioner remained silent. Nevertheless, the young wanted and thirsted for a better life. They only had the Russian model. Could this, Harrison wondered, be an opportunity for the United States?[34]

Salisbury concluded: "Population 1,300,000. Smallest, most backward of satellites. Non-Slav. Few historical ties with Russia. Economically unviable without Soviet subsidies. Unswerving dedication to Stalinist force, police methods, gross anti-Western propaganda. Most distant from Moscow, most dependent on Moscow."[35]

His next port of call was Bucharest. By September 10, 1957, Harrison reported his remaining itinerary to his mother and Jan—Bulgaria, Czechoslovakia, Poland—and told them, "I enjoyed my stay in Bucharest as you will be able to gather from my articles. Had some very nice talks with people there."[36] Romanians were ideologically on the move westward. Young people attended a Moscow youth festival. Western art and ideas at the festival excited them. "Conversations with Rumanian writers, artists and sculptors indicate," wrote Harrison, "that the collision of Western and Eastern ways that took place in the Soviet capital has already had deep repercussions in Bucharest. A process of critical re-examination of Soviet methods of Socialist realism has set in."[37] The Soviet party line remained fixed: against impressionism in literature; against formalism in music. Romania had long been oriented to the West, especially Paris. Though shocked by some Western art, Romanian intellectuals and youth recognized a vitality in Western art, not previously suspected by them. Romanian artists could be a bridge to the West. Harrison thought he detected a "tendency to break with the Moscow line and show much more friendliness toward Western writers and techniques."[38]

The following day Harrison reported on Romanian "long-hair cats" interested in jazz and rock 'n' roll. He visited a university youth house where he saw an obvious fascination with things Western. Romania had abolished compulsory Russian-language study, and instead students were opting for English, French, and German. They staged one-act plays by Eugene O'Neill and watched old adventure classics like Tarzan and Laurel and Hardy comedies. America had youthful enthusiasts in Romania.[39] Harrison found American writers were a strong literary influence. "Rumanian taste," he reported, "is much more catholic than Russian and writers are permitted much greater diversity of opinion and style." Vladimir Dudintsev's novel *Not by Bread Alone* scandalized Moscow. Romanian literary critic Zaharia Stancu, editor of *Gazeta Literara*, called the commotion in Russia "much ado about nothing." Stancu, in Harrison's mind, reflected the older generation's Westernization.[40]

When Harrison reached Sofia, Bulgaria, he decided that Eastern European solidarity—excepting Albania—was not to the Soviet Union, but to themselves. There was support toward a six-power Balkan conference and evolving a common policy between Romania and Yugoslavia. Bulgaria announced its support. Even Moscow, it was believed, backed it. And that brought Albania's interest in it.[41] On September 26, Harrison reported that Roswell Garst, head of Pioneer Hybrid Corn Company of Iowa, had visited Romania selling seeds two years ago. Superior U.S. products were better propaganda than anything that might be said by the American government's Voice of America or independently operated Radio Free Europe. Corn was Romania's cash crop. Garst's corn was returning eighty to one hundred bushels to the acre. It was widely conceded that if Khrushchev had not fallen in love with Pioneer-301 hybrid seed, "Rumania might never have a chance to embark on her 'American revolution.'"[42] If Garst and hybrids were not enough, Romanian radio duplicated American popular quiz and hit parade shows. TV used American-style soap operas and serial dramas. As Salisbury put it, "Rumanian State Broadcast officials make no secret of the fact that they are raiding United States television and radio for ideas."[43]

Harrison concluded: "Rumania—Population 17,000,000. Potentially prosperous agricultural satellite. Non-Slav. Historical relations with Russia sometimes good, sometimes bad. Stalinism distorted agriculture and industry but progress now being made. Rising antagonism toward Moscow. If Rumania could switch locations with Bulgaria, she would join with Bulgaria; she would join Marshal Tito in independent communism tomorrow."[44]

Bulgaria was Salisbury's biggest surprise. Reporting on September 22, he was able to announce First Secretary Todor Zhivkov's call for a "resumption of full diplomatic relations with the United States 'immediately.'"[45] Zhivkov said there were no obstacles on the Bulgarian side for quick renewal of full relationships—diplomatic, cultural, commercial, and tourist. In his interview with Salisbury, Zhivkov told him it was time for Bulgaria to make a thorough study of the West. He promised further de-Stalinization and suggested Bulgaria was ready for the Philadelphia Philharmonic to play George Gershwin's *Rhapsody in Blue* in red Sofia. He called for disarmament and banning all nuclear weapons. Zhivkov was open to cultural exchanges and wanted improved relations with Bulgaria's neighbors. Though Bulgaria hewed closely to the Moscow line, there were separate roads to socialism. Peaceful coexistence was necessary. Most importantly, Bulgaria modified heavy industrialization in favor of agriculture, making it Eastern Europe's greengrocer.[46]

In a series of three articles on Bulgaria's new look, Salisbury showed the brighter side of a doctrinaire regime. Bulgaria had copied Russia down to its own version of Red Square, even with a GUM-style department store named TSUM, a Lenin-like mausoleum for its Comintern hero Georgii Dimitrov, and a Gorky-style street with Kremlin-like towers. Underneath this facade, change abounded. Stalinist heavy industry gave way to Bulgarian tobacco, fruit, and wine. "No longer is Bulgaria plunging headlong on a course of heavy industrial development, aping the Soviet Union's First Five Year Plan, with no account of Bulgarian natural resources. No longer are Bulgarian vineyards and orchards being hacked down to create fields of corn and wheat on the Soviet model." Though there were no signs of discontent, there was a growing gap between ideology and deed. Renewed relations with the West, Salisbury thought, strengthened Sofia's hand in Moscow. [47]

Everywhere Harrison saw relaxed living conditions and heard rock 'n' roll, despite stern ideological proscriptions. TSUM's main showroom window sported a Renault car at a cost of about four-and-a-half years' salary of the average Bulgarian. Nightclubs featured hot jazz, boogie-woogie, Tin Pan Alley, and rock. Whiskey was served. Bulgarians were filled with a curiosity about all things Western. [48] The centerpieces of change were casinos on the Black Sea, designed by Swiss tourist specialists. They marked an effort by Bulgaria to become the Miami Beach of a Florida-style communism. "The heart of the bold tourist bid," wrote Salisbury "is a beautifully designed new resort called Golden Sand on the Black Sea near Varna." The complex included twenty-one hotels, 520 beach bungalows, nine restaurants, a theater, and a casino. Added to all of this glitz, "Bulgaria has turned away from a Soviet inspired plan for a grain-potato-cabbage economy." [49] American styles and English-American literature were replacing Russian as the preferred course of study, and amid this was the country's most popular professor, Viktor Sharenkov, called "the American." He had taken his advanced degrees at Columbia University and returned home in 1948. His casual attitude, so American, won the hearts of his students. He symbolized the renewed interest in America. [50]

Harrison summarized: "Bulgaria—Population 7,500,000. Next smallest, next most backward of satellites. Slav. Warm historic ties with Russia. Economy grossly distorted by Stalinist heavy industrialization. Quietly going into business as green-grocer and resort-keeper of Eastern Europe. People cooling toward Moscow, government deviating steadily from classical Marxism." [51]

Resentment smoldered beneath visible changes in Eastern Europe. That was no more strongly felt than in Hungary one year after its 1956 revolution. Salisbury first faced Hungary's dark side while visiting a youth refugee camp in Bela Crvka, Yugoslavia, with 520 internees under eighteen years old. He spoke with fourteen-year-old Lazlo and Edit, his two-and-a-half-year-old sister. They had crossed the border with their mother, who subsequently died.

More than nineteen thousand Hungarians had entered Yugoslavia. More than eight thousand remained after a year. Their grandmother in Budapest wanted them to return. She refused to give them the name and address of her sister who lived in America. There was the faint possibility they could go to the United States if they had a relative there. Lazlo studied English in the camp and wanted to be an American naval officer. There was little likelihood of this, and eventually they would be forced to return. Waiting, according to Salisbury, sapped their morale.[52]

On October 2, Ferenc Munnich, a prominent government official, spent three and a half hours answering Salisbury's questions. About Joseph Cardinal Mindszenty, an anticommunist cleric who had fled the communists and remained in the American legation, Salisbury reported that Munnich said his government "might be willing to allow the prelate to leave Hungary under certain circumstances, which he did not define." The government was open to proposals that would end the eleven-month sanctuary of the cardinal. Salisbury was not permitted to speak with the cardinal. Salisbury's efforts to interview Archbishop Joseph Groesz also failed.[53] Munnich attacked the prelate and U.S. policy for "persistent interference in the internal affairs of Hungary." Further, he "denied [strongly that] former Premier Imre Nagy, now in exile in Rumania, would ever again play a political role in Hungary." Only a few score had been executed because of the October 1956 uprising. Of the 170,000 who fled the country, 26,000 had returned. Ninety percent of the estimated one billion dollars in damages had been repaired. His most astonishing comment, according to Salisbury, was that "many Hungarians had gone abroad because they had feared that the 'counter revolutionaries' would start a wave of 'Fascist atrocities' as they thought it better to go abroad to escape the coming terror."[54]

Salisbury observed that general conditions were tense as the first anniversary of the October 23 revolt approached. The government spent its time haranguing workers and students, and "Great efforts have been made to end the sit-down strike of writers, which has been in progress since the revolt was crushed."[55] Precautions were evident with heavy armed patrols. The government realized that only the most confirmed communists still supported it. It was obvious that Russians were invisible, except in the countryside. In the capital, they stayed in their barracks. For Harrison, "A sure sign of the hate that the ordinary Hungarian bears toward the Russians is the fact that no displays of Soviet books and magazines are to be found in Budapest."[56] He saw a grim resignation in the streets. Hungarians were also bitter about the United States, especially propaganda broadcasts, as they felt America had egged them on during the revolt and then let them down. Harrison noted that Laszlo Balogh, a Budapest insurgent, had been condemned to death just as he datelined his October 4 dispatch.[57] Even Hungary's current premier, Janos Kadar, was also threatened from the right. He was "deeply engaged in an almost constant battle to hold his own against hard-line Stalinists, who wished to stiffen the Hungarian party against any moderate course." Kadar followed Khrushchev's softer line against the "get-tough" policy advocated by the right.[58]

While Harrison was still in Budapest, the free writers' union capitulated and agreed to go back to work. It still hoped the government would spare their colleagues remaining in prison. They maintained that unrest was a result of what had been promised and what the communists delivered. Salisbury excused their retreat as due to their dire economic conditions after holding out for a year.[59] Youth also reflected the general apathy existing in Hungary. "In place of the intellectual ferment of a year ago," Salisbury wrote, "the university today is a cowed and sullen institution." The only sign of protest was the persistence of rock 'n' roll.[60]

For the Hungarian population in general, prices were rising while wages were dropping. Even Soviet loans, supplies, and credits did not avert the economic slump. For Harrison, it was difficult to determine "how the workers feel about the rising cost of living, the suppression of the workers' councils and the whole progress of events since a year ago." Only the peasants had gained since the revolt. They had been relieved of compulsory state deliveries, and their incomes had risen. Hungary had not solved what to do about the heavy industrial pattern imposed by Stalin. Half-finished factories stood out like white elephants, with no sense of when they would be finished or used.[61]

On this down note, Harrison summarized his Hungarian experiences. It looked as if the system was in for further liberalization—socialist democracy and an easing of the five-year plan. The government had reestablished peace, but "it is the peace of a graveyard and the quiet of a detention ward." Only Soviet tanks propped up Kadar's government. Harrison believed that "no Hungarian can see any future for his country."[62] He concluded: "Hungary— Population: 9,750,000. Excellent base for mixed industry and agriculture. Non-Slav. Long historic antagonism with Russia. Stalinism crippled Hungary economically. Last November Soviet guns crippled Hungary's revolutionary spirit. People burn with hatred for Russia. A weak regime made weaker by complete dependence on Moscow."[63]

Before departing Eastern Europe, Harrison interviewed Polish Premier Jozef Cyrankiewicz. His mantra was a call for a new effort by the Great Powers to negotiate basic issues of armaments and security. The government asked for coexistence and cooperation, not balance of power. Poland's greatest interest was a guarantee by the major powers of the Oder-Neisse line, the border set with Germany in 1945. The East called it permanent; the West called it temporary. Unlike his Eastern European colleagues, Cyrankiewicz appreciated Western economic aid. He was interested in long-term investment to improve Poland's coal mining, electrification, and railroads. He even praised the coverage of Poland in the *New York Times*.[64] Harrison concluded: "Poland—Population 27,000,000. Largest Eastern European country. Slav. Long historical antagonism with Russia. Suffered severely under Stalinism. Held in Eastern orbit only by geography. Nowhere else in Eastern Europe is there greater independence of thought, greater contempt for Russia and Russian ways. A Communist regime whose strength is founded upon anti-communism and anti-Russianism."[65]

Although no separate articles appeared on either Czechoslovakia or East Germany, Salisbury did summaries of each: "Czechoslovakia: Population—13,000,000. Most prosperous of satellites. Slav. Warm historic ties with Russia. Only satellite where Communists had solid popular base (38 per cent of the vote) before taking over. Only satellite where Russians are still popular. But Western culture silently is displacing Stalinist models in art, music and literature."[66]

"East Germany: Population—18,000,000. Most advanced satellite industrially. Non-Slav. Long historical antagonism with Russia. Unviable politically without Soviet. Economically hamstrung by Germany's division. Eastern Europe's best consumer goods source. The cooler the populace to the Soviet Union the more dependent the regime upon Moscow."[67]

After returning home, Harrison wrote a stunning series of articles evaluating communism in Eastern Europe. In these articles, he examined five themes: diversity, Westernization, poverty, democratization, and the so-called "third force." As he put it, "Riots in the streets of Warsaw, the Bulgarian rock 'n' roll craze, Albania still living in the age of Stalinism, the quiet Czechs, the quieter Hungarians (their quiet etched in bitter hatred), the eccentric Yugoslavs, the contented Rumanians—this is Eastern Europe today. The common note is change. The hallmark is diversity."[68] There were important lessons to be learned in all of this.

Though each regime was authoritarian, beneath these dictatorships lay chronic crisis, instability, and deep frustrations. Soviet policy failures heightened the dangers of severe problems, aimless rioting, and possible war. Added to this unhealthy brew, the United States' policy seemed "bewitched, bemused or bewildered." His insight into the future was revealing: "the twilight area of the Balkans remains Europe's great breeding ground of war and dispute." Even so, Soviet power would remain dominant in the area for the near future. As for Yugoslavia's neighbors—Poland, Hungary, Romania—they would break away in a twinkling, if it were not for Soviet tanks. Communism in Eastern Europe was, in Salisbury's words, "disintegrative, deteriorating, unvital." Dialectical materialism could point to creative poverty in the satellites. Only Albania could fit into the Soviet Union as a sixteenth republic, while all the others were drifting further and further away. Thus Eastern European communism came in many different models: rough in Tirana, garish in Bucharest, do-it-yourself in Belgrade, circumspect in Warsaw, garden variety in Sofia, crippled in Budapest, hamstrung in East Berlin, displaced in Prague. "Eight different regimes," Salisbury pointed out, "eight different orders, each colored by national character, tradition and prejudice."

In Stalin's day, all but Yugoslavia were ruled from Moscow. Stalinism had spread over Eastern Europe like a blight. The only unity Salisbury now found was the Red Army. Except for Albania, all were groping for a better way of life than that accorded to them by communism. Second-raters had replaced Stalin's men, who could do nothing to prevent the drift away from Soviet Russia. "The specter that haunts Soviet policy," Harrison warned, "is the creeping and relentless spread of antagonism toward the Soviet Union."[69]

Western nations, especially the United States, had more friends behind the Iron Curtain than anywhere else in Europe. The carping against America in Western Europe was replaced with "Americans can do no wrong" in Eastern Europe. One Romanian quoted by Salisbury put it comically: "Rumanians are 99 percent anti-Communist, 99 percent pro-American—and 100 percent supporters of the regime!" With few changes, that could be said about most of the other satellites, if perhaps a little less so in Albania and Hungary.

American popularity was just the opposite of Soviet unpopularity. This could not be attributed to either U.S. policy or propaganda. To quote Otto von Bismarck, Germany's nineteenth-century Iron Chancellor, "God has a special providence for fools, drunks, and the United States of America."[70] However that might be, one Yugoslav thought it was only American pragmatism that saved rude and ignorant Americans. Harrison put it more thoughtfully: "American popularity behind the Iron Curtain is founded on two factors: hostility toward the Soviet Union and an enormous reservoir of goodwill for the United States centering on the persistence of the 'American dream.'" Salisbury severely criticized America's preoccupation with liberation rather than making new friends. Eastern Europe was not a lost cause even though "enormous effort is sometimes poured into naïve undertakings of questionable value."[71]

When Salisbury studied Eastern European economies, Marxist economies dedicated to ending capitalist exploitation, he found they were based on low standards of living, low pay, and sweated labor—all resulting in low productivity, shoddy workmanship, and zero morale. The result was black marketeering, theft, trading, and odd jobs to make up the difference. The monopoly of Soviet techniques had grossly distorted Eastern European economies. In Yugoslavia and Poland, the collective farm was dead. Plants stood half-finished. Communism in the satellites, as far as Harrison was concerned, seemed broken beyond repair. For example, he compared two towns, one just inside Austria—pleasant and prosperous—and the other just across the border in Czechoslovakia—dilapidated, dismal, and depressed. He concluded: "That contrast is the measure of a failure of communism as a system to set up in any nation of Eastern Europe an attractive, efficient or stimulating way of life."[72]

Though Albania was the exception, thinking persons in the satellites were "profoundly disturbed by doubts of communism, its ethics and works, as demonstrated in their lands since World War II." They did not reject socialism. They wanted a socialism based on democracy, morality, and concern for humanity. Their intellectuals "have turned violently against Stalinist-style police-supported regimes." Milovan Djilas was representative of such thinking. Coincidentally, the sharpest criticisms were within the various communist parties. Khrushchev's anti-Stalin crusade ignited critics. They pointed to the widening disparity between communist word and deed. Youths were most disillusioned. Few areas of the world had been more saturated with the ideas of Marx, Lenin, and Stalin. Yet in most of those areas, the thoughts of Rousseau, Jefferson, and Wilson appealed more.[73]

Harrison finished this series on Eastern Europe by assuming the area was emerging as a powerful "third force." By this he meant a neutral or quasi-neutral area lying between East and West. The job of U.S. policy was to nurture this neutralism without the dangers involved in rollback or liberation propaganda. Cold War propaganda had to be replaced by friendship. The gap between U.S. performance and opportunity had never been wider. The United States needed to cultivate contacts and spread technical assistance, or what is now widely referred to as soft diplomacy. Harrison used that metaphor: "Soft rather than hard sell is clearly indicated."[74]

Attending a luncheon of the Council on Foreign Relations in New York, he heard disenchantment with America's foreign policy toward the East, especially with President Eisenhower and Secretary of State Dulles. There was too much reliance on NATO rather than a softer approach as outlined in Salisbury's East European articles.[75] On October 25, 1957, the day his last article on Eastern Europe appeared in the *Times*, he attended a question-and-answer session, addressing ten questions. The session was an important addition to his articles on Eastern Europe. His audience wanted to know if the Kadar regime was "extremely fearful" of violence on the first anniversary of the Hungarian revolt. Special meetings, he remarked, were held with students and workers, warning them of severe retaliations and making a great show of force. He observed the methods of tyranny by Kadar and Stalin were substantially different in that Kadar's weak regime relied on Soviet support for its maintenance. Otherwise, it would be powerless. He was asked about the underground movement. Harrison had only been in Budapest ten days and had not watched any such activities. Though the media had reported that forty Russian divisions were to be sent to Hungary as a new occupation force, Harrison discounted this rumor.[76]

One person wanted to know why he believed America's nonrecognition policy was sterile. In Salisbury's opinion, the American government needed to reexamine its policy of de facto nonrecognition of the Kadar regime. By this he did not want people to suppose he believed the Kadar regime had any special virtue. The longer the Kadar regime remained weak and dependent on Russia, the longer the Russians stayed in control. If the fall of the Kadar regime resulted in the establishment of one closer to the ideals of Hungarians, he would favor an American policy leading toward the fall of the government. It seemed that if Kadar fell, he would be replaced by a Stalinist regime like that of Matyas Rakosi (1948–1953). That would institute a harsher life for Hungary.[77]

One questioner asked if Hungarians expected anything from those who had escaped. Although they wanted "sympathy and support," their future depended largely on themselves. Another asked if the United States softened its propaganda approach, would that bring eventual neutralization of Eastern Europe? About propaganda, Harrison believed the United States should do what it could to get "straight news and objective reports" of conditions in the West. "United States programs should be based on America—American beliefs, American policies, American traditions, and the American way of life."

The question on religious life elicited the most interesting of Harrison's answers: How much religious life was suppressed? Were Hungarians free to visit their religious institutions? Harrison thought the outstanding feature of current Hungarian life was religious observance because by filling their places of worship Hungarians symbolized their nationalism and patriotism against foreign subjugation. Salisbury believed there was a great chance in Hungary for the West. In their time of tribulation, the Hungarian people chose the church as their symbol of national patriotism and unity. He thought it was no accident that neither the Russians nor the puppet Kadar regime had dared to lift a finger against church attendance on Sunday, demonstrating that Hungary's spirit of independence burned brightly.[78]

Asked if he had had a chance to meet with Hungarian writers and editors, he answered no. He had been deliberately blocked. From his telephone calls to such people, it was obvious they had been intimidated. Even in his interview with acting Hungarian premier Ferenc Munnich, he dealt with a hardliner who never deviated from the party position. Yet Harrison's questions were submitted in advance, and Munnich's answers were tape-recorded.[79] So what chance did writers and editors have to speak openly?

Salisbury also appeared before the New York City Press Club. There he received sharp criticisms of his Albanian reporting. To one such critic's subsequent letter, he responded, "I am utterly at a loss to understand why a patriotic Albanian like yourself should deliberately try to quarrel and categorize the first American who has been interested enough to lift the keys of his typewriter in behalf of your poor, unhappy, unfortunate and ill-developed land in a great many years."[80] This person's invective continued, and Harrison wrote him a second time: "Perhaps my greatest shock arises from your suggestion that rather your nation be smothered in tortured silence than that a voice with whom you do not entirely agree be raised in its succor." Actually, many Albanians had praised his articles and talks.[81]

Salisbury was becoming a sought-after speaker on the Soviet Union and Eastern Europe by virtue of his time spent there and his energetic reporting. W. Colston Leigh, Inc., the top lecture-circuit organization in America, hired Salisbury for a speaking tour titled "Revolt in the Satellites: Mirage or Reality?" The agency advertised him as an eyewitness observer. "Are the satellite countries," the broadside leaflet asked, "shaking loose from the Soviet orbit?" A person could find out the answer by attending: "For an authoritative and as comprehensive answer as possible, Harrison Salisbury of the *New York Times* has made a prolonged fact-finding survey of the countries on the rim of the Iron Curtain."[82] The flyer billed Harrison as "An excellent speaker whose cross-country lecture tours have produced unanimous audience enthusiasm." As a further marketing tool, Harrison's law firm arranged with the *Times* for a thousand copies of his articles on Eastern Europe to be forwarded to "outstanding citizens here and abroad."[83]

Harrison's articles on the satellites did not go unnoticed by the United States Information Agency (USIA), which oversaw Voice of America and other media outlets. It had received inquiries about them. The agency sent out a memorandum in response. In a cover letter to Harrison, a member of the agency stated, "I should like to emphasize that the points made in the memorandum should not be construed as an attack on your fine articles [and] the Agency feels that nothing is more important to the United States than the kind of reporting Mr. Salisbury is doing."[84]

The memorandum itself relied on self-justification, recognizing that USIA should not be in the business of preaching the liberation of enslaved peoples. Voice of America (VOA) should not harangue but present facts. The memorandum especially took issue with Salisbury where in one article he stated that the "United States Government has taken 'not a single step' to preserve the good will of the Bulgarian people." Yet, the memo maintained, "Voice broadcasts include such items as courses in health and medical care, Harvard lectures on Bulgarian-American relations, and stories illustrating the traditional friendship of Americans for the Bulgarian people." USIA kept qualified personnel in Belgrade. However, it was nonplussed by Salisbury's quote from a Yugoslav official: "One of the most incomprehensible of the criticisms reported by Mr. Salisbury was his quote of a Yugoslav who said, 'You send us cultural attachés who know nothing about Yugoslavia.'" Both representatives of USIA in Belgrade, the memo pointed out, spoke fluent Serbo-Croatian and were well trained and carefully selected. The memorandum stated that its intent was "merely to set forth certain information which may not have been available to Mr. Salisbury at the time he wrote these articles."[85]

In response, Salisbury wrote a friend at the agency, Abbott Washburn. He called the memorandum a "curious document." For him, the document seemed to be "rather more of an attempt at rebuttal and self-justification—an effort to minimize and denigrate the various observations which I made about the situation in Eastern Europe." Harrison elaborated that it was a "strikingly shoddy piece of public relations but also the kind of document which could be utilized by critics of USIA as evidence that the agency is more interested in defending past accomplishments than in letting in a little fresh air and generating some new ideas to take advantage of the opportunities which actually exist." Harrison wrote that he could have made an even sharper critique of USIA, but he wanted to be constructive. Salisbury concluded: "If this defensive, argumentative, backward-looking memorandum of Mr. Dennis with its bureaucratic concentration upon self-justification represents with any accuracy the response of USIA to a fresh look at our prime propaganda target—well, then, I fear our prospects of coping with new threats which the Soviet poses to us will be sorely handicapped."[86]

In 1980 Salisbury would reflect on Eastern Europe and the Tito era in Yugoslavia. "When he is gone," Harrison thought, "there will be only Molotov left." Whimsically, he speculated, "I've arrived at the idea that Yugoslavia will muddle through and that the Russians won't get a look in. My theory," he went on, "is that if they try to play with anyone in Yugoslavia it will be the kiss of death for their cat's paw and that nothing would so unify Yugoslavia as a Russian play."[87] Of course, that was not to be. Whatever the circumstances, Yugoslavia would not muddle through. With the Russian Goliath gone and Tito dead, the ethnic conflicts within Yugoslavia were too great for any ideology to withstand, and the south Slavic state, created in the fires of World War I, disintegrated. That would be the case in other parts of Eastern Europe, such as Czechoslovakia and the Solidarity workers' rebellion in Poland. Ethnicity would win, and the dreams of any Danubian or Eastern European federation would crumble. Harrison proved right about the collapse of the communist order in Eastern Europe. He lived just long enough to see it happen.

Salisbury's reporting on the failure of communism in Eastern Europe turned out to be an accidental scoop. However, daily life as a regular reporter in the *Times* bull pen rarely offered an accidental scoop; it took extraordinary focus and effort to succeed. Harrison possessed both.

Chapter Six

"Without Fear or Favor"

Harrison Salisbury, winner of the 1955 Pulitzer Prize for foreign journalism, took his desk against the south wall of the *New York Times* newsroom at 229 West 43rd Street unceremoniously. Already he was known for his pugnacity and tenacity, for being "remote and unreachable." As the new person in the *Times* bull pen, he drew Iphigene Sulzberger's recurring assignment. Each year Adolph Ochs's daughter, after returning from her European holiday, complained about New York City's filth compared to London or Paris. And each year the newest reporter on the floor covered the city's garbage problem with a quick call to the city's sanitation department and a quicker article. Not Salisbury. He refused the casual call. Instead, he rode garbage trucks and interviewed refuse workers and officials in New York and elsewhere. His investigative reporting netted him a page-one series and permanently ended Iphigene's yearly campaign. She never returned to that subject again, because he was so thorough. Years later, after he had been promoted to assistant managing editor in 1964, he thanked her for getting him started. Iphigene died in 1990 at the age of ninety-seven, and Scotty Reston declined to do another eulogy for the family. Arthur O. "Punch" Sulzberger asked Harrison, who gladly took on the assignment. He praised her for a "subtle editorial influence on the *Times* and her ability to mold her 'warm, opinionated family into a band of keepers of the faith.'"[1] And what about New York City's garbage?

"No city in the world," Harrison asserted, "comes within ten million dollars of spending what it costs New York each year to keep it clean. No great city in the world, with the possible exception of a few in Asia, has a greater reputation for dirt, disorder, filth and litter. Why?" His answer was twofold: population density and an inadequate number of garbage workers. Possible solutions ranged from police enforcement of city codes to roving sanitation patrols. The only real cure was a larger sanitation and refuse force. Even so, New York City cleaned 53 percent of its area daily and the remainder three times a week.[2] With that bravado, Harrison launched his home career with the *Times*. He would cover topics from crime to racism to politics and everything in between.

◆◆ 1 ◆◆

Harrison followed up his garbage debut with a wide assortment of articles on urban renewal in Yonkers, gangs in Brooklyn, the city's welfare reform, national elections, and post-Stalinist Russia. They were characterized by his turning a seemingly simple story into investigative reporting and then making a study of a larger problem and evaluating it. A good example of this reporting was his analysis of Brooklyn's juvenile delinquency.

His findings were summarized in a series of seven acclaimed *New York Times* articles that ran from March 24, 1958, to March 30, 1958, which he turned into a book.[3] Harrison, despite being forty-nine years old, in typical fashion went to meet these juvenile delinquents, interviewed their neighbors, teachers, social workers, and so forth. He spoke with police and other law enforcement. He found juvenile delinquency to be a "symptom, not a disease, and the disease knows no geographical and no social boundaries."[4] At the end of his book, *The Shook-Up Generation*, he elaborated: "We cannot fail to see in adolescent gang hostility a distorted reflection of the atmosphere of the world itself."[5] More strikingly, he labeled shook-up as upset or disturbed. Its consequences constituted "one of the principal social problems of our day."[6]

It was youth rebellion beyond the powers of resolution. In their gang wars, or "rumbles," the most vicious flowering of juvenile delinquency, weapons such as zip guns, revolvers, knives, and bludgeons were used. Each gang patrolled its own turf and kept its own peace, or cool. Members, from the "Big People" to the "Little People" had to have heart and not punk out. They were constantly ready to kill or "jap" the aliens or enemies. Otherwise, they extorted money for protecting others or "coolies." Some eighty to one hundred or more gangs existed in New York City. The guy gangs had their ladies' auxiliaries or "debs." The gang's war counselor sent spies or "snakes" to opposing gangs. Cools and rumbles were negotiated. Though Harrison praised Leonard Bernstein's musical tragedy *West Side Story*, his study revealed that Bernstein fell far short of the "black despair of the rumble and the impermanent cool."[7]

These juveniles were deeply troubled social outcasts from the dysfunctional homes of broken families. Harrison's average gang-member interviewees were usually deficient in intelligence. Their leaders, if convinced of his sincerity, revealed a pathetic eagerness to talk about themselves. "Probably 95 percent of them come from broken families or families in name only. They get neither understanding nor interest at home."[8] He interviewed "Smokey," whose fifteen-year-old girlfriend was pregnant. His own fate symbolically represented many of the others. He was a star of the streets. Smokey needed and desired the gang's adulation. He was usually drunk all day, probably used narcotics, and his mental condition was dubious. His girl would likely fall into prostitution. After many such interviews, Harrison "wondered whether it was really beyond the ability of a rich city like New York to make the streets as safe and free for boys like [Smokey] as they were for me."[9]

New urban ghettos spread with the construction of mass public housing. One family out of twenty lived in these in New York City. In them were concentrated the families of welfare cases, the ill, the halt, and the crippled—whether socially, physically, or spiritually. Gangs sprung up in the broken stability of the projects. They were political and social deserts, built where the city tore down old slums. Harrison realized it was not the housing system as such that contributed to delinquency, but how each was run that made the difference. "Here," he wrote, "are all the social evils of the great city which most of us comfortably living middle class Americans thought had long been relegated to the annals of the past." They were ripe recruiting areas for young prostitutes, pushers, and pimps. In the old slums, he contended, delinquency was a recent phenomenon, and now it bore a made-in-America label.[10]

Twenty thousand families, constituting less than 1 percent of New York City's population, accounted for 75 percent of the city's juvenile delinquency. Good families could do more for adolescent trouble than any other remedy. Many troubled youth did not read well enough to study basic lessons. "The problem of working with upset youngsters is not after all," Harrison stated, "so complex and mysterious. What it principally requires is common sense, understanding and good heart."[11] Social clubs and churches helped. Harrison had little doubt that violent juvenile delinquency could be reduced to manageable size quickly if common sense, civic leadership, and community responsibility were used—all without large expenditures. It could only be treated at its source—the local community. "The answer [to why the problem existed and got worse]," he wrote, "is shameful. No comprehensive, co-ordinated, vigorous effort is being made to apply on a city-wide, year-in, year-out basis known methods for improving the conduct of the young."[12]

He meant the following: restore the social component to housing projects; institute more flexible income requirements for tenants to stop siphoning off the able and ensuring a social mixture of more than just the lowest incomes;

produce active social work to reduce housing-area conflicts and encourage use of joint community organizations; support active social programs that improve housekeeping and family life habits; encourage tenant organizations and end punitive evictions; promote enlightened police work, with the addition of special youth squads; and institute active improvement programs like sports for kids. Harrison pointed to communities where these things had worked. If untreated, the problem would become one of national security. [13] For his efforts on juvenile delinquency, Salisbury won the first Award for Distinguished Social Reporting from the Committee Chairman of Greater New York in 1958.

Salisbury did not rest with articles on urban renewal, garbage, and juvenile delinquency. He continued his interest with Russia and contributed numerous articles on the USSR and communism, as well as an award-winning series on Eastern Europe. He tried to get into red China and wrote articles on various aspects of Asia. As race relations in America sharpened, he contributed on that subject and was asked by his editors to tour the South.

It was Salisbury's protégé David Halberstam who suggested he travel south and study the civil rights movement. Salisbury had not done that since covering Huey Long's funeral in Baton Rouge twenty-five years earlier. By 1960 he knew the national American scene, was acquainted with Adlai Stevenson and Richard Nixon, and reported on big-city politics. In March he found himself in Nashville, visiting with Halberstam, and getting background on the New South. The *Times* had published on March 29, 1960, an ad captioned "Heed Their Rising Voices." It solicited funds for Martin Luther King, was signed by a list of notables, and quoted a *Times* editorial of March 19 that asked Congress to heed the rising voices of black protest. Grover Hall, editor of the *Montgomery Advertiser*, called it "lies" and demanded the *Times* dissociate itself from that ad. Alabama's secretary of state proposed prosecution of the *Times* for falsifying Alabama, and the state's attorney general considered legal action. [14]

Against that background, on April 1, 1960, Harrison went south, as he put it, "on an extended swing to examine in greater depth a contrasting group of cities—Nashville, Baton Rouge and Birmingham." [15] He also went to Raleigh and Montgomery. April 6, 1960, found him at the Tutwiler Hotel in Birmingham, Alabama. The sit-ins had just reached this "hard-rock center of resistance to integration." He drove around, stopped at the cast-iron Vulcan statue atop Red Mountain, lunched at The Club, and listened to tall tales about Theophilius Eugene "Bull" Connor, Birmingham's police commissioner, whose aphorisms folks bandied about: "We're not goin' to have white folks and nigras segregatin' together in this man's town," or "Damn the law— down here we make our own law." That gave Harrison a grim foreboding. "The more I saw and the more I heard, the more I knew that I was treading dark and bloody ground." [16]

In room 1060 of the Tutwiler—he had first been assigned room 1117—Harrison checked his notes and then, on his 1942 Remington portable, typed his story. Before leaving town, he called in to the *Times* and dictated it from Birmingham's airport. The *New York Times* put it on page one, dateline April 12, with these headlines: "Fear and Hatred Grip Birmingham: Racial Tension Smoldering after Belated Sitdowns." His article outraged Birmingham whites. "This is the big lie. Perhaps it was the biggest of all. Salisbury has done his damage," fumed the editor of the *Birmingham News*, E. L. Holland. The next day his paper ran the following story: "*N.Y. Times* Slanders Our City—Can This Be Birmingham?" As Salisbury put it, "All hell broke loose" and "Birmingham raged." The city demanded retraction.

Hate letters poured in to the *Times* editorial desk, but *Times* editor Turner Catledge turned them down. However, he sent a reporter to check Salisbury's facts, which were vindicated, and published a "Birmingham Statement" by city officials, which painted the place as "lovely" and asserted that "fear does not abide." Nothing soothed the city's commissioners. Bull Connor and two other commissioners filed a $1.5 million libel suit against Harrison and another $1.5 million against the *Times*. Three other commissioners each asked $500,000. A city detective sued for $150,000. Governor John Patterson and Montgomery city officials joined in a similar libel suit against the *Times* for publishing that ad, "Heed Their Rising Voices." They wanted three million dollars. Added together, the suits totaled around ten million dollars. That became part of a "Southern strategy" to suppress coverage of the civil rights movement. It did. Harrison did not return for four years, and few *Times* reporters ventured to Alabama. Harrison put it this way:

> I was indicted [Bessemer, Jefferson County] on forty-two counts of criminal libel. I was subject to instant arrest if I set foot in Alabama. If I went to Birmingham to defend myself in Federal court on the civil libel, I would be clapped into jail in Bessemer in the criminal case for which I might be subjected to several hundred years of consecutive sentences.[17]

Harrison's damaging article, the one causing the firestorm, started by comparing the haze of acid fog covering Birmingham from the Tennessee Coal and Iron Company's Fairfield and Ensley works to the atmosphere sensed by some citizens, both black and white, of growing fear of violent civil strife. Even though recent black sit-ins protesting lunch-counter segregation only slightly touched Birmingham, convulsive tremors were felt. "The reaction," he wrote, "has been new manifestations of fear, force and terror punctuated by striking acts of courage."[18] Just about the only things whites and blacks shared in Birmingham were the streets, water supply, and sewer system. Everything, everything else—ballparks to taxicabs, libraries to schools—was segregated. There was even a drive to segregate "white music" from "black music." As Harrison put it, "the whip, the razor, the gun, the bomb, the torch, the club, the knife, the mob, the police, and many branches of the state's apparatus" reinforced Birmingham's rigid segregation. Nor did the races talk to each other freely. Telephones were tapped by the police—that was why his room at the Tutwiler was changed. Mail was intercepted and opened. Informers and spies were everywhere. There had been at least twenty-two church bombings. Whites and blacks shared a community of fear.

A Birmingham newspaperman told Salisbury the city was on the verge of blowing up. One businessperson had warned him to take care in what he reported. Lives were at stake. A black lady told him there was a limit to what people will stand. The days of Margaret Mitchell's *Gone with the Wind* had vanished. That was especially true when on April 2, 1960, the sit-ins arrived in five downtown lunch counters. Demonstrators were arrested for trespassing and held eighteen hours before even being allowed to make bond. The next day three black ministers and a white student were arrested and all charged with vagrancy. The police held them three days by local custom. This was Bull Connor's favorite device. Bull was a former sportscaster and an ex-police commissioner during the thirties. He reemerged after World War II as police commissioner. One minister was Bull's frequent victim, and his home and church were bombing targets. A college student at Birmingham Southern College was charged with white intimidation and restricted to the campus for his own safety. The college president refused to expel him. Students petitioned Alabama's governor to uphold their rights of peaceful protest. That could cost the college over a million dollars in legal fees.

In nearby Bessemer, things were worse. A white lady was flogged until she admitted dating a black man. The sheriff refused entertaining her charges against them. The sheriff's deputies beat another person who participated in a freedom prayer, and then his sister and mother. Again, no charges were entertained. The FBI was called in. Black and white children came and left schools at different times to avoid contact. As Harrison recorded, "The list of beatings, intimidations and violence could be continued almost indefinitely."[19] Is it any wonder the ad and Salisbury's article caused an uproar in Birmingham and Montgomery and massive legal challenges?

Those Salisbury had interviewed in Birmingham were harassed. Reporters went to jail. Law firms in Alabama refused to handle the *Times* cases until finally, a small firm in Birmingham—Bedlow, Embry & Bedding—took his case, the kind of law firm that got black litigants a life penalty instead of a death sentence. The various suits would drag on for years. (Later, one of the attorneys, Eric Embry, was elevated to the Alabama Supreme Court.) On Sunday, May 14, 1961, a year after Salisbury's article had run, true to prediction, Birmingham blew up. Thugs attacked Freedom Riders at Birmingham's bus station with iron pipes and blackjacks. No police showed up. The *Birmingham News* belatedly agreed with Salisbury's first assessment. It ran a front-page story admitting Harrison's controversial headline that fear and hatred stalked its streets. On Salisbury's desk at the *New York Times* big-city room at 229 West 43rd Street, editor Clifton Daniel put a copy of the *Birmingham News* with this note attached: "To Mr. Salisbury: Vindication! ECD."

Harrison returned to Birmingham in September 1964 to appear in U.S. District Court before Judge Grooms in his libel case. The trial lasted one week and the *Times* lost. He was hustled out of town as a posse from the Bessemer sheriff had come after him. Only federal marshals, ordered by Judge Grooms, turned the Bessemer posse back. But a year later came a turning point for freedom of the press: "the U.S. Circuit Court of Appeals gave us a sweeping victory. Costs of $3,220.25 were awarded to the *Times* as well as vindication of my Birmingham reporting." Twenty-one years later, Harrison would be invited to a celebration in Birmingham. Bull was dead. Gone was the grim atmosphere. Birmingham was reborn.

As to the Martin Luther King advertisement in the *Times*, the U.S. Supreme Court ruled on March 9, 1964, in *New York Times Co. v. Sullivan* that "the actual malice standard which has to be met before press reports about public officials or public figures can be considered to be defamation and libel . . . requires that the plaintiff in a defamation or libel case prove that the publisher of the statement in question knew that the statement was false or acted in reckless disregard of its truth or falsity."[20]

In 1963 Turner Catledge insisted that Harrison become national editor of the *Times*, with the high-sounding official title of director of national correspondence. As Salisbury put it, "reluctantly I bowed to Turner Catledge's insistence" and became a *Times* executive. However, he had concluded, even before working with the *Times*, "the essence of journalism was reporting and writing. I wanted to find things out—particularly things which no one else had managed to dig out—and let people have the best possible evidence on which to make up their minds about policy."[21]

Soon after his appointment, President John F. Kennedy was murdered in Dallas on November 22. Salisbury, on hearing the news, dropped his lunch, darted to the *Times* building, and ordered Tom Wicker, as the on-the-scenes eyewitness to President Kennedy's assassination, to start writing and not to stop: "Just write every single thing you have seen and heard. Period. He did." Harrison concluded, "To this day not one material fact has been added to *The New York Times* account of the assassination and the events that followed it."[22] That account was published in 1963. Harrison wrote the introduction to the report, which he also edited.

The *Times*, wrote Salisbury, was the first to reveal certain facts about JFK's assassin, Lee Harvey Oswald—his life and activities before JFK's death. It remained only interested in what had happened and who was involved with the purpose of supplying the public with essential information. It did not participate in the various theories emerging. In Salisbury's opinion, the Warren Commission did its job competently. Nevertheless, despite this, a Kennedy legend emerged. It wrapped itself around a martyr's mystique and reflected the deep guilty feelings of a mourning nation. Added to this were various contradictory reports of eyewitnesses and the Dallas police. The "arch stones of the state seem to shift," he wrote. A handful of central questions remained germinal: "Whence came the shots? How many were fired? Was there one assassin? Or two? Or more? Was it a conspiracy? Who was behind the deed? Was it a madman? What was the motive?" These remained the keys and distinguished them from everything of a secondary nature.[23]

The commission established that the shots all came from the book depository and only from Lee Harvey Oswald's gun. Because there was no confession due to Oswald's murder by Jack Ruby, a dark theory emerged: it was a conspiracy. For Europeans, especially, this seemed plausible, given their history with the Archduke Francis Ferdinand and Sergei Kirov's murder by Stalinist agents. For Americans, a solitary killer was not implausible, given previous presidential assassinations and attempts. All these theories fell into three categories: left-wing conspiracy, right-wing assassination, or a lone killer. The conspiracy theories shared the idea that there was a "cover up" of facts by elements within the government. As Salisbury put it, "The plain intent, of course, is to cast into doubt in advance the findings of the Warren investigation."[24] Often such advocates called for impeaching Chief Justice Earl Warren or Allen Dulles, former director of the CIA and a member of the Warren Commission.

Much was made of a checkered-shirted man seen standing in the book depository's doorway. But his shirt did not match that of Oswald's shirt. About Kennedy's wounds, the Warren Commission established beyond a question that all the shots were from the gun itself and that the person who purchased the gun was Oswald. The angle of the bullets' trajectory was, in reality, not sharp, nor did it take an expert marksman to hit Kennedy. Further, an analysis of Oswald's personality provided a convincing answer about the killer's paranoia. Harrison noted, "No material question now remains unresolved so far as the death of President Kennedy is concerned [and] the evidence of Oswald's single-handed guilt is overwhelming."[25]

About the problem of the lingering doubts, Salisbury concluded, "Not, I submit, because the evidence is not toweringly clear. But rather because there is in each of our hearts some feeling, however small, of responsibility; some feeling that each of us had some share in the crime because we had a role in a society which made it possible, which gave birth to a young man who by a long, dreary, painful path became distorted in an assassin." It was something akin to "communal guilt."[26]

♦♦ 2 ♦♦

Without Fear or Favor is one of Salisbury's factually densest books. This is true even if *The 900 Days* or *The Long March* or his memoirs—*A Journey for Our Times* and *A Time of Change*—are included. That is because it deals with what became his intellectual pursuit and professional passion, one of America's greatest institutions, the *New York Times.* He published *Without Fear or Favor* in 1980, six years after his retirement as a full-time journalist for the *Times*, yet when the author was still at the apogee of his career as an author. Its subtitle revealed Salisbury's intentions: The New York Times *and Its Times.* It revealed, as the paperback cover also reflected, "An Uncompromising Look at *The New York Times.*" It was nothing short of that and angered many of his former colleagues. Its topical organization perplexed some readers. However that may be, it won the *Los Angeles Times* book prize for 1980. It is neither an easy book nor a quick read, even if Arthur Schlesinger Jr., John Kenneth Galbraith, and David Halberstam praised it. It is nothing short of an exposé, another of Harrison's big scoops, where the *Times* was Harrison's hero, and he dedicated the book to Iphigene Sulzberger, "this extraordinary woman." One of the most valuable stories he tells is his insider's account of one of the twentieth century's biggest scoops: the Pentagon Papers.

Saturday, June 12, 1971, so the scoop went, was wet and sultry in the nation's capital. It was Tricia Nixon's wedding day to Edward Finch Cox in the Rose Garden. "Everything was very homey," wrote Salisbury, "and the White House seemed an island of calm in a storm-tossed world." During the reception Dan Henkin, Defense Department PR man, spoke with Ron Ziegler, White House press secretary. Henkin had heard from Jerry Greene of the *New York Daily News* that the *New York Times* would carry a story beginning on Sunday about what Managing Editor Abe Rosenthal called the "Vietnam Archive." According to Greene, it was "some god-awful powerful project" about the Pentagon. Ziegler did little or nothing about the rumor, though he may have mentioned it to National Security chief Henry Kissinger, or to Henry's assistant, General Al Haig, or even to the president. Whatever the case, Nixon remained relaxed and unconcerned.[27]

Few in DC knew what the *Times* was cooking, except the man who had headed the study for Secretary of Defense Robert S. McNamara in the first place, Leslie Gelb. When a member of the *Times* team, Hedrick Smith, made a cautious call to him for general information, Gelb drew the right conclusion—the *Times* proposed its publication. He did not pass this on to the Nixon administration. Nevertheless, Al Haig, playing on Ziegler's remark, went to work on the tip. He called Walt Rostow, President Johnson's security adviser, and finally Rostow fingered Daniel Ellsberg, his former student, as the probable source of the *Times* information:

> "Who leaked it?" Rostow asked.
> "We think it is a guy named Ellsberg," Haig replied.
> "The son of a bitch!" Rostow responded. "He still owes me a term paper."[28]

The chase was on.

At 4:30 that Saturday afternoon of Tricia's wedding, the flow of copy from the third-floor city room at the *Times* ended. Then the story's first installment was composed into the fourth floor's hot-leaded type and steel forms for casting into plates. It then went to the subbasement for a full run at 6:13 p.m.—thirteen minutes behind schedule—at two hundred thousand copies an hour, a first print arriving at 6:16 p.m. in the city room. Then, and only then, did Managing Editor Abe Rosenthal see a four-columned, two-line headed, six-page story. Abe insisted on captioning it "Vietnam Archive: Pentagon Study Traces Three Decades of Growing U.S. Involvement." It was Abe's biggest triumph, the first of nine excerpts from a seven-thousand-page collection.

Salisbury, as op-ed editor, had intently followed the making of this great *Times* scoop. He had spent the weekend in the Berkshires, dining, as he put it, with "addicted *Times* readers." Harrison quietly swelled with pride and vindication over the scoop of his colleague Neil Sheehan's super story. Yet there was not a single mention of the Pentagon Papers' publication among his friends over drinks.

The beginning of the *Times* publication of the Pentagon Papers that Saturday afternoon, June 12, 1971, coincidentally restored and vindicated Harrison's stature after his journalistic assassination by the Johnson Administration in January 1967 following Salisbury's reports from Hanoi (see chapter 7). Moreover, it was a watershed in the life of American journalism. Harrison poignantly remarked, "the Vietnam Archive would create a new dimension in American journalism which ultimately would profoundly affect American policy, American politics, and even as many came to believe, the shape of American life."[29]

Daniel Ellsberg, a military analyst for the Defense Department who was on loan working for the Rand Corporation in Pasadena seventeen months earlier, had secretly copied what would come to be known as the Pentagon Papers. In mid-1967, President Johnson's Secretary of Defense Robert S. McNamara had ordered a study of the Vietnam War. It took over a year to complete, approximately three thousand pages of narrative and another four thousand pages of appended documents—some 2.5 million words, forty-seven volumes.[30]

The study covered American involvement from 1945 to May 1968. Ellsberg tried to interest senators—J. William Fulbright, chair of the Foreign Relations Committee, and George McGovern, a leading Senate opponent of the war—to release the documents on the floor of the senate, where they were immune from prosecution. Their rebuff discouraged Ellsberg. He tried to circulate some copies privately at the Institute for Policy Studies. Finally, he shared them with *Times* correspondent Neil Sheehan. Neil and his wife, Susan, took the sixty pounds of papers from Ellsberg's Cambridge apartment and copied them. Neil negotiated with the *Times* to publish them, except for four diplomatic volumes. He was put to work secretly in room 1106 of the New York Hilton to edit them for publication.

When Sheehan had come to him with the story, Arthur O. Sulzberger took his decision to publish the papers to the *Times* law firm of Lord, Day and Lord, which refused to defend publication, ending its forty-year association with the *Times*. Attorney General John N. Mitchell objected to the publication and asked for return of the documents to the Department of Defense on July 14, 1971; the *Times* refused and sought legal defense by another law firm, Cahill Gordon. The *Times* rejoinder to Mitchell stated that it must "respectfully decline the request of the Attorney General, believing that it is in the interest of the people of this country to be informed of the material contained in this series of articles." Actually, Harrison was hesitant. He feared Nixon would try to destroy the *Times*. "I took the view that publication of the series by *The Times*, citing the documents and quoting from them, would have the effect of forcing out the texts themselves through privileged congressional sources."[31]

Mitchell sought a legal halt to publication and intended to compel the paper to return what the government believed to be unlawfully obtained materials that were damaging to national security. Federal District Judge Murray I. Gurfein had to consider the government's complaint: a temporary restraining order to prohibit "further dissemination, disclosure or divulgence" of the Pentagon Papers. Further, the government demanded a permanent injunction against twenty-two *Times* executives and employees who were busy preparing the remaining materials for immediate publication. Mitchell also asked the defendants to return all the Pentagon Papers. An affidavit was attached, which asserted the Pentagon Papers were "Top Secret-Sensitive" and their publication prejudiced America's defense interests, resulting in "irreparable injury to the national defense."[32]

Alexander Bickel of Cahill Gordon, the new law firm for the *Times*, argued for the heavy burden of the government's case. It rested, he maintained, on prior restraint of publication. In order to meet that heavy burden, all the government had presented was an "affidavit couched in the most general terms by [Fred] Buzhardt and this did not satisfy the conditions." There were no specifics. "Again and again," Harrison wrote, "[Bickel] asked

Judge Gurfein whether he wished to be the first judge in the history of the nation to impose prior restraint upon a newspaper."[33] The *Times* did not ask for immunity. It was ready to publish and go to court for the consequences. "But it was not prepared to accept precensorship by a government which sought to impose the restriction before it saw the newspaper and its published contents." Judge Gurfein issued a temporary restraining order for the government that Tuesday, thus suspending publication until the hearing, set for Friday morning, would determine the merits of the government's case.[34]

After a sea of affidavits was issued from both sides, after the judge requested a listing of documents, and after oral arguments were presented on Friday, the contesting parties finally met at 2:45 p.m. on Saturday for Judge Gurfein's opinion.[35] He conceded that First Amendment rights were not absolute. But he was not convinced of a serious breach in the nation's security. Such a breach must be extremely limited to warrant prior restraint of publication, such as during wartime the "divulging of the sailing of troop transports or the numbers and locations of troops." Otherwise, precensorship of the press was the primary evil dealt with in the First Amendment. The only problem involved in the Pentagon Papers was the question of "embarrassment," and, Harrison quoted the judge, "we must learn to live with it." The judge continued the temporary restraining order so the government had time to seek a stay from the Court of Appeals. It sustained his order. A parallel procedure was followed in Washington, DC, against the *Washington Post*, with the same results. The case proceeded to the U.S. Supreme Court for a hearing on Friday morning, 11:00 a.m., June 25, 1971.[36]

Often referred to as the "nine black beetles of the Temple of Karnak," the Supreme Court justices marched into the temple led by Chief Justice Warren Burger. Burger had refused the government's motion for *in camera* proceedings, which would have restricted public attendance in the court. Solicitor General Erwin N. Griswold argued that just because the Constitution said Congress shall enact no law abridging the freedom of the press, that did not exclude the Constitution from saying just the opposite—that Congress could enact such a law. Salisbury suggested that this curious reverse argument was an attempt to argue that black was white: "In the name of suppressing a 'leak' it [the government] was seeking to establish a monopoly of leaks; in the name of 'security' for the nation it was seeking to impose security for itself." Harrison interpreted Griswold to mean "no law meant the right to impose a law." As to Griswold's argument that the First Amendment was not absolute, the *Times* had already agreed to that in Bickel's argument to Gurfein.

After four days, on Wednesday, June 30, 1971, the Supreme Court announced its verdict six to three in favor of the *Times* and *Post*: "Any system of prior restraints of expression comes to this court bearing a heavy presumption against its constitutional validity." The government, in the whole court's opinion, had not met that burden. Each justice, however, submitted his own opinion—everything from the absolute guarantee of the First Amendment to granting the government wider discretion. [37]

At the *Times*, Abe Rosenthal and Punch Sulzberger were "extremely ec-static." They resumed publication of the Pentagon Papers immediately. President Nixon had an opposite reaction. It was not just Ellsberg's doing, it was a larger conspiracy. The president, according to John Ehrlichman's notes from the following day's meeting with Nixon in the Oval Office, "suggested it might be a good idea to put a 'non-legal team' onto the conspiracy. This was the first mention in Ehrlichman's notes of the idea for the Plumbers." There might be other groups beyond the Massachusetts conspiracy group. As Salis-bury indicated, "that set the stage for the break-in of the office of Dr. Lewis Fielding, Ellsberg's psychiatrist, the commissioning of a CIA 'psychiatric profile' of Ellsberg and other White House operations of the summer of 1971. These led to the Watergate scandal and Nixon's downfall." [38]

On Saturday, June 17, 1972, at 2:30 a.m., almost a year after the Supreme Court allowed publication of the Pentagon Papers by rejecting the government's injunctions as unconstitutional prior restraint, the Washington, DC, police arrested on burglary charges five men in the Democratic National Committee Headquarters of the Watergate complex. The five carried 35-millimeter cameras, walkie-talkies, lock picks, tear-gas guns, and bugging devices. Four from Miami were involved in anti-Castro activities with CIA connections. The fifth, James W. McCord Jr. of DC, was a former CIA man, security coordinator for the Committee for the Re-Election of the President (CREEP), and linked to White House consultant Howard E. Hunt. Hunt worked for Nixon's special counsel Charles W. Colson. Eight men from the *Washington Post* covered the story—among them Carl Bernstein and Bob Woodward. Salisbury put it bluntly: "Watergate had started." [39]

Whereas publishing the Pentagon Papers was a *New York Times* coup, the Watergate break-in and Nixon debacle were scoops of the *Washington Post*. One of the Miami four, Bernard L. Barker, had made telephone calls from Miami to G. Gordon Liddy's office in the White House, where he had worked for Ehrlichman. Worse, a check for twenty-five thousand dollars could be traced in Barker's account and on up the political food chain to Republican campaign funds—that is, to CREEP. [40] The FBI soon connected payments from the 1972 Committee for the Re-Election of the President to a slush fund for the Watergate burglars. Evidence mounted. A leak by Secret Service men revealed the president taped everything in the Oval Office. The tapes were subpoenaed. They implicated the president, who had attempted to cover up the break-in. After a number of court battles, the U.S. Supreme Court ruled the White House had to turn them over to the Senate Watergate

Committee. It appeared certain President Nixon would be impeached. Nixon resigned the presidency on August 9, 1974. Later, Gerald Ford, his successor, pardoned him.[41]

♦♦ 3 ♦♦

In 1966, when Turner Catledge planned for his retirement as executive editor of the *Times*, he considered three persons to replace him—Clifton Daniel, managing editor since 1964; Sydney Gruson, the foreign editor; and Salisbury, national news editor. But the three of them were older, and among the younger men, only one had Catledge's endorsement: Abe Rosenthal. Salisbury was already in his fifties and stood in Rosenthal's way. Rosenthal "deeply detested" Harrison, because he seemed readily to adopt left-wing causes and persons—much the way that *Times* foreign correspondent Herbert Matthews had done by promoting Fidel Castro. There ran a satirical subway advertising poster card depicting a smiling Fidel Castro with the caption, "I got my job through *The New York Times.*"[42] Abe thought Salisbury and Matthews "goddamned ideologues" and added, "There'll be no fucking Herbert Matthews while I'm at the paper."[43]

Salisbury's career at the *Times* was controversial. *Times* employees respected him but held little affection for him. He remained a loner in the *Times* newsroom. True, his talent and versatility enabled him to write well on any subject from a few paragraphs to multipage spreads, from roaming the South to leading the first coverage of the antiwar movement. He remained godlike and feared. Though he had been right about Stalin, his Soviet-censored articles painted him pink. He never shed that image among conservative readers, however incorrect it was. The few who admired him, like Halberstam, also garnered Abe's dislike. Halberstam's departure from the *Times* took support away from Salisbury.[44]

Most importantly, in 1966–1967, Harrison's reporting from Hanoi on the civilian damage due to American bombing, especially in Namdinh, deprived him of further support for a top *Times* position. The *Times* reeled away from the Johnson administration's ferocious attack on Harrison and the *Times*. A frightened Daniel wrote Catledge, "Harrison, in general, betrayed a tendency of so many correspondents—of seeming to identify himself with the place from which he was deriving his information." That was the beginning of the end for Harrison's rise to managing or executive editor. Catledge pushed Harrison off to "special projects" and promoted Rosenthal to assistant managing editor. "Salisbury's reportage from Hanoi effectively ended any chance for further advance in the news department."[45] Catledge "did the political hatchet work that cleaved away such potential competitors [from Rosenthal] as Harrison Salisbury and Ted Bernstein."[46]

After a storied career with the paper, Harrison prepared to retire from the *Times* on January 1, 1974, not long after his sixty-sixth birthday. He intended to plunge into a writer's career by focusing his efforts on China. Nevertheless, his interest in the *Times*, its vigor and health as the nation's newspaper of record, continued. This was the age of Abe Rosenthal. The paper was having a renaissance. Salisbury had once defined the newspaper business as a "field of public information dispersal." In that context, the *New York Times* held a unique place because of its "good name," which was its "only real asset." That, he believed, was priceless. Any undertakings jeopardizing the gray lady's dignity as America's newspaper of record in exchange for temporary profits or by its use of careless standards diminished rather than augmented that asset.[47]

When Rosenthal became its executive editor in 1977, it was already about four years after Harrison's formal retirement, although he had continued as a Sunday special correspondent. He wrote Abe in late 1978, "I am stunned and amazed and pleased at the marvelous pace you have given *The Times* with its return to the living." He cited a new vigor in "really original reporting from Washington," which had not been done in a very long time. Harrison liked getting the "inside story" and a "stupendous scoop" from international news, as he did from "inside the White House." Of course, there were still weaknesses. The paper's grasp of the "political scene" was still "not very secure," and some of the writing was "once more caught in clichés." Much of the paper's news was too keyed to TV, and that, in Salisbury's view, was "pathetic." These criticisms notwithstanding, Harrison cheered his former colleague: "Congrats to you and all your hands on bringing back a great paper."[48]

Because Harrison was busy working on *Without Fear or Favor*, his own book about the *Times*, he had occasion to interview Rosenthal frequently and to do many of Abe's requested memos reviewing his stewardship of the paper. Salisbury admitted conducting more conversations with Abe—at length, in depth, and frank—than anyone else he had spoken with before. They just talked and talked. Salisbury boasted he knew Abe better than anyone except Abe's wife, Ann, or his alter ego, managing editor Artie Gelb—"Abe 'n' Artie." And their friendship went back to Abe's days as an international correspondent in India, Poland, and Japan. Both were dedicated to the *Times*, to covering news without fear or favor. Professional friendship saved their ties through thick and thin. Their styles differed. "I was always," Salisbury wrote, "much more a gung-ho reporter, a drop-dead scoop artist with deep roots in the Chicago style of *The Front Page*. Abe was philosophical and conceptual, not a street reporter." This made Abe a "writer's writer," a reporter with style and panache. The difference created friction between them. "We could enjoy each other's talents, but at close quarters the hair sometimes rose on the backs of our necks."[49]

Beyond differing styles and alternating winds of hot and cold friendship, Salisbury remained concerned with how Rosenthal ran the *Times*. Abe tended to prefer glitz or "pop" stories while Harrison bemoaned the fact that "Serious sociopolitical studies for which the *Times* had become famous took second place." Politics, as Salisbury put it, "got the Roman candle treatment." Abe 'n' Artie waxed and waned on New York Mayor John Lindsay. That, Lindsay's wife told Scotty Reston, "cost my husband the Presidency of the United States." Along with Punch Sulzberger, they endorsed Daniel Patrick Moynihan's primary senate bid over Representative Bella Abzug, leading the editor of the editorial page, John Oakes, to quit in anger. On the literary side, they championed novelist Jerzy Kosinski, Abe's close friend. On the gourmet side, there was everything from Café des Artistes to Zabar's and the gentrified delis.[50]

There was a certain kind of "Abe problem" Salisbury found typical and vexing—cutting corners to get an important story by any means necessary. For example, in March 1974 Salisbury wrote Dr. Fritz Heeb, the Russian writer Alexander Solzhenitsyn's Swiss lawyer, to expose some of Rosenthal's methods. In 1969 Solzhenitsyn had arranged for an "intermediary" lawyer to act as his literary agent outside the USSR to guarantee Western royalties, since previously none was paid on published translations because they had not been previously copyrighted.[51] Due to an important issue—the *New York Times* possible publication of excerpts from or, perhaps, the entirety of Solzhenitsyn's "Open Letter to the Soviet Leaders"—Salisbury wanted to reconstruct as accurately as possible the actual circumstances about this to Dr. Heeb. He asked Heeb to keep this letter in the strictest confidence. Fortunately, due to Salisbury's close ties to Solzhenitsyn's American translator Thomas Whitney and to the author's confidant, Olga Carlisle, he had read Whitney's translation of Solzhenitsyn's "Open Letter" earlier, "when it was completed in rough form by Mr. Whitney." But he "could *never* have managed the task of producing excerpts of any literary or informational character in the few days available for this work."[52] That job fell to Theodore Shabad, an international reporter with a particular interest in Russia.

Many inexplicable things had complicated the "Open Letter's" publication. There had been changes of text, changes of publication dates, and changes in Solzhenitsyn's own plans. Furthermore, Rosenthal seemed to believe the document to be a news rather than a literary item and, therefore, free of charge, especially because the cost required to acquire rights and print it as a literary piece was considered extravagant. However, Rosenthal got his Paris correspondent to obtain a copy from the YMCA Press in order for the *Times* to publish it "without any authority at all" when Salisbury intervened and objected. That halted publication. By then Solzhenitsyn had also decided it was not to be published prematurely. Nevertheless, in spite of all these objections and problems, Max Frankel, editor of the Sunday magazine section, had remained interested in publishing the whole version, but even he realized that the price was outrageous and the lead time too short. Finally, the *New York Times* did publish a long article by Theodore Shabad. It contained big excerpts. By way of explanation, Shabad indicated the Sunday *Times* of London was also publishing the "Open Letter" entirely in its own English translation as well as the YMCA Press in its original Russian book, both on March 3, 1974, the same day Shabad's piece came out. As far as Rosenthal was concerned, the "Open Letter" was just that, a letter to Russia's political leaders, and, therefore, should be treated as a news story, although it was over thirty pages long and in the form of a letter purely as a literary device. [53]

Curiously, Shabad's article in the *New York Times* on March 3, 1974, consisted of a series of very long quotes, loosely strung together with Shabad's commentary. From those quotes, Shabad insisted on the following: Solzhenitsyn blamed the West for Marxism and lack of spirit; he claimed that Khrushchev's anti-Stalin campaign was an act of penitence; he warned of an upcoming war between Russia and China if Siberia's empty space was not developed—because of China's population pressure—in which sixty million Russians would be killed; he sought constraints on economic growth for ecological reasons; he demanded dismantling the Soviet Empire; and he pointed out that the Russian state was always authoritarian and would remain so even without the communists, but it must be benevolent and allow intellectual freedom. [54]

In a letter to Salisbury, Solzhenitsyn poured out his rage on the *Times*. He complained that the world situation had changed considerably since he had first sent off his letter to Soviet leaders in September 1973—there had been a revival of the Western spirit and a furious Soviet campaign against his book *The Gulag Archipelago*. Those changes only represented 10 percent of the text: "*all thoughts* remained in place, *all practical proposals* to the Soviet government, as it is written in the preamble, as also in the estimation of the West (according to the miserable conduct of Europe during the oil crisis) was preserved in the first heading by large letters: THE WEST ON ITS KNEES. And so it is, Mr. Salisbury." Solzhenitsyn emphasized, "And in that the *New York Times* sees a *principal* difference of evaluation?" He cast aside details such as whether the "Open Letter" was literary or news, whether he wanted too much money, whether the text was too large to publish, or whether the *Times* obtained the text under false pretenses from the YMCA Press.

Rather, Solzhenitsyn concentrated on Shabad's "shallow" commentary. He found it "malicious, with a full distortion of the sense of the document and position of the author." It was "inadmissible to write that *principal* changes are introduced, when such kinds are not. It is inadmissible to distort citations of a whole paragraph." The *Times* secret photocopy of the document, according to Solzhenitsyn, was theft. Then, to quote the document as the final copy, against the expressed will of the author, was the same kind of action taken by the KGB (the Soviet secret police) when it embellished one of his plays and published it against his will. Furthermore, he contended that Greg Whitney of the *New York Times* had promised him that the "Open Letter" would not appear without his corrections. When Salisbury suggested putting all this behind him, Solzhenitsyn objected: "No, such things do not remain simply behind, they are corrected." Nevertheless, he saw no other path of correction than for Salisbury to translate Solzhenitsyn's personal letter to him and turn it over to "Mr. Rosenthal and his circle."[55] Salisbury never did. On that note, the matter ended, but it left Salisbury suspicious of Rosenthal.

◆◆ 4 ◆◆

To be sure, Salisbury gave Rosenthal's era at the *Times* begrudging credit for financially salvaging the paper. In reality, they were "chums," yet no love was lost between them. Salisbury candidly admitted to Cy Sulzberger, another unenthusiastic supporter of Abe, his dissatisfaction:

> I deliberately ducked the Rosenthal work having heard from my spies of many inaccuracies and deliberate errors. I am sure your opinion was on the mark. As for AMR, he is indeed a shit and oddly enough possesses some good qualities as well. But I am not an admirer of his tenure at the NYT as executive editor. Not a good span. But a mixed bag in some ways—terrible to work for, wildly emotional, and as he has grown older and become a columnist, an unpaid agent of the Israelis. I think two of such, Safire and AMR, are one too many for the Good Grey Ladies and I think both your uncle and old Mr. Ochs would not have tolerated it.[56]

Many at the *Times* complained that Rosenthal maintained a hit list. The *Times* staff became a focus of gossip as reporters came and went, often the result of Abe's ire. Abe ordered M. S. Handler to stop writing on Malcolm X, who then disappeared from the pages of the *Times*. Handler's career sank. Ted Bernstein's championing of the *Times* bull pen led to his fall. But as Harrison put it, "Nothing exceeded in ups and downs the career of Seymour Hersh." He got hired on with his My Lai story and rose quickly with his investigations of Watergate, almost equaling Bernstein and Woodward at the *Washington Post*. But Hersh wandered away, as did many other talents such as David Halberstam, whom Abe "exiled" for ten years. Halberstam took revenge by reediting the *Times* as an exercise in Composition 101 at dinner parties to the delight of friends. Abe boasted of how he sent stars in the *Times* diadem to rusticate in faraway places—Christopher Wren, John Burns, Ray Bonner, Jim Sterba, Roger Wilkins, Alder Whitman, Ben Franklin, and so on. The most notorious of these exiles was Pulitzer Prize winner Sydney Schanberg. He was famous for his Cambodian reporting. In New York City, he exposed city scandals. Abe abruptly terminated him in 1986. Abe wondered why people hated him, as he once remarked to Salisbury. Whatever the answer, Harrison was certain, "Neither his friends nor his enemies understood him."[57]

Harrison asked Abe how he had carried out his mandate. He answered, "I kept the paper straight." What did Abe mean by that? Harrison made a list of "straight." He published the Pentagon Papers, his greatest triumph. He did well with minorities and made the paper more readable. He admitted stealing any idea not nailed down, and he "made no bones about it."[58] No one, Salisbury admitted, had changed the *Times* more, with open columns, graphics, art, pictures, and even introducing color. He had "invented a newspaper with enormous appeal to upwardly mobile readers."[59] Most importantly for the owners, he had made a profit. It was the greatest financial turnaround in the paper's history. Abe, in Salisbury's estimation, was a genius, and "without his transformation the *Times* might not have survived."

Nevertheless, there was a downside to Rosenthal's revolution: it came with "institutional chaos," and that might not have been necessary. In the end, Abe's power at the *Times* corrupted him.[60] Surely, Harrison revealed, Abe loved the paper. He had no hit list, according to Salisbury. He had a temper. As a transforming agent, "he had changed the paper and he had changed the people, he had changed reporters and editors and the whole atmosphere of the city room, and what he was doing made people angry."[61]

Rosenthal justified stern measures by referring to a recurring nightmare: he would awake on an ordinary Wednesday morning and "there was no *New York Times*."[62] In 1968 *Times* stock was at fifty-three dollars a share, and by 1976 it had dropped to fourteen dollars a share. In a one-month period in 1972, circulation fell by thirty thousand to a new low of 814,000. It was at this point, with Abe quickly moving up management's ladder, that task forces were established and professional market consultants engaged. They discovered the *Times* readership below age thirty-five was miniscule, that interest in foreign and national news almost nonexistent. Oppositely, arts and entertainment features drew readership. Younger readers wanted lifestyle columns. That found expression in new special sections for home and garden, travel, fashion, entertainment, and the arts. Abe hung a huge poster of opera star Beverly Sills outside his office. He veered toward soft journalism by adding more of it, while keeping the paper honest. He demanded his reporters "tell it like it is." The paper would remain ideologically neutral, respect the facts, be serious, and not be afraid to ask the hard questions and give the tough answers.

Abe remained fearful of the paper's leftward cant, and he was hostile to the counterculture. He and Punch Sulzberger restored circulation and profits so that at his retirement in 1986, Abe could say the Gray Lady turned a profit of two hundred million dollars. He was quoted as noting that "reporters and editors look a bit more around them to see what is going on in other fields and try to make an effort to represent other shades of opinion than those held by the new left, the old left, the middle-aged left and the anti-war people."[63]

According to Salisbury and, for that matter, Rosenthal himself, Abe's greatest achievement was when, in 1971 as managing editor, he published the Pentagon Papers. Harrison referred to this case as not just a "great confrontation" between the press and government, but as the rise of the *Times*, and along with it the media in general, as a fourth coequal branch of government.[64] The Supreme Court's six-to-three vote in favor of the *Times* publishing the Pentagon Papers reinforced first amendment freedom without threat of civil and criminal penalties against the *Times* specifically, or against the media in general.[65] For this important act, Rosenthal got high marks from Salisbury.

Yet Harrison was critical, so critical that Abe labeled Salisburian images as "wrong time after time."[66] Rosenthal went on to say of Salisbury, "Harrison is an intelligent man who grinds axes at all times. We all do that to some extent. But not as he does, as a way of life." Salisbury was, in one author's view, the "quintessential hard-charging reporter, whose unimpeachable sources extended inside the Kremlin and the Chinese Politburo, or so he claimed."[67]

Rosenthal had climbed steadily to the top of the *Times* managerial power structure, while Salisbury and other luminaries were deflected. "Sulzberger also had, again with a great deal of agonizing and demarches, closed off the rise of other *Times* eminences, such as Harrison Salisbury."[68] Perhaps Salisbury was spiteful, even jealous, of his old friend. One writer called Harrison a "longtime ill-wisher" of Rosenthal and an "unsympathetic" biographer.[69] Salisbury, it was charged, treated Abe as an "angry, argumentive, supremely ambitious egomaniac."[70] Harrison called Abe a writer rather than a reporter and "overemotional" at that. He also criticized the paper's rightward turn under Abe, even though both sides of an issue remained the ideal of objectivity.[71]

Rosenthal struck back at Salisbury. Once he refused Salisbury's efforts in 1975 to get a visa through the *Times* to visit North Vietnam and Cambodia over regular news department people. Or there was the time in 1968 when Salisbury was directing *Times* reporters covering the Democratic Party Convention in Chicago. J. Anthony Lukas labeled police behavior as "brutality."

Rosenthal in New York changed that word to "overreaction." Salisbury complained, "You're taking the guts out of the story!" Abe shot back that he was removing the "goddamn editorializing."[72]

In-house politics at the *Times* were sharper than the razor's edge. Salisbury typified the left wing of the paper's inner circle along with Tony Lewis.[73] Sniping at one another was common, with gossip and the rumor mills explosive. Gay Talese wrote of Salisbury as a "loyal *Times* executive but not a supplicant." As both a distinguished writer and a respected journalist, he would never starve, nor could he be pushed out or shoved aside easily.[74] But this bickering popped up even after Salisbury's death. For instance, Edwin Diamond insisted that Salisbury was anxious to include everything bad about Abe with only the exception of his sexual dalliances.[75]

All literary and journalistic wounds die slowly, however much rationalizing and apologizing there is. After Salisbury's retirement on January 1, 1974, he could, as Talese once noted, carry on an equally distinguished career as a prolific writer.[76] From 1974 to his death in 1993, Salisbury did just that. By the time of his death, he had written twenty-nine books, edited numerous others, and written countless articles and dispatches. For this work, he was elected to the National Institute of Arts and Letters in 1972. He became its president on January 31, 1975. In 1988 he was chairperson of the American Writers' Delegation to China. And so it went.

There was, before we leave Harrison's career as a prominent journalist and enter his life as a literary lion, an all-important *Times* assignment: Hanoi at the end of 1966 and start of 1967. His reports from behind the enemy lines in the North Vietnamese capital shook world opinion and gained him celebrity status. However, for these articles, he was denied another Pulitzer Prize by a single controversial vote. He had become, quintessentially, the reporter who knew too much.

Chapter Seven

Hanoi Harry

America's Vietnamese involvement began innocently enough, but a decade later it ended in disaster. As early as 1960, communist North Vietnamese leaders formed a National Liberation Front (NLF or Vietcong) to combat the Western-backed South Vietnamese regime under the dictatorship of Ngo Dinh Diem. In 1961, the then vice president Lyndon B. Johnson visited Saigon and suggested aiding Diem. Kennedy advisor General Maxwell Taylor and presidential staffer Walt Rostow went there and recommended sending U.S. military consultants disguised as flood relief workers, though Kennedy rejected the idea. By mid-1962, however, an initial seven hundred troops increased to twelve thousand as America's military assistance command. Ambassador Henry Cabot Lodge arrived in August 1962 and backed mutinous generals against Diem. They staged a coup in November and murdered Diem. General Nguyen Khanh seized power in January 1964. By then American aid had reached five hundred million dollars, and the U.S. military presence stood at fifteen thousand.

Secretary of Defense Robert McNamara visited Saigon in March for his new boss, President Johnson. The secretary supported increased aid and refined bombing plans against the North. In August 1964, North Vietnamese patrol boats attacked the USS *Maddox* in the Gulf of Tonkin, and American aircraft retaliated in their first bombing strike against the North. The Senate's Tonkin Gulf resolution of August 7, 1964, gave Johnson a free hand. Johnson struck with Flaming Dart and then Operation Rolling Thunder—the systematic and sustained bombing of the North in February 1965.

Throughout, the *New York Times* tried to get one of its reporters to Hanoi. When the *Times* succeeded in December 1966, American troops had reached four hundred thousand and Rolling Thunder was fully operational.[1] Not since Tillman Durdin in 1955 had the *New York Times* had a "Man in Red Hanoi." The *Times* believed a high-profile Western journalist needed to dramatize the Vietnamese War because of the escalation of America's bombing campaign and the steep rise of the antiwar movement in 1966. The *New York Times* began carrying stinging antiwar editorials by John Oakes and Herbert Matthews. The moment was ripe for Hanoi Harry. Some of Salisbury's colleagues quipped, "If Hanoi would only keep him, the U.S. might stop the bombing!" Another story circulated around the newsroom: Harrison had once dropped a memo on the floor. A cub reporter picked it up for him. Harrison snapped, "That memo stays where it fell!" Turner Catledge, the *Times* executive editor, called Salisbury a one-man band: he reports, he writes, he edits, he directs. Harrison may not have been Citizen Kane, but he had survived more than five years in Stalin's Russia and won a Pulitzer Prize.[2]

By 1966 Harrison had begun relentlessly campaigning for a North Vietnamese visa. It was not on the wings of an idle whim that he made his December 1966 trip to Hanoi. Yet Hanoi would be his triumph and tragedy. "Yes, it would be the scoop of my life and a great feather in the cap of Clifton [Daniel] as managing editor of the *Times*."[3] But it also arrayed the "powers that be" against him and the *New York Times*. Meanwhile, American bombing of North Vietnam escalated, and he believed that he might "arrive in Hanoi at a significant *turning point* in the war."[4] Of his various efforts to secure Hanoi's visa, the most important was a letter from Anne Morrison in support of his request. She was the widow of Norman Morrison, the Quaker who immolated himself in front of the Pentagon in 1965, and she represented Hanoi's patron saint.[5]

On the morning of December 15, 1966, the *Times* foreign editor, Seymour Topping, handed Harrison a cablegram with these words, "You're in." A visa to Hanoi did, indeed, await him in Paris. It was a ticket to his greatest scoop—"one of the war's biggest scoops."[6] Though that trip was to be a secret, Clifton Daniel decided once confirmation arrived and Harrison was airborne from Phnom Penh to Hanoi, "I think we ought to advertise a bit and let people know that we have a man in Hanoi." It seemed a good idea. "Neither of us realized that my first dispatch from Hanoi would have an impact far beyond that of any announcements we might make over WQYR, the radio station of *The New York Times*, or any ads we might run in the big Sunday paper."[7] When the story of Salisbury's coup broke on Christmas morning, it made every newspaper's front page the world over. It blared from radio and TV newscasts.

On Friday, December 23, 1966, Harrison had landed in Hanoi at 7:15 p.m. A North Vietnamese official emerged from a Soviet black Volga and greeted him. He was taken to the rambling old high-ceilinged Metropole Hotel, renamed Reunification, and he resided there for two weeks until three in the morning on January 7, 1967, when he departed on an ICC (International Control Commission) plane via Vientiane to Hong Kong. Of his twenty-three dispatches—about what the American public called the "dirty little war"—he issued fifteen from Hanoi and eight from Hong Kong.[8] Salisbury was the first American reporter invited to Hanoi to be officially cleared by the State Department. On his return, he secretly briefed LBJ's administration and testified before Senator J. William Fulbright's Foreign Relations Committee.[9]

His dispatches caused LBJ's people considerable consternation, inspired a media rhubarb, and ultimately ended in a Pulitzer Prize fiasco. Why? Because, he revealed, "Contrary to the impression given by United States communiqués, on-the-spot inspection indicates that American bombing has been inflicting considerable civilian casualties in Hanoi and its environs for some time past." The White House ordered this messenger discredited. Unknown to Salisbury or the public, there were secret memos from Secretary of Defense Robert S. McNamara to LBJ, CIA and DIA reports, and the Joint Chiefs' memorandums indicating the ineffectiveness of the bombing. These did not reach the public until the *Times* published articles in 1971 based on the purloined Pentagon Papers.[10] They indicated sharply divided LBJ consuls on the bombing.

In October, two months before Salisbury's departure, McNamara made secret recommendations that, when they were revealed, would support Salisbury's subsequent dispatches. McNamara conceded, "emergency deployments and actions [as well as] bombing of the North [had] exacted a price." His concern remained that he saw "no reasonable way to bring the war to an end soon." He wrote, "Nor has the Rolling Thunder program of bombing the North either significantly affected infiltration or cracked the morale of Hanoi."[11] As early as September, data showed bombing the North "had no measurable direct effect on Hanoi's ability to mount and support military operations in the South at the current level."[12] This was because of renewed communist supplies from Russia and China—a situation unlikely to be altered. In November, McNamara concluded, "our bombing is yielding very small marginal returns not worth the cost in pilot lives and aircraft."[13] As later revealed, "NVN [North Vietnam] has demonstrated excellent ability to improvise transportation, and because the primitive nature of their economy is such that Rolling Thunder can affect directly only a small fraction of the population."[14]

McNamara reached these conclusions against the background of increasing deployed attack aircraft. "In North Vietnam, almost 84,000 attack sorties have been flown (about 25 percent against fixed targets), 45 percent during the past seven months."[15] The United States could, McNamara suggested, concentrate on North Vietnamese targets or shift to supply and infiltration routes. Yet he recommended "against increasing the level of bombing of North Vietnam and against increasing the intensity of operations by changing the areas or kinds of targets struck." At the proper time, "we should consider terminating bombing in all of North Vietnam, or at least in the Northwest zones, for an indefinite period in connection with covert moves toward peace."[16] Hanoi had diverted three hundred thousand civilian personnel from their jobs to keep military supplies flowing. Increased sorties would not alter Hanoi's success. Further destruction only met with further repair. There was no noticeable impact. Insurgency continued apace.[17]

The military brass disagreed. The Joint Chiefs opposed a bombing pause. It would show irresolution. Escalation, they argued, would decide the war in the next sixty days; it never did. They called for a "sharp knock." Stopping Rolling Thunder would be "nonproductive" or "counterproductive." They concluded: "The bombing campaign is one of the two trump cards in the hands of the President [and] should not be given up without an end to the NVN aggression in SVN [South Vietnam]."[18]

LBJ favored bombing as well. He savored a victory that would halt the spread of communism in Southeast Asia. The White House reacted swiftly against Salisbury's reports. It also accounted for the ferocity of administration officials and members of the capital's press corps, to whom was leaked selective information. Stanley Karnow, in his prizewinning Vietnam history, noted, "For a while in early 1967 it seemed that Salisbury had replaced Ho Chi Minh as the administration's prime adversary."[19] The White House's and its policy defenders' hypocrisy was lamentable, but believable. McNamara stood alone against LBJ; Salisbury stood alone against the media. Harrison later wrote, "McNamara no longer believed in the air war; he no longer believed Hanoi could be bombed to the peace table. The Joint Chiefs exploded. They opposed every point made by McNamara. They wanted more troops, more bombing, more everything. Total victory."[20]

The White House, presumably at LBJ's direction, tried "professionally killing" Harrison Salisbury, the messenger. That failed. Harrison survived. It finally took the Pulitzer Prize's advisory board to "professionally assassinate" him.

◆◆ 1 ◆◆

Harrison's Hanoi dispatches exploded like political dynamite on the White House lawn. While Harrison was still in Hanoi, TV luminaries held a panel discussion about them at the Waldorf Astoria. Audience questions peppered NBC's Peter Jennings, CBS's Walter Cronkite, and ABC's Edwin Newman. "Why," for instance, "is Salisbury the only American correspondent there?" Jennings said he was not the only one, but rather, "the one with the controversy swirling about our bombing of the North." Salisbury had, according to Jennings, "a reasonably serious effect on general American thought, but whether he has had any effect on American policy we won't know for some time." Hanoi, Jennings alleged, stirred up controversy through Salisbury.

Cronkite, recalling Harrison as his former boss at the United Press and an old Kremlinologist, compared getting to Hanoi to Russian roulette. "I would think," Cronkite continued, "that's how he was selected, and I personally would put my stamp now on its being a great idea that he got there. I think that this has opened up a window for all of us." Everyone knew there was propaganda in Salisbury's dispatches, not deliberate on his part, but because they put it there: "after all these are the sources of information which he has to plumb—these are the people who are going to plant the propaganda. We all know that." Salisbury raised several issues for the first time that were now up for full public discussion. He might even have had something in his briefcase from LBJ to Ho Chi Minh, Cronkite intimated. Things would get muddied. Cronkite stressed that Salisbury was telling all the truth that he could from Hanoi because he was censored and yet wanted to stay the full time allotted without being kicked out. Cronkite doubted Salisbury's dispatches would change United States policy, but he "certainly has opened some areas for discussion again, including the credibility of our reports from the Pentagon, the military side of the war." Salisbury's interview with Premier Pham Van Dong, Cronkite speculated, had exposed an opening for secret discussions, even if the premier planted that idea.

Newman noted the ambiguous situation that placed Salisbury in Hanoi. He believed Salisbury influenced U.S. policy, if nothing else than by opening public discussion. It was, after all, possible to speak with Hanoi's leaders, which the United States had not yet done—at least, not that anyone had heard of directly.[21]

Publication of Harrison's dispatches in the *New York Times* began Christmas morning and continued through mid-January. They made a compelling argument against the bombing. Contrary to what American opinion might expect, he wrote, "The mood of Hanoi seemed much more that of a wartime city going about its business briskly, energetically, purposefully [yet its atmosphere was one of] grimness and foreboding." Recent air raids before the Christmas cease-fire had caused damage within two hundred yards of the Reunification Hotel and near the Chinese and Romanian embassies. Harrison's walk along Pho Nguyen Thiep Street and in the village of Phuxa just four miles from Hanoi's center led him to contradict LBJ's contention that there were no civilian bombings. These bombings did inflict civilian casualties, whether intentionally or accidentally. Residents found little credibility in U.S. bombing communiqués, which maintained precision bombing.[22]

Harrison walked from the Reunification to Pho Nguyen Thiep Street in Hanoi's working-class district. It had been hit one afternoon a week earlier by a rocket, possibly by an air-to-ground missile known as a "bullpup," which caused houses on both sides to collapse. He spoke with a young medical student, Tran Ngoc Trac, who lived at number 46. He had just started off to work when he heard a plane overhead. Tran dropped facedown and an instant later the bullpup exploded. In number 44, two women and a child were killed. Numbers 36 to 50 were damaged or destroyed, and numerous other residents were wounded. The Phuc Lan Pagoda lay in ruins. Tran noted that Americans had warned residents not to live near military targets. "Where," he asked, "was the military target?" At Phuxa, villagers said, "Imagine, the antipersonnel bomb was loaded in July," according to the legend on an unexploded casing, "and within a month it fell here on this village." A fragmentation bomb which fell on the village released three hundred baseball-size iron spheres, each carrying another three hundred ball-bearing-size pellets.[23]

Harrison's two most controversial dispatches, both published on December 27, concerned Namdinh, a textile center fifty miles southeast of Hanoi, and the country's third largest city. One carried "questionable" data, mentioning eighty-nine civilians killed, 405 wounded, and the Black River dikes breached. The Department of Defense, according to the Democratic Republic of Vietnam (DRV), never confirmed these attacks. Salisbury challenged LBJ's depiction of "steel and concrete" military targets hit with precision. He also, in passing, cited the enormous weight of explosives dropped from U.S. planes. Civilians took the brunt of it. Ground-level inspection indicated LBJ's dream targets were a delusion; rail, roads, bridges, and highways were easily repaired, widely dispersed, and easily available. Reinforcements for the Vietcong simply flowed around damages. Unfortunately, civilian destruction outside military targets was greater than to the targets themselves.[24] A marine joke circulated: an insurgent told his supplier, who had just brought his load of one mortar shell south, "Go back to Hanoi and get me another!"

Seeing Namdinh reminded Harrison of a grim World War II line: "one of our cities is missing." Now it had happened to an obscure North Vietnamese railroad town. Namdinh's mayor, Tran Thi Doan, insisted Namdinh had no military targets. It was, she said, "simply a silk and cotton textile town." From its cathedral tower, Harrison looked out on "block after block of utter desolation." On one deserted street, Hang Thao, or Silk Street, virtually every house was "blasted down." Nguyen Tien Canh, member of the city's council, said, "Americans think they can touch our hearts"—he meant U.S. intimidation by continuous attacks. It was civilians like Nguyen who took the brunt of the "enormous weight of explosives." And Namdinh was far from exceptional. [25]

Hanoi, during an air alert, raised a hurricane of fire—surface-to-air missiles, antiaircraft, rifles, pistols—against U.S. jet fighters. Waitresses donned helmets and used their rifles. Drills were serious and important. This civilian participation checked the population's feelings of helpless defenselessness. Everything and everyone wore camouflage. [26] North Vietnam's President Ho Chi Minh warned that both Hanoi and Haiphong would be leveled. In anticipation of total destruction, blueprints were being prepared for constructing new cities. Thus there were no new buildings in Hanoi and one-third of its population was scattered to the countryside, especially many women and children. Foxholes lined streets and were under each child's school desk. Earthen walls reinforced schools and hospitals. People wore heavy straw hats to guard against bomb fragments. Harrison found his hotel's restaurant food tolerable—though air raids frequently interrupted his meals—and prices steady. [27]

Incidentally, Harrison remarked on December 28, all casualty estimates and statistics came from North Vietnamese officials. This should have been obvious to his critics. Where else could his data come from? Nevertheless, Salisbury's earliest Namdinh dispatches, dated December 25 and 26, and printed on December 27, 1966, caused an LBJ administration and media frenzy aimed at "killing" the messenger and diverting public attention. Both the flap and the diversion were hypocritical, as Harrison later recognized, "every war propels some obscure city or town into the limelight, a community which has existed in respectable anonymity for hundreds of years and now suddenly is on everyone's lips." He named Guernica, Coventry, Stalingrad, and Rotterdam, calling attention to Namdinh, which he made world famous in his Christmas dispatch. [28] It was a city near the old French-built Route Nationale No. 1, and it closely paralleled a one-track railway, twenty miles from the Gulf of Tonkin, and straight across the Red River's delta. Namdinh was North Vietnam's third largest city and a textile center, with a silk mill, fruit-canning plant, rice mill, thread cooperative, and farm tool plant—hardly prime targets. After it had suffered fifty-two air raids, it lay in ruins. [29]

Actually, a U.S. briefing officer in Saigon had announced three air attacks against Namdinh that had occurred in the spring of 1966: April 29, May 19, and June 1. This briefing was only unearthed because of the "inquiry and insistence of correspondents in Washington" and revealed the bombings had been directed at its railroad line and yard and its river facility. [30]

When he got back to the Reunification Hotel that Christmas evening, he sent his first dispatch to the *Times*, the one that "shocked the Pentagon and produced a rash of denials, assaults on my personal reliability and hastily fabricated explanations."[31] There were "no very remarkable targets in Namdinh." Assistant Secretary of Defense Arthur Sylvester, chief Pentagon spokesperson, quickly challenged him to walk down Namdinh's main street, where he would find a large antiaircraft installation. None could ever be located. "The nearest thing to a military installation which I saw on Namdinh's main street was a rather pretty militia woman, or traffic officer. She had a small revolver on her hip, but I doubted that it would have been effective against a supersonic attack bomber." Sylvester's assistant, Phil G. Goulding, claimed Harrison's dispatches misled his readers. Harrison maintained that what he had written could be said even "after all the statements and all the verbal brickbats had been hurled": "the mystery of Namdinh remained." He came to regard the destruction of Namdinh as "one of the tragedies of the Vietnam war, and perhaps the fatal fallacy in our whole bombing policy." That was, he mused, because all military objectives, even when totaled up, did not amount to much. Yet the United States was "hitting these with a tremendous amount of muscle." He concluded that North Vietnam paid a tragic price to prove the validity of America's bombing policy. "The people of Namdinh and their residential area," he wrote, "had suffered heavy punishment—regardless of what might or might not be the intent of our military strategists."[32]

Salisbury's Namdinh dispatches were headed by this italicized summary: *"extensive bombings and the enemy's speed in repairing communications."*[33] The Pentagon argued that Harrison had stated, "No American communiqué has asserted that Namdinh contains some facility that the United States regards as a military objective." Actually, it was Namdinh's mayor who said that. It took the former *Times* correspondent in South Vietnam, Neil Sheehan, extensive research in that paper's archive to find those three obscure communiqués.[34]

The Pentagon's major criticism of the Namdinh dispatches was the supposed failure of Salisbury to attribute his sources. George C. Wilson, Pentagon correspondent for the *Washington Post*, revealed on January 1, 1967, that Salisbury's casualty data was the same as a document prepared by the "Committee for the Investigation of U.S. Imperialists' War Crimes in Vietnam of Nam Ha Province, October 1966," *Report on U.S. War Crimes in Nam-Dinh City*.[35] The Department of Defense complained that Salisbury had not attributed this communist source. Salisbury replied, where else would it have come from but his communist hosts? Otherwise, he either invented the data or by some miracle gathered it in a single afternoon. Both scenarios, Harrison maintained, were unlikely. Everyone knew that. The attribution question provided LBJ's administration, the *Post*, and various others with a diversion.[36] They jumped on it. Nevertheless, when all was finally said and done, Salisbury had the better of the argument. In the end, attribution or not, the data itself proved correct.

The *Wall Street Journal* on January 6, 1967, deflated the Pentagon. The Department of Defense, the *Journal* showed, had leaked this information to the *Washington Post*. It previously had acquired the report when it was widely circulated in Moscow. However, it later turned out that the Pentagon's and the report's data confirmed each other. Nevertheless, the *Washington Post*'s Joseph Alsop attacked Salisbury for promoting communist propaganda for ending the bombing. Likewise, the *Post*'s Joseph Kraft smeared Harrison for putting himself at the center of his dispatches and using polemics. He accused Harrison of being a communist dupe, falling for their propaganda. The *Post*'s John Chamberlain joined the chorus of its writers. Was this journalistic jealousy on the part of the *Post*? Others added their newspapers' columns, one referring to the *Times* as the *Hanoi Times*. Another compared Salisbury's dispatches to Heinrich Himmler's Nazi propaganda.[37] Walter Lippmann, defending Salisbury, suggested both Hanoi and Washington used propaganda to promote their positions. That should not prevent Salisbury from reporting what he saw and heard.[38]

The *Times* retreated because of the frenzy his early dispatches initiated. It reviewed a White House press conference: LBJ's press secretary, George Christian, when asked whether LBJ had any reactions to recent public discussions of bombing policies spurred by Salisbury's dispatches, replied, "None." The president was satisfied that only military targets were hit. LBJ approved no civilian ones. Asked about distinctions between approved targets and accidents, Christian left those details to the Department of Defense. Nor had Johnson ordered any investigations. Had the president's orders been disobeyed, another journalist asked. Christian answered, "No." These answers, the *Times* continued, indicated "he [Christian] was authorized to [say] so by the President."[39]

Salisbury much later speculated about the LBJ administration's take on his dispatches: "Not a hint of a crack in the imposing façade of the U.S. establishment was visible. I knew that my reports had stung LBJ, but I saw no sign that, as the Pentagon Papers were to reveal, they had generated an 'explosive debate about the bombing.'" America's air war was open to criticism, as McNamara had noted and the Joint Chiefs had rebutted. It was time, as Salisbury put it, for LBJ to "shore up his position."[40] Walt Rostow, LBJ's special assistant, and Secretary of State Dean Rusk coached LBJ on talking points for his news conference of December 31 at his ranch: avoid getting into a debate over Salisbury's dispatches; reply to reporters' questions along broad lines; act ready to discuss a cease-fire; regret loss of life; emphasize striking only military targets and the impossibility of preventing collateral damage; note the Viet Cong and North Vietnamese made no such distinctions.[41] LBJ did just that. Historian Stanley Karnow quotes LBJ as saying the bombings were "the most careful, self-limited air war in history."[42] After LBJ issued these platitudes, fed to him by Rostow and Rusk, the White House launched his administration's and the media's campaign against Salisbury.

The *Times*, intimidated by the backlash and seeking a balance to Salisbury's dispatches, published two seemingly apologetic articles. The first, dated December 29/30 by Neil Sheehan, "Raids' Precision Seen in Reports," carried Sylvester's remarks that the low death toll in Namdinh indicated "precise, careful bombing." Sylvester, in a telephone interview, contended that out of sixty-four raids, only eighty-four civilians were reported killed. If accepted as accurate, he suggested, that reflected precision. "I don't know if 8 or 89 people have been killed there," using those figures for discussion. The *Times* continued, "Although he repeatedly declined to say whether the Defense Department's evidence confirmed or denied Mr. Salisbury's reports, Mr. Sylvester criticized his dispatches for alleged misstatements of fact." Internally, the Defense Department used the same data Harrison did, and it knew independently of Salisbury and the *Report on U.S. War Crimes in Nam-Dinh City* that the data was correct. But it hypocritically denied that data under the cover of "attribution." As to the *Times*, it had it own "fetish about attribution; a city room joke for years was that even when a thunderstorm deluges the city, the weather bureau must be named as the authority for the announcement that it rained."[43]

Sylvester complained that Salisbury missed a large antiaircraft installation in the city's center and other kinds of targets around the city. The *Times* quoted Sylvester: "If, as Mr. Salisbury stated, there are no military targets in the city, it is difficult to understand why the Communists defend it so heavily, as testified by pilots who attacked the military targets." The Pentagon's aerial photographs, some officials privately said, showed little damage. Sylvester was unwilling to reveal those photos.[44]

The second article, by the *Times* military expert Hanson Baldwin, explained the bombing at length. High-ranking officers, Baldwin explained, were almost unanimous on its effectiveness. For example, Admiral David L. McDonald, chief of naval operations, believed civilian casualties, as reported by Salisbury, were grossly exaggerated. Officers argued that proximity of civilians to military targets made damage unavoidable. Dikes, they claimed, were never targeted, nor were several power plants, factories, and docks. The bombing program, they all insisted, had been "misrepresented and misunderstood." Successes were achieved despite supposed restrictions—not bombing within twenty-five miles of the Chinese border or within a thirty-mile circle around Hanoi or ten miles around Haiphong.

Secretary of the Air Force Harold Brown said over twelve thousand sorties each month were flown, sometimes putting 400 to 450 planes overhead simultaneously. Brown boasted that from March 1965 to September 1966, air attacks destroyed or damaged seven thousand trucks, three thousand railway cars, five thousand bridges, and five thousand barges. Repairs diverted two to three hundred thousand North Vietnamese. Planes eliminated over two-thirds of known oil storage. Baldwin quoted British journalist Norman Barrymaine, who had traveled to Haiphong just before Salisbury's Hanoi trip and had, supposedly, "reached conclusions almost diametrically opposed to some of those reflected in Salisbury's dispatches." Bombing had, according to Barrymaine, reduced travel to a crawl, necessitated night travel only, and impeded distributing essential supplies. He went on to write, however, "Although the bombing has wrought havoc with transport, I saw no sign of economic collapse." He also noted, "American losses have been very heavy."[45] If the secretary had read Barrymaine more carefully, as it turned out, that reporter was not so contrary to Salisbury after all.

Additional pieces in the *Times* further sought to balance Salisbury's dispatches. One, unsigned and dated January 1, 1967, explicitly called attention to Sylvester's criticism of Salisbury as reported in the *Post*. Salisbury's Namdinh data was "identical to those given in a Communist propaganda pamphlet." Though the *Post* harped on the attribution problem, it also said Salisbury's later dispatch of December 27/29 finally and explicitly attributed his data to DRV officials: "The *Post* said officials [in the Johnson administration] who had compared the two sets of figures were furious." Clifton Daniel was quoted: "It was apparent in Mr. Salisbury's first dispatch—and he so stated in a subsequent dispatch—that the casualty figures came from North Vietnamese officials."[46] Nevertheless, the *Times* had distanced itself from Salisbury.

A *Times* editorial, "The Tragedy of Vietnam," was also conciliatory. While being "critical of Administration policies toward Vietnam [the editors] urged a cessation of the bombing of the North for the political as well as humanitarian reasons." It rejected "sweeping deductions and false conclusions" Americans drew from Salisbury's dispatches. But information released by both the White House and Defense Department was "secretive, evasive, misleading or untruthful [and therefore] stimulated misunderstanding and misinformation." Civilian damage was unavoidable, and only military targets were aimed at, though some were in close civilian proximity. Rather than further escalation, there should be a "unilateral end to American bombing of North Vietnam, but it does not mean an acceptance of Communist propaganda that Americans are deliberately murdering civilians."[47] This *Times* admission marked a retreat when confronted with the Salisbury frenzy generated by the media criticism and a government attack. Letters poured into the *Times* expressing both reader outrage (one-third) and approval (two-thirds). [48]

Two more *Times* articles, interspersed with Salisbury's dispatches, pointedly argued the government's side. One reported that Lieutenant Colonel D. K. Salmon, a fighter squadron leader, saw surface-to-air missiles go up, fail to detonate, and fall back, exploding their 350-pound warheads on the ground. These were on the edge of Hanoi. The article ended by quoting Salmon on U.S. bombs: "I saw absolutely none off the target."[49]

On January 10, 1967, the *Times* carried Drew Middleton's article "Hanoi's Bomb Damage." Middleton, like Hanson Baldwin, complained about communist propaganda and that "something might happen if it stopped looks very [much] like an admission that it is doing great damage to Hanoi's war effort." Hanoi's propaganda, according to Middleton, stressed innocent civilian lives lost. The article almost called Salisbury a communist dupe: "Mr. Salisbury, and Eastern European correspondents before him, were told that the bombing offensive was not successful and, in fact, counter-productive on the ground that it stimulated the North Vietnamese people to even greater military exertions." The war's opponents contended camouflage made bombing ineffective. DRV officials like Premier Pham Van Dong demanded an unconditional cessation of bombing and raised the threat of China's entry into the war. [50]

Unfortunately for Salmon's, Baldwin's, and Middleton's then-current assessments, Assistant Secretary for Far Eastern Affairs William P. Bundy later admitted a bombing error in a 1969 oral history interview: "it was one of those rare cases where our aircraft either went over Hanoi or did drop bombs in Hanoi, we'll never know which, I suppose. At any rate, lots of anti-aircraft went up and came down. Or bombs dropped, or both, and the result was a mess." That was when, Bundy thought, Hanoi decided to invite Harrison. [51] The LBJ administration knew more of the truth than Baldwin, Salmon, or Middleton, who, it could later be said, were themselves duped by the administration.

Two magazines typified the pro-and-con treatment of Salisbury. *Time*, after summarizing the Salisbury frenzy, assumed that he had gotten "little more than a guided—or misguided—tour." *Time* insisted he painted a distorted picture. Otherwise, why would Hanoi open its doors to selected visitors? Hanoi "hoped by this distorted picture, to reinforce the widely held impression that the U.S. is a big powerful nation viciously bombing a small country into oblivion, and thus spur international demands for an end to the air war." *Time* also quoted Secretary Brown on the effectiveness of the air war and its equivalence to the Vietcong's guerrilla warfare in the South. A second *Time* piece scorched Harrison's interviews with North Vietnamese officials. Rather than reciprocity in negotiations, *Time* insisted there would only be a "quid pro nil." Had not, *Time* asked rhetorically, LBJ repeatedly offered to meet them halfway?[52] *Time* failed to mention that "halfway" did not include a pause in the bombing.

Illustrative of support for Salisbury was *I.F. Stone's Weekly*. Harrison had, according to Stone, put a spoke in the wheels of the Pentagon's efforts to intensify the air war. Washington's animosity to Salisbury and the *New York Times* bordered on more than resentment. Harrison had enlarged LBJ's credibility gap in the eyes of the public. A week before Salisbury's first dispatch, world opinion, led by the Vatican, had condemned the heavy bombings of December 14 and 15, putting the Pentagon on the defensive. Stone referred to the reputation of both Salisbury and the *Times* as difficult for the Johnson administration to kill. Baldwin's effort to counter Salisbury, in Stone's opinion, made matters worse for the Department of Defense. Baldwin had to admit that dumping a half-million tons of explosives each year amounted to more than used against Japan in the entire Pacific area during the four years of World War II. Stone remarked, "The myth that we have been bombing the North with surgical precision is dead."

Then Stone took on Washington's media. "The disturbing aspect of the Salisbury trip is the reaction of the Washington press corps. That America's foremost paper could send a correspondent to the enemy capital in the middle of a war and expose the misleading character of our own government's pronouncements was extraordinary." Stone lamented that instead of being greeted by applause, Salisbury was met with "as mean, petty and unworthy a reaction as I have ever seen in the press corps." Even Joseph Goebbles, Hitler's propaganda chief, Stone claimed, "would have been charmed." Stone quoted samples of what he termed "frenzied journalism," in *Time*, *Newsweek*, the *Washington Post*, and the *Washington Star*. He held up Chalmers M. Roberts in his *Post* article of January 2 for what Stone called "Ponji Stick Journalism," a reference to poisoned-tipped bamboo spikes used by the Vietcong. Stone also claimed Crosby Noyes of the *Washington Star* wondered how the U.S. government could allow visits to Hanoi at all. Stone characterized that remark: "Poor Joe McCarthy! He died too soon."[53]

♦♦ 2 ♦♦

Harrison's dispatches continued, now stressing the role of propaganda, then demonstrating its use by North Vietnam to build morale, and always enlarging his readers' knowledge of a little-known country. Once he focused on patriotic concerts and ballets, which emphasized Vietnam's unyielding battle against foreign enemies. One ballet depicted ferrymen crossing the Red River in the midst of U.S. air strikes. Others showed the Vietcong storming a

U.S. military outpost or capturing U.S. pilots. As Harrison revealed, "The theme of the Vietnamese David conquering the United States Goliath is struck constantly." At another time, he visited the State Revolutionary Museum, which exhibited the country's struggles against invaders. Officials pointed with pride to Vietnam's great victory over the French at Dienbienphu in 1953. The museum was a chamber of horrors, exhibiting many lethal weapons.[54]

On Saturday, December 31, 1966, Salisbury's seventh and eighth dispatches revisited the Namdinh controversy. Harrison actually mentioned the Pentagon's Sylvester, who had maintained that Namdinh appeared in three Saigon communiqués, and its military installations had been attacked sixty-four times. City officials, not Salisbury, had challenged that assertion and insisted their city contained none. Salisbury saw no evidence of military targets, unless an agricultural equipment plant had been converted for military use. He did see intensive destruction of civilian and business areas, reminding him of similar scenes he had witnessed during World War II of Berlin, Warsaw, and Stalingrad.

In the eighth article, also published December 31, Salisbury explained to curious readers how he had gotten to Hanoi, his travel requests while there, and the nature of censorship in the North. No color pictures were allowed, for example, because there were no facilities to develop them to be inspected. Only once were his pictures objected to—pictures of girls working looms. All his cables were submitted to the North's Foreign Office. None was censored. Since travel outside Hanoi was dangerous due to the bombings and strafings, his trips were limited.[55]

In his ninth dispatch, appearing in the *New York Times* on New Year's Day 1967, he admitted the conflict was a "rough affair" for the North, causing "difficulties, handicaps and hardships" in overcoming the bombing. Colossal numbers of civilians were needed for transport and repair work. The country instituted rationing, decentralization, and increased foreign imports, but despite needing all of these, Hanoi felt it could continue the war. In his tenth dispatch, the only one from Phatdiem, seventy-five miles south of Hanoi, he explained how church services had to be moved out of the largely bombed-out Catholic cathedral. Father Nguyen The Vi mentioned that only a tiny candle was allowed during mass. Phatdiem, a provincial rail center, had been repeatedly bombed and strafed by American pilots. There were no visible military targets Harrison could see, though these might exist. Officials contended there had been 150 attacks since 1965, with the worst on April 24, 1966, which killed seventy-two and injured forty-six. On November 20, 1966, a man came home following a bombing to find his wife and five of his children dead. The city's hospital workers had to be dispersed. It was a "steel and concrete" structure and, therefore, too dangerous to occupy.[56]

One dispatch was colorful filler on the importance of bikes in moving vital supplies south, each bike carrying six hundred pounds. Bicycle chains, like pearls, became precious gifts: "Without the bicycle," Harrison contended, "Hanoi's life would come to a halt." They were not rationed, but expensive. If by magic bikes could all be "immobilized [then] the war would be over in a twinkling."[57]

Another dispatch on Catholic charity reported on Monsignor Georg Hüssler and German Evangelical Pastor Martin Niemöller's visit. They contributed to the North Vietnamese and NLF's Red Cross and assessed the need for medical supplies. Their trip indicated Pope Paul VI's deep concern and instituted personal contact between the pontiff and North Vietnamese Catholics. Eighty-two parishes still existed in the North. In 1962 the Most Reverend Trinh Nhu Khue had been named archbishop of Hanoi. He estimated that three hundred to four hundred priests were still serving in North Vietnam.[58]

Harrison's eleventh, twelfth, and fourteenth dispatches summarized his conversations with DRV Premier Pham Van Dong and the NLF's representative in Hanoi, Nguyen Van Tien. These important interviews in Hanoi raised public speculations over cover-ups, secret diplomacy, or clandestine conversations between Salisbury and Secretary of State Dean Rusk and his assistant Bill Bundy. Even special assistant to LBJ Walt Rostow urgently wrote the president about this matter. The premier subsequently issued a sanitized public version of Harrison's previously published interview that removed any hints he had earlier made to Salisbury about the possibility of secret negotiations between Hanoi and Washington.[59]

The nonsanitized report, first published as part of Harrison's eleventh dispatch, contained remarks by North Vietnam's Premier Pham Van Dong that caused worldwide agitation and "a number of apparently *forthcoming statements* couched in very general language [which the State Department concluded] are essentially *mood music*, accompanying a strong attempt to get us to stop bombing without reciprocity."[60] The so-called *forthcoming* statements with *mood* music were spins put on the premier's words by the State Department. As first reported by Salisbury, then later sanitized by Premier Pham, the critical words Pham now left out of the sanitized version were: "possible," "settle," "other things," and "generosity." Salisbury reported Pham's indication that by mutual respect other things could be mentioned. Especially important, Pham had excised his assertion in Salisbury's report that the United States must accept Hanoi's four basic preconditions before negotiations could begin—ending bombing, accepting the 1954 Geneva settlement, stopping the fighting and withdrawing, and recognizing Vietnam's sovereignty. In other words, secret talks could start preliminary to accepting anything. As things had stood, the United States especially rejected recognition of the independence, sovereignty, unity, and territorial integrity of Vietnam. Also, the United States had violated the 1954 Geneva Convention, which barred foreign forces.[61]

At this time, Salisbury remained unaware of any previous secret negotiating initiatives, all of which had failed, such as Marigold—an effort by Polish diplomats from June to December 1966 to initiate secret and direct talks between North Vietnamese and U.S. officials.[62]

Salisbury's remaining dispatches again reviewed apparent discrepancies between his and the U.S. government's claims of whether only military targets were bombed and whether they had been announced or not. Did U.S. bombing only accidentally cause civilian damages? Unintentional accidents did occur, and some were massive. About the subsequent announcing of raids, local Namdinh officials, whom Salisbury quoted, were wrong, not Harrison. As Karnow noted, "Hundreds of Pentagon researchers were assigned to prepare line-by-line rebuttals [of Salisbury], and their findings were leaked to rival newspapers like the *Washington Post*."[63]

Salisbury's interview with the premier cast doubts on perceptions of Hanoi's diplomatic rigidity. He also challenged the widely held view that the National Liberation Front was merely the North's puppet. His twelfth dispatch asserted the NLF's independence of the North, at least in the view of its representative in Hanoi, Nguyen Van Tien. The NLF was, Nguyen claimed, a separate entity and all matters must be taken up by it, and its leaders must have a place at the peace table. "The direction of the struggle," Nguyen insisted, "is run by the South, not the North." Reunification would only be discussed based on equality and be a gradual, step-by-step process. The NLF had its own program: national independence, democratic freedom, peaceful development, neutrality, reunification. The front's complexion, Nguyen Van Tien insisted, was politically diverse, comprising a multiparty system.[64] If these differences were real, Harrison thought, could a deal be negotiated along these lines?

Salisbury's last eight dispatches, sent from his respite in Hong Kong on January 10 and 11 and published between January 11 and 18, summarized his experiences "behind the lines," as he later did in his subsequent book of that title, published in April. The first Hong Kong dispatch predicted the beginning of a "parade" of Western journalists to Hanoi—a prophecy that came true. He called this a "momentous decision" for Hanoi. The churchmen were the first contingents, but Harry Ashmore, former editor of the *Arkansas Gazette*, and William C. Baggs, editor of the *Miami News*, quickly followed. They met with President Ho Chi Minh on January 18. They believed Ho seemed interested in a formula for mutual de-escalation of the fighting.[65] Their initiative resulted in LBJ's secret letter to Ho of February 2, 1967, delivered on the eighth and calling for reciprocal de-escalation, and Ho's response of February 15, demanding an unconditional end of the bombing—

both only made public by Hanoi on March 21. As with Salisbury's dispatches, this failed effort, labeled Sunflower, was criticized by Chalmers M. Roberts in the *Washington Post* in September.[66]

It was clear these groups, like Hüssler and Niemöller or Ashmore and Baggs, as Harrison speculated, would be taken to the same streets, the same villages. They would, sooner or later, fan out across the whole country and be able to judge who was telling the truth—Salisbury or the LBJ administration and its admirers. Visible evidence of damage caused by bombing would be apparent to outsiders who walked down the streets of Namdinh or who tried to reconstruct in their minds what the village of Phuly may have looked like before bombs obliterated it. It was against these impressions of human suffering that air strategists' arguments about precise military objectives would have to be placed.[67]

Dispatch seventeen played on an earlier theme of Salisbury's: bombing, though severe, was not decisive. Throughout the night, supplies still moved south, whether by bamboo poles on women's shoulders, by squads of bicycles, or through detours such as makeshift pontoon bridges or repaired railways. Replacements of all sorts from China and Russia littered fields near damaged rails, bridges, or highways. Labor for repair work was plentiful.

In his third dispatch from Hong Kong, the eighteenth in the series, Salisbury revisited his most controversial subject, bomb damage as viewed from the ground. He asked: What was the United States seeking to bomb, and what was it hitting? LBJ insisted the United States only bombed "steel and concrete." Supposedly, pilots fulfilled their orders precisely. The DRV claimed it was a "deliberate policy of terror bombing, with civilian and nonmilitary objectives as the target." Where was the truth? After two weeks of "painstaking observations and inquiry [he could] only report what he saw and heard." Bombs fell on the just and the unjust. He surveyed widespread hits on civilian housing and institutions. Though some of the civilian damage of the December 14, 1966, bombings before the Christmas pause may have resulted from misfiring surface-to-air missiles, everyone he spoke with—Northerners or foreigners—"believe that the major areas of damage in the attacks of December 14 resulted from [American] missiles. Rightly or wrongly, the opinion in Hanoi is that the damage was caused by the Americans, not the North Vietnamese." There were bound to be errors from planes flying low at six hundred miles an hour and dropping two-thousand-pound bombs as well as antipersonnel weapons—bullpups and lazy dogs.[68]

The fourth dispatch from Hong Kong, published on January 14, 1967, demonstrated how, though difficult, North Vietnam's industrial output continued despite its dispersion of people and equipment. Continued bombing escalation led to more and more cities evacuated and their industries dispersed. Women workers at a textile plant, for example, spent one-third of their time in production, one-third on defense, and one-third at their homes.

Even U.S. nght missions, 30 percent of the total, were increasing, and that meant more civilian and nonmilitary targets would be hit. Yet North Vietnamese spirits remained high.

In his fifth dispatch from Hong Kong, he wrote about North Vietnamese hero worship of such persons as Nguyen Van Troi, who tried to kill Defense Secretary Robert McNamara when he visited Saigon in March 1964. Past glories such as Dienbienphu were celebrated in government propaganda. The heroic feat of feats was downing an American plane and capturing its pilot. The North claimed 1,600 downed and hundreds of pilots held at the infamous "Hanoi Hilton."[69]

The sixth article from Hong Kong reiterated Harrison's interview with Nguyen Van Tien and Nguyen's claim that the NLF was independent of the government of the North. As Salisbury noted, each had "basically different foreign policies [which] seems to have gone almost unreported in the Western press." Both were committed to reunion and a single Vietnam. Annexation by the North was disavowed. Rather, reunion would be worked out as "between brothers," according to Nguyen. He insisted that forcible reunion would be a "stupid, criminal" thing. He further argued that all military action in the South was fully under NLF direction. He also talked of a future coalition government and a nonaligned and neutralist Vietnam. Four-fifths of the South, he claimed, was under NLF control and ten million lived in liberated areas.[70] Again, Salisbury queried, could not arrangements for peace be made more along these lines?

Salisbury's last two dispatches from Hong Kong, numbers twenty-two and twenty-three in the series, widened the reader's perspective of China's and Russia's roles. The red giants were feuding with each other. China was in the throes of the Great Cultural Revolution. Further, China pressed the North Vietnamese about the theory of People's Wars, which the Soviet Union rejected. Nevertheless, the North was dependent on both for supplies, especially rice from China and sophisticated war matériel from Russia. North Vietnam needed them, and it feared their struggle might hurt its own. It was, Salisbury believed, Ho's tact and skill that kept China and Russia as his suppliers, but it was an open question how much longer that might last.[71]

In his last article, Salisbury argued the Vietnamese War had reached a turning point—it would either move to an eventual peace or suddenly escalate, after the previous two years of bombing. He thought he saw signs of a below-the-surface movement toward peace. Each side was moderating; neither was immune to world opinion. The paths to peace were thorny, as there was deep suspicion on both sides. Salisbury referred to tantalizing North Vietnamese comments: "If the U.S. would . . . then we could take tea together," or "If the U.S. stops bombing, then we won't sit with folded hands." Yet the North Vietnamese were adamant about submitting. They were ready to "go into the caves" if necessary. Salisbury remained optimistic that if the parties could get to the conference table, a solution might be worked out and, afterward, all sides would be "excellent friends."[72]

Salisbury's twenty-eight pictures and two maps, which ran with his articles, made powerful impressions. Photojournalism and its accompanying captions often replaced thorough readings. The maps, in each instance, showed Hanoi and its environs, especially the Paul Doumer (Long Bien) Bridge. There was a good picture of the author interviewing Premier Pham Van Dong. Otherwise, the pictures, mostly taken by Harrison, gave the sense of a country at war. His most graphic ones showed civilian damages and injuries: the interior of the church at Phatdiem's Thuongkiem Catholic Cathedral and Vu Kat's child with his missing leg. The photos depicted bomb shelters, workingwomen, and the omnipresent bikes.

Salisbury's book *Behind the Lines*, published in April 1967, broadened his twenty-three dispatches with added details. He admitted, quoting his diary, that he wanted to convey the DRV's confidence while showing the bombing's failure and the possibility of negotiations. He again stressed the DRV's flexibility despite demanding acceptance of its four basic preconditions before any negotiations took place. Salisbury clung to the notion of "private, secret, low-pitched discussions on a completely unofficial basis."[73] Hanoi would not be bombed to the conference table. Despite the "chilling blast of winter wind" his dispatches had encountered from LBJ and the press, he still believed in negotiations, not escalations.[74]

♦♦ 3 ♦♦

While the administration intensified its anti-Salisbury campaign, Secretary of State Dean Rusk already had by December 30, 1966, conclusive proof that the early December bombings before the Christmas pause had left only three craters in the Yen Vien railway yards but forty outside the target area. A report by Thomas L. Hughes, the State Department's intelligence chief, found that twenty-three 750-pound bombs had been jettisoned by pilots to avoid MIG fighters—these were probably the bombs that destroyed the Pho Nguyen Thiep Street houses. Salisbury later concluded, "There were two wars: the one which the White House, the State Department, the Pentagon, carried on in public, and the second, quite different, conducted in secrecy and deceit."[75]

In a 1969 interview, two years after his trip to Hanoi, Salisbury revealed that Premier Pham Van Dong had given him an off-the-record comment on LBJ's deceit: "I'm sorry to say this, Mr. Salisbury, but we've come to the conclusion that we cannot always believe your President. He does not always tell the truth." Pham said this, according to Harrison, "more in pain than in anger." Assistant Secretary of Defense Arthur Sylvester, Harrison confessed, "was the guy who was really on the spot, because it was the Pentagon's version of the bombing which had suddenly blown up in his face, [and he] was certainly looking around frantically for any kind of counter to soften the blow that had come their way." Salisbury thought Sylvester originated the attribution problem for the casualty figures in Namdinh. They were "blown up and beaten around quite a bit." It was a "specious distraction," especially by the fall of 1967 when the public had fully come around to Salisbury's view.[76]

It is interesting to note David Halberstam's take on the LBJ administration's response to Salisbury's articles:

> He [McNamara] paid particular attention to stories about the destruction caused by the bombing. When Harrison Salisbury of the *Times* visited Hanoi at the end of 1966, his articles were violently attacked by the Administration, particularly Defense Department spokesmen, but McNamara was fascinated by them and followed them closely.[77]

By mid-1967 President Johnson turned on McNamara after he testified to Senator John Stennis's Armed Services Committee about trying to stop bombing as a way of attaining victory. In November LBJ unceremoniously removed McNamara as secretary of defense and appointed him head of the World Bank.[78]

It turned out that a CIA study on Namdinh, completed May 23, 1967, arrived at the same conclusions as Salisbury, using some of the same documentation, including the *Report on the U.S. War Crimes in Nam-Dinh City*—the one labeled communist propaganda by Sylvester and his epigones. The report's data, the CIA study found, "seemed to be accurate when measured against detailed studies made on the basis of post strike photography." As it finally turned out, the Pentagon's previous declarations were propaganda—not the report or Salisbury's dispatches on Namdinh.[79]

Despite the anti-Salisbury frenzy, Rostow, Rusk, and LBJ did take his dispatches seriously and, surprisingly, attempted to pursue a path to peace that he had opened up. In chats with John Colvin, the British attaché in Hanoi, Salisbury began summarizing his various interviews with the North Vietnamese leaders, and Colvin secretly passed this information on to the British Foreign Office. Foreign Secretary George Brown told his ambassador, Michael Stewart, who informed Assistant Secretary of State William P. Bundy. Hanoi, according to Salisbury, treated him as an unofficial emissary. The bottom line, Salisbury confided to Colvin, was "if we halted the bombing and troop increases, Hanoi would make some military concession and would be prepared to negotiate." Covertly, and still unknown to Salisbury,

American Ambassador Henry Cabot Lodge had just finished the attempted secret negotiation with Hanoi coded Marigold. This effort, begun in June and ending by December 6, 1966, collapsed over the question of de-escalation, especially because of heavy bombing raids over Hanoi. [80]

Nevertheless, Colvin continued to think that Ho would negotiate secretly if this could be arranged. Bill Bundy took Colvin's report to Rostow, who sent an urgent memo to LBJ that evening, January 3. Rostow believed it probable Hanoi wanted peace but had to bargain secretly due to Vietcong and Chinese communist pressure. He added a handwritten memo: the NLF would "bug out" if it knew negotiations were being conducted. The most important quote was, "If this is so, the message we should send back is this, and no more: 'Your message to Salisbury has been delivered. You will be hearing from us soon.'" The "your" and "you" referred to Premier Pham Van Dong. Rostow did not give this proposal "very high odds" but thought it "worth a try." Salisbury's information coincided with what Brown knew. [81] Within a day, the lowly attaché's message had reached all the way up to the president, but its return hit a snag.

Rusk passed a long message to Ambassador Stewart for Brown to transmit to Colvin that asked Harrison to negotiate. Colvin failed to decode the extended communiqué in time for Salisbury to negotiate during his Premier Pham Van Dong interview of January 3, 1967, published in the *Times* on January 4. Hanoi, using Aesopian language, had suggested clandestine talks—at least, that was Salisbury's interpretation. It was first published in his dispatch but omitted in a republished, sanitized version by Hanoi. Rusk had authorized Salisbury to convey a U.S. interest in secret talks. Salisbury seemed willing, Colvin reported. But Rusk's proposal never reached Harrison because of Colvin's tardy decoding, and Salisbury only found out about it much later. If, and only if, the Salisbury maneuver had been successful, then a direct message would have been sent through Moscow in a sealed envelope, without intermediaries, to Hanoi. Rostow recounted to LBJ that he had earlier spoken to McNamara and Rusk on the need to do this. The failed message, nevertheless, did not offer much, according to Salisbury's later investigation: "It could restate the kind of settlement we would envisage, but its major message should be technical; namely that we believe a secure facility could be provided for our emissaries to meet without diplomatic or journalistic knowledge." The desired bombing halt was not offered, and that was Hanoi's requirement. Harrison was relieved LBJ's message never reached him:

> I would have been extremely uncomfortable in the role of a go-between, although I confess the notion of "Harrison Appalsbury" being recruited for delicate, secret diplomatic duty on behalf of Dean Rusk and Lyndon Baines Johnson did have its charm. [82]

The follow-up to this stillborn initiative occurred on January 13, 1967, at 5:00 p.m., when Salisbury, after returning to the United States, visited Rusk's office at the State Department. Scotty Reston, the *Times* Washington bureau chief, had set the meeting up. It, too, was as clandestine as Colvin's initiative. Rusk's assistant Bill Bundy was present, and because Rusk anticipated a publicity stunt by Harrison, he had invited his own PR chief, John J. McCloskey, to the meeting. Harrison assured Rusk that their meeting would remain secret; Reston also could be counted on for that. So McCloskey left. Salisbury observed, "Rusk was stiff and on guard, especially at the start. He kept trying to start arguments with me."[83]

Salisbury focused on his interviews with Premier Pham Van Dong and other DRV officials, which he summarized for Rusk. In direct, clandestine talks, the DRV would slowly make concessions, indirectly, and reciprocate commensurate to a bombing halt. Pham seemed to want Salisbury to tell Rusk: *pause and stop the bombing and we can secretly talk without preconditions.*[84] The secretary wondered whether the Geneva settlement must be the basis of any future settlement and whether the bombing halt had to be unconditional. Harrison said yes to both, though he thought the latter was not strongly stressed. That was more of a semantic question, as the bombing could always be resumed anyway. Salisbury believed the DRV feared Chinese interference or blackmail and that they would lose their population's high morale. Though Pham admitted nothing directly about DRV troops in the South, Salisbury believed it was always assumed. In one form or another, Rusk kept coming back to that point. Rusk asked, "Did you ask them whether they have sent troops to the South?" Harrison answered, "No, because my questions always assumed that they were doing this and it seemed to me their answers were based on the same."[85]

Rusk sent his own assessment of this conversation with Salisbury to LBJ the next day, January 14. The secretary indicated to LBJ that Salisbury's visit to his office would remain a secret; however, "if questions are seriously raised over the weekend or later [then] we don't want to build him up, but neither do we wish to have our contact with him seem something to be concealed."[86] Rusk focused on Pham's revised remarks, Hanoi's sanitized corrective to Harrison's dispatch, which was originally carried in the *Times* on January 8, 1967.[87] It will always remain an open question whether Salisbury misinterpreted Pham in his original interview or whether Rusk disbelieved both Salisbury and Pham.

Salisbury, the secretary recounted to the president, pressed the premier on Hanoi making some response if the United States were to stop bombing or take other actions. Pham made various replies. First, there was his statement that once the United States had halted its attacks "as far as we are concerned we will take an appropriate stand." Second, the premier remarked that if the United States wanted a settlement, "Of course we know what we should do if the U.S. shows goodwill. If they stop the whole war, we know what we should do. If they stop doing harm to the North, we know what we should do." Third, at another place in the conversation, Pham commented, "The moment the U.S. puts an end to the war, we will respect each other and settle every question." Finally, the premier mentioned at another moment, when hostilities ceased, "we can speak about other things. After this there will be no lack of generosity on our part." Rusk believed the last two points added nothing, but the first two suggested, in Rusk's opinion, that "reciprocal action is required before we can stop the bombing." Rusk pointed out that even after Salisbury's repeated questioning, Pham refused to elaborate on his phrase "an appropriate stand" or the meaning of "we know what we should do." Otherwise, "Dong took the standard line that our bombing was aggression and that we were not entitled to get anything in return for stopping it."[88]

It is worth once again repeating how Rusk interpreted Salisbury's interview with the premier: "Our net judgment is that Pham Van Dong's unreported statements," which were not included even in Harrison's published dispatch of the statements "the North Vietnamese would not let Salisbury print—are interesting as *mood music* [italics added], but give us no real handle beyond what we already had from similar statements and to at least one other source." He seemed to be referring to Marigold. Rusk recognized that Salisbury "appeared to regard himself as a confidential reporter to his government only," and yet there were other interesting elements. The first was that some officials believed the war was a big drag on America domestically, though Salisbury refuted this. Another was that Hanoi worried about how the crisis in China might affect shipments from there and the USSR. Lastly, Pham fretted about Chinese influence over any publication on negotiations—that the Chinese "had a pistol at their back." Any public peace gesture would affect DRV morale adversely. Rusk was inclined to "share Salisbury's conclusion that if Hanoi ever started down the road to peace, it would have to have a clear idea at the outset just where they would come out, and that a conclusion would be reached rapidly." That, for Salisbury, meant working out all the details of a settlement "in the most private and secret way." Salisbury stressed that to Pham, and that point coincided with what Rusk called a package, which could be reached secretly. But it was the sanitized part of Salisbury's interview with Pham that for Rusk was the most important thing.[89]

Salisbury, it seems, only aroused surface interest in LBJ. Publicly, Rusk and Rostow "were denouncing him, while privately they were using the information to try to fashion an approach toward negotiating, but, I'm afraid, this effort to find common ground with Hanoi was scuppered by LBJ just as were all the others."[90] According to Bill Bundy, LBJ had already decided just after Marigold in early December 1966 to "Get ahead with it! Get ahead with it!" Bundy called that "very strong" and again quoted LBJ: "We've done all this diplomacy, now, let's get on with it. Let's do the job!" The president believed Hanoi was only stalling and that the bombing had to be sharply increased—the "hard knock."[91]

The Joint Chiefs had won the argument with Secretary of Defense Robert McNamara. Salisbury's dispatches, arriving in the middle of that dispute, were meddlesome but not decisive with LBJ. At the beginning of February, he ordered a sharp escalation of the war on all fronts. Even so, Salisbury's efforts in Hanoi carried forward of their own momentum. He had a long conversation with U.S. Ambassador Arthur Goldberg at the United Nations on January 20, 1967. Goldberg revealed that a careful memo had been sent to the DRV's representative in Rangoon. "We were willing," Goldberg indicated, "to continue the [Christmas] bombing pause indefinitely if Hanoi was prepared for negotiations." That resulted in failure. Hanoi demanded its four points—end bombings; restore the Geneva settlement; end fighting in the South and withdraw all U.S. forces; and recognize Vietnam's sovereignty—so bombing was resumed. Because of this, "he was convinced that the President would not order a cessation of bombing." Goldberg supported the pause and felt the bombing was a mistake. "But it was," he said, "strongly supported by the Joint Chiefs." He regretted the McCarthy-like tactics used by Sylvester and the Defense Department against Salisbury. Rusk had informed Goldberg about Salisbury's conversation with him, and Goldberg agreed that the "situation required patient, quiet, completely secret and direct talks." Salisbury insisted that a bombing cessation had to be part of the procedure and not a preliminary effort.[92]

A Scotty Reston conversation with Bill Bundy bothered Salisbury, and he wrote Bundy for clarification. This contact initiated an exchange that further explained the Johnson administration's criticism of Salisbury's dispatches. Scotty told Harrison that Bill Bundy "had an idea I had some kind of a vested interest in Communist area coverage, was economically dependent on this and therefore to a 'soft' line in that field." Salisbury gave a quick history of being denounced repeatedly in Moscow for his views and, likewise, in America for being "soft-headed." He just wanted Bundy to know that he was "not dependent on the Russians or any of the Communists for my livelihood." That came from his post at the *Times* as assistant managing editor. Because his opinions satisfied neither Moscow nor Washington, it told him that he was getting closer to the truth in a polarized world.[93]

Bundy denied making a "vested interest" remark; he also rejected having said that because of Salisbury's dependence on his communist expertise, Salisbury took a soft line. "This is," he wrote, "a quite inaccurate and misleading summary of anything I have said or thought." Bundy did admit that Salisbury's "articles have of course occasioned a good deal of discussion in

Washington gatherings." But Bundy was at great pains, especially because Reston got the information secondhand, to clarify his position both with Reston and Salisbury.

The first problem with Salisbury's dispatches, according to Bundy, particularly the earliest ones, was the need of "attribution and distinction, [that is,] your opening articles from Hanoi totally failed to separate what you yourself had actually seen and what you had been told." Bundy labeled this "slipshod" and "handout" journalism: it was "slipshod" in that, even with indirect attribution, "the reader would still find it hard to distinguish your own opinions from what you saw or were told." By "handout journalism" Bundy meant his reporting reflected what Hanoi may have wanted said. Harrison wrote his dispatches, Bundy insisted, with little critical analysis. The fine line of objectivity may have been crossed because reporting in such a hostile environment needed some cooperation by the regime itself. By waiting, rather than hastily posting, Bundy believed Salisbury might have avoided these pitfalls in his earliest dispatches.

Salisbury should have done more preparatory homework and taken a harder look at communist claims and data. As Bundy put it,

> I would have thought an experienced reporter going to Hanoi would have been thoroughly familiar with the many reports, not confined to foreign newspapers, of Nam Dinh, and would therefore have taken a harder look than you did at claims that there were no military targets there [and] familiarized himself with past formulations [and noticed that] there had been anything more than the most nuanced change, if that, in what you were being told about the four points.

Bundy closed his critique by thanking Salisbury for an "honest and helpful account" to the secretary of state and suggesting that Harrison was not pro-red but overly optimistic. It was not whether or not he had crossed the line of objectivity: he had been hasty. That was a new wrinkle in the criticism of Salisbury. Though Salisbury might get a Pulitzer Prize, Bundy would only give him a "B" for his dispatches and ended on a hard-nosed remark: "But I suspect that is a much higher grade than you or the *Times* would give me. So let's not be too sensitive with each other."[94]

Bundy's letter, written on January 25, 1967, did not reach Salisbury until May 10 of that year because of Bundy's trying to ascertain Reston's view— but Reston was out of town and Bundy forgot about the matter. When Bundy's secretary called his attention to it finally in May, Bundy decided to send the letter as it stood. That explains Salisbury's tardy reply to Bundy's critique, dated June 5, 1967.

Vested interest was, as Salisbury then noted, not a part of Bundy's objections. Rather, his principal objections were, first, that there was a question of attribution. Harrison insisted that his dispatch clearly separated and indicated what he saw from what he was told. Besides, "the things that I was told were quite minor, largely summaries of damage and casualties which had occurred in the past." For argument's sake, Salisbury even accepted that "casualties should have been sourced [but] I do not concur in the view that anyone was misled by this. As Clifton Daniel pointed out, there was and could be only one source for these figures and I am still awaiting a convincing demonstration that the use of this material in any way distorted the actual picture."

Bundy's second point about preparation, especially about the Premier Pham Van Dong interview, puzzled Salisbury, since he had done just that. He had brought a thorough rundown of DRV negotiating points with him from the *Times* archive. The error in interpretation was not his but the State Department's. A careful reading, Salisbury stressed, would distinguish what he had written "from reactions abroad in the minds of persons who were not familiar with what had been said in the past about the four points." That flaw, Salisbury insisted, "existed either in the Department or in other Western quarters."

About Bundy's third point, concerning being familiar with Namdinh, Salisbury said it had only been referred to once in the *Times* as a "casual reference" by James Cameron. Though the *Times* was not the fountain of all knowledge, what other newspaper would have carried it? But much more important was his fourth point. As he revealed to Bundy, "a close comparison of my observations in Nam Dinh with those of the military and air intelligence people whom I consulted on my return here disclosed no essential difference in our estimations of the damage which had occurred in that city." He rejected the notion of "handout journalism" with some bitterness and as a point of professional pride. It was Salisbury's skepticism, not naiveté, critics misperceived. Salisbury had replied to Bundy because he did not want any misconceptions to go unchallenged.[95]

Also, TV played a role in the Salisbury frenzy. On January 12, 1967, NBC's prime-time program with Peter Jennings hosted an interview with Salisbury and featured ABC's Lou Gioffi. Gioffi pointedly asked Harrison about Namdinh. "You reported," Gioffi noted, "the civilian areas of that town were heavily bombed, with heavy civilian casualties, and so on, while Washington says that there were military targets in there." Gioffi also commented that a returned navy commander insisted the "whole city is ringed by antiaircraft batteries, and military targets, and so on." Gioffi wanted to know which it was. Was Salisbury allowed, or not, to see them, or were they hidden? "What is the truth?" Salisbury said that they hid them, but not well. "It's perfectly easy to see the batteries as you move along the highways, or if you move into a city." He did not dispute the pilot, but, he emphasized, things looked entirely different from the ground. Salisbury continued, "It was not my impression, from the number I saw in their location, that Namdinh was as heavily defended as this Navy flier says it is." About military targets there, that only had to do with freight and supplies moving through Nam Dinh and Nin Binh, a city close by. Goods moved south from Hanoi's port city of Haiphong and fanned out from those two cities of Nam Dinh and Nin Binh. Salisbury remarked that Nam Dinh was heavily hit, and military targets were hit there, but "in addition to whatever military targets we hit, we hit a lot of civilian housing. And there's no question about it. We did."[96]

Jennings cited Senator Barry Goldwater's (R–Arizona) charge that the *Times* had become the mouthpiece of communist propaganda in publishing Salisbury's articles on North Vietnam. Howard K. Smith, as ABC's reporter in Washington, was quoted on the show at length as a sharp critic of Salisbury's dispatches, calling them "careless, erratic, and dangerously misleading." Naturally, U.S. bombs hit civilians, as Smith also had reported for the last year, and that was not very revealing. However, Salisbury broke a rule of good journalism because "he gave no source and left the impression that he knew the figures to be true. Only days later we're told that they came from communist propaganda sources that are not famous for telling the truth." Besides, Smith continued, Salisbury's interview with Premier Pham Van Dong was a "muddle because his account was sharply at odds with the published text of what the premier actually had said." Smith appeared unaware that the interview as first reported by Harrison had later been sanitized and then published again by Hanoi. The quote from Smith finished, "The danger in Salisbury's reporting to the *Times* is that it illegitimately fostered Hanoi's wrong state of mind." Everyone falters now and then, Smith went on, and that could be Salisbury's apology.[97] Unfortunately for Smith, historians have looked more kindly on Salisbury and more critically at his assailants.[98]

John Scali's *ABC Scope* interview with Salisbury, conducted back in early January from Hong Kong, was finally aired on January 14, 1967. Scali also faulted Salisbury for complaining about civilian damage when the U.S. government never claimed it only hit "steel and concrete." Salisbury made "some serious errors" when he later said he did not intend for his reports to suggest otherwise, or to imply that "American planes were causing totally unnecessary casualties by aiming at a peaceful textile plant." In fact, Scali claimed, Salisbury had accepted "false Communist claims that the attacks on Nam Dinh had never been announced, that the city contained no military targets." Then, on how heavily Namdinh was defended, Scali insisted the Pentagon had aerial photos showing clearly there were "500 antiaircraft guns with a 25 mile radius of the city, including 165 in Nam Dinh itself and more than 1,000 in the Hanoi-Haiphong area." But Scali never saw these photos. The Department of Defense only made the claim; it did not release the photographs until much later. Like Smith, Scali accused Salisbury of trying to be an "instant expert" from a "two-week Communist-guided tour."

This stinging attack, of course, along with Smith's, turned out to be not based on fact. They relied on Pentagon propaganda, released by an antagonistic administration. Scali, Smith, and all the others were wrong and biased. They had been pimped by LBJ's administration. When Salisbury complained, Scali, like Smith, hid behind what he thought were Salisbury's factual errors, that is, the false data the Pentagon leaked to him. [99]

Harrison confronted Scali and Smith. In a letter to ABC's William Sheehan, Salisbury declined a TV rebuttal because it would turn things into a "minor kind of Donnybrook."[100] Smith and Scali had a right to their opinions. However, "I did object to Scali's wrap-around, because it seemed to me that if ABC shared John's viewpoint, they had no business putting before their viewers so biased, inaccurate and queasy a report as John seemed to think I had presented." That was Harrison's tongue-in-cheek criticism.[101] To Scali he was more specific. Salisbury told Scali that he had a right "to think I have done a lousy job [and] I certainly would not raise one little finger to keep you from broadcasting that view, much as I might disagree with it." About Scali's later wraparound, "you put me a little bit in a position of a sitting pigeon which you could shoot down at will and with the shots fired from any angle that you happened to feel like." What Harrison meant was that Scali was on live TV after he returned home from Hong Kong and did his wraparound. Salisbury was not then a part of that wraparound session. He could not rebut. Salisbury gave ABC a break to scoop his story. "I assumed that they wanted my report because they felt it had the degree of reliability which ABC viewers had a right to expect." If it were as "lousy" as Smith and Scali later suggested, why was it aired in the first place?[102] Harrison learned that victims of media reprisals rarely recovered their reputations, while the perpetrators go their merry ways.

♦♦ 4 ♦♦

Salisbury testified before the Senate's Committee on Foreign Relations on Thursday, February 2, 1967, from 10 a.m. to 1:20 p.m.[103] The senators' questioning and Harrison's comments added some depth to his dispatches and helped to clarify the public debate over the Vietnam War. Harrison started with a prepared statement, emphasizing his main point: the Vietnam War had reached a turning point. It could lead to a negotiated settlement or to a precipitous escalation. Also, despite an escalation, everything would continue at the same level to move south.[104]

Chairman Fulbright then asked about the Namdinh controversy. "I had the feeling," Salisbury said, "and maybe I am unfair in this, that the question of the sourcing of those figures was introduced really to sort of start a false hare on this matter because the statistics themselves were really not very impressive."[105]

Fulbright yielded to John Sparkman (D–Alabama), who gave the Senate's notorious hawk Frank J. Lausche (D–Ohio) a moment to complain of a one-sided hearing. He resented Salisbury's presence, seeming to confirm the "effort of the chairman to create a portrait that doesn't quite accurately reflect the position of our country,"[106] Sparkman continued. He suggested Salisbury thought U.S. policy in North Vietnam was "unsound," which the journalist corrected to "unproductive" or "counter-productive." Fulbright had termed it "unsound." Sparkman remarked that earlier Salisbury agreed and said it was having a "considerable effect." So what did Salisbury mean by it being unproductive? Harrison considered the positive and negative aspects of the policy. The former meant that vast damage took labor away from the rice paddies and cost the North casualties and material. It also resulted in an increased will to resist because of the rise in national patriotism. The one—patriotic fervor—canceled out the other—damage. This all happened with the result that the flow of men and materials continued despite the bombing.[107]

Bourke B. Hickenlooper (R–Iowa) thought public impressions of Salisbury's articles were that the U.S. bombed only urban areas of no military significance. Harrison argued that only a superficial reading could give that opinion. Highways, railways, and bridges were the principal targets—as well as oil storage and transshipment areas, motor depots, and antiaircraft installations— all often found in metropolitan areas. He did not see MIG airfields and heard there were orders not to attack them. Salisbury pleaded ignorance on whether the DRV had to repay for goods from abroad. If so, he answered, the contributors would be waiting a long time.[108]

Mike Mansfield (D–Montana) was, as he noted, "listening and learning." He believed there was a "vendetta being waged against your stories, and I am delighted that you have had a chance in an open forum to rebut some of those statements." The only thing he wanted to know was where, similarly, reporters in South Vietnam went to get their lists and types of casualties. If American, Harrison replied, then from the U.S. military. If Vietnamese, then it was difficult to say, but probably by making inquiries over time. Otherwise, they got them from South Vietnamese sources, just as Salisbury had obtained his data from North Vietnamese sources.[109]

Wayne Morse (D–Oregon) complimented Salisbury for his "factual reporting which we have read for the more than 20 years that you have served as a foreign correspondent abroad."[110] Though critics may not like the facts, Morse congratulated him. Was it, Morse wondered, unreasonable for the

North to distrust the United States? It was not, Harrison responded. Morse continued with an indictment of the United States for its lies about the Gulf of Tonkin incident and the unilateral basis of the U.S. military buildup in the South and fighting an undeclared war. If all of that were true, then Salisbury went along with the senator about the North's distrust. About widening the war to China, the United States could destroy, but not conquer, China—and the Chinese expected that. What about bombing the Paul Doumer (Long Bein) Bridge in Hanoi? Was it not a military target? Harrison agreed and did not know why it had not been bombed, the results of which would be considerable, but they have prepared for that. It would be a severe blow, but not fatal. If, Harrison reasoned, bombing were strictly a military calculation, then, "I see no reason at all why we do not take the bridge out, take out the MIG fields, take out Hanoi. This is what the North Vietnamese expect us to do."[111] Karl E. Mundt (R–South Dakota) said he would be "shocked" if the Johnson administration was not looking into secret negotiations. Salisbury hoped it was. No senators seemed to know—at least publicly—that Marigold had failed or that Sunflower was underway.

Parenthetically, attempts may have been made at various will-o'-the-wisp negotiations: "American officials were responding to some vague but enticing signals conveyed to journalist Harrison Salisbury by Pham Van Dong in early January." It led to LBJ's letter to Ho of February 2, 1967, and Ho's response of February 15, 1967. As previously noted, LBJ would stop the bombing only if Ho ceased the infiltration into the South. Ho replied that the bombing must end unconditionally as well as other acts of war, again spelling out the preconditions. Secret negotiations like Marigold and Sunflower abruptly ended.[112]

Albert Gore (D–Tennessee) knew and respected Salisbury, so he turned his ten minutes over to Lausche. Would Salisbury, Lausche asked, recommend a U.S. pullout? "I certainly do not recommend our pulling out, Senator." What about remaining there in enclaves, Lausche demanded, but Salisbury was not keen on that. Well, Lausche wondered, what about stopping the bombing of the North? That, overall, might be a good move, Salisbury believed. "I am sure that it would not be adverse to our interests if we did do it." It was common sense not to sit with folded hands as the South was supplied. It would not be prudent to stop bombing unexpectedly: "we have a right to know if we stopped the bombing what move they are prepared to take." What extra avenues could be explored to stop the shooting? Salisbury believed it could end if every path were studied, but below the public's radar. There was, in Salisbury's view, less hardness on Ho's requirement that the South Vietnamese government had to be reformed based on the NLF. Lausche disagreed.[113]

Lausche shifted gears to a more confrontational attack. How did Salisbury get in? Harrison recounted his story of persistence and his important position on the *Times*. Lausche tried to compare Salisbury's success in getting to Hanoi to *New York Times* reporter Herbert Matthews entrance into Castro's Cuba. Lausche was implying that Matthews had made Castro acceptable to undecided Cubans and liberal-progressive American opinion. Had Salisbury done that with North Vietnam? "I do not think so." At that point, the chair had to ask for order in the chamber. Lausche continued. Did the *Times* do it? That was, in Salisbury's mind, a subjective question. He believed the *Times* had not. Lausche quit. Fulbright remarked that such provocative questioning was "one of the principal reasons for major difficulties in conducting this committee."[114]

Clifford P. Case (R–New Jersey) resumed the hearing. If the bombings were stopped, he queried, would that not simply prolong the war by two years? It would strengthen the North's resolve. Salisbury believed that if nothing happened, except for world opinion, international pressure would be directed at North Vietnam. For America, there could be an enormous diplomatic gain. Further, he thought, "if the bombing were halted, they would take a reciprocal step, and we would then move into the negotiative period." His concern was not that the U.S. government would fail to get into negotiations, but that "we not get into negotiations before we know what we are going to negotiate, and I think before the bombing stops, before anything happens, there should be an exploration to see whether there can be worked out some terms for a settlement." Case remarked that he assumed everything was being done that could be done and, if not, the administration should be thrown out immediately.[115] Yet, only two weeks later, LBJ's disingenuous letter to Ho was rejected almost immediately.

Some thought, Case reflected, that there were only two alternatives: winning by bombing or leaving. Others added—seizing more and more territory and holding it until victory, that is, a free and independent South Vietnam. Salisbury only agreed if the South did it and not the United States, even if the South required some U.S. protection. He believed negotiations would be a more successful route and, at least, should be tried. Case agreed. What about China? Salisbury thought there was hereditary antagonism. About their own government, ordinary people supported it, but they were ignorant of the rest of the world. They thought of the United States the way they once thought of France in 1946. Could two Vietnams result through negotiations? Yes, Salisbury believed, but it would be difficult.[116]

Stuart Symington (D–Missouri) asked whether the North's supplies included infiltration. It did, answered Salisbury, and had not been slowed. U.S. authorities argued it had been heavily cut. About Namdinh being announced as a military target, it had been. Would Salisbury further comment on why he and the *Times* contradicted the Pentagon? It was, Salisbury insisted, because of Sylvester's faulty premise, which his deputy Phil G. Goulding's letter to Representative Ogden R. Reid (R–New York) promoted: "The stories [in the *Times*] specifically said that the residents of Nam Dinh were not aware of it ever having been mentioned in an American communiqué." Further, Goulding's letter had denied dams were targeted. Salisbury could not challenge that, "I said in the story, which was that bombs had fallen on the dikes." Goulding had additionally stated to Representative Reid that Namdinh was an important transshipment point and had major military targets: a power plant, storage depot, railroad yard, a large transshipment installation, naval facilities for unloading from the Dao River, and heavy antiaircraft defenses—some five hundred in that area, 165 in Namdinh itself.[117] Only residents, according to Salisbury, refuted that, not he.

About casualties, Goulding's letter had claimed Salisbury offered no evidence and accepted as fact what the communists gave him, that is, eighty-nine killed. Even if accepted, this was small for a city of ninety thousand, Goulding remarked. Salisbury indicated that the city had been widely evacuated, and its population reduced to probably thirty to forty thousand. Goulding also claimed it had extensive antiaircraft defenses, a trench-bunker system, and air raid shelters. Of these targets, all Harrison could say was "I was reporting, and I did report, and specifically said that the civilian officials of this city did not believe that their city contained military objects." He only saw that the textile and silk plants were "bombed out of existence." Only the supposed density of antiaircraft installations was worth quibbling about. Salisbury thought U.S. statistics might refer to the entire Namdinh area, not just the city itself. Goulding's letter, in conclusion, reaffirmed that no civilian installations were targeted purposely, but they could be collateral damage. Salisbury remarked, "I have no knowledge of my own that we have targeted civilian objectives, and I think any inference drawn from my dispatches that we did do that is false." Only Hanoi made that charge.[118]

At this point, two articles were put into the hearing's record, one by Joseph Alsop of the *Post*, and another by Tom Wicker of the *Times*. Alsop was convinced bombing decreased infiltration and provided Department of Defense figures to prove it. Wicker suggested otherwise. Salisbury made no comment. Symington asked him if DRV civilian casualties justified his criticism despite South Vietnamese deaths. Salisbury remarked that comparisons between South and North civilian casualties were iffy. This was especially true as a military matter, not considering public opinion. Rather, the question should be: Did the United States get sufficient payoff by making it harder for the North to conduct the war? "I do not think we make it that much harder to be worth this, and to be worth the price which I think we pay in giving them a greater sense of national will and purpose in fighting back." Symington proceeded to his last question by noting the consternation in some and the delight in others that Salisbury's dispatches had created. What would Salisbury do? "I would embark on the quietest and most secret kind of exploration to see if my intuition that there is a possibility that this time we might move on to a negotiation with some idea of a settlement is borne out." He could not be sure that was happening.[119] The senators also put an article by Neil Sheehan into the record on the history of the struggle in the South seen as a guerrilla war.[120]

The hearing ended with Morse complimenting the chair's fairness and the chair condemning Lausche's attempt to "discredit this witness because of something another journalist said [which] did not appeal to me very much."[121] Fulbright's hearing indicated the deepening divisions in public opinion, but a turning point had been reached. Johnson's decision at that very moment for a "hard knock" in the bombing fueled the antiwar movement. Salisbury had shown that the bombing offensive was anything but "surgical." The more LBJ and his entourage claimed precision bombing of only "steel and concrete" targets, the more they appeared to be "liars and deceivers."[122]

♦♦ 5 ♦♦

When the Salisbury frenzy ended, when congratulations and criticisms finished, he still faced a "journalistic assassination." In the eyes of U.S. leaders, Salisbury knew too much; it was not a dissimilar motivation from Stalin's when he had considered killing the *Times* Moscow bureau chief. It was, as in the notorious case of Bull Connor, a personal vendetta against Harrison and the *Times*. Karnow puts it succinctly: "An advisory board composed largely of publishers overruled a jury of newspaper editors that had voted to award Salisbury the Pulitzer Prize."[123]

According to Turner Catledge, then senior editor at the *New York Times*, part of the excitement over Salisbury's Hanoi articles was that "despite the official denials, most readers knew that Salisbury had reported the truth about the bombing." He had the biggest scoop of the year, and it was assumed he would win a Pulitzer Prize.

Catledge served on the Pulitzer's advisory board but followed the practice of abstaining when his own paper was nominated. The Pulitzer jury had voted four to one in favor of Salisbury. The advisory board of twelve, consisting mainly of news executives, voted six to five against—its secretary being a nonvoting member. The board "narrowly voted against giving the Pulitzer Prize to Salisbury." Catledge was convinced that several board members cast their votes along political lines instead of journalistic merits. And he added, they "made no bones about it." They supported the war. Joseph Pulitzer Jr., publisher of the *Saint Louis Post-Dispatch* and chair of the Pulitzer board, then called for a secret ballot. The result was the same, however upset Turner Catledge, Joseph Pulitzer Jr., and the others were. Although Salisbury shrugged it off, his wife told the authors privately that Columbia University's president, Grayson L. Kirk, had broken the tie vote by vetoing Salisbury and that he was the most intensely partisan member of the board.[124] Of course, this decision spilled over into the press. The *New York Times* reported that Edward Albee, winner of the 1967 drama award, believed the "Prize is in danger of losing its position of honor."[125]

John Hohenberg, longtime secretary to the advisory board, later wrote that the jury for international reporting voted four to one in favor of Salisbury. What he did not admit was that Salisbury had by far the best score, the lowest being the best at ten. R. John Hughes of the *Christian Science Monitor* scored a distant third at eighteen, writing on Indonesia. Actually, Ward Just of the *Washington Post* scored twelve, also writing on Vietnam. By selecting Hughes, the prize remained free of the Vietnam controversy. Joseph R. Pulitzer Jr., grandson of Joseph Pulitzer and chair of the advisory committee, strongly supported Salisbury, and he revealed the deliberations and decisions of the jury, omitting only the names of those who voted for and against. Grayson Kirk argued against this move, stating, "I strongly urge them [advisory board members] to protect the integrity of the system by not revealing Jury discussions and votes." Pulitzer sharply disagreed: "Forgive me but I cannot agree that the integrity of the Jury system would be served by not revealing jury discussion and votes. The *Post-Dispatch* will print a full and accurate account of what transpired at Arden House omitting only the identity of the individuals who voted for or against on both the jury and advisory." The advisory board had voted six to five in favor of Hughes. They asked Hohenberg for a fuller report, and he telephoned Michael J. Ogden, chair of the jury for 1967 and executive editor of the *Providence Journal-Bulletin.* The advisory board reconsidered its previous action and took a secret ballot, resulting again in a six-to-five vote in favor of Hughes. That decision then went to the trustees of Columbia University, and the advisory committee's action was upheld. Hohenberg revealed that "the case for Salisbury was put so strongly by his advocates that the Trustees for a time thought of reversing the Advisory Board even though the university counsel had repeatedly warned them that they had no authority to do so." The chair of the trustees, Maurice T. Moore, influenced them, and by a close vote they upheld the advisory board's decision.[126]

Time magazine suggested that those voting in the majority thought Salisbury "had unprofessionally allowed himself to see and report only those parts of the story that his hosts chose to display. And he cited casualty figures without mentioning their source: the North Vietnamese government." However, *Time* also noted that the winner in international reporting was R. John Hughes, a *Christian Science Monitor* foreign correspondent whose "stories provided a straight, factual report of what was going on, though they were hardly exceptional."[127] Herbert Brucker, past president of the American Society of Newspaper Editors, asserted the "awards are made at times for a political reason [and that] the suspicion remained that Harrison E. Salisbury's articles from Hanoi did not get the prize 'because his reporting embarrassed the hawks in and out of the United States Government.'"[128] It was, Gay Talese noted, "a decision that would be widely protested in editorials around the nation, but to no avail."[129] Salisbury himself reportedly said, "I put the judgment of the editors of *The Times* ahead of any other criteria."[130]

In the end, Harrison proved correct. Asia still fascinated him. He now turned his full attention to China.

Chapter Eight

The Middle Kingdom

Salisbury endlessly applied for visas to China; the Chinese endlessly rejected him. He took a trip around China's periphery in 1966, vainly attempting a "break-in" by pushing Chinese diplomatic officials to grant him a visa. Already by 1971, he had spent twelve years "developing my contacts and establishing a presence for myself."[1] During that time, millions in China were persecuted in the Cultural Revolution; Lin Biao's coup against Mao was aborted in 1971; the "Gang of Four," who wanted to continue the Cultural Revolution, was arrested in 1976. After Mao's death that year, Deng Xiaoping took power and ended the Cultural Revolution.

Harrison had finally arrived in the People's Republic in May 1972, behind "Dick and Pat" Nixon, staying there through June. After 1972, he remained interested in China. Salisbury became a Sinophile, a belated China Hand. True, Harrison criticized the "New China," especially Mao's last years. True, he beamed over Deng Xiaoping's "New Long March" to jumpstart China's progress. Then there came the 1989 demonstrations and with them the terrible thirteen days in June on Tiananmen Square. As an eyewitness, he watched helplessly the massacre from his Beijing Hotel window. How could the Chinese leadership he personally knew and championed, he wondered, resort to such unimaginable violence? He never quite recovered.

Harrison once wrote about all of his varied experiences in China as "a tidal shift in world power, comparable to the shift in Europe when she mastered the technology of the gunpowder which China had invented, when she armed her galleons and frigates and privateers and adventurers with their

161

letters of marque and set them to plundering the East."[2] The Asian renaissance, which Harrison foretold, was at hand. At last, he was there to watch it,
to chronicle it.

◆◆ 1 ◆◆

Salisbury's first serious efforts to enter China began in 1956, even before his
trip to Eastern Europe, with letters to his Moscow friend Anna Louise
Strong, America's procommunist columnist. In his memoir, he referred to
her as "The Meanest Queen." He liked her for all her perversity. Strong's big,
opinionated mouth had betrayed Mikhail Borodin, the famous Comintern
agent. Stalin arrested Strong and Borodin as American spies in 1949. She
returned to America. He went to the Gulag, perishing there on May 29, 1951.
Stalin purged his China specialists along with Borodin. Anna Louise Strong
had visited Russia in the 1920s, then China, escaping with Borodin in 1929.
Borodin and Strong founded and edited the English-language *Moscow News*.
She wrote "sloppy books about Red Russia and Red China." She went to
Yenan, China, in 1946, sat at the feet of Mao, and transcribed *The Thought of
Mao Zedong*, her most important book. She only learned of Borodin's death
from a *New York Times* obituary. She had never noticed the fear her Moscow
friends had of her China chatter: she would tell Stalin a thing or three!
Borodin's arrest and exile followed. By 1955, one year after Stalin's death,
Moscow forgave her. She returned to China and stayed there. It was in
Beijing, as Salisbury put it, she found Shangri-la. Strong died on March 29,
1970. Only one ranking Chinese political leader attended her funeral, Zhou
Enlai. Salisbury mentioned that he "wrote her long, chatty letters, full of
American political gossip and my notions of why I should be permitted to
come to China." She read them to her Chinese friends, who all wanted to
meet him, including Sun Yat-sen's widow, Mme Soong Ching-ling.[3] This
persistent Salisbury correspondence annoyed Strong. He quizzed her about
Russian-Chinese relations, suggesting, as Khrushchev had, that they were
bitter. Strong blamed U.S. propaganda and discounted Khrushchev's remarks.[4]

By 1958 the *New York Times* managing editor, Turner Catledge, proposed
sending Salisbury to China to make a comprehensive, factual survey. Catledge believed his readers deserved knowing what happened there. It was
logical to anticipate that Harrison could duplicate what he had done in Moscow. Salisbury sought Strong's influence with Chairman Mao Zedong and
Premier Zhou Enlai.[5] She sent his letter on to Zhou with a comment, "it may
be useful for your office to see that the *New York Times* and Mr. Salisbury
want this request, even enough to write to me."[6] Anna told Salisbury it would

be the "scoop of the ages," and she could sympathize with that. But Salisbury overestimated her influence even though China's leaders honored her on National Day by placing her beside Mao on Tiananmen Gate. Americans, she reminded him, were not being allowed into China as "correspondents" because of the reciprocity idea—for each American journalist in China, one People's Republic of China (PRC) journalist in America. A few weeks later, she told him that they had denied his request. The idea of a Russian-Chinese split, she thought, was something the *New York Times* had cooked up. "From every sign," she wrote, "this will not occur in my lifetime or yours, if ever."[7] It was only the government in Washington's dream. Salisbury responded that scoops had nothing to do with getting a better understanding and a willingness to start a dialogue somewhere. Greater understanding served both countries.[8]

Harrison wrote directly to Zhou Enlai with his appeal. "It is the conviction of the editors of *The Times* that this project is of national importance to both of our countries." It was of such importance that it should take precedence over other "pending proposals of a journalistic nature." Foreign Editor Max Frankel even made an inquiry in Moscow. They told him that Salisbury, an outspoken anticommunist, was "PNG" (persona non grata) in Beijing. Salisbury spoke with Russian First Deputy Premier Anastas Mikoyan about the project. Mikoyan thought it a good idea, and he saw no obstacle; Salisbury repeated that to Zhou Enlai, but Zhou did not respond. Once again, he reviewed the entire situation with Strong, and once again, she said there was no chance, at least not in 1959. "I asked a second time [and] was given a polite rebuke, saying that I had asked fairly recently and been refused."[9]

Nineteen-sixty was neither better nor worse. Harrison's interest did not flag. Lester Markel, editor of the *New York Times* Sunday magazine section, accepted Salisbury's article "Haunting Enigma of Red China" as the lead piece for June 12, 1960. Markel labeled it excellent. He suggested sharpening contrasts between red China and red Russia. Salisbury focused: How much did Mao follow or rival Stalin? What held them together? What drove them apart? Harrison challenged the old view that there were no essential differences, that it was a "single global Communist conspiracy with headquarters in the Kremlin." Sure, they shared Marxian ideology. But, he contended, there were also sharp contrasts. The Chinese only seemed as homogenous as "blue ants" in denim outfits. Russia claimed to be a fully socialist state. China only claimed socialism's earliest stage. Its communized agriculture was primitive, while Russia had advanced to huge state-directed co-ops. Another divergence was varying economic-social needs. The USSR was already a mature industrial state. China had barely begun industrialization. It used high psychological motivation to sustain tempo—"to keep the 'blue ants' working at the highest pitch." Stalin's distrust of Mao and their territorial quarrels over Manchuria also separated them. Their worldviews also conflicted. China's belief in the possibility of violence, revolution, and impe-rialist wars had not diminished. Russia allowed for peaceful coexistence and different paths to socialism. Nuclear war, according to Nikita Khrushchev, would be a global calamity. For Mao, China could afford three hundred million causalities and survive.

Given disparities, Salisbury asked, would China and Russia unglue or stick? In the short run, so it seemed, they would stay together. Each appeared to supplement the other's military advantage in the global balance. It looked as if they made mutual concessions to maintain their alliance. In reality, Salisbury maintained, the picture was far different.

The weight of China's population, he argued, would pressure Russia's Far Eastern possessions. He continued debating the point. China was posi-tioning itself, against the USSR, as the leader of colonial and dependent people's struggles for national liberation. That competition with the Soviet Union led to conflict between them. "If China should come out ahead in the competition, then her mass block would be the largest, in numbers, the world has ever seen." Harrison predicted by 1975 China's economy would equal Russia's on the eve of World War II and, armed with rockets and nukes, would be formidable. That shifted the balance of the Sino-Soviet alliance sharply eastward, which frightened Russia. Then, he speculated, America and Russia might resolve their differences to meet China's challenge. "Chi-na's position, the divergence of her viewpoint from that of Mr. Khrushchev, and the implications of her future role are echoing behind the scenes in Moscow."[10]

From 1962 to 1971, Harrison strained in his efforts to reach Beijing. They failed. He only circumnavigated China's edge, looking for some way in. He went to Hanoi in 1966 to report on the bombing, winning journalistic celeb-rity status and notoriety. But nothing brought him any nearer to the Great Wall. His persistence never flagged. He pestered and pestered once again Strong. He added others to his pestering list. It was an endeavor in frustra-tion.

His correspondence with Anna Louise Strong, as well as with the famous author of *Red Star over China*, Edgar Snow, revealed his tenacity. Harrison's justification was simple. President John F. Kennedy offered new opportu-nities for reciprocity. "I am not at all unhopeful of the possibility of a belated but necessary transition in Sino-American relations." He was encouraged about interest in small steps to advance large ones. War was unlikely. He faulted China for being uninterested in a new approach. Or it might be an American "lack of direct contact with Chinese events, Chinese policy and Chinese personality." How were Americans going to know China better, or vice versa? His answer: permit "some writers or correspondents or call them what you will to come from America to China; write about the country, talk to the people, interview the leaders, see what is going on, bring the real feel of China to the United States."

Things remained frozen. "I would be most grateful," he pleaded with Strong in 1961, "if you found the time to drop me a line giving me your assessment of the relations between the two countries, the prospects for the future and the possibilities of getting to China to do something myself on a firsthand basis." She replied, on the contrary, China desired better relations with the United States, despite U.S. bases on Taiwan and its Seventh Fleet in the straits. President Truman had favored Taiwan, and now Kennedy proposed its permanent detachment from China. So, she asked, where did the obduracy lie? She noted Snow's interview with Zhou Enlai, when the premier indicated exchanges should help to "eliminate estrangement [and] improve relations," but that "aroused a storm" in the American press. Journalists railed at Chinese interference with America's press freedom.[11]

Snow wrote Salisbury in 1961. He had recently traveled to China because of "auld lang syne, going back to civil war days." China recognized Snow as a writer, not a correspondent. His interview with Zhou Enlai made it clear, "China won't admit correspondents or settle any other 'concrete' issue until or unless the U.S. is prepared to negotiate about 'principles' and 'fundamentals'—that is, when and how the U.S. armed forces are to withdraw from Taiwan." Of course, if the U.S. voluntarily ended its embargo, withdrew Chiang Kai-shek's forces from Quemoy and Matsu, and stopped invalidating passports for Chinese travel, the PRC might relax its restrictions. In the meantime, Harrison ought to try getting in as an author or writer. No news organization had questioned Secretary of State Dulles or his successors' right to accredit business corporations while denying individuals a visa to the PRC. "Wherever Mr. D. got the notion that he could 'accredit' anybody to a government the U.S. does not even recognize, incidentally, and from whom he could demand no normal courtesies or protection, has always been a moot point." Snow added, "I don't think there is any objection to you personally in Peking. Someone in the F.O. [Foreign Office]—I have forgotten who—mentioned to me that you had applied but that nothing could be done now. You have become an integral part of a major policy issue which they won't break up into pieces."[12]

Salisbury planned a trip to Mongolia, he told Snow, and thought it would be good while there to go on to Beijing. He requested entry as a writer.[13] He bothered Strong. "I have by no means given up hopes of coming to China." Harrison mentioned writing Snow and speaking to international journalist-photographer Felix Greene. Neither Snow nor Greene was optimistic. Also Salisbury was not. "At any event, I am certain that a book by myself on China would have impact, would help to get things moving—just as I am certain Ed Snow's book [*The Other Side of the River*] is going to have an impact, and Greene's book [*Awakened China: The Country Americans Don't Know*], etc."[14]

Salisbury's comings and goings received a dash of cold water from Strong, even though she loaned out his books to Chinese leaders. He reapplied as an author to the Chinese Foreign Ministry in 1961. Strong wrote, "I do not know whether it will have success or how long it may take, but I doubt if the desire of the Chinese for your visit would be materially hastened by an application to come as a writer of books, instead of as a newspaper correspondent. Your status is too well known for that, it includes both functions and you remain best known for your work in the *New York Times*. The Chinese have rules and regulations." They only got around them for Snow because he was "an old friend of China and of the Chinese people. That he might [write] a book went without saying, but was not the essence of his welcome." The Chinese were simply not as convinced, as Salisbury seemed to be, that "things you want to do will be worth to China all the effort it will undoubtedly cost. This view may change with time, but I see few signs of it yet."[15]

Harrison put himself "firmly and plainly on record" to Strong as a frank and honest reporter who respected differences in a diverse world. He remained convinced "no greater service could be achieved for the cause of Chinese-American understanding than an extensive, detailed, sympathetic, understanding—but objective—series of articles on what has happened to the great country of China in the past 11 years." He wrote to Strong from Moscow, on his way to Ulan Bator, emphasizing that if the United States and PRC were ever to begin understanding each other better, then a start had to be made and journalists were the "ones to make this start."

When Harrison returned to America, Snow was in New York, doing the lecture circuit for his recent book. Harrison wrote Strong, "I cannot help wishing that a person like me with the ability to reach enormous and influential audiences could have the opportunity of coming to China and beginning the long and difficult and necessary task of bringing this country up to date on what has happened since 1949. It is more than a pity that this cannot be done; it is criminal."[16]

In one of her final letters to Salisbury, Strong wrote that the Chinese had growing public interest in America. Zhou's bottom line, given in an interview with Reuters, was American removal of its forces from Taiwan and the straits, as well as cessation of U.S. efforts in Vietnam—taken by the premier as an attempt to contain China. Strong reiterated Zhou's complaint: "Under such condition, any quest for knowledge from the USA is bound to be suspect." The less Americans knew the better. Enough could be gained from the files of the *Peking Review*. There were already more than thirty foreign correspondents functioning in Beijing, but no Americans. She herself had tried freelancing, but no one abroad was interested. It was thought to be trading with the enemy. She closed, "For all these reasons, I think I should be deceiving you if I encouraged any premature hope. One day, of course, Americans will be coming, but when I cannot guess."[17] Harrison's attention turned to others.

China policy, according to Snow, feared a U.S. attack comparable to Hitler's invasion of Russia. "The assumption," he wrote, "that the Chinese have absolutely no reason to fear American aggression results in a distorted analysis of their thinking and their objectives. It altogether leaves out of account, most of the time, any role of response to American provocations. It unwarrantedly assumes that the Chinese cannot fail to understand that all our moves are peaceful and defensive in intent." This included Chinese thinking about the viewpoint of the *New York Times*. Salisbury conceded Snow was correct. Even so, Harrison continued to "pester everyone whom I know who might possibly have any influence with Peking because I think the subject is so important." However, he did not have much hope.[18]

That led him, especially after the *New York Times* published Gerald Long's and Edgar Snow's interviews with Premier Zhou Enlai, again to annoy the aging seventy-eight-year-old Anna Louise Strong in 1964.[19] He mentioned those interviews of Long and Snow. American interest in China had increased tenfold. Zhou was in Africa, where Snow spoke with him. Paris recognized Beijing. There was gradual movement for the United States in that direction. The role of the *New York Times* would be considerable. "I need hardly tell you," he emphasized, "my conviction that this forward progress in the evolution of better relations between the two countries would be radically advanced were it possible for a reporter of the *Times*, and I again nominate myself, to come to China and engage in even a limited period of firsthand reporting." He repeated that in 1965. On her eightieth birthday, Chairman Mao attended a party in Strong's honor, and Harrison wrote her a congratulatory letter and mentioned that, if the chance should arise, "you might put in a word for me getting into China." He told Snow the same thing—it preyed on his mind. American feeling toward China, he believed, was one of "extremely active curiosity and of general warmth." Americans needed the inside scoop from direct reporting, "as for example reporting by myself."[20] No modesty here!

Harrison excitedly prepared to orbit China for ten weeks, an idea of Clifton Daniel's, beginning in May 1966. Catledge asked the State Department to remove restrictions from his and his wife Charlotte's passports should they, during their travels, gain admittance to North Korea, North Vietnam, or China. Harrison asked his friend Cyrus Eaton, chair of the Chesapeake and Ohio Railroad, to put in a "good word" with friends he had in Beijing. Unfortunately, the Chinese thought Eaton was too friendly with

Soviet scientists and educational leaders, and they paid no attention to him. Eaton suggested trying Chinese ambassadors in each of the countries Salisbury visited. [21]

♦♦ 2 ♦♦

Salisbury and his wife traveled more than twenty-five thousand miles along China's frontiers—from the jungles of Southeast Asia to the Siberian-Chinese border. The dust jacket of his book *Orbit of China* commercialized it: "Wherever he went—remote Himalayan villages or glittering Hong Kong— Mr. Salisbury sought from peasant and princes the story of China—her explosive impact on Asia and the world." [22] In a series of articles in the *New York Times* in 1967, he summarized his findings. The PRC, he commented, dominated Asia in 1966 and could master the world by 1985. After seventeen years, there had been a tidal shift in the continental balance of power. Throughout his travels, there was "concern and deep worry"—about what a power, "seemingly possessed by an aggressive expansionist ideology, will do once she has a nuclear striking force." Did America, his interviewees asked, grasp the nature of what was happening? If not, at least they were apprehensive. It would only take China's military ten years to dominate Asia. Behind China's nuclear strike capacity stood only a mixed industrial potential. [23] Salisbury suggested that Mao saw the Vietnam War as the first stage of China's encirclement by the United States. Mao feared domestic revisionism and sought to "steel China's youth" as a way of purging the "capitalist roaders" while simultaneously hardening China's youth for the coming struggles with the United States. Growing food shortages and an increasing population "imparts to China's policy toward the outer world a constant tone of aggression, of hysteria and of menace." [24]

Harrison focused on the ideological struggle between the PRC and its neighbors. Evidence for this was extraordinary. He saw the Soviet buildup and tightened security all along its China borders. Chinese claims to portions of Siberia further aggravated Russians. [25] Salisbury dealt with Chinese-Indian rivalry. India had built up its defenses since the Chinese 1962 invasion. India now viewed China as its number one enemy. Harrison cited Indian officials as believing India was the essential rock of Asian stability, holding Chinese power from flowing west to the Persian Gulf. [26] Salisbury suggested that Japan, spurred on by a growing threat from China, would rearm with atomic weaponry. Japan's interests in China exceeded all Asians in news, trade, and tourism. The Japanese wondered if they could balance China's future power with similar military strength. [27]

The *London Times* in its Literary Supplement gave the book a glowing review: "He has given us a stimulating and persuasive book as well as a great deal to think about."[28] Salisbury's ended on a somber note, quoting Alfred Lord Tennyson: "When all men starve, the wild mob's million feet will kick you from your place." He had concluded from reading Lafcadio Hearn, the nineteenth-century Greek-born writer about Japan, that China would finally win the struggle with the West. Harrison put it slightly more optimistically: "there is still a chance that ingenuity and intelligence might spare us the catastrophe." Catastrophe was not inevitable, but hypocrisy and hesitation could doom the West to disaster.[29]

In his last letter to Strong before her death in March 1970, Harrison maintained that he would eventually be allowed into China. She had criticized inaccurate *New York Times* reporting on China. He excused the *Times* ; no *Times* reporter was in Beijing to get it right. His letter from Hanoi reinforced his conviction that the time was ripe for a total reevaluation.[30]

Back from his influential trip to Hanoi, he now focused on Snow, while adding Jan Myrdal, the Swedish social scientist, to his list of influential foreigners to sway Chinese leadership for his visa. He told Snow how "literally flabbergasted" he was at the "fantastic reverberations stemming from my reports" from Hanoi. He believed a "similar venture to China would be productive and have an equally important impact on American opinion."[31] He wrote Cyrus Eaton that though the times, given the Vietnam War, were not propitious for getting a visa for China, yet, "with the deterioration which has occurred between Moscow and Peking, I can hardly fail to believe that there must be some counsels in Peking which are interested in bettering their position vis-à-vis Washington."[32]

What prescience of mind Harrison had by anticipating Nixon's China initiative by three years. He wrote Snow the same thing that he had told Eaton. As Secretary of State Dean Rusk dreamed of the yellow peril and thought of the American fight in Vietnam as a blow to Peking, Harrison told Snow, "Mr. Johnson sometimes indulges in ideas of some kind of a détente with China, although I doubt very much that it has taken any substantive form in his mind." Again, that possibility opened in Salisbury's thoughts.[33]

Myrdal wrote him that few Western writers would get to China in 1969. Even he and his wife were being postponed. Harrison would only be considered at the "very highest level," because it was not just a case of a visa, but one of policy. Even the Warsaw Rounds (back channel talks between the United States and the PRC) had discussed the entry of American journalists into China.[34] Harrison agreed. He was pessimistic, as late as July 1969, that Nixon would attempt anything. Then, suddenly, in the depths of his depression that anything between China and America could change, there came the ping-pong players' invitation to China in April 1971 and the Kissinger-Nixon initiative in China. Everything transformed overnight.[35]

Salisbury wrote Premier Zhou Enlai. He had been struck by Snow's visit to Beijing and his "references to Chou En-lai's remarks about applications from friends of China in concrete cases and in concrete ways." By June 1971, he was again begging Snow to give his application a push because it was "extremely important." He added, "I have no doubt that your word would make a very great deal of difference."[36] He had told the premier that his letter was reinforcing his cable request: "I am certain that you are well aware of the fact that over many years I have been devoting myself very strenuously to the cause of enlightenment of Americans in general with respect to the People's Republic." He renewed his and Charlotte's visa applications on July 12, 1971, to Zhou Enlai. He told the premier he planned to do "not only comprehensive newspaper articles but [a] book for the widest popular distribution in [the] United States, bringing to mass readership [a] portrait of new China."[37] Without fanfare, his odyssey ended on May 25, 1972.

As his Ilyushin-18 flew into Beijing from Canton, he could see an ochre world, divided into rectangles, with village after village extending endlessly to the horizon. He drove through the city after 1:00 a.m. Its *hutungs* lay dark and silent in the morning mist. There was little car traffic, only the crunch of bicycle tires. His perilous journey to China had been long and arduous—all the way from a Chinese shop on Western Avenue, Minneapolis, to the countless letters and cables to friends of the Chinese leaders, to his orbit of China and its theory of polycentrism, not monolithic communism. "My words and my evidence and my conclusions were treated as a rather poor joke."[38] Everyone in the United States knew—supposedly—of the Russification of China. "To them there was no China. There was merely a Red Empire; Headquarters, the Kremlin; Ruler, Stalin."[39]

Eisenhower, Dulles, and all the rest of the cold warriors rendered that verdict. Senator Joseph McCarthy purged the State Department of those who thought otherwise. Dean Rusk perpetuated it. *Washington Post* journalist Joseph Alsop popularized it. Even the Moscow-Beijing cold war did not defeat it.[40] Salisbury even wondered whether Nixon's trip to China really taught American leaders the lesson of Mao's New Chinese society. Was Mao what the Russians called him, a new Genghis Khan, as Salisbury wrote, "Or did I now stand in the presence of a New Man, a new being born out of chaos, and endowed with moral qualities such as had never been seen before?" He would spend two months in China trying to find out.[41] Then those two months stretched into repeated visits to the end of his life. The first result was his book *To Peking and Beyond: A Report on the New Asia*, published in 1973.

He related that his first glimpse of the PRC was in 1966 from a guardhouse at the Lo Wu station, terminus of the twenty-seven-mile railroad running from Kowloon through the Leased Territories to the Chinese frontier. There he saw stern soldiers of the People's Liberation Army (PLA). That prepared him to expect a grim encounter in 1972. He "walked across the bridge at LoWu, typewriter in one hand, briefcase in the other, camera around my neck. Unlike other communist countries, the border official said, 'Welcome to China.'" As he put it, "First impressions are important. My first impression of China stood in stark contrast to my expectation of China, and to my experience with Communist countries in general and the Soviet Union in particular." Regardless of the Cultural Revolution, the terror, the rioting, the attacks on foreigners, he found everything clean, neat, friendly. "Why, I thought, it's pleasant to be in this country! I didn't know why, but I felt at home. And it was a feeling that never left me."

On the train from Lo Wu to Canton, he further considered this initial impression and his fleeting glances from the train windows of what had been widely depicted of China as the land of "blue ants"—a nation of eight hundred million human robots. Of course, Harrison realized, "For any judgment on this, a train window was hardly sufficient. It would require firsthand knowledge, visits to the communes, talks with the peasants, and a close-up look at what might prove to be a blend of China's oldest folkways with some of the new weapons of the 20th century's armory of technology." He began his quest for the real China. Would it be a country of blue ants or a strange, but not hostile country—or one of dignity and respect? His first efforts were with students and faculty at universities—Tsinghua, Wuhan, and Fudan.[42]

The key to his first voyage of discovery was to understand the Cultural Revolution. Everywhere he went, he asked about it. "If there is in China a New Man, if China is creating the pattern of the world's future, the secret, I think, must lie in the Cultural Revolution." He had asked about it when in Hong Kong in 1966. The answer he got was that a power struggle had broken out within the Chinese leadership. But there were those who also believed it was no ordinary struggle. It was a deliberate tempering experience for China's youth to prepare them for a future war with the United States—a doomsday psychology because of the Vietnam War that said America needed a foothold on the Asian continent from which to attack China. Other interpretations existed—for example, Mao had gone mad or the country had fallen into complete anarchy. None of these interpretations fit. He first turned to Tsinghua University for answers.[43]

Tsinghua University was the birthplace of the Red Guards, of the Cultural Revolution itself. It was there on May 29, 1966, that students of the university's secondary school first called themselves Red Guards. Though repressed, Mao rescued them in a letter of August 1, 1966: "I hereby give you my enthusiastic support." "By June the students and faculty were ranged in violent disagreement over the educational system, methods of study, the rights of students, the content of courses, the attitudes of professors, the whole aim and objective of education." They were opposed by work teams of about five hundred senior party members, headed by the president of the

PRC Liu Shaoqi's wife, Wang Kuang-mu. These opponents did not quiet strife at the university. The Red Guards were victorious. They cleansed the thought of Tsinghua University, and their movement spread to other universities. Faculty and administrators were sent to "May Seventh" schools, founded by Mao for remolding thought in two-year terms, living a peasant's life and studying Marxism-Leninism and the *Thought of Chairman Mao*. Those who sided with President Liu Shaoqi's revisionist line were called "capitalist roaders." This was repeated at Wuhan and Fudan Universities. [44]

One of the Shanghai Cultural Revolution's leaders told Harrison, though Salisbury was skeptical, that Liu Shaoqi and his supporters had swung hard to the right, reversed policy in agriculture, and returned to reliance on private farming. Internationally, Liu favored reconciliation with the Soviet Union. Liu's group of sixty was branded traitorous. Mao attacked their publications. On May 16, 1966, the Cultural Revolution had officially begun with the first "Big Character" poster (wall posters, hand-lettered ideographs) exposing Liu as a reactionary capitalist roader. Mao wrote one on August 5, 1966: "Bombard the Headquarters." Mao's enemies were those in power who took the capitalist road. On August 18, 1966, Mao appeared on Tiananmen Square wearing a red armband inscribed with the word *soldier* and received the Red Guards, wishing them well. He repeated this five more times and, by then, thirteen million Red Guards had come to Beijing. They also swarmed over the countryside. Ultra-leftists like Defense Minister Lin Biao joined Mao's crusade as well as Foreign Minister Zhou Enlai. [45]

From May 1966, peaking that summer, and into 1968, the Cultural Revolution rolled along, teaching the "roaders" to learn from the people. "By this time, most of the old leadership had been driven out. Revolutionary Committees, in which the army played a major role, began to be set up and people were starting to go to the newly formed May Seventh schools—schools established on the basis of a directive of Chairman Mao of May 7, 1966." Enrollees were sent to work with their hands, cleanse their thoughts, and get back to Marxist-Maoist basics. One official even told Harrison it was a "wonderful experience—the great experience of my life." He lived and worked for others. Now they had to learn from peasants and workers who told them what to do. Harrison reflected on what he had learned. "I can only describe [the schools] as combination of a YMCA camp and a Catholic retreat—with no offense intended to either." [46]

Now that he had learned from Chinese what they thought the Cultural Revolution was, Harrison began to study its results—the "New China"—one created through the remolding of ideology and moral transformation. He looked at the following specifics to generalize on each of them: countryside, communes, industry, cities, sex, students, culture, population, and medicine. Red China transformed agriculture from arid to irrigated, well tilled, and dotted with urban centers. Harrison visited Anyang, four hundred miles from

Beijing. It contained textile and steel mills, chemical and tobacco industries. Its rural countryside prospered. Though still primitive compared to American standards, it was a miracle of change. The Red Flag Canal brought water into a system of interconnecting channels. At the Double Bridge Commune, production had been boosted. Families lived better.[47]

At Liu Ling in Yenan where Mao settled after the Long March, Jan and Gunnar Myrdal did a classic study titled *Report from a Chinese Village.* Harrison followed with a report on current collectivization there, comparing it to Russia's. Unlike the USSR's destruction of family plots, China socialized its production gradually. For example, when the Long March ended in Yenan in 1935, collectivization took more than twenty-five years. Communes displayed diversity, absence of state interference, and peasants free to sell surpluses on the private market. There was still little mechanization in 1972, and China remained 80 percent rural. Harrison predicted rapid urbanization and an industrialized agriculture by 2000.[48]

In Wuhan he saw how the Chinese overcame obstacles created when the Russians pulled out of China in August 1960, leaving the country to manage itself. There were severe setbacks, but the Chinese finished their projects—roads, rails, dams, land reclamation. For instance, Wuhan pre-1949 was smelly, fly ridden, and disease prone. Afterward, modern health procedures overcame problems in the "four-pests" movement against flies, mosquitoes, rats, and mice. China used DDT massively and sanitized fertilizers. The problem of industrial wastes was yet to be solved, as was urban planning to accommodate the influx of population. "I did not for a minute believe the uneasy assurances of the officials that, by some miracle, Wuhan would stop growing."[49]

Harrison found sex a taboo subject. China placed high value on abstinence and marriage deferral. There was, he wrote, "an official morality, a kind of Boy Scout-Girl Scout atmosphere that was encouraged and advanced by the party propagandists." China subordinated and sublimated sex. "They had no time for sex and no energy for it." The universal attitude was there could be no such thing as homosexuality. Reliable figures on China's population could not be found. "China consistently understates her population, and understates remarkably continuing rate of growth." That was a military secret. He believed China would exceed one billion by 1980.[50]

The remainder of the book dwelled on tensions between Russia and China, especially China's building of bomb shelters. He considered his dinner with Zhou Enlai the trip's high point. On June 16, 1972, Harrison, Charlotte, and a group of Old China Hands with their spouses dined with Zhou Enlai in the Great Hall of the People. Harrison asked the premier why China had consistently refused him a visa since the end of 1956. According to Harrison's wife, Zhou answered, "We were afraid of angering the Russians, as you were a well-known anti-Stalinist and a cold warrior."[51]

In his first book on China, Salisbury wrote that the premier continued, "'Yes, you are quite an honest friend.' He added that one reason they had not invited me to be the first *New York Times* correspondent in China was that it would have involved inviting the 'leading anti-Soviet champion.' They did not want more Russian complications over such a minor question."[52]

The book touched on the elimination of Lin Biao, who had tried to replace Mao in 1971, and predicted Asia, especially China, would eventually displace America on the world stage.[53] Nixon, he asserted, had done the right thing in reconciling America to China. It was a great move toward international peace, security, and understanding. One question remained. Could America and Europe rise to the challenge?

◆◆ 3 ◆◆

Salisbury sent Premier Zhou Enlai a letter expressing thanks for the "remarkable opportunity" of studying China from the inside. He praised Ed Snow's final book *The Long Revolution*, and he asked for the privilege of coming to China often for the cause of Sino-American friendship. Salisbury would fill the void left by Snow's death in 1972. "There can be no replacement of Snow, but if there is anything I might do to help to fill this gap, I would like to offer my good offices."

By the following March 1973, he wrote expressing hope the premier found his book *To Peking and Beyond* accurate and would help in bettering Sino-American relations and understanding. He wanted a chance to return to deepen his own understanding by more fully exploring China, especially its remote regions. He wrote Zhou again in January 1974 to renew his request to visit the PRC in late spring or summer. In this letter he mentioned the idea of a project to follow the route of the Long March and write an account of it, similar to his *The 900 Days*. "I think . . . the story of the Long March if retold in the same fashion would be one of the most dramatic and inspiring tales that the world could read." He followed that with a letter to Chiao Kuan-hua, deputy minister of foreign affairs, asking for a visa, suggesting travel plans, and mentioning the route of the Long March. He had in mind "a narrative based on the heroism, sacrifices and courage of the individual people involved in this epic undertaking."[54]

In his memoir, Harrison recounts his astonishing discoveries in his various efforts to become the new Edgar Snow. Harrison Salisbury's career was the reverse of Snow's: He went first to Russia as a correspondent in 1944 and then, after retirement, to China in 1972. Snow started in 1929. However, the results were much the same. In his memoir, he wrote, "I was more than forty years behind in getting to China." He had finally arrived there "at long last in

1972." How he got there was a story in itself. When Salisbury finally did arrive in China in 1972, China's Premier Zhou Enlai apologized. Salisbury insisted there was a "nub of truth" in Zhou's remark about his anti-Soviet stance. Though, after the 1989 Tiananmen Square incident, Salisbury became critical of the Chinese Communist Party. Since childhood, he had had China on the brain. Ever since his mother had taken him to the "Chinaman's shop" in his hometown of Minneapolis, that "Chinaman's shop *was* China, a place of mystery, romance, excitement—exotic, a world which drew me like a magnet, so different from plain flat Minnesota." So also was his father's curio case with its bamboo opium pipe and tiny red-and-green embroidered shoes. "This was the China of my youth, and my imagination grazed over it endlessly, so endlessly that when I entered the writing seminar at the university, my first sketch was about the Chinaman and his shop."[55]

As luck would not have it, Salisbury tried to get to China as a journalist for United Press. He spoke with John Dewey's onetime student Hu Shih, and he conversed with Henry Luce and his missionary father. Finally United Press sent him to cover World War II in London, North Africa, the Middle East, and Moscow. There he met Edgar Snow and Anna Louise Strong. Through them, his China education proceeded, but he still had not arrived in China.[56] Through them, he met Mikhail Borodin, once Stalin's agent in China. After Strong's exile from the USSR in 1949 and her residence in China in 1958, Salisbury learned of Borodin's sad end and Strong's new career as a China apologist.[57] But still he remained in Moscow, residing at the Metropole Hotel's room 393—the place where he had his great insight into America's and Russia's China paradox: Stalin had purged his Chinese experts and banned China from the Soviet media; at the same time, Senator Joseph McCarthy successfully purged America's Chinese specialists. Salisbury lamented that he—a nonexpert on China—"could discern enough to suspect that something was rotten between the two big Communist countries. Is it not reasonable to expect that the President of the United States, his Secretary of State and all the other secretaries, intelligence analysts, members of the Senate, members of the House and assorted wise men would scent a faint clue?" He remarked that McCarthy was simply the poster child for Secretaries of State Dean Acheson and Dean Rusk.[58] Both countries had silenced their China experts.

Salisbury decided that after Mao's two-month trip to Moscow in 1949–1950, after vanishing from the Russian media and being treated like a "petty petitioner" by Stalin, he would have "broken with Russia and gone over to the American side, had it not been for our ostentatious hostility." That was how General Secretary Nikita Khrushchev revealed it, and Salisbury wrote later in 1988, "I am inclined to accept Khrushchev's story." The treaty Mao and Stalin signed, after all, was only slightly broader than the one Stalin signed in 1945 with Chiang Kai-shek. The China card was America's to play,

Salisbury contended, but President Truman feared the Republican war cry, "The Democrats Lost China."[59] Stalin was surprised at Truman's decision to defend South Korea, where he thought he could "squeeze Mao out like a pip from an apple." That inveigled "China into a war with the United States." According to Salisbury, Stalin "knew, as we didn't seem to understand, that Mao was his stubborn, implacable antagonist." The United States had "figuratively put out the eyes of our best China specialists. . . . We blinded ourselves and by so doing stumbled into two terrible wars—Korea and Vietnam—neither of which need have been fought." It took two of the most unlikely people—Nixon and Kissinger—to get it right in 1972 and "put us on the right track at last."[60]

So who lost China? Stalin did for Russia. McCarthy did for America. "The symmetry of Stalin's and McCarthy's 'loss of China' was so delicious, the ignorance so colossal, the implications so profound I can still hardly believe it."[61] Relations between Russia and China became so intense, the military buildup on either side of the border so great in the 1960s, that Mao could finally play the American card and invite the ping-pong players to China in April 1971, after hinting to Edgar Snow in the fall that Nixon was welcome.[62] The rest—Kissinger and Nixon—was history.[63] At last, Salisbury realized his childhood dream and saw, finally, the real China and not the image of an exotic place created in his childhood days in Minneapolis.

Salisbury had read Soviet memoirs designed to rehabilitate Russia's Sinologists—those in the 1920s and 1930s who were purged and executed. Stalin, he wrote to "Old China Hand" Jack Service in 1977, preferred Chiang Kai-shek to Mao. Only after 1949 did he have to pay respect "grudgingly" to Mao. "Not only did Chiang seem to him the devil he knew, but he did not have the contrary and independent and crotchety air of Mao, nor did Chiang talk back to Stalin; nor did CKS shove Stalin's team (Wang and Co.) into the background."[64]

In 1979 Harrison wrote China's Foreign Minister Huang Hua about returning to China to write two books. One would be an update on *To Peking and Beyond*. The other was what he called a "picture-and-textbook on China Today." Photographs would be important. That book he published in 1983 as *China: 100 Years of Revolution*.[65] The publication of his book on the *New York Times* (*Without Fear or Favor*) interfered. Nevertheless, he wrote Yao Wei, his close friend in China's Foreign Office's Press Department in December that he was putting together the picture book, then called *China in Revolution*. But far more importantly, he wanted to do a book on contemporary China. That book finally resulted in *The New Emperors*. It was to be his last major book, published in 1992, one year before his death.[66]

China: 100 Years of Revolution was a stunningly illustrated book with a readable story of China's modern evolution. First, he quickly assessed Old China. Then he dealt with the Western penetration and China's descent into venality and corruption. That sowed the seeds for revolutions, not just one led by Mao, but also many headed by visionaries and saviors. Salisbury traced the rise of Dr. Sun Yat-sen and Chiang Kai-shek. The largest part of his essay focused on the period from the 1920s to the Gang of Four. He sketched Mao's rise and victory through the Long March, war with Japan, and the Civil War. It was a wonderfully panoramic story of, as the dust jacket proudly announced, "a billion people, mercilessly exploited from without not only by Western powers, but also by their Russian Communist 'friends,' and from within by jealous warlords and vying political factions." Harrison's firsthand experiences since that 1972 trip made this book possible.[67] He dedicated the book "In Memory of Premier Chou En-lai."

For the second book, he began interviewing top Chinese officials. In July 1980 he spoke with Vice Premier and Vice Chairman of the Party Li Xiannian at the Great Hall of the People. They candidly discussed China's prospects at home and abroad. "Since you are an old friend," Li opened, "I should tell you these things and I think Ch. Mao himself was responsible for these things. And, practically, in the last years of Chairman Mao's life he could not respect the ideas of others than himself, including those of Premier Chou Enlai. The first mistake, which all of us shared in, was the Great Leap Forward." He excused the leadership because it was weak in economic experience. Nonetheless, China could not just copy the Russian model. There had to be pragmatic reforms in China's economy. When mistakes were made, the leadership must be modest and correct them. But the biggest mistake was the Great Cultural Revolution. "We have to agree that Chairman Mao made a wrong assessment of the situation prior to the CR [Cultural Revolution] and I think he exaggerated the class struggle and thought that a bourgeoisie still existed within the Party. I think that was an inappropriate notion." He finished, "The 10 years of the CR were a disaster for China." No economic progress was made and education stopped. On foreign affairs, Mao was more successful, as he came to realize the Soviet Union was a greater threat than the United States. China, Japan, the United States, and Western Europe could curtail the Soviet Union and check its strategic deployment in Africa and Asia.[68]

Salisbury became close to China's Foreign Minister Huang Hua. He shared his thoughts on the incoming Reagan administration with Huang. The president would continue Nixon's policies, and his comments about Taiwan were a product of "colossal ignorance"—they would remain rhetorical. "Will Reagan actually do anything consequential regarding Taiwan? Not likely. Too many knowledgeable people in the Republican establishment would oppose this." Nixon and Kissinger would especially see to that. Secretary of State Al Haig was brought in to balance Kissinger's influence. Kissinger would have accepted the secretaryship, but Reagan feared he would be publicly seen as the "real" president. The team of Nixon, Kissinger, Haig, and Reagan would make foreign policy, which would be good for the PRC. [69] Salisbury liked his role as an analyst for China's big shots.

As 1980 ended, Harrison wrote a friend, "This has been a great China year for me." He was there all summer and into the fall, especially on the outer rim, the far northwest, and Tibet. He wrote, "but the images, impressions and information—lord, I will be a longtime absorbing and collating them and eventually, I hope, putting them into some kind of a book." [70] At the same time, he was busy writing the first volume of his memoirs, *A Journey for Our Times*. He admitted to his friend that it was hard to write about himself, but he would get the knack of it. Salisbury's supreme confidence even bothered his friends.

During 1981 and 1982, Harrison kept up a vigorous correspondence with Huang Hua and others on what would be his most successful and important book on China, *The Long March*, published in 1985. It was to be his most arduous effort and came close to killing him. He had arrived in Beijing on March 1, 1984, and returned home on June 19, 1984. On May 10, 1984, Charlotte reported his heart beat irregularly, and he felt so exhausted he believed he could not finish the expedition over the Long March's trail. Charlotte, Jack Service, and Harrison had reached Huili, near Fire Mountain. His knees had turned to rubber. He was swaying. Harrison spread out on rocks after taking a fall. He dragged himself up to a building above the Golden Sands River. Some of the boatmen who had ferried Mao's band forty-nine years earlier were still there. They helped the fallen journalist. Harrison had to be carried the next day by stretcher. Doctors came to a guesthouse at Qiong Hai to do blood tests and an EKG. His 1975 heart trouble and pacemaker covered up a heart attack, or so the doctors believed. He had strained his heart for sure. They got him to the Sichuan Medical College Hospital, where for four days a team of seven heart specialists examined him. Charlotte wrote, "Because of fatigue and dehydration, he suffered loss of blood and oxygen to his heart, but breathing oxygen and drugs can fix that." By then he was thin and had to avoid getting tired or catching colds. Charlotte had no doubt the doctors had saved him. [71]

After finally publishing *The Long March* in 1985, he set to work on a book he tentatively titled *The New Long March*. It was meant to be a triumphant story of Deng Xiaoping's restoration of China in the wake of Mao's destructive Cultural Revolution. Instead, it was interrupted by the tragedy of the Tiananmen Square massacre. Consequently, it became a dual biography of Mao and Deng.

The Tiananmen Square massacre of June 1989 ended Salisbury's long love affair with China. It left him saddened, even perplexed. He abandoned his optimistic outlook and wrote critically of the PRC in his last book about China, *The New Emperors*. As he put it in *Tiananmen Diary: Thirteen Days in June*, the communist world was "dissolving before my eyes." He wrote this with the assurance of an insider: "I think I know China as well as, if not better than, any member of the Standing Committee of the Politburo." Further, when it was all over, he could make an eyewitness testimony from his room at the Beijing Hotel of the atrocities of the People's Liberation Army. He had promoted and sometimes defended Deng's government. Now he had soured on "men I have regarded favorably and known so long [who] have played a cowardly and despicable role." Deng had blown it. He had thrown away his great reputation in a mighty carnage. [72]

The origin of the demonstrations went back to the autumn of 1986 and a campaign against party secretary Hu Yaobang's liberalism. He resigned on January 16, 1987, replaced by Zhao Ziyang. Hu's death, April 15, 1989, touched off "immediate demonstrations at Beijing and other universities, rapidly snowballing into marches on Tiananmen Square." [73] As early as April 26, 1989, in a "Plan A," Deng's government decided to employ military force against demonstrators, but only after Soviet General Secretary Gorbachev's visit on May 1–7. Zhao remonstrated, even complaining to Gorbachev. The party elders and Deng secured the PLA's support. In the bloody aftermath, party elders would drive Zhao from office and compel Deng to abandon his "Reform and Opening" policies. Salisbury, of course, had no premonition of this. He did not imagine April's student movement for greater democracy or its escalation in May and June presaged disaster. But viewed against the government's inability to cope with economic problems, it seemed inescapable that a "get tough" decision was inevitable. "It would solve nothing basic, but it would terrorize the population and give the party a chance to impose absolute control on an unruly citizenry." [74] That, he thought, accounted for the massacre with its extraordinary firepower and randomness. The junta halted at nothing to retain its power. The thousands of students mowed down on Tiananmen Square were only a fraction of the public liquidated elsewhere in the country. The government's line, broadcast over national television, was that almost nothing happened except to what it called "bad men" and "bandits." Deng's speech of June 9, 1989, Harrison believed, betrayed a "baffled, almost bewildered old man, painfully clutching at his vision of a new, open, and reformed China, a China that will go forward to economic vigor and meet his goals for the year 2050." [75] Who needed democracy?

Harrison came to Beijing from Tokyo on June 2, 1989. He saw no sign of troops and found the Beijing Hotel, just off the square, almost empty. From his seventh-floor windows he looked out directly on Tiananmen. That evening he and his Japanese TV crew went out to have a look around, but they could take only stills as no taping was allowed. They saw clusters of youth, a tent colony, and the Goddess of Freedom statue in the center of the square— the students' symbol of liberty looming high, stark, and white. "I had a good look at the Goddess of Freedom, still standing, made of plastic and not very beautiful."[76] It had been put up three days before. Its placement in the square's center further irritated officials. On TV they called it outrageous. The students were asking for more democracy over the loudspeakers, haranguing passersby. Harrison paused at roadblocks when returning to his hotel, encountering students at the Martyrs' Column. A bulletin board had notices and posters. One student recognized him from his face on his best-selling book *The Long March*. He promised these students to tell the truth when writing about the demonstrations.[77] They would not live to read it.

Back in his hotel room, he tuned in to BBC, and then he went to bed. About 2:00 a.m. on the third, he awakened to heavy gunfire on the square, then quiet. BBC and VOA were reporting twenty-three dead and hundreds wounded. By 4:00 a.m., he noticed large armored vehicles moving onto the square, bursts of artillery fire, and rounds of automatic shots. By 6:00 a.m., BBC reported casualties all over the city and a "big carnage" in Tiananmen. Tanks were mowing down protesters as they pleaded for dialogue. By 5:00 p.m., BBC news announced thousands killed and "tanks crushing people sleeping in their tents."[78] Hundreds had linked arms and been shot. He wrote in his diary, "The impression grows that they are bungling again, bungling the end of Tiananmen just as they have bungled everything about the square since the students first turned out to mark the passing of Hu Yaobang."[79] By midnight, he collapsed from exhaustion on his bed.

At 3:10 a.m. on the fourth, he awoke to massive firepower and large deployments of troop carriers roaring and revving nearby. Column after iron column went by his balcony. Bullets ricocheted or pockmarked the hotel's sides. By 7:00 a.m. on June 5, CCTV ordered him to Beijing's airport to catch a plane for Wuhan. BBC claimed the death toll in the thousands. He telephoned Charlotte, who told him, "Also she had seen incredible footage of the PLA mowing down the kids on Tiananmen." He packed his gear and, by 8:00 a.m., met the van for the airport. He saw tanks occupying the hotel's courtyard and soldiers shooting at anyone on the street. His minibus made its way through the complex of *hutungs* rather than the highways. By 8:00 p.m., his plane reached Wuhan. There, on his trusty 1942 Remington portable, he typed his op-ed piece for the *New York Times*. "I proclaimed the end of the Deng Xiaoping era of enlightenment and opening a new regime that would be run by the doctrine of 'authoritarianism,'" he wrote.[80] From there, he wandered from Jiujiang to Lushan to Nanchang to Canton and a plane home. He was anxious to leave because he feared being used as a hostage in exchange for Fang Lizhi, the famous dissident holed up in the U.S. embassy.[81]

All the Chinese TV chatter was about the brave soldiers and showing endless visits of dignitaries to the hospitals to honor them. It characterized students as "bad men" and "bandits." It reversed the order of events. Demonstrators attacked troops, who reluctantly opened fire. Innocents died in the melee. Harrison, however reluctantly, ended this note: Deng was responsible, with Yang Shangkun as his chief of staff. The party elders cheered, while Zhao Ziyang fell from power. Salisbury lamented, "To think I know the men who did this."[82] Had he been a dupe for China all of these years?

In the aftermath, the title of his *New Long March* book, the one intended to praise Deng Xiaoping, now changed significantly to *The New Emperors*. The new title reflected Harrison's realization that China remained authoritarian, perhaps forever. In a letter to his sister Jan, he lamented, "I am just back from China having quite by accident stumbled in on Tiananmen, at the Beijing hotel when it all went up in the god damndest spate of bullets I've ever seen and that includes a good many wars." He saw no good direction for China. Deng, he wrote, "is just at the edge of dotage. Yang Shangkun is running the army. There is a council of geriatrics and a few younger (sixtyish men) and a slain generation of wonderful young people and fine intellectuals."[83] He could not foretell China's future. He spoke with Professor John K. Fairbank of Harvard, who called him a worm for suggesting the Chinese could be educated and enlightened. He talked with George F. Kennan, who sympathized with China and added that no one understood Russia.[84] He wrote Yao Wei, "I cannot tell you how appalled I am at the way things have gone beginning with Tiananmen."[85] Yet, until the end of his life, he remained cautiously hopeful about China. "I think it will get back to the Deng Xiaoping path. Don't see any other. I could be very wrong."[86] He was right only in the sense of China as an amazing story of modernization. He did not mention that China remained a communist authoritarian state.

Cautious optimism remained a Harrison characteristic. When current events dismayed him, he retreated to the quiet of his study. There, amid his books and research materials, he was contemplative and wrote histories. When contemplation failed him, his imagination ranged widely, and he wrote fiction. The results of these efforts turned Salisbury into a man of letters. The journalist, like Lewis Carroll's Cheshire cat, became historian and novelist.

Chapter Nine

Historian and Novelist

Throughout Salisbury's career, he wrote books about his important journalistic experiences and a memoir. Yet out of Salisbury's various writings, four of his twenty-nine books were ambitious histories, two on Russia and another pair on China: *The 900 Days* (1969) and *Black Night, White Snow* (1977); *The Long March: The Untold Story* (1985) and *The New Emperors: China in the Era of Mao and Deng* (1992). The Pulitzer Prize–winning journalist became an admired historian. These moving narratives revealed him as a master of his sources, a penetrating analyst, and a stylist. He also wrote two successful novels—*The Northern Palmyra Affair* and *The Gates of Hell*—making him a man of letters.

Of his two major books on Russia, the first dealt with the Nazi attack on Leningrad and its heroic defense. The second was a study of Russia's twentieth-century revolutions. Russia's revolutions also began in Leningrad, then called St. Petersburg (1905) and Petrograd (1917). Thus the city of Peter was a natural choice for Salisbury's scholarship. Harrison maintained deep affection for this magnificent city and its art, a place he considered Russia's cultural capital. He had, as a journalist, covered Leningrad at the end of the Nazi siege in 1944.

About China his interest was piqued after his articles on Hanoi stunned the world. After his first, long-anticipated visit in 1972, he came to China often. His Chinese friends were excited with his request to write of Mao's Long March. The Salisburys and their friend, old China hand and specialist Jack Service, made the long march themselves. From this eyewitness account and numerous interviews with those who had made it with the "Great Helmsman," he wrote the book. His interest in China and his curiosity about two of the men who had made the People's Republic (PRC), Mao Zedong and Deng Xiaoping, led him to write their dual biography.

These narrative histories were brilliant commentaries on his two lifelong interests, familiar to all students of the subject as the Russian bear and Chinese dragon. The bear and dragon share the same continent, and in many ways, their actions and interactions make them partners to a similar fate. The mystery of each linked Harrison Salisbury to them.

♦♦ 1 ♦♦

Salisbury's first Russian historical narrative, *The 900 Days*, begins with June 21, 1941, the summer solstice and eve of the Nazi-Soviet Armageddon. He faults Stalin and his clique for the near disaster; after all, they had confidently assured Russians of the 1939 Nazi-Soviet Pact's durability. Soviet citizens were distraught by war in Europe and rumors of war for the USSR, though they feared challenging the Soviet dictator's assurances. Two of Stalin's closest confidants were architects of the Nazi-Soviet Pact as well as arch rivals: Andrei A. Zhdanov, Leningrad's party boss, and Georgii M. Malenkov, the Politburo's red star. Zhdanov helped launch the collaborationist peace policy with Nazi Germany, and Malenkov was its chief defender. Stalin fully approved the German collaboration. Warnings were, Stalin believed, "provocations." Neither he nor his closest associates were in a mood to provoke Hitler. Even more than his compatriots, he clung to the Nazi-Soviet Pact until the bitter truth of a massive German invasion of June 22, 1941, revealed otherwise. Then he suffered a nervous breakdown, secluding himself for a month while Soviet Russia soldiered on. Stalin's gullibility and Zhdanov's and Malenkov's servility were the basis of Salisbury's thesis: they led Russia needlessly to disaster's edge.

Salisbury presses Stalin's culpability. At a Politburo meeting the Saturday afternoon just before the attack, he adopted a proposal of Marshal Semyon Budyonny that a line of deep defenses be set up from Kiev to Riga. Yet hours later there were the first messages of German planes approaching Sevastopol, antiaircraft fire, and bombings—all reported to Admiral Kuznetsov at 3:15 a.m. on June 22. He spoke at once to Malenkov, who refused to believe it. Similar reports from the Baltic to the Black Seas piled up. General Georgii Zhukov, chief of the Soviet general staff, told Stalin directly. Like Malenkov, he still insisted it must be a German provocation.[1]

On Sunday morning, June 22, at 2:30 a.m., Marshal Timoshenko's Alert Number 1 orders had been belatedly received at Leningrad's Military District, leaving only another hour before the Nazi attack. Those orders called for the Soviet military to occupy firing points with live ammunition and camouflage planes, to prepare tank traps, and ready antiaircraft. Other measures, such as firing on German planes, were strictly forbidden. Not until 5:00 a.m. did Moscow tell Leningrad's party secretary, "German planes had bombed Kiev, Minsk, Sevastopol, Murmansk."[2] Only then were the secret and sealed red packets with mobilization orders ripped open. But it was not until 7:15 a.m. that Marshal Timoshenko and General Zhukov signed Directive Number 1 of the Defense Commissariat. By then, the USSR had been under attack for nearly four hours. Soviet armed forces were commanded to destroy the invaders though restrictions still remained. The Soviet air force was to conduct reconnaissance, but it could fight only to a depth of sixty-six to one hundred miles inside Russia. Permission was granted to bomb Konigsberg in Prussia and Memel in Lithuania, but Soviet planes were prevented from flying over Romania or Finland without special permission.[3]

At 3:00 a.m., Hitler's Berlin had issued its last message to Moscow, reading, "Very Urgent. State Secret." It ordered all cipher materials and radio sets destroyed. Ambassador Count von der Schulenburg, in a last dispatch from Moscow, recounted his final conversation at 5:00 a.m. with Molotov. The ambassador and his attaché Gustav Hilger, though they knew an attack was advancing, patiently listened to Molotov's efforts at appeasement: "Surely," Molotov pleaded, "we have not deserved that." In Berlin, Foreign Minister Joachim von Ribbentrop finally asked Soviet Ambassador Dekanozov to his office and repeated what Schulenburg had said to Molotov: it was Germany that had been attacked. Hitler had taken "defensive measures." He admitted objecting to Hitler's war against Russia, begging Dekanozov to tell Stalin that.[4]

Out of many credible warnings that the Soviet leaders had received, the most valuable were those coming from the NKGB's (People's Commissariat for State Security) master spy, Richard Sorge, alias "Ramsey." He was a German communist and Soviet intelligence agent working as a Tokyo news correspondent. Along with "anonymous" letters, German reconnaissance flights over Soviet territory, noticeable troop concentrations, and direct warnings from all and sundry sources, Sorge's monthly reports were providing the Soviet leaders with crucial details. For example, in late December 1940, he reported eighty German divisions concentrated on Soviet Russia's frontiers and another twenty shifted from France to Poland. In early March 1941, he transmitted a telegram from Ribbentrop's office giving the time of the attack as mid-June. He gathered this information from the German ambassador to Tokyo, Hermann Ott—his friend and confidant. As late as May, Sorge reported on Hitler's overall goals not only to destroy the USSR and use its raw materials and grain, but also to occupy the Ukraine and force Russians into labor camps. Sorge revealed that 170 to 190 divisions were being massed, no declaration or ultimatum of war would be issued, and Hitler expected the USSR's collapse within two months.

With such information from Sorge and others, all well known to Stalin, Salisbury reached two conclusions. First, "Stalin could not have had more specific, more detailed, more comprehensive information." Second, "Nothing in the Bolshevik experience so plainly exposed the fatal defects of the Soviet power monopoly when the man who held that power was ruled by his own internal obsessions."[5]

What were these obsessions? Salisbury explained: "Stalin, Zhdanov and his associates were living in a world turned inside out, in which black was assumed to be white, in which danger was seen as security, in which vigilance was assessed as treason and friendly warning as cunning provocation." Anyone suggesting otherwise would have been shot.[6] The reasons for such an inside-out view of reality were many. Salisbury concedes Stalin knew the times were changing, and the Germans were preparing for war. He hoped to hold it off for six months. As late as June 6, he approved plans for shifting to war production, but only to be completed by the end of 1942. Salisbury notes that "none of the intelligence data altered the fixed opinion of Stalin and his closest associates, Zhdanov, [Lavrentia] Beria, and Malenkov, that there would be no immediate Nazi attack." Zhdanov, as head of the party's Propaganda and Agitation Department, enforced the "no war" line. That meant allowing no military moves along the frontier for fear of provoking Germany. Salisbury insists Stalin thought war could only result because of provocations, not by Hitler but by "military revanchists" within the Soviet Union. Salisbury asserted, "Stalin trusted Hitler but not his generals!"

There was the possibility that Stalin thought he had an ace in the hole. Rumors circulated abroad that Stalin would pay an exorbitant price to avoid war, such as turning over Russian airplane production to Hitler or allowing German exploitation of the Ukraine. To cement this "peaceful capitulation," Stalin even considered "going to Canossa" by making a personal pilgrimage to Berlin to seal another deal with Hitler. After sifting through a wide variety of Soviet data, Salisbury remains convinced: "The evidence is overwhelming that the Nazi attack came as total surprise and shock to Stalin." He had fallen into the flaw of believing his own propaganda and infallibility.[7]

At noon on June 22, 1941, Molotov—not Stalin—spoke to the nation. He announced that the USSR had been attacked without a declaration of war or any claims, despite a nonaggression pact being "scrupulously observed," and without the "slightest complaint" from Germany. Molotov called on Soviet citizens to rally behind the party, the government, and Stalin: "Our cause is just. The enemy will be crushed. Victory will be ours."[8]

For Salisbury, the two men most responsible for the mortal crisis facing the USSR and, especially, Hitler's first target, Leningrad, were Stalin and Zhdanov. Stalin retreated to a locked room and Zhdanov was on holiday in the Crimea. Who was to lead? The new *stavka* or Supreme Command that was set up on June 23 simply reorganized the High Command, but dominated by Timoshenko and Zhukov; it could hardly deal with the complex matters of state requiring the Politburo's and Stalin's personal attention. The Committee of State Defense, headed by Stalin and consisting of Beria, Malenkov, Molotov, and Marshal Klement Voroshilov, filled this vacuum on June 30. In essence, Beria and Malenkov dominated this junta. These two had managed, in the Kremlin's Byzantine politics, to shift the entire blame for the failed policy of appeasement onto Zhdanov's shoulders: "It is more than possible," Salisbury continues, "that his colleagues saddled Zhdanov with responsibility for the incredible disaster of Soviet foreign policy, of which he had been a leading architect—for the gargantuan error in miscalculating Hitler's appetites and psychology."[9] Zhdanov never resumed his primacy and was given the unhappy task of saving a doomed city, Leningrad.

Zhdanov swung into action on June 27 by establishing his own Leningrad Defense Committee, or the "Big Five," consisting of the party secretaries, chairman, and mayor. It had to preserve and protect some of the Soviet Union's most important industrial enterprises like the Kirov (Putilov) works, which made military hardware, the Izhorsk metallurgical combine, and Baltic shipyards. Added to this was securing or shipping out over one and a half million precious art objects from the Hermitage Museum and camouflaging the great Smolny architectural ensemble. To do this, the population was mobilized—with an obligatory "People's Army" of over two hundred thousand, increasing the strength of the regular army, and rapidly creating defensive works with required labor battalions—field fortifications, trenches, and tank barriers. Children were sent for protection to summer camps to the west and southwest, directly, it turned out, in the Panzers' paths, but Salisbury noted, "no one supposed the enemy might get this close."[10]

Sensing Leningrad's crisis was at hand, the defenders were thrown into panic. Marshal Voroshilov and Andrei Zhdanov were named co–supreme commanders to defend the city on July 10. Leaders who failed were called immediately to Moscow and shot. At that point, the Germans were estimated at 340,000, with 326 tanks and 6,000 artillery—a superiority of 2.4 to one in infantry, 4 in artillery, and 1.2 in tanks, with about 1,000 planes to Leningrad's 102. Voroshilov had diverted some of his mechanized corps and rifle divisions southeast to prevent a German flanking movement around the Luga Line east of Lake Ilmen near Novgorod. Yet he retained half of the People's Army to defend the remainder against Hitler's best Panzers, especially concentrated at Luga city itself. It was nip and tuck as the Germans just arrived at Porechye, slightly ahead of its defenders. Salisbury warned, "If the Germans broke through here, they had a smooth highway sixty miles to the Winter Palace. There was not a single organized unit, not one manned defense position to halt them all the way to Leningrad."

It took Voroshilov's personal bravery at the head of the volunteers to hold the hastily created defensive line. And the danger to Novgorod lessened as the 8th Nazi Panzer Division retired for refitting. Hitler was forced to shift the 3rd Panzer Group of Army Group Center to a northeast axis to cut connections between Leningrad and Moscow and shore up Army Nord's right flank. Hitler visited von Leeb's headquarters on July 21 and admonished his marshal to finish off Leningrad speedily. Lieutenant General K. P. Pyadyshev, commander of the Luga Operating Group, was shot as a warning that the line would be kept to the last man as rumors of German breakthroughs circulated. Yet these were only minor penetrations. Hitler's victory parade had to be postponed repeatedly. "The Germans were held up on the Luga front from July 9 or 10 to August 8—close to a month. The blitzkrieg was thrown off pace, the Nazi timetable out of balance."[11]

By August 10, Colonel General Franz Halder, chief of staff of the Nazi Supreme Command, noted in his diary that von Leeb's gains were very insignificant. He feared the front was "becoming frozen in positional warfare [and that] we underestimated the Russian colossus." The front devoured Soviet manpower. However great the loses on each side, the Germans were able, despite what they called a temporary crisis, to take advantage of an opening between the two Leningrad fronts, the north and northwest, due to an unfortunate shift in the Forty-Eighth Army, retreating to the east rather than falling back to the north, leaving a twelve mile gap the Nazis squeezed through to cut off the Leningrad–Moscow railroad and encircle the city. On August 21, Hitler reemphasized that, as Salisbury indicated, "the principal Nazi objective was not the capture of Moscow but (in the north) the encirclement of Leningrad and junction with the Finns." That would, Hitler said, "free the forces for attacking and destroying the Center Army Group Timoshenko, which was defending Moscow."[12]

As Hitler was decreeing Leningrad's demise, Stalin was by late August recovered from his initial breakdown and increasingly interfering with the northern Palmyra's defense. Egged on by Beria and Malenkov, he sought to micromanage the work of Zhdanov and Voroshilov. Stalin, who had by that time recovered, assumed the title of supreme commander or generalissimo on August 8, and he was directly in touch with key places by the VC (highpriority or high-security telephone). According to Salisbury, the Stalin system suffered from all the weaknesses of overcentralization: micromanagement, long delays, and confusion. As he followed every detail of Leningrad's crisis, he interfered in its internal defenses. For instance, he strenuously opposed Zhdanov's and Voroshilov's creation of the Council for the Defense of Leningrad on August 20. On the twenty-first, it proclaimed, "The enemy is at the Gates!" By urgent consultation on the VC, Salisbury revealed, "Stalin was in a rage. Why had they set up the Council for the Defense of Leningrad without consulting him?" Stalin refused to be appeased by their explanation of a need for block-by-block plans for the city's defense. Stalin argued they were evading responsibility. On August 21, he ordered that the council be reviewed and its membership revised, and he rebuked Voroshilov and Zhdanov. Salisbury suggests Stalin may have been convinced of a plot or feared arming citizens. When Admiral Vladimir Tributs proposed a counterattack because he believed the Germans lacked reserves, "Stalin turned it down out of hand." And Salisbury concludes: "There can be no doubt that the savage row between Stalin and the Leningrad defenders, Zhdanov and Voroshilov, was of import not only in the defense of the city but in the higher game of Kremlin politics [that is] between Stalin and those of his associates who sought, by one means or another, to advance their personal fortunes, regardless of its effect on the war."[13]

Now the Baltic states came under Nazi fire. The Tallinn (Revel) disaster Salisbury compares with Dunkirk, but much worse—a "sheer catastrophe." Though the Eighth Army was to guard Tallinn in Estonia, in fact no plan existed. The German army had moved so swiftly that, had not the Baltic Fleet resisted, it might have driven less than a hundred miles along the Baltic highway and captured Tallinn instantly. The Soviets had never imagined Tallinn might be attacked, but by August 8, the Germans had cut the city off and captured Kunda to the east. At this juncture, Admiral Vladimir Tributs took charge of the city's defenses and mobilized his fleet's guns against the enemy. It was too little, too late. On August 26, Moscow ordered Tallinn evacuated. By then, the Baltic Fleet was already at the mercy of German mines, aircraft, and, especially, submarines. Tributs began the 190 ships' evacuation—220 miles to the Kronstadt island fortress just on the immediate approaches to Leningrad—in four convoys. This hegira cost him ten thousand lives, twenty-five large transports, sixteen warships, and many other vessels of his flotilla.[14]

Meanwhile, the Soviet high command shifted its forces facing the Finns from the Northern Front to reinforce Leningrad's defenses, even though the Finns attacked north of Leningrad on July 31. No alternative remained if Leningrad was to be protected from the Nazi advance to the south. The Finns recaptured Vyborg and forced the Russians behind the old Mannerheim Line separating Russia and Finland. At the same time, Karelia was lost. The remaining twelve thousand soldiers from the Tallinn convoy plugged the hole of the 7th Army under General Meretskov and stabilized the north for the remainder of the war. The Finns would never join the Germans for a final assault on Leningrad.[15]

Often in warfare, some previously insignificant spot attains the greatest significance. So it was with the tiny railway station at Mga—a fly spot like so many others connecting Leningrad to the rest of Russia. On August 29, 1941, German paratroops captured Mga, and to the south Panzers took Novgorod. Luckily, by then Leningrad's Public Library had already shipped 360,000 priceless items and the Hermitage sent 350 box loads eastward by train to safety. Artistic ensembles had fled along with the treasures of the great palaces ringing the city.[16]

Just before all rail connections to the north were cut off, Admiral Kuznetsov with two members of the State Defense Committee arrived in Leningrad with Molotov and Malenkov to assess Leningrad's fate, "whether it could or should be held." It was already too late to evacuate all children, women, and old persons. On the VC phone with Stalin, it was decided to save the city: KV sixty-ton tanks from the Kirov and Izhorsk factories would go straight onto Leningrad's defense with four aviation regiments, ten infantry battalions, and every reserve unit—some seventy. Joining Molotov and Malenkov was Zhdanov, the one who had insisted on saving the city. Stalin put Zhukov in command of Leningrad's defenses; he removed Voroshilov. By then, the Shlisselburg fortress had nearly fallen on the Neva River and the circle around the city closed by September 8. Though Stalin ordered scuttling the remaining Baltic Fleet, he himself would not sign such an order. Nor would Kuznetsov or Marshal Shaposhnikov. Stalin had seemed prepared to abandon the city. Instead, Voroshilov was sacked and Zhdanov and Zhukov were given one last chance. They would have to save Leningrad quickly or Stalin would sacrifice it.[17]

Salisbury captured the significance of Mga's fall: "What gave Mga importance was that once the Nazis firmly grasped the town they severed all the rail connections between Leningrad and the remainder of Russia—the 'mainland' as it came to be called—and they cut all the highways."[18] The 48th Army, instead of retreating northward, drifted to the east, leaving the gap the Germans quickly filled. With the fall of Mga, and the cutting off of rails and highways, the Germans also drove to the gates of Leningrad and within artillery range of such important factories as Izhorsk—producer of the KV sixty-ton monster tank as well as the T-34, other heavy armor-plated tanks, and various other military equipment. However, they did not breach the Izhorsk Line just outside the city. The encirclement and fall of Leningrad would have allowed Hitler to carry out his strategic sweep from the north to encircle Moscow from the rear. All that held them from success were the Neva bridges, especially the rail bridge at Ostrovski. Colonel Bychevsky's men succeeded in blowing it up, thwarting Hitler's plan, but Leningrad had been encircled, not defeated. Leningrad itself could now be shelled by German long-range artillery.[19]

Perhaps most painful of things to come was the bombing destruction of the Badayev warehouse from September 6 to 8. It had contained the city's greatest food supply storage. This event, more than any other, foretold the coming famine. Only a few days later, Dmitry Pavlov arrived, appointed as Leningrad's food czar at the request of Mayor Pyotr Popkov. Both calculated no supplies would arrive for some time to feed Leningrad's 3,400,000 inhabitants. Only ration coupons could purchase food. The main market, Gostiny Dvor, burned for days. Losing one's ration card was a death sentence; some were forged. The most terrible battle, the battle for the city itself, was just beginning. It would be a nine-hundred-day siege.[20]

The only fortification remaining, though surrounded by Germans, was the small Russian battery at Shlisselburg. Otherwise, all along the Neva River's south bank by August 31, the Nazi legions stood, but they never crossed that formidable barrier, nor did they penetrate thirty miles northward to juncture with the Finns. Why they did not remains a mystery. Five days later, Hitler decided to tighten the ring and starve Leningrad out, not to seize it. Instead, elements of von Leeb's army were released for the drive on Moscow. General Georg-Hans Reinhart's armored corps moved south for the drive on Moscow. The opportunity to cross the Neva, join with the Finns, and seal Leningrad off from Lake Ladoga was forever lost. Thus an ice bridge could supply the city across the lake.[21] Hitler had failed either to take Leningrad or to starve the city into submission, even after the long siege. The survivors—less one and a half million who starved, froze, or were killed by the invaders—turned to rebuilding.

Salisbury saved some of the best of his narrative and analysis to the very end of his fiftieth chapter. The renaissance of Leningrad began—its reconstruction and restoration. It was, as one visiting correspondent in February 1944—the author himself—was told, "a dream on a scale of magnificence worthy of the traditions of Peter." Heavy industry was given priority by the State Defense Committee. And yet, "The sums advanced for rehabilitation and restoration were niggardly." Leningraders had to lower their ambitions, postponing many of them. Party Secretary Kuznetsov and Mayor Popkov presented revised plans in the summer of 1946; they would have been parts of the fourth and fifth five-year plans. More than fifteen years passed before another word was publicly expressed concerning the Leningrad Renaissance. This was no accident. With foreboding, Salisbury stressed, "Not for one moment during the war, during the nine hundred days, had there been a moratorium in the secret political struggle within the Kremlin." This reflected the "morbid sphere of Stalinist politics." Murderous and suicidal politics intensified. Zhdanov rejoined the party secretariat in Moscow, his power second only to Stalin's. Mayor Popkov became Leningrad's party chief. At once, an anti-Western crusade began, the Zhdanovshchina.[22]

Leningrad's remaining cultural elite was purged—writers and artists were always the first victims. By the summer of 1948, Malenkov's power was apparent. It was he who now signed the secretariat's orders. On August 31, 1948, the party announced Zhdanov's death. The remaining figures of the siege period disappeared—all those closely associated with Zhdanov. Even the Museum of the Defense of Leningrad closed in 1949. The purges were carried out secretly, and poison was the main instrument. All of this became known as the Leningrad Affair, an effort by Stalin to eliminate his rivals. Salisbury put it aptly: "The Leningrad epic was wiped out of the public memory insofar as this was physically possible, and, as in Orwell's 'memory hole,' the building blocks of history, the public record, the statistics, the memoirs of what had happened, were destroyed or suppressed." The blockade had consumed a million and a half people, whereas the "affair" destroyed many who had survived. Salisbury concluded that after a quarter of a century, Leningrad still had not recovered. "The deadly sequence of Stalinist events [had] left a mark nothing could erase." Nevertheless, and in spite of that self-inflicted hell, the memory of the nine hundred days lived on.[23]

The noted British historian A. J. P. Taylor reviewed Salisbury's masterpiece in the *New York Review of Books*. Even though he praised this epic, especially from the Russian side of Salisbury's account, Taylor also offered criticisms. Sometimes, Taylor maintained, Salisbury divined what leaders were thinking short of what his sources indicated. More gravely, the German side of the story was lacking. "One day the final account will bring the two sets of sources together, and we shall understand German failure as well as Soviet success." And even graver, according to Taylor, Salisbury had a political theme—an implicit indictment of Stalin: Stalin miscalculated and initially collapsed; he regained himself and executed the war rigidly, his suspicions turning to his paranoia in the postwar Leningrad Affair. Taylor branded this interpretation "a misleading trail." Rather, the situation itself called for brutality, which fit Russia's past history. And Stalin's blindness as to the war's outbreak was not worse than FDR's before Pearl Harbor; it was "exactly the same." Stalin, according to Taylor, just did not believe Hitler would attack before the war in the West was won. As for Stalin's lack of preparations, a threat to Leningrad seemed a remote possibility. "In fact," Taylor indicated, "one is merely left with the banal conclusion that Stalin made as many mistakes as anyone else." As to Salisbury characterizing Stalin's conduct of the war as "very hard," Taylor countered, "Stalin was willing to sacrifice a million or more inhabitants of Leningrad, if this would harass and delay the Germans. Human lives did not count in the scales of victory. This is quite different from saying that Stalin deliberately provoked death and destruction at Leningrad or welcomed it." Furthermore, Zhdanov was not sent there by Stalin to ruin him. He had nowhere else to go.

The Leningrad Affair was typical Stalinism, in Taylor's opinion. Zhdanov's comrades were eliminated because Zhdanov died and his faction lost. It was "fantastic" to imply they were destroyed because they were the "outstanding leaders during the siege." What can Salisbury mean, Taylor asked, "than that Stalin was responsible for the Leningrad blockade as directly and in the same sense as he was responsible for the 'affair'? It is totally and monstrously untrue. The man responsible for the Leningrad blockade was Hitler." Taylor concluded, "Mr. Salisbury has concentrated so much on the Russian side that the Germans outside Leningrad seemed to have escaped his attention." Salisbury was not one to let such a barrage go by unnoticed.

Harrison replied. Stalin's wartime leadership was more than "very hard," according to Salisbury. He maintained that it was "capricious, often incredibly misdirected and never free from Stalinesque paranoia, 'suspicion,' as Khrushchev called it." Nor could Stalin be exculpated for the Leningrad disaster. Stalin countermanded his commanders' preparations and only belatedly, too belatedly, gave in. And so it went throughout the war. Nor could FDR's Pearl Harbor miscalculation be compared to Stalin's blindness to Hitler's intentions. "Stalin, on the other hand, blindly and fantastically *refused to believe* Hitler was going to attack and even after the Nazi assault began *still refused to believe* that Hitler had ordered the offensive." Further, Stalin was willing to sacrifice Leningrad to save Moscow, and he was willing to erase the official memory of its heroes."[24] Though Taylor was correct about the German side of the story, Salisbury had the better end of the argument. His *The 900 Days* remains the classic account.

As a master of the scoop, it is curious Harrison devoted time and effort to events already often recorded. By the 1970s, the bibliography of Russia's twentieth-century revolutions—from eyewitnesses to serious historians—was legion. Harrison justified another account by saying he wanted to tell the story as it actually happened, going to primary sources and uncovering new documents. He warned his readers that his account was from the bottom up: from the common people to the famous names. Viewed from that angle, historical surprises caught Lenin and Czar Nicholas II unprepared. Only the poets had premonitions of Russia's two revolutions that destroyed the ancient regime and created a new order—one so radical that it challenged the world's capitalist system for almost the remainder of the twentieth century. Lenin's victory was germinal, yet it did not unfold in Olympian grandeur. Rather, it occurred through blundering and chance, where leaders only occasionally decided what happened.[25] As in *The 900 Days*, where Salisbury attacked Stalin and his henchmen, in *Black Night, White Snow* the author exposes the myths surrounding Lenin and his Bolshevik elite of professional revolutionaries. Fate dealt Lenin a lucky hand. He and his successors overplayed their cards, leading to their own destruction seventy-four years later.

Salisbury's second Russian narrative begins and ends with executions: on May 8, 1887, Lenin's brother Alexander Ulyanov and his four fellow conspirators were hanged by order of Czar Alexander III at the Shlisselburg fortress in St. Petersburg for planning to kill the royal family; on July 16, 1918, Lenin ordered the liquidation of Czar Nicholas II, his family, and their attendants at the Ipatyev House in Ekaterinburg to prevent a royal restoration. Lenin followed the dicta of his model revolutionary, Sergei Nechayev: gather the Romanov dynasty and assassinate them all. This advice, Lenin said, "is simplicity to the point of genius."[26] Between these two points, Salisbury spun his story. It started with Czar Alexander III asking how long his family would be saved from revolutionary destruction.

Salisbury first chronicles Russia's nineteenth-century revolutionary movement from Nikolai Chernyshevsky's *What Is to Be Done?* to Lenin's *Development of Capitalism in Russia.* An interesting insight is Salisbury's comment that the czar's finance minister Sergei Witte's analysis of industrialization in Russia was the same as Lenin's.[27] Salisbury's knowledge is impressive as he relates once more the tragic events of Khodynka Fields during the coronation of Nicholas II, when an unruly crowd trampled thousands to death. He reviews Georgii Plekhanov's introduction of Marxism. By the 1890s, Salisbury concludes, Lenin had "welded the extremist ideals of Chernyshevsky, the dedication of [Nikolai] Dobrolyubov, and the economic critique of Marx into a philosophy of politics and life."[28] By the first fifty pages, it is clear that Salisbury's range of knowledge is large.

From these revolutionary origins, Salisbury turns to the problems of the Russian monarchy, particularly the bad start of Nicholas II's reign, namely, the incident at the coronation in 1896 at Khodynka Fields. He followed the Russian defeat in the Russo-Japanese War of 1904–1905 and the first chance of a revolutionary victory with Lev Trotsky at its head. Salisbury has little to say of Trotsky throughout. Curiously, he passes over the Duma experiment in democracy from 1905 to 1917 and quickly prepares the reader for the events leading from the Russo-Japanese War to World War I. It was during the Duma period that the czar showed a "fatal inclination toward harebrained schemers and schemes." The most important of these was, of course, Grishka Rasputin, the Czarina Alexandra's holy man and confidant, who exercised a healing power over the hemophilic Aleksei, heir to the throne.[29]

Two schools of historiography emerge: those who believe the Romanov dynasty would have collapsed of its own dead weight even if World War I had not occurred, and those who credit the war with bringing the monarchy down. Salisbury, like his mentor the British historian Bernard Pares, considers the war as the major factor. He is at pains to chronicle the mishaps and mistakes of the czar and his ministers in handling the war, including the two interesting warnings not to go to war: Rasputin's and that of the minister of interior, Pyotr Durnovo.[30] Count Witte called the war "madness."[31] This part of Salisbury's history culminates with Rasputin's debauchery and his assassination by Prince Felix Yusupov.[32] Following the lead of Pares, Salisbury counts Rasputin as Russia's dictator in the empire's last days.[33]

The February Revolution of 1917 took everyone by surprise from the czarist bureaucracy to the most radical revolutionaries. The slide from the Provisional Government to Bolshevism also came as a surprise. When the dynasty collapsed, it took down the entire social order that Peter the Great and his successors had built up from the seventeenth century onward. Inept liberals and their moderate socialist allies were unable to fill the vacuum. Moreover, the war continued at the insistence of the Western powers. Salisbury gives his readers vivid moments, as when Nicholas II equivocated over his abdication. The narrative picks up with Lenin's arrival from Switzerland in a sealed train car with the connivance of Kaiser Wilhelm II. Salisbury dashes through the July Days and the Kornilov Putsch. That gets him to the heart of his story.[34]

Salisbury wishes to recount the October events surrounding the Bolshevik coup not as pageantry, but as banality: "Seldom has the contrast between legend and reality presented a wider gap."[35] The leaders of the Provisional Government could have arrested the Bolshevik high command with five hundred Cossacks attacking Smolny, headquarters of the Bolsheviks. Likewise, three hundred volunteers could have taken the Winter Palace. But neither side understood each other's vulnerability. The balance changed quickly when Lenin's Military Revolutionary Committee persuaded eight thousand troops at the Peter and Paul Fortress in Petrograd to either remain neutral or come over to its side. Salisbury lamented, "Until these early morning hours a single company of cadets with a few machine guns and an armored car could have easily captured the Military Revolutionary Committee, most of the Bolshevik leaders, and Smolny itself."[36]

Lenin's sense of timing and his iron will convinced his central committee to initiate the coup. It is remarkable that "Lenin—and Lenin alone—backed the idea of the October coup; that almost all of his associates opposed him and thought him violently mistaken; that he singlehandedly overcame their opposition and was prepared to go to *any* lengths (including conspiring against his own party) to achieve his goal; and that the historical record has been deliberately suppressed and distorted for sixty years to conceal the dimensions and depth of the conflict."[37] Thus began the siege of the Winter Palace on October 25. That led to the fall of the Provisional Government and Lenin's declaration of Soviet power under the banner of "Peace, Land, and Bread."[38] Salisbury noted how much everything depended on improvisation. Trotsky suggested the new government's name: a Soviet of People's Commissars. The general population thought Lenin's government also would be swept away in a few weeks. It took daring, Salisbury concedes, to hold back a countercoup by Kerensky aided by General Krasnov's Cossacks. Faced with counterrevolution, the Red Terror began.[39]

Relentlessly, events moved toward force and more force. Those who stood against the Bolsheviks, Lenin declared "enemies of the people." To enforce the Red Terror, the Cheka (Extraordinary Commission for Combating Counterrevolution and Sabotage) was created on December 7. Lenin dispatched Trotsky, the first Commissar of Foreign Affairs, to Brest Litovsk to arrange a peace with the Central Powers, which was consummated on March 3, 1918. The capital moved to Moscow. The Czar's family and attendants were imprisoned in Ekaterinburg at the Ipatyev House. As Russian counterrevolutionaries with their Czech allies came close, Lenin ordered the execution of the Romanovs.[40] "There were a few moments of quiet. Then came a noise in the neighboring room—the executioners were assembling. Outside car motors started up. The hour was 3:15 A.M. (by daylight time). [Yakov] Yurovsky entered the room followed by his command of eleven Chekists. He stepped forward and said: 'Nikolai Alexandrovich, by the decision of the Urals district committee we are going to shoot you and your family.'" With that, they were shot and cut to pieces, and their bodies thrown into an abandoned mine.[41]

Robert Conquest in the *Times* called Salisbury's treatment of yet another rendition of the Russian Revolutions "an ebullient, impressionistic picture of the whole period [and] a well-contrived whole, of a type not previously given us." Salisbury exposed the one-sidedness of Soviet research, though it is massive. As to the heroic Soviet gospel of Lenin's final victory, Salisbury discovered a "blaze of apathy and incompetence, only victorious because of the even more transcendent ineptness of the Provisional Government." Conquest was critical of Salisbury's "dealings with the moods" of the intelligentsia, though they make an "immensely readable anecdotal tour de force." Moreover, Salisbury, in Conquest's evaluation, played on the inevitability of the revolution once the war began, and that meant less attention to other alternatives. For instance, Conquest felt that the author "sneered" at the possible success of the Stolypin reforms. Moreover, Stolypin's repression was "painted blacker than it merits." The Salisbury picture of hopelessness extended to other areas such as war weariness in 1916. "What Salisbury brings out extraordinarily well is the way the regime fell only because of the devoted idiocy, or rather lunacy, of the Czar and (above all) the Czarina." This is especially illustrated by the royal obsession with the Czarevich's hemophilia and with Rasputin. The February Revolution may not have taken place, as Salisbury estimates, but for the curious nature of the Romanov family. Equally, Salisbury points out, the October Revolution was determined by one person, Lenin. Conquest congratulates Salisbury's picture of Lenin, not as a "slightly rough-edged liberal" but as a "narrow-minded (and bloody-minded) fanatic, as neurasthenic in his own way as any intellectual or Czarina." Therefore, the new regime emerged with the same "political primitivism, of obsessive despotism" as the former regime.[42]

Salisbury's epic tales, *The 900 Days* and *Black Night, White Snow*, run through some of the sadness and violence that make up Russia's twentieth-century history. Each shows his gift for narrative storytelling as well as interesting insights along the way. More importantly, they reveal the author's attitude toward Russia. Like many Americans before him, he shows a compassion for the Russian people but a dislike of Russian rulers and their governments, be it czars or commissars. He aims his heaviest condemnations at Stalin and his cronies for leaving Leningrad to the mercies of Hitler, Stalin's revenge against the heroes of Leningrad, Nicholas II's stupidity, and the barbarity of Lenin and his associates. None of it is a pretty picture. The dilemma for Salisbury has been the same for his fellow Americans, beginning with Siberian explorer George Kennan all the way to that Kennan's distant relative, the diplomat George F. Kennan, to separate the picture into a sympathetic portrait of Russians and a dislike of their leaders. In assessing the two, leaders and peoples, he found the same disparity when he studied China and the Chinese.

Two of Salisbury's other twenty-nine books—these two on China—parallel his remarkable narratives on Russia. They are *The Long March: The Untold Story* and *The New Emperors: China in the Era of Mao and Deng*. The former reminds us of *The 900 Days*, while the latter we can liken to *Black Night, White Snow*. How is this so? In *The 900 Days* Harrison attacks Stalin for refusing to recognize the Nazi danger and, by so doing, opening Leningrad and Soviet Russia itself to near total destruction. In addition, after narrowly avoiding annihilation and overcoming the Nazi onslaught, Stalin destroyed the very heroes who won the victory at Leningrad in order to cover his own mistakes. Likewise, Mao destroyed some of the most important heroes of the Long March during the Cultural Revolution. Both Stalin and Mao understood that these former comrades, namely Zhdanov's cohorts and his fellow members of the Politburo who had saved Russia and Deng Xiaoping and his associates, would alter their policies. In their "cold-eyed" reasoning, these persons must be destroyed. Stalin initiated the Great Terror and Doctors' Plot, and Mao the Cultural Revolution. Salisbury understood the mechanism at work. His historical narratives underlay that analysis. What he wrote about Mao and the Long March could have applied to Stalin's role: "That this brotherhood disintegrated in the madness of Mao's final years adds a note of tragedy to the heroic drama."[43]

Harrison took years preparing to write *The Long March*. It started as an idea back in 1972 when he first went to China. He had often discussed the project with Jack Service, the "famous old China Hand, the diplomat the State Department expelled in McCarthy days but who fought in the courts and got his job back."[44] Salisbury's wife, Charlotte, had exclaimed, "What a story! What a scoop! If he could only persuade the Chinese to let him go." So when the Chinese embassy called to approve the project in February 1984, he was ready. It would be, his wife wrote, the trip and scoop of his life.[45] That scoop was translated into Chinese and became mandatory reading in China's secondary schools after Mao's death.[46]

Harrison and Charlotte arrived in Beijing on March 2, 1984, and left three and a half months later. He returned in the fall. They visited Mme Soong's Museum as well as Dr. Rewi Alley, friend of the Chinese Revolution, who sent Salisbury many books on the Long March. Jack and Caroline Service arrived on March 16. Salisbury busied himself by interviewing survivors of the Long March, especially Huang Hua. A major theme developed: the Russians misunderstood the Chinese Revolution and only saw it in Russian terms. That accounted for the Red Army's loses at the time Mao was pushed aside by Wang Ming and the so-called twenty-eight Bolsheviks. Harrison also spoke with the former foreign minister Ji Pengfei, a Long March survivor. Ji cited crossing the Dadu River as the most difficult moment of the march. Harrison typed his notes every evening. He noticed that the four generals he interviewed were all victims of the Cultural Revolution. Every veteran of the Long March he spoke with was "either in prison, under house arrest, or on a pig farm, being humiliated, persecuted, tortured, during that time."[47] Finally, on April 3, they packed and left Beijing for Nachang and by April 11 arrived in Ruijin, in Honan Province, the former red capital of the Central Soviet Area in 1934. It was the departure point of the Long March.[48] As Charlotte put it in her diary, "The Fifth and last encirclement campaign came after Mao was out. Bo Gu and Li De were running things, and they believed that standing fast and facing the enemy Kuomintang of Chiang Kai-shek was the best strategy. It was a disaster, the final blow. The Communists realized they had to move on."[49]

Harrison took it from there. Zhou Enlai announced the red retreat on October 9, 1934. It was to start in a week. Nationalist leader Chiang Kai-shek planned mopping up the "Red Bandits" in his last campaign by moving against Riujin, the Central Soviet Area's capital, an area established five years earlier by Mao Zedong and his ally Zhu De, known as the Zhu-Mao base area in Hunan. Li De had committed the reds to static tactics, but their losses were too great. Now all agreed to break out of Chiang's attempt at encirclement, deploying two hundred thousand against eighty-seven thousand as well as threading through blockhouses, a tactic designed especially by German General Hans von Seekt. It was not a spur-of-the-moment idea, though they did not escape before Chiang destroyed the Nineteenth Route Army. Sometimes the reds marched fifty miles at night in long box formations, with the Central Military Command at the center for protection. In November and early December 1934, Mao's forces moved to the southwest corner and slipped over the border into Guandong Province—with warlord Chen Jetang's connivance. Its secret asset was breaking the Nationalist army's communications codes, never suspected by the Kuomintang (KMT).[50]

In a narrative pause, Harrison sketched the life of Mao and his women, which followed closely works by Edgar and Helen Snow. Noteworthy was Mao's famous 1927 *Report on an Investigation of the Peasant Movement in Hunan*. Its bottom line, Mao told Edgar Snow, was, "Whoever wins the peasant will win China; whoever solves the land problem will win the peasant."[51] One must march at their head and lead them. Mao, according to Harrison, spent his youth "gobbling up books like bowls of noodles."[52] His motto was "Seek truth from facts."[53] Mao took this motto from his Changsha Normal No. 1 school. He spent some of the Long March on a litter where he discussed his ideas with Zhu De and Lin Biao.[54] As to the women, the thirty cadres, like Mao's then wife (He Zizhen) or Zhu De's (Kan Keqing) or Zhou's wife (Deng Yingchao), they soldiered on, even though Mao's was pregnant and Zhou's had TB.[55]

Besides overcoming Chiang's blockhouses along the Red Army's route, the marchers had to cross the Xiang River flowing north from Guangxi Province into Hunan. Zhou had already negotiated a thirteen-mile corridor for safe passage with the local warlord. Nevertheless, the KMT attacked. The Red Army lost more than half of its men and supplies, but it managed to escape total destruction. The Comintern's supremacy over the reds under Otto Braun's leadership collapsed. It marked the rise of Mao Zedong. From the Xiang River, the reds had to climb Laoshun Mountain. Mao proposed abandoning the effort to join with He Long and to shift course from northwest Hunan and move into Guizhou. Mao's strategy was accepted at a conference at Zunyi in January 1935. A new revolutionary command was formed, and Mao was made commander of the Red Army. Military direction was given to his two closest supporters, Zhu De and Zhou Enlai. Salisbury put it succinctly: "Zunyi was over. The Long March continued. Mao was in charge until he died in 1976. China's course had been set for at least half a century to come."[56]

Only a remnant remained of the original force. It had escaped the KMT's trap at the red corner of Jiangxi. But Chiang intended to get them at Guizhou or block them from crossing the Yangtze. The Red Army entered the Karp area of Guizhou. Mao's objective was clear—to find a path north to join the Fourth Front Army of Zhang Guotao. By dividing into many columns, he hoped to confuse Chiang. But the way was still blocked. Though suffering loses, he fooled Chiang by an unexpected tactic—doubling back and making another pass at Zunyi. This bewildered Chiang's forces. The reds swooped down Loushan Pass on February 27, 1935, catching KMT forces by surprise, and won their biggest Long March victory. It again looked to Chiang that Mao would force a Yangtze crossing, which Mao was eager for him to think. He sent units to Guiyang, while Mao raced to the Golden Sands River. "Chiang had, in effect, opened the path for Mao to streak for the River of Golden Sands." The reds moved to the east, bypassing Guiyang by twenty-five miles.[57]

Chiang Kai-shek seemed certain of Mao's return to Hunan and Jiangxi. Instead, Mao sent shock forces ahead to secure crossings of the Golden Sands River. Recuperating his strength, it looked as if Mao wanted the capture of Kunming. Rather, he skirted Kunming. Lin Biao led Mao's crack regiments and made a crossing on April 29, 1935. The remainder of Mao's forces raced to Longjie. Not able to float a bamboo bridge, they pushed on to the Jiaopingdu crossing by May 6. Bravely, they secured Lion's Head, won over the boatmen, and made the crossing. It was an epic moment. "The Red Army was across the River of Golden Sands. It had slammed the door on pursuit. Not yet was Mao Zedong wholly free from Chiang Kai-shek. But he was north of the Yangtze." That was China's great dividing line. The Red Army had been saved, but what would Mao now do?[58]

Mao had decided to move north through the Yi country and cross the Dadu River at the Luding Bridge. If successful, that would allow him to join Zhang Guotao's Fourth Front Army. It meant another race for time. Mao must avoid antagonizing the Yi minority and race to the Dadu ahead of Chiang. Money and goods were offered and an oath taken. To secure Luding Bridge, Mao sent the Fourth Shock Regiment under Yang Chengwu "to break the trail and carry out the surprise assault." Lin Biao issued the order: "You must march at top speed and take every possible measure to accomplish this glorious mission." This two-day mission had to be done in one day. The Fourth Regiment jogged, guns in hand. At Luding, they invited a suicide attack, gained the bridge, and made the Red Army's crossing possible. With that, fear of Chiang's pursuit ended. No enemy could stop Mao from juncture with the Fourth Front Army in northwest Sichuan. However, the Great Snowy Mountains separated them. This was perhaps the worst experience for those of the Long March. Finally, in June 1935, around one hundred thousand of Zhang's army and thirty thousand of Mao's met at Aba.[59]

Relations between Mao and Zhang were cool, and that made a united command difficult. Mao contended that the farther west they went, the less influence they would have on China's political scene. Zhang sought greater safety in the west. By August, a compromise was worked out. Their forces were divided into two columns—left and right—each one mixed, as was the central command, and Zhu De was made commander in chief, with Zhang as chief political commissar. Mao retained the chairmanship. From the Great Snowies, they had to cross the grasslands, what Harrison called an "inland Sargasso Sea." So many drowned that it was thought to be the worst trial on the march. It was also the worst political moment—Zhang had halted at Aba and would not let his left column go farther north.[60]

Mao convened the Central Committee, and it unanimously urged Zhang Guotao to head north. Zhang responded on September 9 by ordering the right column to reverse, recross the grasslands, and rejoin his Fourth Army. Indeed, it appeared Zhang threatened to attack. However, Mao continued north and Zhang moved south. "Zhang Guotao was going south; Mao was going north. A meeting at Ejie by Mao approved, 'Resolution Concerning the Mistakes of Comrade Zhang Guotao.'" Mao now had to take the narrows at Lazikou Pass by direct assault. He headed to Hadapu. Mao had returned to Han China. They were headed north, but to what final destination? It was now time to fight the Japanese. Mao's forces raced to Shaanxi's loess country. To the north were the Great Wall and the plain of the Yellow River. It was the burial site of the Yellow Emperor, founder of China. "The Long March of 25,000 li, the *Chang Zheng,* the six-thousand-mile journey had ended."[61]

Zhang's decision cost him ten thousand troops lost in battle with Chiang Kai-shek. His Fourth Front Army was destroyed. He was marooned in the south. Only a few thousand survived and arrived in Shaanxi, due to an arrangement with Mao's agreement with Chang Kai-shek to fight the Japanese jointly. Zhang's remnants arrived on December 14, 1936. Mao and Zhang were reconciled. The Long March was over.[62]

Harrison concluded *The Long March* with two chapters contrasting Mao and Deng Xiaoping. Mao, he wrote, conceived the Cultural Revolution, his "cold-eyed" survey of the world. Mao grew impatient with his revolution. Like Stalin, it was time to rid himself of the old leadership and try the young. It had been fifty years since the Long March ended, "It has even proved powerful enough to overcome the vagaries of the final years of Mao Zedong himself and move forward on a fresh new path—one which Mao would hardly have chosen. But the reckoning is far from complete."[63] That reckoning Harrison would analyze in his last major book, *The New Emperors*.

Steven C. Averill, reviewing Salisbury's *The Long March*, noted that the author had the approval of the PRC to remake the journey and to utilize the full scholarly resources then available, especially personal reminiscences of Long March veterans as well as historians and museum officials. The results, according to the reviewer, "are quite impressive." Averill goes on to say, "The broad outlines of the Long March have long been well known, but

Salisbury's book provides much new and vivid detail about conditions on the March, while at the same time evaporating much of the hagiographic haze that has enveloped its events and personalities in previous Chinese accounts." Salisbury's discussion of the politics of the Long March is important, especially revealing the inaccuracy of Otto Braun's memoirs, details of the Zunyi Conference, and negotiations between Mao and Zhang Guotao. The reviewer notes, "That in the end one is left still with a host of questions about both the substance and the dynamics of these meetings is due less to Salisbury's abilities as writer and analyst than to the real or artificial lacunae remaining in the memories and materials made available by the Chinese to him." The reviewer credits Salisbury's ability, nevertheless, to sort out whatever political shadings the PRC fed him, especially on Mao's role. Averill concludes that this is the "best single account of the Long March" likely for some time.

Harvard scholar and Sinologist Ross Terrill agreed with the reviewer. *The Long March* was, Terrill emphasized, a masterpiece and the one book of Salisbury's on China that he completely respected, even though it exonerated heroes of the Long March. In addition, said Terrill, "Though Harrison never learned Chinese, he used his interpreters and translators very well." Averill pointed out that Jack Service, "an Old China Hand of the first order," had accompanied Harrison. The book greatly benefited from this.[64]

Salisbury used a sophisticated organization of flashbacks to fill in the biographies of Mao and Deng in *The New Emperors*, rather than a straight chronology. He began with the surrender of Beijing to the reds on January 21, 1949, the victory parade of February 3, and Mao's slipping into the city on March 25. Unlike the communist confiscations of property and executions of landlords and rich peasants in the countryside, Mao cautioned against such treatment of urban capitalists. He needed their cooperation and the support of noncommunist parties. Making Beijing, rather than Nanjing, his capital gave him added legitimacy, as did rejecting the Nationalists and Americans, especially rebuking Stalin's suggestion of a coalition with Chiang Kai-shek. In harmony with exercising such caution, Mao invited John Leighton Stuart, U.S. ambassador to Nationalist China, for commencement exercises at Yenching University, where he had been president. The U.S. State Department vetoed that, an indication of future PRC-U.S. troubles. Harrison cast another shadow before his readers—Mao's days as part-time poet and philosopher were ending. He told his fellow poet Liu Yazu not to turn his back on China's future. Mao and his comrades had to focus their attentions, after proclaiming the establishment of the PRC on October 1, 1949, to "putting the nation in order and preparing the foundations for the New China."[65]

The country's leaders operated from the new government's compound, Zhongnanhai, adjacent to the Forbidden City. According to Salisbury, Mao had learned more from such Chinese classics as *The Romance of the Three Kingdoms*, *The General Mirror for the Aid of Government*, and the *Annals of the Dynasties* than he had from Marxism-Leninism. He studied the transition from the Ming to the Qing dynasties with special care. "Thus begins a new era in the history of China," Mao proclaimed from the Gate of Heavenly Peace. "We, the four hundred and seventy-five million people of China, have now stood up."[66] As chairman of the new republic, Mao assigned his marshals and generals the proconsular tasks of building New China: Zhou Enlai as foreign minister; Zhu De as the army's commander-in-chief; Liu Shaoqi as vice chairman and soon president; Chen Yi as chief of Shanghai; Deng Xiaoping as proconsul of southwestern China, soon to be the "Third Line" fortress against American military designs; Gao Gang as proconsul of Manchuria—and so it went.[67]

It so happened that not only was Mao's last wife, Jiang Qing, off in Moscow and missing from the October festivities, but so was the Soviet Ambassador Lieutenant General N. V. Roshchin, former military attaché at Chongqing, Chiang's World War II retreat. Russia formally recognized the PRC the next morning. Salisbury put it simply: "'Cool' is too weak a word to describe the nature of Soviet-Chinese and Stalin-Mao relations over those years." Mao never forgot the years of eating Soviet humble pie served up by Stalin. Everything Stalin had overlooked, from the Shanghai massacre of 1927, to the freeing of Chiang in 1936, to Stalin's help of Chiang during the war—all of that—made Mao aware of having to go it alone: "Mao therefore had no illusions that Stalin would be a cooperative partner, and he was not made more comfortable by the fact that the Russians were still trying to help Chiang Kaishek survive or, at rock bottom, to detach China's western province of Xinjiang."[68] To make matters worse, Stalin was paranoid over Tito's defection. Thus, while everyone else was watching China, Stalin kept China from Russia's view, even though Stalin admitted this to Liu Shaoqi and apologized. Nevertheless, Stalin's man in China was Gao Gang, Mao's viceroy for Manchuria:

> It was clear to anyone who bothered to examine the evidence that in the summer of 1949, when Mao was so concerned over his relations with the Soviet Union, Stalin and Beria were not only putting puppets into parts of Eastern Europe, they had secretly acquired their own man in Manchuria, the most strategic stronghold in all of China, ready to stab Mao in the back at their command.[69]

Or, as Salisbury candidly put it, "Stalin was paranoid, more nervous about the Communist world than ever before. His fear and suspicion of Mao were great."[70]

Even so, Mao boarded the train for Moscow on December 6, 1949, to celebrate Stalin's seventieth birthday on December 21. Though Stalin let "Mao hang long enough in the breeze," the Chinese dictator had not come all that way for nothing. He called for Zhou Enlai to make the journey so that a Sino-Soviet Treaty (signed February 13, 1950) could be drawn up covering defense, friendship, and mutual aid. Most importantly, each would come to the other's side in the event of aggression by Japan or any nation allied with Japan. Russia retained the old tsarist rights in Port Arthur and Dairen, the South Manchurian Railroad, and mineral rights in Xinjiang. Only a piddling three hundred million dollars in credits were promised to China.[71] Salisbury concluded that the world thought Russia had subjugated China and Moscow was the communist capital, with Stalin the Red Emperor: "This assessment of the Chinese-Soviet treaties was swallowed whole by the United States, and almost all of the Western world." With Mao as Stalin's puppet, it was assumed, U.S. recognition was out of the question.[72]

It was in this atmosphere that Stalin approved Kim Il-sung's initiation of the Korean War, without China's prior knowledge. When Kim's efforts failed at Inchon and General Douglas MacArthur moved north of the 38th parallel toward the Yalu River, Mao decided on intervention, catching the Americans by surprise. It also caught Stalin by surprise. Stalin calculated on a full-scale American attack on China and the collapse of Mao. Mao had trumped Stalin. Nevertheless, lacking artillery and with no air power, Mao was able to fight the United States to a standstill. It cost China diplomatic isolation and reliance on Russia until President Richard Nixon visited in 1972.[73]

By 1955–1956, the first Chinese five-year plan had been completed, a close model of Soviet plans. Mao came to believe, however, that China could do better by originating its own policy and fashioning it to take advantage of its unique resources, especially manpower. In an effort to discover ways forward, Mao instituted the Hundred Flowers Movement—"Let One Hundred Flowers Bloom; Let One Hundred Schools of Thought Contend"—often referred to as the "Double Hundreds." Given Khrushchev's "Secret Speech," it may have been that Mao had taken the first step toward relaxing controls instead of following Soviet repressions. Powerful party members were openly opposing Mao: Liu Shaoqi and Deng Xiaoping. Yet within a year, Khrushchev reversed himself and purged the "antiparty group." Mao desisted. Perhaps he had used this slogan to expose rightists and prepare for the Great Leap Forward. He was, after all, uneasy with Zhou Enlai and Liu Shaoqi, "whom he was beginning to perceive as increasingly unsympathetic to his twists and turns."[74]

In Harrison's opinion, Mao believed Zhou and Liu had failed in economic management. Simultaneously, he wanted to outpace Stalin's five-year plans and equal the achievements of China's first emperor, Qin Shi Huang, unifier of China, creator of the terra-cotta army at Xian and the Great Wall north of Beijing, in the third century BC. In 1958 Mao anticipated rapid industrialization. The peasants were collectivized with much the same results as in the USSR—resistance and destruction of crops and livestock. "Not one associated publicly challenged the commune plan or the Great Leap. Not Zhou, not Liu, not Deng. Mao had spoken, and Mao was never wrong."[75] Mao believed the common kitchen would stimulate a unified civilian organization parallel to the army. It did not. Furthermore, he imposed on China's masses their primitive backyard steel mills, whose tiny smelting pots' productions would overtake the few great steel plants of China. Not only did their poorly built smelters produce inferior iron, but they took the peasantry away from agriculture and encouraged the destruction of China's forests to make charcoal. Mao's failure was colossal. "Neither Zhou nor Liu nor Deng nor anyone else in a position of authority uttered any warning. The silence was deafening." The Great Leap Forward had not advanced Chinese industrialization over all the others nor instituted pure communism. Instead, it plunged China into one of its worst famines. It raised the threat of American military interference. Mao raced to Moscow for military assurance, and he got a declaration from Khrushchev that an attack on China would be considered an attack on the USSR.[76]

On July 2, 1959, Mao held the Chinese communist's Lushan Conference; it brought on the "greatest quarrel since the founding of the People's Republic." With his wife Jiang Qing at his side, the chairman declared, "the problems are many, the experience is abundant and the future is bright." Mao thought Deng not hostile to his policies, and Zhou and Liu only lukewarm. He needed them to keep the country going.[77] There was, nevertheless, a sense of foreboding. Marshal Peng Luhai and Mao's secretaries Hu Qiaomu and Li Rui criticized the chairman's policies. Mao composed a denunciation of them, eventually a formal indictment, for an "anti-Party conspiracy" or plot to overthrow Mao's regime. Yes, chaos had been created. But no one halted him. They cheered him on and bore some responsibility. Peng was replaced as defense minister, and Lin Biao took his place. Li Rui began an eighteen-year jail sentence. It was a preview of the Cultural Revolution.[78]

In the aftermath, Khrushchev came to Beijing for three days of talks in October 1959. He flew back to Moscow and ridiculed the Great Leap Forward, denounced the communes, questioned the Hundred Flowers Movement, and ceased giving large-scale aid to China. Peng disappeared. By 1962 intimates such as Mao's first private secretary, Jian Jiaying, suggested a modified family responsibility system—a primitive precursor of Deng Xiaoping's agricultural initiative of 1978. The Cultural Revolution was just beginning its denunciation of the four olds: old thoughts, old culture, old customs, and old habits. The antiparty clique was exposed as Soviet spies and traitors. Mao was preparing his comeback from the Great Leap by turning over economic direction of the country to Liu Shaoqi and Deng Xiaoping: "No more backyard steel mills. No more tacky rhetoric. Quiet, off-the-record experiments in profit motivation for the peasants (it worked like a charm but ended when Mao found out about it)."[79]

It would not be easy restoring China, but neither could it go on starving. Deng and Liu purchased six million tons of grain on the world market. The country could not go on starving; as Deng put it, "Communism is not poverty." Marx, Lenin, and Mao went out the window, or, in another homey phrase, referring to the quality of ideas, Deng said, "It does not matter whether the cat is black or white. So long as it catches the mouse it is a good cat." Nevertheless, when Edgar Snow interviewed Mao in 1965, Mao told him, "Liu must go." Mao remembered that he decided that on January 25, 1965, evidently the day of the chairman's last angry row with Liu. Henceforth, "Liu Shaoqi was to become capitalist roader number one; Deng, capitalist roader number two. Liu was to die, Deng to survive. Thus, starting from January 25, 1965, China's most bizarre political movement—the Cultural Revolution—would gather momentum, ultimately to encompass the whole country and its entire people."[80]

At the center of the inner circle of the Great Proletarian Cultural Revolution stood Mao's head of the secret police, Kang Sheng, his associate Chen Boda, and Marshal Lin Biao. However, more visible was the Gang of Four: Mao's now estranged wife Jiang Qing, and three veteran party workers—Zhang Chunqiao, Yao Wenyuan, and Wang Hongwen—all three entered the Politburo and two served on its Standing Committee.[81] Why did Mao unleash these persons? Harrison lists three possible reasons: first, to recapture the power that he believed was sliding away from him; second, to overcome the wrong course for China initiated by his associates; three, to set a different course than Russia's for China. However, Harrison admits, "Whether all this underlay Mao's fatalistic decision will never be known." He ventures his own interpretation: it was a "revolution not only to save his revolution but to perfect it, endangered as he believed it to be by contamination, impurities, and even treason from within. It must be saved from the men who had helped to create it."[82]

By the spring of 1966, Mao had determined to clear away the Four Olds. He told his secret police chief Kang Sheng, "We must overthrow the king of hell and liberate the little devils. We need more Monkeys to disrupt the royal palace." The Red Guards, armed with lists of enemies of the people provided by Kang's secret police, forced their victims to their knees, tied their hands behind their backs in the airplane mode, slashed off their hair in yin-yang style, and beat them unmercifully with brass-buckled belt whips in their heads and faces and kicked them savagely. These little devils were unleashed by Mao and freed to wreck his vengeance on the society that he ruled. "Their formula for extracting a 'confession' was identical to that employed by Stalin's Beria against the old Bolsheviks—no secret psychology, no truth drugs, just 'beat and then again beat.'" Though they severely threatened Zhou Enlai and Deng Xiaoping, they actually dragged Liu Shaoqi off to torture in the airplane style. Jiang Qing cried out at a mass meeting on September 18, 1968, "I'm in charge of the most important case in China. He deserves a slow death by a thousand cuts, ten thousand cuts." "Flog the cur that had fallen in the water," yelled Zhang Chunqiao, one of her Gang of Four associates." [83]

Although Marshal Lin Biao had invented the "little red book"—*Quotations from Chairman Mao*—it did not save even him from Mao's wrath. He had received official anointment as Mao's successor at the Ninth Party Congress in 1969 and was made vice chairman and official heir. He suggested that Mao become a super president, a living god, a philosopher-emperor. Such a scheme would turn over to Lin the actual levers of power. Mao had to remove Lin. As one of the leading backers of the Soviet alliance, Lin saw Mao's move toward the United States in 1971 as his end. He planned a putsch, but word leaked out. He fled to Mongolia, where his plane crashed with no survivors. That left Zhou in a powerful position as Mao embraced the Americans, inviting Henry Kissinger to Beijing. Nixon would soon follow. It also weakened the Gang of Four. Salisbury put it succinctly: "The hour of Zhou Enlai had dawned, and the end of the age of Mao was at hand. That of Deng Xiaoping was not far distant." [84] Zhou led the presidential delegation.

The Shanghai communiqué sealed the transformation of the United States from enemy to friend to eventual ally. The axis of power had shifted. Zhou swiftly moved to rehabilitate Deng Xiaoping. By August 1972 he had asked Deng to write a self-criticism to Mao. Deng admitted mistakes but swore allegiance to Mao and the Cultural Revolution. In February 1973 he was allowed to return to Beijing. Mao was in rapid decline, and Zhou was dying of abdominal cancer. Deng criticized the Gang of Four, and Mao agreed. In January 1975 Mao named him vice chairman of the Central Committee and a member of the Politburo's Standing Committee. "He now had authority to move fast and hard." Zhou and Deng declared the four modernizations: agriculture, industry, science-technology, and national defense. In Salisbury's words, "Deng Xiaoping's salvation, and China's, as he saw it, was to outrun the terrible ticking of time, as Zhou Enlai and Mao Zedong lay dying and Jiang Qing rallied her forces in the struggle for succession." Deng attacked Jiang over the film *The Pioneers*, which she did not like. She had banned the film. Mao revived it and "supposedly called Jiang 'ignorant and ill informed' and 'stupid and benighted.'" The campaign against the Gang of Four began at the end of 1975. Deng would not back down. On January 8, 1976, Zhou Enlai died and was hailed as the man who had saved China from Mao's madness. Mao died on September 9, 1976. An era had ended. [85]

Marshal Ye Jianing, a collaborator of Zhou and Deng and one of China's ten marshals, supported the conspiracy of army and party seniors who overthrew Jiang Qing and the Gang of Four. The key player in their arrest was Huo Guofeng, then first vice chairman of the party. He simply put it to neutrals and waiverers: How long would you last with the gang in power? Put another way: Whom do you trust? On October 11, 1976, they arrested the gang and put them on trial. Deng took charge on December 11, 1976. "Our goal," he said, "is to create a country which is prosperous and happy and without exploitation." Mao's communes were wiped out. Families were given a plot of land, and they signed a contract of responsibility. They could share in their profits, make their own contracts with the state, and sell wherever at the best price the market rendered. Deng opened China to the West. He rehabilitated victims through a review commission. Money and material incentives worked. The Gang of Four went to jail. As the Deng Revolution expanded, peasants were allowed to divide the land and plant what they wanted. They could hire labor, lease more land, and farm for a profit. They could set up small industries. Roads, rails, and highways were built. A new megalopolis was created, half-rural and half-urban. As Salisbury put it, "China had entered an era of glitz in which Donald Trump would have felt at home."[86]

In the autumn of 1986, Chinese politics entered a growing democratic phase, though Deng and the party elders were not comfortable with such outward symbols of it as the "Democracy Wall" where the people could put complaints. Social criticism became open, and critics such as Fang Lizhi were student heroes. Hu Yaobang seemed to side with the new democratic currents and was retired. A campaign against "bourgeois liberalization" began. Rumors circulated that Deng had lost control and was finished. A widely seen documentary, *The Yellow River Elegy*, suggested that China throw away its dynastic legacy and march with the West on the fast track. Hu Yaobang died in April 1989, and his memorial service in the Great Hall of the People instigated a student demonstration that gained momentum; a million people filled Tiananmen Square in May. The Politburo split over whether to negotiate with the students, as advocated by Zhao Ziyang. Deng resisted and declared martial law. When the student-made Chinese Goddess of Democracy appeared on the square at the end of May, a deal still may have been negotiated. Nevertheless, on June 2 Deng approved the clearing of the square by military units of the Twenty-seventh and Thirty-eighth Armies, which appeared on June 3, and a savage battle ensued. On Sunday, June 4, the square was emptied. The hardliners had won, but Deng slipped from the public eye. Neo-Maoism revived. Salisbury ended his dual biography on a melancholy note: "[Deng] had saved his mandate at the price of mortgaging its content to elderly men and women opposed to his objectives. He had been willing to abandon the reality of Marxist practice in order to jump-start China on an accelerated path to the high-tech future. Now, it seemed, he had sold his future for the sake of a fuzzy present."[87]

Salisbury's dual biography took slings and arrows as well as cautious praise. Ross Terrill thought his last book on China, though not bad, made some factual gaffs. It was, nevertheless, a fresh look. "Salisbury's [book] (who makes 5 or 6 awful slips beyond any Waldron mentions), but serious ones, nonetheless, for the theses of the book, i.e., that Kang masterminded this and that. The result is that it exaggerates his role."[88] Others chose their own slings and arrows; for example, Jon Pomfret, reviewing in the *Far Eastern Economic Review*, called the book entertaining, but believed it ignored the "ideological underpinnings" of collectivization and omitted mention of nationalization of industry. In fact, according to Pomfret, "one wonders why Salisbury had to burden his book with such an absolutist idea that gets in the way of the story." The book was best when Salisbury forgot theory and stayed with what he saw. Ann Stevenson-Yang enjoyed Salisbury's narrative. "Like many journalists, Salisbury excels in scrupulously detailed and telling description, but his book lacks binding analysis." She continues, "But if Mao was less interested in Western Marxism than in China's reformist dynasties, Salisbury has not proven it in this volume." Finally, the reviewer concluded that Salisbury failed to "illuminate the great mystery of Mao Zedong: how such imagination and empathy could coexist with such willful ignorance and cruelty." Frederick C. Teiwes in the *China Quarterly* excoriated Salisbury, as did Michael Fathers in the *Independent*. Though a great story, Fathers remarked, "Salisbury's latest contribution to history is flawed. Not because he has got his facts wrong, but because he has accepted at face value everything he has been told." Fathers continued, "he churns out every revelation and opinion uncritically, sometimes interposing but seldom illuminating." Teiwes was very severe, saying, "sadly the book disappoints on virtually all levels." There were many instances of "questionable analysis" and "flawed accounts." He criticized the book's "sloppiness with basic facts." He insisted, "Perhaps the saddest aspect of all is that Salisbury began with a promising theme and excellent access, and if he had focused his enquiry more sharply, paid more attention to the existing scholarly literature which is barely acknowledged, and approached his interview sources with more discrimination, this final book could have provided some of the benefits of his earlier contributions." Nevertheless, one reviewer concluded, "For all these limitations, *The New Emperors* remains a powerful and persuasive account of China's history throughout much of the twentieth century." The reviewer, James Ferguson, claimed, "It is a book of academic importance, but is also accessible to the general reader. Its limitations of perspective are partly based on the commitment and sympathy of the author to his subject, and also to the difficulty of interpreting recent events whose effects had not yet become fully apparent."[89]

A parallel theme runs throughout these four major nonfiction works, establishing Harrison Salisbury's claim to preeminence as author and historian. That theme is his detailed analysis of the fragility underlying the two most powerful communist regimes of the twentieth century. Extended reigns of terror by these regimes undermined their credibility. Though neither has been entirely replaced, each society nurses fledgling democracies. That transformation raises the question about the prohibitive costs incurred by communism in creating a modern industrialized state: whether Marxism and mayhem is superior to capitalism and caution. Harrison's four books, careful chronicles of the rise and fall of communist autocracies, also are stories of their gradual metamorphosis into democracies. Their tales are ongoing and even at the start of the new century, the jury is still out. Nevertheless, these books are lasting contributions to our understanding and remarkable literary pieces.

Salisbury's narratives pioneered the "new" history: using interviews and eyewitness accounts as his primary sources. Edgar Snow and Teddy White had also employed these techniques to great storytelling advantage. David Halberstam, Bob Woodward, Carl Bernstein, Walter Isaacson, and others would follow them. These journalists-turned-historians were a new breed, combining mastery of style with fresh research methods. Their generation of readers put aside traditional historians for sound, but entertaining, journalistic historians.

♦♦ 3 ♦♦

While the histories were natural extensions of his journalistic work, Salisbury also published two novels. The first in 1962, *The Northern Palmyra Affair*, and the second, *The Gates of Hell*, in 1975. Neither is a fictional masterpiece, yet each makes a worthy story. The latter was a main selection of the Literary Guild and became a mass circulation paperback. The earlier one has a tightly drawn plot, unfolding like a Sherlockian mystery. The latter takes the form of an epic Tolstoyan novel. They provided the author an outlet to display his unrivaled knowledge of Russia—down to the tiniest details of personal lives. Harrison could say much more in a fictional framework—and get away with it short of his reputation being assassinated—than by reporting truth to power in a nonfiction work.

Besides standard characterizations of evil Soviet types versus heroic ones, the plots make for page-turning excitement, regardless of occasional historical factual failings.[90] The Leningrad Affair, so skillfully analyzed in his *The 900 Days*, becomes a penetrating storyline in *The Northern Palmyra Affair*. The purge of the Zhdanov clique in post World War II Leningrad is reduced to a focus on a great sculptress, Harrison's heroine, Irena Galina. She has returned to Leningrad in the 1930s from voluntary exile and study in Paris to resume her love affair with a prominent architect, Morozov, who later engages in redesigning the war-ravaged northern Palmyra—Leningrad. By then the youthful Irena has had another affair with the poet Voronsky and had a son, Mikhail. Irena has gained fame by an exhibition of her sculptures in Paris. These are busts of famous Russian politicians, artists, and intellectuals. At the time of her death, she had finished her "End of the War Group," an antiwar statement, still covered in her studio. A rejected lover, the poet Smirnoff, denounces her. She is forced into internal exile in Tashkent with her son, where she dies. Mikhail takes her body back to Leningrad for burial, and he invites her old friends and students to her funeral. This provides a trap for the KGB to arrest "enemies of the people" and cart them off quietly. It makes for a clean sweep of top Leningrad officials such as General Orlov, Security Chief Chaikovsky, Party Secretary Ivanov, and so forth. Mikhail and Nadya, his mother's pupil, escape the net set by the evil Galpert. Orlov's speech at the cemetery, the reading of a Voronsky's poem "Ballad of a Poster Maker," and Chaikovksy's surprise arrest are dramatic high points of the novel. Galpert smiles as the novel ends with his telling his Muscovite superiors that all the victims will confess their crimes eventually by KGB methods of "beat, beat, beat."[91] As one reviewer said, "Mr. Salisbury admires them [his heroes]. At the book's end, so do we."[92]

Salisbury's second novel, *The Gates of Hell*, takes its title from what the Muscovites refer to as the infamous Lubyanka prison gates in central Moscow. The statue of the first Cheka director, Felix (Iron Felix) Dzerzhinsky, once stood in the square. This expansive historical novel moves along two railway tracks, which are destined to cross and the trains to crash. One train carries the head of the KGB, the actual historical figure Yuri Andropov, as he prepares his case against the hero of the novel, Andrei Sokolov, who is lightly based on the career of Solzhenitsyn. Andropov spends a morning doing so by trying to understand the motives of two Americans, the Morgans. They have unsuccessfully tried to convince Sokolov to leave Russia. They depart, but not before being skin-searched and robbed of two parting gifts taken by the KGB—a samovar and an icon. The icon yields a yellowed scrap of the real Alexander Herzen's 1860s paper *The Bell* and contains the phrase, "Ring out the Bell!" Just before Andropov's noon Politburo meeting, where he must justify KGB treatment of the Morgans and what he thinks should be done to the famous writer Sokolov, he realizes his winning strategy: eventually exile Sokolov. The bell statement turns out not to be a message to Sokolov's friends in the West to publish his *Gulag Archipelago*–like work *The Black Book*. Rather it was earlier smuggled into Russia by Herzen himself. Brezhnev praises Andropov's analysis, thus refuting Andropov's Politburo enemies.

The novel is largely interspersed with the writer Andrei's life, from growing up in Rostov, his romance and marriage to Rosa, and his war years as an artillery officer, to his arrest in 1945 and various internments, his release and rehabilitation in 1953 after Stalin's death, Rosa's remarriage and Andrei's new love to Stasia and marriage, his famous career with the publication of *Taishet* and *Lubyanka*, and his final arrest and exile to West Germany with the printing abroad of *The Black Book*. Readers will notice the parallel to Solzhenitsyn's *One Day in the Life of Ivan Denisovich*, *The First Circle*, and *The Gulag Archipelago*. Special moments of high drama in the novel are the exposé of Andrei at the Politburo meeting and Andrei's speech after arriving at West Berlin. Like Andrei's model, Solzhenitsyn, his many trials and tribulations in the Gulag are exhaustively treated. As the cover jacket promised, "A towering hero whose passion for Russia was his birthright, whose conscience was formed in the crucible of the Gulag, and whose genius and courage defied the awesome power of the Soviet state and its servants, even as they ruthlessly tore him away from the arms of the woman he loved."[93]

Harrison entered his eighty-fourth year in 1993. Behind him lay a career of outstanding journalism, both domestic and foreign. As an author, he had written, by that time, twenty-eight books, four of them histories, two novels, and the remainder summaries of important assignments and scoops that were mainly focused on Russia, America, and China. It was now time to reflect on his achievements. He chose to do that in a unique way: he interpreted his era by pointing out unlikely heroes. Over the years of the twentieth century, he was a pesky seeker of the truth, exposing lies, reporting truth to power. Now he spotlighted the careers of unsung heroes who had also cast pearls of truth before the swine and suffered the consequences. His last book, number twenty-nine, did that in the tradition of the great gadfly.

Chapter Ten

The Great Gadfly

Sometimes the journalist's duty takes him far from home. Sometimes he finds his subject in the community where he lives or in his own country. But his duty to my way of thinking is always the same: To seek out the truth as best he can, to present it as simply and forcefully as possible, and to hope that his readers will then act with wisdom and intelligence in the directions of a better community, a better nation or a better world.
—Harrison E. Salisbury, December 27, 1967[1]

Harrison E. Salisbury's career spanned more than six decades, from the 1930s through the early 1990s. It encompassed a career with United Press through World War II, freelancing between jobs, with the *New York Times* until his retirement at the end of 1973, and as author and literary gadfly until his death in 1993. Throughout, he found time to publish twenty-nine books, write many articles and dispatches, and appear on many lecture circuits. He was, most notably, the recipient of a Pulitzer Prize for international reporting in 1955, and again in 1957, as shared with all the foreign journalists of the *New York Times.* He got the Overseas Press Club Award and the George Polk Memorial Award for foreign reporting in 1957 and 1966. After retirement, he was president of the American Academy and Institute of Arts and Letters from 1975 to 1976 and of the Authors League from 1980 to 1985. His career as a foreign correspondent took him to every imaginable place on the globe. His three areas of greatest interest were Russia, China, and America. When he passed away in 1993, he was widely recognized as one of the giants in American journalism and an author of distinction. His circle of friends included the high and mighty. Their tributes to his life were meaningful and sustained. They agreed that he was a seeker of truth—a harrowing pursuit

filled with mortal danger. Indeed, Harrison was the great gadfly, one who, as
the dictionary says, "upsets the status quo by posing upsetting or novel
questions, or just being an irritant."[2] A sampling of his wide-ranging opinions, especially the cockiest of them, gives vivid evidence of this.

◆◆ 1 ◆◆

From his earliest dispatches, Harrison was concerned about truth and justice,
as evidenced in his piece on Senator Huey Long's assassination. This interest
continued and grew stronger, especially toward the end of his career at the
Times and in his retirement. He often did a series of articles and speeches for
various organizations, making him stand out as one of America's chief critics. They represent a remarkable cache of social and political criticism.

The sixties were an important time for Salisbury. Turner Catledge had
asked him to take the job of national editor in 1962. He had remarried in
1964. Punch Sulzberger appointed Clifton Daniel as editor in 1964, and
Daniel asked Salisbury to be his assistant managing editor. It was the high
tide of Salisbury's active career as a journalist, though he eschewed management as much as possible in favor of writing. He continued to advocate
forthright journalism, as when he wrote Catledge in 1968 suggesting a bolder
approach to the news in all its aspects, especially race relations. That meant
reporting the ideas of Stokeley Carmichael or Rap Brown, no matter how far
they differed with the *Times*. Ignoring them would not make them vanish.
The paper had been remiss.[3] It meant reporting truth to power, whatever the
personal consequences.

One of Harrison's lasting contributions to the *New York Times* was his
initiation of the op-ed page on September 26, 1970. The *Times* was one of the
first papers to do so, and Harrison was often referred to as the page's origina-
tor, although he shared that distinction with former editorial page editor John
Oakes. "I created the Op-Ed at a moment when the country had entered an
uncharted, unproclaimed, and largely unrecognized revolution."[4] Its goal, as
he put it, was to "present an alternate opinion to those expressed by *Times*
editorials and columnists." It was an instant hit and immediately copied by
news competitors. It gathered almost one hundred big names a month, gar-
nering one to two hundred submissions each week.[5]

Harrison's original idea was for it to represent the whole range of opinions and ideas as expressed by institutions, *Times* columnists, and other
writers, thinkers, and policy makers, signed or unsigned. It would be a forum
for the exchange and clash of ideas, not exclusively political, but covering all
intellectual interests. There had been so much opposition at one point that he
had given up on it. His idea included cartoons, sketches, or photographs on a

six-column page, two for ads or a news index. It would fall under the editorial department's control. Op-ed would be weighted for opinion "contrary to that expressed editorially by the *Times*, but of course by no means limited to it." Though keyed to the news, op-eds were to go beyond the news in a "more philosophical way than is possible in the news columns." Its editor would have wide freedom, and yet be responsible to the editor of the editorial page. "I do not," he wrote, "view my own role as that of dictator over the Op-Ed Page but rather as a guide and counselor with, however, veto authority."[6]

Three powerful editors had fought for its control—John Oakes of the editorial page, Lester Markel of the Sunday *New York Times*, and Turner Catledge (and later Abe Rosenthal) of the daily *New York Times*. However, Punch Sulzberger gave it to the *Times* leading curmudgeon, Salisbury.[7] Salisbury explained this new contribution to journalism he had cocreated as a "place where men and women could express themselves on what was closest to their hearts, strongest in their passions, most fiercely in their principles. The criteria for Op-Ed could not have been more simple: to have something challenging to say and to say it with eloquence."[8]

There would be no curtains for the op-ed—Iron, Silken, or Bamboo. This was emphasized by accompanying images or what Harrison termed a "symbiosis of creative forms." He recognized that art contributed something new: "The task of Op-Ed images is to create an environment which extends and deepens the impact of the word." It was not a cartoon or a caricature. Rather, the graphics established the atmospherics or milieu. The artists tended to be Europeans, while most of the authors were Americans. The reason, perhaps, was the more sensitive artists needed distance from the subject of the writer to capture the essence of the story. In the op-ed both authors and artists epitomized the critic. That is what mattered most to Harrison.[9]

Already in 1969, the meddlesome role of America's number one gadfly had begun to capture public attention, as it had with his Hanoi dispatches in 1966–1967. That had catapulted him to international prominence and fame. In a perceptive talk he gave in 1966 to a college audience, he compared the relative positions of Russia and China in 1945. He conceded that Stalin's Russia had reached the apex of its power, whereas China was midway between recovering from war and beginning a revolutionary period. With Mao's victory in 1949, China's emergence started. Its past two hundred years had been a dark age. In 1966 China was still cut off from the West, even from Russia. China concluded that Russia might even be in league with the United States. It was not impossible for Chinese leadership to decide the West, including Russia, had encircled it. China's greatest problem was its rapidly expanding population. Would this problem shatter all prospects for peace? Salisbury most feared a Peking that perceived the world with no differences between Washington and Moscow. If that were the case, he speculated, a program needed to be instituted by the United States that related China to the rest of the world.[10]

His "orbit of China" and his Hanoi dispatches deepened this speculation. He had a proclivity to think outside of the box. The prestigious establishment journal *Foreign Affairs* invited him to do a piece on Southeast Asia. Salisbury titled it "Image and Reality in Indochina." With the death of President Franklin D. Roosevelt, it began, restraints were taken off the great prewar colonial powers. Between 1945 and 1950, France reengaged in Indochina. Mao's success in 1949 and France's weakness in Indochina restored American interest. It looked to Washington as if communism would roll across Asia under Soviet tutelage. President Harry S. Truman agreed to a ten-million-dollar French credit to prop up the French puppet Bai Dai regime against communist Ho Chi Minh's North Vietnam. Instead of finding rapprochement with Mao, America saw a "singular unity and direction of a Muscovite communist menace in Asia (which in fact did not exist) and the two communist powers perceived a unified aggressive U.S. policy (which in fact did not exist)." That idea behind him, Salisbury went to his next hypothesis about the cause and origin of the Korean War: "I believe," he wrote, "the war was instigated by Stalin but that his target was not, as is supposed, the United States but actually communist China."[11] Those stings hurt his establishment readers. He had to explain.

Stalin, Salisbury emphasized, had little confidence in foreign communist leaders and had a troublesome record with Mao, whose strategy appeared opposed to his. Tito's break further exasperated his paranoia. Stalin had been busy purging Eastern Europe and ridding himself of China experts and sympathizers such a Mikhail Borodin and Anna Louise Strong. He clung to Northeastern China and Outer Mongolia. It seemed to Stalin that the United States did not include Korea in its Pacific defense line. Secretary of State Dean Acheson had not mentioned it in a National Press Club address of January 12, 1950, nor had other U.S. officials when referring to America's defense perimeter. "There could be no reason for the omission of Korea (although Acheson continues to argue otherwise)," thought Salisbury, "except that it was not, in fact, on the U.S. defense perimeter." Therefore, Stalin felt he could take that for granted. If Korea could be overrun, Stalin would dominate Mao from Mongolia, Manchuria, and Korea. Stalin gave the North Korean dictator Kim Il-sung permission to attack, thus triggering the Korean War based on mistaking U.S. policy. Instead of noninterference, he got massive retaliation. Salisbury concluded that Stalin's position was distorted, but so was Truman's.[12]

The United States blamed China for the aggression. Truman ordered General Douglas MacArthur to defend Korea; he sent the Seventh Fleet to the Formosa Straits; he gave military aid to the Philippines; he deployed a military mission to Indochina. Yet the Chinese had little or no part in this, though Stalin probably regarded North Korea's attack of the South as reckless. China's intervention in September to October 1950 confirmed that. "If his [Stalin's] gambit for getting a stranglehold around Peking had failed, at least he had succeeded in embroiling two of his major antagonists." Nevertheless, even the Chinese had deluded themselves into thinking that American intervention in Korea was a springboard into China itself.[13] Given this background, Salisbury considered Indochina directly.

President Dwight Eisenhower's secretary of state, John Foster Dulles, shared the Acheson-Truman doctrine that Ho Chi Minh was the southern flank of China's common front. Neither the Korean truce nor the Geneva Agreement of 1954 shook his belief. "But neither then nor later was it true, as Dulles and many U.S. policy-makers supposed, that Ho was a 'puppet' of Peking or that Peking was a 'puppet' of Moscow." By 1965–1966, Salisbury postulated, American distortion and misperception had peaked with President Lyndon Johnson's bombing campaign—just at the time of Salisbury's Hanoi dispatches at the end of 1966 and beginning of 1967. Hanoi itself, as Salisbury's interview with officials there confirmed, came to regard the Unites States in the image of France. "It was generally asserted and assumed that the United States simply wished to replace France as the exploiting colonial power in Indochina." Mao saw it as another attempt at a springboard to attack China, even to the extent of collaborating with Russia. Perhaps, Salisbury continued, it was one more rationale for the Cultural Revolution, launched in mid-1966, to strengthen China's youth for the coming war with the United States. Moreover, Moscow feared the Vietnamese War could turn into a U.S.-USSR war. Yet as it wore on, the war increasingly pitted China against Russia. Once America began pulling out, Harrison maintained, the North would strike the South, not fearing a U.S. reescalation. He ended this article on an extraordinary note: "And perhaps one of the greatest illusions is the American belief that Hanoi, having been, as it feels, cheated both in the French settlement of 1945 and the Geneva settlement of 1954, is likely to put much credence in any end of the war which is not achieved by tilting the military balance in its favor."[14] Saigon fell to Hanoi on April 30, 1975.

♦♦ 2 ♦♦

In the mid-1960s, Salisbury gave a speech at St. Lawrence University in Canton, New York. America, he contended, not the communist states, had undergone the most profound changes—a triple revolution. The Iron Curtain remained almost stagnant since 1945. By contrast, the twenty years since World War II had seen in the United States revolutions in technology, productivity, and organization. Under communism, there were fragmentations, rivalries, and people's movements. He had not yet been to China, but "I think," he said, referring to America, "that we achieve revolutionary effects in this country at a pace which makes those revolutionary movements look as if they were standing still." He liked illustrating this by describing a conversation Eric Johnston, head of the U.S. Chamber of Commerce, had had with Stalin. Johnson had suggested to Stalin that American experts on retail trade and distribution help Russia. Stalin complained, "Before you can distribute you have to have something to distribute." Harrison pointed out to his college audience: "It is literally true though not as true today as it was then, that the system simply does not produce enough goods to satisfy the needs of its people." What would happen, Harrison wondered, if you could drop a million copies of the Sears and Roebuck catalog from a U-2 spy plane? That is all the CIA needed to do, he joked: "It would be the end of the Communist world."[15]

By the end of the sixties, Salisbury had grown less optimistic about the land of the triple revolution. In 1974 he published a criticism of the American press. He faulted the Fourth Estate for abdicating its social and political responsibilities for security—decreasing its own exposure to harassment from the public and government. He called his age one of disillusionment and disarray. Harrison blamed President Richard Nixon, Watergate, and the Pentagon Papers controversy for the public's lack of belief in the credibility of their government, their cynicism, moral collapse, and venality—even a global public angst. In a leap of fantasy, he sketched a scenario of how a proposed U.S. invasion of Cuba might be carried out and the press's response on discovering it. He asked, "Would the President and his Secretary of State intervene to try to keep the *New York Times* from publishing word of a planned American invasion of Cuba? . . . Certainly they would." His fictionalized scenario was farfetched, but nevertheless, he argued, censorship would linger and the media would show "remarkable sycophancy in supporting whatever President Ford and Secretary Kissinger propose." The media would attack one another: that happened to Harrison's Hanoi dispatches; that happened with the publication of the Pentagon Papers; that happened during the Watergate conspiracy.[16]

Salisbury admitted, amid rampant sycophancy and commercialism, there were notable exceptions. For instance, there was Seymour Hersh's exposure of My Lai, or David Halberstam's detailed reporting from Saigon. Nevertheless, consolidating the media into great chains and monopolies worked against the courageous journalism of dedicated reporters. Even though television followed valiant reporting, "Without print, however, there is no reason to believe that these breakthrough achievements of journalism would have occurred." Television and radio were secondary. In the future, the public would continue relying on major networks, newspapers, and occasional assistance from news magazines. Government would continue manipulating. The public itself, in this crisis of the Fourth Estate, suffered from the credibility gap and responded, "So what else is new?" Public skepticism, resulting from degradation and debasement of the Fourth Estate, led to limits on freedom. There was, in his mind, a "symbiotic relationship between free print, free thought, and a free society." No society, in his opinion, could rely for its salvation on the integrity of a few individuals and their media outlets. Rather, its salvation required everyone's work. "It rests with society at large and its insistence that reporters tell it like it is, regardless of the high and mighty of the land and of the consequences."[17]

On April 19, 1978, Harrison delivered a speech, "American Society after 20 Years of Radical Change," at Columbia University's annual University Seminars dinner. In it he identified major areas of radical change: race relations and equal rights under the law; women's liberation and gender equality; environment and the green movement; the antiwar movement and world peace; government reform and participatory democracy; education and the youth rebellion; religion and family values. The list, to be sure, was not exhaustive. "I believe that we have gone through in the last two decades and a little bit more, the most profound series of changes which American society has ever encompassed since the days of the Founding Fathers." It all started, according to him, with *Brown v. the Board of Education* in 1954. That signaled the end of segregation. As he put it, "beginning with that event this nation has undergone a progressive examination and radical criticism and radical change of many of our great institutions." Desegregation went from Woolworth's five-and-dime store sit-ins to the banishment of discrimination in public places. It was accomplished without "falling apart, without—as has happened in some other countries—falling into the most desperate and bloodiest civil wars." From there, all the other changes followed, like links in a chain, beginning with inequities in race and color to a "veritable explosion in this country of movements for eliminating inequities of other types." Of all the movements for diverse sexuality, women's rights were the most notable, but not alone: "to remove as far as humanly possible all legal barriers and social barriers so far as we can so that all of us are actually standing on the same ground with the same kind of rights and privileges." Those rights and privileges would be not just a matter of standing alongside one another or of sloganeering.[18]

The other radical changes sprang up from popular movements among the people. Environmentalism demanded security in natural factors—clean air to breathe, clean water to drink, a clean land to settle. The Vietnam antiwar movement spoke not only against political leadership, but also for the grassroots. So did what might be called the Watergate Movement—a broad coalition calling for a popular voice in government and demanding purity in its actions. He called it participatory democracy. Much of it had to do with the rebellion of the young. Finally, there were basic changes in the family, marriage, and religion growing out of the reforms of Pope John XXIII. All this happened quickly, yet more fundamentally than in 1776. The American people began to transform the world.

Harrison looked for Russian parallels, such as 1917. The old regime was too rigid. It crumbled. America was different in replacing the old. "We haven't," he concluded, "proclaimed ourselves as new geniuses with a great revolutionary doctrine. We haven't pinned up a set of principles on the wall and raised a flag for the world to rally about. But we have gone forward making a practical demonstration of what can be done."[19]

Besides America, two other areas returned as major themes of his writings in retirement: Russia and China. In 1983 and again in 1990, Salisbury wrote challenging, upsetting, and irritating articles on Russia, "The Russia Nobody Knows" and "Roll Over Lenin," both of which ran in *Penthouse*. William F. Buckley Jr. interviewed Harrison, along with Robert Conquest and Christopher Hitchens, on "Firing Line Special Edition: Harvest of Despair," on September 4, 1986, about a Canadian film documentary of the great Soviet famine of 1931–1933 that major American networks rejected but which PBS showed.

In the first article, "The Russia Nobody Knows," he maintained Russia changed little from the czars to the commissars, contrary to the "cardboard façade of Communism and the cold war."[20] He admitted it took a long time before he realized Lenin and Stalin failed. If you wanted to understand the actual Russia, "you had to peer deeply into the soil in which Russia's fears, hopes, frustrations, and real goals are nourished." Instead of communism taking root, youngsters were westernizing to the jitterbug and boogie-woogie. The Kremlin did not stop Western pop culture from penetrating the Iron Curtain. This other world was not the Kremlin's, not the Sovietologists', not the cold warriors' in Moscow and Washington. It was Russia's private world. It went on regardless of who occupied the Kremlin. Harrison differed from the so-called experts, those who came to Russian studies from an academic approach—one often influenced by contemporary affairs and Marxism-Leninism, with all its political jargon. So much, as far as Harrison was concerned, for scientific studies, so much for long-range calculations over opportunity and expediency. In the planned society, "no one ever knew what was going to happen next." Still, he had to read *Pravda*. It was more important to know what *Pravda* did not say. In his study of Russia, he found Stalin fit the pattern. Harrison looked for Russia in the birch forests rather than the wooden words of communism.[21]

The "Firing Line" interview was a contentious affair with Salisbury dominating the discussion about the Canadian film. Salisbury inserted a historical note on the Ukraine for the viewers with the object of showing its nationalistic spirit. It was too independent for Stalin. At the time of collectivization, it resisted. Stalin starved Russia's breadbasket into submission at the cost of at least seven million lives. It was a holocaust, contrary to what Walter Duranty of the *New York Times* then reported. He retired as Moscow correspondent of the *New York Times* on April 1, 1934, though with an annual retainer of five thousand dollars to work three or four months a year in Moscow. Alfred Ochs, publisher of the *Times*, had lost confidence in him. Many on the *Times* saw Duranty as "little more than a press agent not only for the Bolsheviks but for the worst Bolshevik of all, Stalin."[22]

When Buckley commented that Salisbury thought Foreign Minister Maxim Litvinov a hero, Salisbury interjected that Litvinov was not an executioner: "He was outside of this. This [was] not his realm [though he knew about it]. [But] he stood out against Stalin on a whole lot of issues, Bill, and boy, anybody who stood out against Stalin under those conditions gets a vote from me."

Reporters did not break the famine story. They were for communism, at first. However, they began to change when they saw what was happening—except for Walter Duranty of the *New York Times*, who received the Pulitzer Prize in 1932 for his reporting of the famine. Duranty always tried to cozy up with Stalin but did not get the first foreign correspondent's interview—Eugene Lyons did. "[Duranty] did not, and he was sore as hell because he didn't."

Harrison again turned to Stalin's killing of millions of Ukrainians. It was an act as horrible as the Nazi genocide of the Jews. Perhaps it was worse, only in the sense that Stalin victimized his own people "repeatedly from the very earliest times again and again and again." Harrison continued, "He wiped out everybody who was close to him and then his circles grew broader and broader and broader until in this final madness of the Doctors' Plot in the period in which he was about to die, he was going to kill off the Ukrainians, he was going to ship all the rest of the Jews in Russia off to Siberia. God knows who he wasn't going to kill."

Buckley and the interviewees believed the networks should have aired the Canadian film, *Harvest of Despair*, however grisly a parallel it was to the Nazi genocide of the Jews.[23]

The second *Penthouse* article, "Roll over Lenin . . . Tell Gorbachev the News," was an obituary on Lenin's Soviet Russia. It was not a rosy picture on what would follow the USSR. "Anyone who claims he can write the future in large, easy-to-read Cyrillic is either a boob or a charlatan."[24] The editor selected Harrison's article as a cover feature under the title "The Soviet Union's Self-Destruction." Harrison was not one to fall in line with the crowd, proclaiming Gorbachev's success in radically transforming Soviet communism into a socialist democracy. The great gadfly simply stated, "Lenin's Russia is dead." He took pleasure in having Ronald Reagan "thrust the final killing lance into the floundering and dying monster that he once called 'the Evil Empire.'" No technology, no miracle by Russia's elites, no perestroika could save it. The arms race would prove it could not produce both guns and butter simultaneously. He quoted a Soviet economist, "You bastards! You are going to win the Cold War. You are going to make us spend and spend to keep up with you. And our lousy economy can't stand that!" With a gross national product only half of America's, the USSR's side of the arms race "ground into the flesh of every citizen." The stakes got higher and higher as Kennedy, Johnson, Nixon, and Carter poured it on. When Reagan "plopped Star Wars into the pot, someone had to cry uncle. Gorbachev did."[25]

Salisbury indicated that even as early as Stalin's death in 1953, Soviet leaders knew their system was on the rocks. They did not know how to handle the "most colossal screw-up a nation ever faced." It reminded him of the disaster created by the Japanese militarists. It took Japan fifty years to rebuild. The Russians could not match the Japanese work ethic and quality. Worst of all, Harrison insinuated, "Moscow today [is] a haunting resemblance to the Russia of the last days of the czar." He meant overheated, hysterical, and corrupt. Anything was for sale, but in dollars only. It was the same nightmare as faced Czar Nicholas II, but "not quite so stylish nor so decadent." Muscovites argued about which moment they were again living through—late 1916 or January 1917. After New Year's Day 1917, it was all over for the monarchy. When would it now end? Muscovites said it took seventy years to get into this mess. It would take another seventy to get out of it. If you spoke to them of glasnost and perestroika, their eyes glazed over. They would respond, "What else is new? Where's the sausage?" Of the differences between Boris Yeltsin and Mikhail Gorbachev, they said, "They're all the same." They expected blood in Red Square any day. Not even the most radical "500-Day Plan" could save them. Pessimism ruled. It was worse than Hitler's invasion in 1941. It was worse than Stalin's final madness in 1953.[26]

When did Soviet Russia begin to die? Salisbury picked July 17, 1918. On that day, Lenin ordered the execution of the royal family and its attendants. It was, Salisbury said, the central act of the Bolshevik Revolution. In 1990 Moscow's Maly Theater presented "I Will Repay." In it, Lenin gives the order to execute, not just the czar and czarina, but to exterminate the entire royal family. Lenin "put in place the whole apparatus that Stalin so skillfully used in his murderous climb to power and even more murderous rule." Given this history, two views of the future emerged: one of chaos and bloodshed, or Russia reduced to its Slavic core. Holders of both views realized that "Lenin's Communist Soviet Union is now as dead as its creator."[27] Harrison summarized the United States' historical relationship to Russia when he remarked that the hottest topic in Moscow in 1991 was the nature of American democracy. As always the great gadfly, he remained gloomy: "Whether they would be able to work it all out before total chaos set in was an open question. Nobody was certain."[28]

♦♦ 4 ♦♦

Salisbury left two interesting pieces about China at the end of his life. The first dealt with American reporting on China from the days of Edgar Snow to 1990. The other was a provocative interview he did on Brian Lamb's TV series *Booknotes*. Lamb focused on Harrison's eyewitness account of the 1989 Tiananmen Square massacre.

The romance of American reporters with China began on July 6, 1928. Edgar Snow docked at Shanghai. Though out for adventure, he grabbed a job reporting, married Helen Foster in 1931, and arrived in northern Shaanxi in 1936 for his classic account of Mao, *Red Star over China*. Anna Louise Strong, Agnes Smedley, Henry Luce, and Teddy White followed. They initiated the romantic-realist school of journalism: "It is first-hand eye-witness reporting placed in the context of personal experience which seeks to illuminate complex social and/or political problems." The style was still in vogue. Dan Rather would report from Tiananmen Square for CBS at the start of the demonstrations in June 1989, until the soldiers pulled the plug on him.[29]

Lamb told Salisbury, "You write that maybe a Chinese leader's call for the elimination of chopsticks with the replacement of the knife and fork may have caused the whole thing."[30] Harrison admitted a long train of circumstances brought him to that conclusion. One day Hu Yaobang, Deng's right-hand man and president of the PRC, told Salisbury of his campaign for China to abandon chopsticks. They were old-fashioned, unsanitary, and a symbol of ancient China. That caused a furor. They represented China's essence. Chopsticks became the basis for a political campaign against Hu: if he ate with a fork and knife, he could not be trusted. Hu Yuobang was too progressive. Chopsticks played a role in Deng Xiaoping's dismissal of him. Chopsticks connected him to the reform movement led by students in Tiananmen Square. He became the students' champion of reform. When they demonstrated after his death on April 15, 1989, he was their model of reform. They flocked to the square in May and demonstrated. He had been general secretary of the party and head of the Communist Youth Organization. He used to serve Salisbury American-style knife-and-fork meals of steaks instead of noodles. China, he said, was moving into the Western world and, of course, that meant no chopsticks. Conversation was lively, especially on American topics. Hu Yuobang favored Nixon as the greatest postwar president, and he and Nixon exchanged letters and books each month. Hu was very much Deng's disciple, especially in 1977–1978. They were pragmatists. Hu clung to Deng's frequently quoted idea that it does not matter whether the cat is black or white as long as it catches mice.

Lamb asked about how the book came to be written. Salisbury claimed it was an instant book. By that he meant both the hard and paperback editions appeared simultaneously. It became available a month after submission. The book was fast paced and written in diary style. How, Lamb wondered, was Harrison able to do so many things so quickly, especially at the age of eighty? Salisbury admitted he was energetic. He'd worked rapidly and intensely all of his life. There were errors, but nothing major. He had zipped the book off, and there was not much time for proofing.

Salisbury had had no idea a big story was breaking. He and a crew from NHK TV (Japanese Broadcasting System) went over to do a documentary for the fortieth anniversary of the Communist Revolution in China. They only chanced to arrive on June 2 and got a front-row seat for one of the biggest stories of 1989. He had been hired due to his expertise. Japanese Broadcasting had come to him because he was well known as a specialist on China. They wanted a program with a historical basis, not spot reporting. The Japanese gave him a free hand and discussed ideas and an outline. They would photograph major events of Mao's movement chronologically, especially doing preliminary work in China and New York City for about one month. They expected to conduct interviews with leading politicians, including Deng. Harrison would stand at the Great Wuhan Bridge, explaining it as Mao's first great industrial accomplishment. But on arrival in Beijing, the students were on the verge of being shot. After the massacre, Harrison and his Japanese TV team got out to the countryside to do location shots, not the interviews. They had to substitute earlier interviews and archival pictures. They increased Harrison's commentary to finish the documentary film in time for the October 1 anniversary.

Salisbury explained his career for Lamb—UP, the *New York Times*, Moscow, Hanoi, and so forth. His book *The Long March* made him famous in China. He'd come there about a dozen times, usually six weeks or more at a time, and sometimes four to six months, over a fifteen-year period.

Lamb was interested in his writing procedure. Salisbury used *The Long March* to illustrate. He said he first read everything in English and interviewed everyone in the United States in connection with it. He sent a list to China of about forty persons who were an important part of it. Eight were already dead. When he got to China, he already had a good working knowledge of what remained to be done. He was going to follow Mao's route, but not their doubling back and forth. He received permissions to go, though many places were closed to all other travelers. Harrison had been working for a dozen years to get all those permissions. He spent two and a half months on the Long March trail—by foot, mule, cart, and jeep. He interviewed all the important surviving people. He got into the Chinese archives. Some of them were inconclusive or propagandistic. "I think I gave them a pretty good lesson in what an American newspaperman or researcher expects by way of facts." Salisbury only used a tape recorder in exceptional circumstances and preferred his own notes. Each evening on his old 1942 portable Remington he typed his handwritten notes, which were kept in the form of a journal or diary. Often he reproduced the exact record in his book.

For Tiananmen, he had not planned a book, but afterward realized that "indeed this would be a book and it had historical interest." His notes appeared right there, mistakes and all. He had little chance to do some correcting. Though tired, he worked at it between four and seven in the morning. He took breakfast, then reread and reworked the narrative. He hoped it would "give people a precise account of exactly what happened at Tiananmen." The students were on a crusade to improve the government, not to rebel. Instead of working with them, the government "rose up and crushed them in an effort to demonstrate that they still had the power and that nobody could tell them what to do." The New China with a democratic process that had been evolving over Deng's ten years was "blasted away" in a few hours, but not forever halted. The beat would again be picked up, but the cost was great. The students were called bandits or bad men, the same term Chiang Kai-shek used to describe Mao's movement.

Dan Rather's TV reporting was accurate. So was Harrison's book. Though the Chinese constructed an alternate theory, the Tiananmen Square massacre was the responsibility of the party elders and Deng, not the bandits. "I think he [Rather] gave us a very accurate picture of these idealistic young people and he gave us at least a little glimpse of the arbitrary action of which the regime was capable when they pulled the plug on his broadcasts." They also blamed the foreigners. Harrison and his Japanese TV crew escaped Beijing and went to film their documentary in the countryside. They left the capital on June 5 and flew to Wuhan, where manifestations of Tiananmen were all about.

Once he returned, he called his editor, who wanted a quick book. He handed over a raw copy, full of penciling. The editor took it and made a clean copy for publication in early August. It was on bookstands by September 1, 1989. There were some incorrect little facts here and there, "But there is nothing wrong in the book. I think it has the right mood. It has the right explanation for why the Chinese acted as they did. And I think I have accurately portrayed the response of the students and most particularly of the people of Beijing." In addition, he still planned another book, if he could get back to China: a dual biography of Mao and Deng, which he had been working on for the last three years. He thought the students' ideas would eventually win, but he could be wrong. Harrison expected another struggle, perhaps even a civil war. He hoped it would not happen. Salisbury wished for a New China that would again pick up the beat, though it would not happen tomorrow, or in two years.

Would China never be the same again? Lamb asked. Harrison agreed in the sense of the students' conception of the New China, that is, the model of what Dan Rather and the others saw in the student movement. They were thinking about the student movement. They were wrong about that but not about China never being the same.[31] Once again, Harrison had played the great gadfly.

♦♦ 5 ♦♦

One week after Salisbury died, his last book was published. He titled it *Heroes of My Time.* Not just anyone claimed Harrison's attention. The people he admired may have had flaws, but they were not afraid to stand alone in the face of adversity. He liked writers, especially journalists, those who exposed evil, corruption, and crimes. His choices also revealed something of himself: "I know a bit about this. I have sometimes found myself the only one in a crowd to cry that the emperor is wearing no clothes."[32]

The most interesting feature of his heroes is that they, like him, fit the definition of gadflies. All were upset at the status quo, and all acted as irritants against it. His ultimate hero was an unknown person who stepped in front of a moving column of tanks on Tiananmen Square, waved his hand for them to stop, and then disappeared into the crowd. He left no name, no trace, only that quick glimpse that told the world one brave man did not fear to stand against the armor and the guns. Harrison's selection of such contrary persons included only a few celebrities, persons such as Alexander Solzhenitsyn, Nikita Khrushchev, Zhou Enlai, and Robert Kennedy. The rest were relatively unknown, even unrecognizable, such as Iphigene Sulzberger, Liu Binyan, and Sister Huang Roushan. They had their blemishes and were often unpleasant persons. Nevertheless, Harrison insisted, "Each of them had something to offer each of us—the rarest of qualities in today's cardboard world—personal bravery."[33]

Take, for instance, his startling inclusion of Khrushchev. This communist dictator had the courage to expose Stalin's crimes. More importantly, according to Harrison, he recognized that capitalism had achieved Marx's goal, while communism remained far distant. In retirement, Khrushchev began to admit some of his misunderstandings—Mikhail Sholakov was a fraud; Boris Pasternak was not.[34]

One hero he included was a sure bet for anyone who knew Salisbury: Alexander I. Solzhenitsyn. Here was a stinging voice who dared to challenge American values head on. In Solzhenitsyn's Harvard Yard speech of 1978, he denounced American youth for objecting to the Vietnam War, excoriated rock 'n' roll, indicted the U.S. intelligentsia for cowardice, trashed the Declaration of Independence for evoking the pursuit of happiness, reviled the welfare state, and saw America as indifferent to good and evil. Here was the courage and frankness of one who even defended the right of people not to know. Solzhenitsyn had, in Harrison's estimation, poured all of his life into that speech. "I thought," Salisbury remarked, "he had made a grave but understandable mistake in this conclusion." The conclusion was that "American civilization was not really a serious one." What was more, as far as Salisbury was concerned, was that, as a revenge on Solzhenitsyn, the "New York literary community dropped his name down the memory hole."[35]

Salisbury had previously corresponded with Solzhenitsyn concerning publishing matters. They first met in person when the Russian gave his "A World Split Apart" address at Harvard's Class Day Afternoon Exercises on Thursday, June 8, 1978. Harrison came to Cambridge that rainy morning to prepare for WGBM-TV of Boston an analysis of the Nobel laureate's remarks. Tom Whitney, English translator of the first two volumes of *The Gulag Archipelago*, had invited the Solzhenitsyns to his Connecticut home for the following weekend. The Whitneys' guests for Saturday's dinner party included the Salisburys, Arthur Miller and his wife, and William Styron and his wife. Harrison's notes about these two occasions render a personal, perceptive view.

Harrison arrived at Harvard Yard just after Solzhenitsyn had received an honorary degree. He reviewed an advance text of the speech, labeling it, "an extremely strong approach, the strongest he has made, and the first in which in logical and coherent form he has placed his essential criticism of the West." It was, Harrison thought, also an assault on the evils of communism. The United States was weak, according to Solzhenitsyn, misunderstanding Soviet Russia's threat, unable to summon the necessary courage because of America's materialist glut. The Bay Colony's Increase Mather, Harrison speculated, would have been more receptive to Solzhenitsyn's words than contemporary Harvard dons, especially in terms of the speech's good and evil themes.

Solzhenitsyn had harsh words for American liberalism, attacked the press, defended the right not to know, and excoriated American ultra-legalism as contrary to a higher law. He blamed Renaissance humanism for that. The West offered no model for Russia. Russians would find their own way out of the suffering caused by communism. Morality had a role in diplomacy. He cautioned against the Chinese as future Stalinists.[36] Salisbury believed the address "a very Russian speech. A biblical speech. I could see him as a prophet of the Third Rome, pronouncing anathema on the infamy of the Roman church and its break with Byzantium."[37]

There were unusual delays as the Harvard crowd reassembled after their postcommencement "spreads" for Solzhenitsyn's two o'clock address. Harrison took the opportunity to introduce himself to Mrs. Natalie Solzhenitsyn and said hello to Mrs. Irena Alberti, the "factotum" of Solzhenitsyn's ensemble. Her chore was to read the speech's English translation simultaneously over the loudspeakers. She greeted Harrison warmly and told him to defend Solzhenitsyn in the WGBM-TV show.

Finally, the speaker and his Harvard entourage passed down the yard and onto the platform. Solzhenitsyn spoke in Russian at a moderate pace, with a minimum of gestures. Alberti's flat and technical English reading drowned out the speaker. Salisbury claimed Solzhenitsyn was a "speaker of enormous force and range," so that Alberti's blotting out was unfortunate. Almost everyone remained seated instead of bolting out over the great author's harsh remarks. Instead, there were, Harrison recalled, twenty-five rounds of applause throughout and a tumultuous ovation at the end. Solzhenitsyn was pleased with how enthusiastically young people responded. Harrison was impressed that Harvard's elders initiated most of the applause, especially over Solzhenitsyn's antimaterialism remarks. Harrison pointedly noted there was no applause when the speaker called for the United States to stand up to Soviet provocations.

Afterward, Harrison rushed to the platform, tapping Solzhenitsyn on the shoulder. He turned and spoke, "Yes, Gospodin Salisbury." Harrison continued, "He brightened, a big smile came over his face and he said, 'Garrison!' At last, we met. I told him the speech had been terrific and that I was doing a commentary on it and would see him tomorrow."

Harrison sauntered over to John Kenneth Galbraith's home where some friends had met. At the doorway, John K. Fairbank and Adam Ulam—Harvard's China and Russia experts—chatted. Ulam maintained Solzhenitsyn said nothing new and no one was interested in him. That remark was, for Harrison, "A classic attitude of the Harvard Russian department if I ever heard one." Harrison believed the speech was a more precise statement. Solzhenitsyn now carried his argument back to the Middle Ages. "Oh, says Adam, but there is nothing new in that." Harrison later wrote that "the Harvard intellectuals were not bowled over by Solzh's philosophy; thought it out of tune with the times, etc., etc.—all the usual expectable reaction."[38]

The following day the *Times* ran a brief article on Solzhenitsyn's speech, calling it a "bitter view of a West grown slack, pusillanimous and evil through devotion to man's appetite instead of God's design." It was delivered, the reporter wrote, "In tones of an evangelist excoriating sinners [and] delivered in Russian and amplified over his voice by an interpreter speaking English [as well as] a philippic against the press."[39] Harrison criticized the *Times* article as too brief and lacking excerpts. "I can't for the life of me understand why *Times* did not run text or at least a half page of excerpts. I really suspect it is due to the genuine Jewish antipathy for Solz which is based on their feeling which I think is probably soundly based tho not articulated by Solzhenitsyn; uncomfortableness with his blatant and strong Orthodoxy; and general feeling that he is too radical and absolute for their taste."[40]

Over a lavish Saturday night banquet at the Whitneys, Solzhenitsyn contributed further understanding to his speech. He took, according to Harrison, "enormous pleasure at the reception in Cambridge. He had regarded his move as very daring, going right into the camp of the enemy." Several times during the evening, he referred to the speech's warm applause by the young. America, he thought, was open-minded and could change. He reiterated that religion was "the very central question of his speech because religion and belief were at the center of the moral dilemma of the day." Salisbury concluded that Solzhenitsyn was "jovian, apocalyptic, Russian in every drop of his blood. There is *nothing* like Russia. Nothing like *Russia's* suffering. Nothing like *his* experience. Tochka. Period."[41]

Three journalists made Harrison's short list of heroic gadflies: David Halberstam, Homer Bigart, and Edgar Snow. Halberstam was there because of his role as a model to a generation of American reporters: "a symbol of the aggressive, no-holds barred, heads up American journalism that produced Vietnam, Watergate, and so many other exposés of the seamy side of American policy and practice."[42] Halberstam's style embodied "boundless curiosity, passion, a sense of what was right and wrong." He became the "most luminous" critic of America.[43]

Homer Bigart was the best war correspondent of his times. He was very professional, unafraid to give the facts. He maintained a skeptical attitude and a terse, no-frills style. His greatest achievement was reporting on the Korean War. "He always regarded war as mean, ugly, distasteful—no positive qualities."[44]

As for Edgar Snow, he produced a "world scoop." It was one of the "great journalistic breakthroughs of the twentieth century." It had not only changed China, but it had also been the most influential piece of journalism of his generation. *Red Star over China* put him in the pantheon of American journalism.[45]

Salisbury was sympathetic to poets as heroes. He picked three of his friends from his Moscow days—Yevgenny Yevtushenko, Andrei Voznesensky, and Bella Akhmadulina. Yevtushenko he called a civic poet. He was one who looked for truth and wrote polemics against falsity, for instance, warning against the return of Stalinism. Voznesensky was lyrical in the tradition of Pasternak. Akhmadulina was the most personal and lyrical. At first, Khrushchev patronized the three. Then he turned against them. When Yevtushenko finished reading from *Baby Yar* for the first time, there was dead silence and then stormy applause. "Nothing in my Moscow years," Harrison wrote, "moved me as did these three poets. They became a part of my life." [46]

The Chinese he selected were either victims or patronized victims—a curious lot. The first of these was Deng Pufang, the son of Deng Xiaoping. When Deng was named the "Number Two Capitalist Roader" in China and driven into obscurity, the Red Guards attacked Deng Pufang, beat him senseless, and threw him out of a fourth-story window. That broke his back and paralyzed his lower body. After the Cultural Revolution, the family was rehabilitated and Deng eventually ruled China. Pufang made it his mission to help the handicapped. That required changing China's philosophy toward those who suffer disabilities. He set up centers of treatment. In 1983 he created a National Association for the Disabled. [47]

Liu Shaoqi's family, the family of the martyred ex-president of China, destroyed in the Great Cultural Revolution by Mao's Red Guards, were also victims. Liu's widow, Wang Guangmei, came close to death, but she lived and reappeared to restore her husband's work. [48]

Both Soong Chingling, Sun Yatsen's widow, and Zhou Enlai, at great risk to themselves, patronized some of Mao's victims. Soong, sister-in-law of Chiang Kai-shek, supported the communists, though never becoming one. When Harrison asked her about Mao, she said, "I distrust him less than the others." In Harrison's words, "She respected Mao for his revolutionary achievements and his bringing unity and nationhood to China, but she did not like him personally—his peasant ways, his peasant manners, his barnyard vulgarity." [49]

As to Zhou, Mao's great accomplice, he was a central enigma—at the same time Mao's rival and pet dog. Harrison could not account for this: "I don't know the full answers today, but I know a lot. Zhou's sangfroid, his charm, his social ease had roots in his personal background." Harrison excused him by saying that "if he could survive he could still save the country." After all, he wrote, "If Zhou had given no other gift to China than that of putting Deng on the track to power, it would have been enough." [50]

Sister Huang Roushan came closest to the anonymous person who stopped the line of tanks. She gave her life to the cause of the lepers. Harrison found in her work the "pride and joy" of faith. In her, he recalled, "I had met a saint." [51] Like her, an American teacher of English in China, Brigid Temple Keogh, through self-sacrifice, achieved a noble goal by helping to bring literacy and education to China. [52]

Two of his heroes, Bobby Kennedy and Malcolm X, though contrasting personalities, fit into Harrison's pantheon. They both underwent life-changing experiences that led them to philosophical transformations. Malcolm X, whom he called the "black Savonarola," had been to Mecca. As a result, he came to understand that "Color alone was not the key. This simple observation brought profound readjustments in his thought."[53] He now embraced an inclusive philosophy of all races.

It was the same with Robert Kennedy—from a shrewd, smart, impersonal approach, the death of his brother Jack brought him an understanding of death and compassion.[54] This compassion could also be seen in Harrison's remaining choices. Iphigene Sulzberger was the quiet liberal-centrist voice behind the *New York Times*.[55] Roger Wilkins and Pat King championed "the virtues of responsibility, sacrifice, and commitment."[56] Compassion could be seen in Sue and Lawrence Brooks, who cherished "Public service, duty to country, belief in the fraternity of man—a strong skepticism and insistence on matching facts to reality."[57]

These were the heroic gadflies, whom, at the end of his life, he cherished. They were seekers of truth, unafraid of having their eyes gouged out in its pursuit, reporting truth to power. Throughout his life, Harrison had taken his cue from such persons. He titled the penultimate chapter of his autobiography "Death for Noble Deeds Makes Dying Sweet." There he wrote about the unquenchable idealism of Americans, especially Lawrence and Sue Brooks. They were his models.[58]

In 1985 he and Charlotte spent a leisurely month in Florence at the center of the Italian Renaissance. At the hall of Botticelli in the Uffizi, he saw the heart and spirit of the Renaissance: "I knew as I looked in that room, inspired by Michelangelo and designed by Vasari for Cosimo, that I would never be the same: I had crashed like a jerrybuilt condo." Here was the Renaissance at its "ultimate eloquence."

Only then did he realize that 1917, the Bolshevik Revolution, and 1953, Stalin's death, were only sputterings, as were those of Solzhenitsyn at Harvard Yard. The Renaissance was *the* revolution. He knew Russia, China, and the United States. He sat at the apex of their triangle. However, it was the reality of Florence that finally captured him. He quoted the great Renaissance figure Leon Alberti: "Man is born not to mourn in idleness but to work at magnificent and grandiose tasks."[59] He might have added Alberti's other remark: "Man is the measure of all things." The gadflies he admired and lionized had labored at such "magnificent and grandiose" tasks. Harrison was one of them. His best essays, speeches, and dispatches, his twenty-nine books, reflect the spirit of his heroes and himself. Marxism was a throwback to the dogmatism of the middle ages, and its Leninist variety a throwback to Eastern Orthodoxy. The Renaissance popes had rejected the Middle Ages in favor of the Florentine spirit of humanism. Lenin and Stalin, Marx and Engles, even Solzhenitsyn, were wrong. The painful twentieth century finally renounced their thunderings. Salisbury now, nearing the end of his life, understood the ultimate meaning of being the gadfly all his life—to reject dogmatism as humbug, in whatever form it appeared, and to stand for humanism in all its varieties.

Harrison Evans Salisbury quietly passed away on July 5, 1993, at the age of eighty-four. He slumped onto Charlotte's shoulder as she drove them home from a holiday in Providence, Rhode Island. According to his wishes, Charlotte had his body cremated. His ashes were scattered over the rolling hills of Connecticut. In Rome, Italy, there is a garden memorial of irises dedicated to him at the American Institute of Arts and Letters. [60]

Conclusion

How do a couple of biographers dig deeply enough into a man's life, into his very soul, without betraying their subject, and yet do him full justice? As they work on draft after draft, the intimate web of family stretches out to their subject's friends, colleagues, acquaintances, and the vast march of events in his era—those who captured his attentions, the passersby, the events big and small, crowded into his life and the life of his era.

Harrison's personal story is a narrative of courage and adventure, of daring thought and writings. In these pages we endeavored to tell his story as it was, without unnecessary embellishment, for it needed none. Rather, Salisbury was a seeker after the truth. He was not an advocate for this ideology or that. In these days of advocacy over news, confusion reigns. What are the facts? What is the analysis? He knew the difference. Let op-ed pages and editorials confine themselves to interpretation and advocacy. Let the news be the news, unfettered save for investigation and thoughtful analysis.

Harrison Salisbury's life warranted this study because he exemplified a standard under assault that was quickly vanishing from the news as he saw it. We are increasingly fed a steady diet of TV news, blogs, and tweets. Daily newspapers are collapsing; even the "Gray Lady" is in decline and may fail.[1] The fourth estate, perhaps in Salisburian judgment a fourth coequal branch of the federal government, may not survive the assault of superficial opinion.[2] Indeed, one wise man suggested,

> The best lack all conviction, while the worst
> Are full of passionate intensity.[3]

Salisbury sustained a conviction that the media, particularly the *New York Times*, would accurately inform citizens of democracy of the facts and, to the best of its ability, the truth of a story with enlightening analysis.

In these pages, we sought to demonstrate Salisbury's effort to, as Adolph S. Ochs proclaimed, "give the news impartially without fear or favor regardless of any party, set or interest involved." Harrison came close to being assassinated on two occasions, the first physically and the second professionally, while he covered Moscow and Hanoi. Those assignments yielded his most outstanding contributions to foreign journalism. He picked up again on that aspect in his retirement by investigating China under communism. In Moscow, he discovered the terrible truth of Stalin's Russia. In Hanoi, he found the awful truth of America's devastating bombing. Later, and belatedly, he found the truth of Mao's Beijing. In these cases, he also came to realize the courage of Russians, Americans, and Chinese trying to reinvent themselves and to create humane societies. In the process, he wrote literary and historical masterpieces—for Russia, *The 900 Days* and *Black Night, White Snow*; for China *The Long March* and *The New Emperors*; for America *Without Fear or Favor*. And, of course, his bylines numbered in the thousands.

In America, he explored the diversity and complexity of his own society. He remained an optimist. His story was always one of Americans reinventing themselves as they struggled to overcome poverty, racism, and corruption. The story was not always pretty. His American heroes, astonishingly, were often ordinary folks who daily performed acts of bravery—Brigid Keogh, David Halberstam, Malcolm X, Robert Kennedy, Homer Bigart, Iphigene Sulzberger, Edgar Snow, Roger Wilkins and Patricia King, Sue and Lawrence Brooks. He raised these Americans to heroic status.

Surely, Harrison Salisbury was a great American man of letters, as his twenty-nine books and numerous articles and essays give testimony to. His own Pulitzer Prize of 1955, his shared Pulitzer in 1958, and his controversial lost one in 1967 lend witness to his journalistic achievements. He rose to the top echelons of America's greatest newspaper, the paper of record, the *New York Times*. He filled its pages with dispatches and stories almost too numerous to count. He contributed to magazines and lectured Americans from one end of the country to the other, from its left shore to its right shore. And we, as a nation, are the better for it. Perhaps legions of the new generations of journalists and writers, TV pundits, and bloggers will learn lessons from his many dispatches or from his autobiographies—*Journey for Our Times* and *A Time of Change*—and take fresh heart from his unflinching courage.

The pre–World War I world in which Harrison Salisbury grew up underwent considerable transformations during his lifetime: from kings and kingdoms to dictators and dictatorships to democracies and republics. His home at 107 Royalston fell victim to the wrecking ball. Cities modernized. His dingy hotel room in the Metropole became a modern suite. Soviet power collapsed. His room at the Beijing Hotel had bullet holes removed after the Tiananmen Square's riots. But the road to the new China recuperated. America emerged as the world's only remaining superpower. Russia struggled to find a democratic path. China remained communist in name only. Harrison had settled into a hyperactive retirement amid the rolling hills of wooded Connecticut and across China. From them, he cast his lightning bolts. He stayed cautiously optimistic, telling his wife each morning, "Dear, what shall we worry about today?" A month in Florence, Italy, resigned him to Leon Alberti's maxim "Man is the measure of all things." Paraphrasing the great Florentine, we could say of Salisbury that he was born not to mourn in idleness, but to let his imagination float freely over his works at magnificent and grandiose tasks, always reporting truth to power bravely. Let that be Salisbury's epitaph.

Acknowledgments

This book is the final volume of a trilogy on American-Russian relations in the twentieth century, with a focus on the Far East. The first was *The First Cold War: The Legacy of Woodrow Wilson in U.S.-Soviet Relations* (Columbia: University of Missouri Press, 2002). That volume, also published in Russian by Olma Press in 2002 and in Chinese by the Peking University Press in 2007, traces the straight American policy line toward the Soviet Union from Woodrow Wilson to Ronald Reagan. The second volume, *Distorted Mirrors: Americans and Their Relations with Russia and China in the Twentieth Century* (Columbia: University of Missouri Press, 2009), also published in Russian by Vagrius Press in 2009 and in Spanish by the University of Cordoba Press in 2009, profiles significant Americans who helped make the policy the United States followed toward the Soviet Union (largely negative) and China (largely positive). Included in these profiles are a number of Salisbury's contemporaries, including Eugene Lyons (Russia; and the only American journalist to get a face-to-face interview with Stalin) and Edgar Snow (China). Given Harrison Salisbury's long involvement with the Soviet Union and the People's Republic of China, this was a natural third volume. Salisbury himself was covered in *Distorted Mirrors*, though briefly.

We wish to thank our colleagues who have read this work and given us valuable suggestions which have been incorporated into the final manuscript: Jin Guangyao, professor of history, Fudan University, Shanghai, People's Republic of China; Boris Shiriaev, professor and chair, Department of North American Studies, School of International Relations, St. Petersburg State University, Russia; Judyth Twigg, professor of Russian government and John Herman, professor of Chinese history, both of Virginia Commonwealth University; and Ross Terrill, research associate of the Fairbank Center for Chinese Studies of Harvard University. All provided considerable expertise that was invaluable.

We also want to thank the late Mrs. Charlotte Salisbury for meeting with us and giving her remarkable insights. To Sue Ann Messmer and Gloria Carnes, staff in the Office of the President Emeritus at Virginia Commonwealth University, we express our thanks for their great help in all aspects of preparing this manuscript, and to the Board of Visitors of Virginia Commonwealth University, we express our gratitude for all the support provided to this project. Finally, this project could not have been accomplished without the kind cooperation and sustained support of Jennifer Lee at the Columbia University Rare Book and Manuscript Library and Eileen Hinthorne, then executive director, at the Research Collections and Preservation Consortium, Inc., at the Forrestal Campus of Princeton University.

To our spouses, Mary L. Davis and Lois E. Trani, we again express our profound thanks and devotion, and for our children and grandchildren— Charles Davis and his daughter, Addison; Peggy Suzuki and her daughter, Koharu; Anne Chapman and her children, Tegan and Woodrow; Frank Trani and his children, Oliva, James, and Renn—we say thank you for bringing joy into our lives.

Notes

1. JOURNEYMAN JOURNALIST

1. David Levine, drawing accompanying an article by Lee Lockwood, "Salisbury's Stake," *New York Review of Books*, August 3, 1967.

2. Interview with Charlotte Y. Salisbury, May 29, 2008. See also Mrs. Salisbury's obituary by Walter F. Naedele, "Charlotte Young Salisbury, 98, Author," *Philadelphia Inquirer*, May 9, 2012, http://articles.philly.com/2012-05-09/news/31642276_1_harrison-salisbury-chinese-authorities-china-epic.

3. On the current state of American journalism and the rapid decline of the newspaper industry, see Alex S. Jones, *Losing the News: The Future of the News That Feeds Democracy* (New York: Oxford University Press, 2009).

4. Russell Baker to Charlotte Salisbury (hereafter CS), September 21, 1993, box 1, Harrison E. Salisbury Papers (hereafter HES Papers), Columbia University (hereafter CU); Max Frankel to CS, July 6, 1993, box 137, HES Papers, CU; David Halberstam to CS, August 4, 1993, box 138, HES Papers, CU; David Remnick to CS, n.d. (1993), box 139, HES Papers, CU; Hedrick Smith to CS, July 26, 1993, box 139, HES Papers, CU; Arthur O. Sulzberger Jr., to CS, July 12, 1993, box 139, HES Papers, CU.

5. Helen Frankenthaler to CS, July 14, 1993, box 137, HES Papers, CU; John V. Lindsay to CS, July 7, 1993, box 138, HES Papers, CU; George F. Kennan to CS, September 13, 1993, box 138, HES Papers, CU; Richard Nixon to CS, n.d. (1993), box 139, HES Papers, CU; Gwendolyn Brooks to CS, August 21, 1993, box 137, HES Papers, CU.

6. Eric Pace, "Harrison E. Salisbury, 84, Author and Reporter, Dies," *New York Times* (hereafter *NYT*), July 7, 1993. See also Turner Catledge, *My Life and* The Times (New York: Harper & Row, 1971), quote on 291.

7. John B. Oakes, "Harrison E. Salisbury (13 November 1908–5 July 1993)," *Proceedings of the American Philosophical Society* 139, no. 2 (1995): 193–95.

8. Arthur Miller, "Harrison E. Salisbury, 1908–1993," *Proceedings of the American Philosophical Society* 139, no. 2 (1995): 80–85.

9. "Remembering Harrison," pieces by David Halberstam, Clifton Daniel, Thomas Whitney, Gloria Emerson, Arthur Miller, Roger Wilkins, Vladimir Pozner, Betsy Ward (quoting Solzhenitsyn), and David Schneiderman, *Nieman Reports*, fall 1993, 4–12. Interview with Jean Halberstam, December 2, 2011.

10. Ross Terrill, Diary, July 6, 1993, Boston.

11. Harrison E. Salisbury (hereafter HES), *A Journey for Our Times: A Memoir* (New York: Harper & Row, 1983), 6.

12. John Reed, *Ten Days That Shook the World* (New York: Vintage, 1960), ch. 4.

13. HES, *Journey for Our Times*, 1, quote on 2; HES, *A Time of Change: A Reporter's Tale of Our Time* (New York: Harper & Row, 1988), acknowledgments.

14. HES, *Journey for Our Times*, 3–5.

15. Ibid., 7, 10, 13, 26.

16. Ibid., 29–31, 33, 35–37, 39–40, 47 for quote, 49.

17. Ibid., 31, 33, quote on 35; Percy Salisbury to HES, n.d. (1922), box 255, HES Papers, CU.

18. HES, *Journey for Our Times*, 50–58, 60, 66; see also *The Polaris*, 1924, 74, 95, 108, and the university's *Gopher Yearbook*, 1927, 180; 1928, 162; 1930, 167, 352, 448, and 562.

19. HES, *Journey for Our Times*, 70–75, quotes on 89.

20. L. M. Harkness, "To Whom It May Concern," April 23, 1929, box 255, HES Papers, CU.

21. HES, *Journey for Our Times*, 78–80, 85–88; see also the front page of the *New York Times*, January 15, 1930, under the heading "Minnesota University Suspends Student for Year for Smoking."

22. Sue Salisbury to her family, December 27, 1931, box 255, HES Papers, CU.

23. HES, *Journey for Our Times*, 88–90, quotes on 89; HES to Jean, October 26, 1929, box 9, HES Papers, CU.

24. HES to Jean, February 26, 1930, box 9, HES Papers, CU.

25. HES, *Journey for Our Times*, 93–94 for quotes.

26. HES to "Dearest," December 1, 1960, box 256, HES Papers, CU.

27. HES to Jud, n.d. (1930?), box 256, HES Papers, CU.

28. "Al Capone," *Wikipedia*, http://en.wikipedia.org/wiki/Al_Capone (accessed September 12, 2009).

29. HES, *Journey for Our Times*, 95–96, quotes on 101 and 108.

30. Ibid., 111 for quote, 113, 115–16.

31. Ibid., 117 and 119 for quotes.

32. HES to "Dearest," December 1, 1960, box 256, HES Papers, CU.

33. Mary Jane and HES to Fred and wife, March 1935, box 255, HES Papers, CU.

34. Ibid.

35. David M. Kennedy, *Freedom from Fear: The American People in Depression and War, 1929–1945* (New York: Oxford University Press, 1999), 238, 239 for quote; see also T. Harry Williams, *Huey Long* (New York: Alfred A. Knopf, 1969), 866, 876.

36. HES, *Journey for Our Times*, 122–30, quote on 130.

37. Kennedy, *Freedom from Fear*, 278.

38. HES, "Harrison Evans Salisbury to His Family Re: Huey Long Assignment," September 1935, box 255, HES Papers, CU.

39. HES, *Journey for Our Times*, 135, quotes on 142, 143, 144.

40. Ibid., 149.

41. Ibid., 148–62.

2. FOREIGN CORRESPONDENT

1. Harrison E. Salisbury (hereafter HES), *A Journey for Our Times: A Memoir* (New York: Harper & Row, 1983), 180–204; HES, Journal, February 6, 1943, box 185, HES Papers, Columbia University (hereafter CU); HES to Margaret, January 25, 1977, box 5, HES Papers, CU. Also see Walter Cronkite, *A Reporter's Life* (New York: Ballantine, 1996), 89ff., 116; Lynne Olson, *Citizens of London: The Americans Who Stood with Britain in Its Darkest, Finest Hour* (New York: Random House, 2010), 169, where Olson agrees that Harriman undercut Winant.

2. HES to Earl J. Johnson, September 17, 1971, box 6, HES Papers, CU.

3. Ivan Maisky, *Memoirs of a Soviet Ambassador: The War, 1939–43* (New York: Charles Scribner's Sons, 1968), 353.

4. HES, *Journey for Our Times*, 188.

5. Ibid., 167, 176–77, quote on 177.

6. HES, Journal, July 14, 1943, box 185, HES Papers, CU.

7. Ibid.

8. HES to Mary Jane Salisbury (hereafter MJS), May 17, 1943, box 256, HES Papers, CU.

9. HES to "Dearest E.," May 31, 1982, box 256, HES Papers, CU.

10. Ibid. Olson quotes Salisbury to the effect that sex hung in London's air like a fog. See Olson, *Citizens of London*, 388.

11. HES, *Journey for Our Times*, 190.

12. Ibid., 194.

13. Ibid., 198–99.

14. Ibid., 201–2.

15. Ibid., 204.

16. Ibid., 205–6, quotes on 205.

17. HES, "What I have left out of my Memoirs," May 3, 1982, box 256, HES Papers, CU.

18. HES, *Journey for Our Times*, 206.

19. Ibid., 207.

20. HES to MJS, December 29, 1943, box 184, HES Papers, CU.

21. Donald E. Davis and Eugene P. Trani, *Distorted Mirrors: Americans and Their Relations with Russia and China in the Twentieth Century* (Columbia: University of Missouri Press, 2009), 114.

22. HES, *Journey for Our Times*, 209, quote on 211.

23. Ibid., 211–14, quote on 214. Mikhail Gorbachev admitted Russia's guilt. The Russian Parliament finally approved Gorbachev's statement. See *NYT*, November 27, 2010. See http://en.wikipedia.org/wiki/Katyn_massacre (accessed November 25, 2009). HES, "Nazis Slew 135,000 while in Smolensk," January 27, 1944, box 184, HES Papers, CU.

24. HES, *Journey for Our Times*, 223–25, quote on 221.

25. Ibid., quote on 225; HES to E, April 3, 1944, box 184, HES Papers, CU.

26. HES, "Leningrad Notes," n.d., box 184, HES Papers, CU; quote in HES to E, April 3, 1944, box 184, HES Papers, CU.

27. HES to E, April 3, 1944, box 184, HES Papers, CU.

28. Whitman Bassow, *The Moscow Correspondents: Reporting on Russia from the Revolution to Glasnost* (New York: Paragon House, 1989), 111–13. Also see *NYT*, February 15, 1944.

29. Bassow, *Moscow Correspondents*, 112.

30. Ibid., 113.

31. Ibid.

32. HES, verbatim of cablegram to Hugh Baillie and Earl Johnson, February 23, 1944, box 184, HES Papers, CU.

33. HES to Stalin, February 23, 1944, box 184, HES Papers, CU.

34. HES to Dekanozov, February 24, 1944, box 184, HES Papers, CU.

35. HES to Baillie/Johnson, March 6, 1944, box 184, HES Papers, CU.

36. HES to Baillie, March 8, 1944, box 184, HES Papers, CU.

37. Ibid.

38. Ibid.

39. Ibid.

40. HES, *Journey for Our Times*, 238.

41. W. Averell Harriman and Elie Abel, *Special Envoy to Churchill and Stalin, 1941–1946* (New York: Random House, 1975), 321–22, quote on 322.

42. Ibid., 329.

43. HES to MJS, May 8, 1944, box 184, HES Papers, CU; Harriman and Abel, *Special Envoy*, 329. Stalin's position became clear when Ralph Parker of the *NYT* asked him why several democratic Polish leaders were arrested the following year. Stalin replied that a reconstructed government had to pursue a policy of friendship with the USSR, not a cordon sanitaire

policy, and have "ties with the Polish people, and not without them." See Parker to Stalin, May 11, 1945, and Stalin to Parker, May 18, 1945, "Reply to The Times Moscow Correspondent's Question Concerning the 16 Arrested Polish Diversionists," http://marxists.org/reference/archive/stalin/works/1945/05/18.htm (accessed February 15, 2010).

44. HES, Journal, June 6, 1944, box 184, HES Papers, CU; John R. Deane, *The Strange Alliance: The Story of Our Efforts at Wartime Cooperation with Russia* (New York: Viking, 1947), 107–25, quote on 124. Salisbury writes about this interview with Orlemanski and his junket east in *Russia on the Way* (New York: Macmillan, 1946).

45. HES, "Stalin Interview," June 26, 1944, box 184, HES Papers, CU. For the Lyons interview of Stalin, see the *New York Telegram*, November 24, 1930.

46. HES, "Stalin Interview," June 26, 1944, box 184, HES Papers, CU.

47. Ibid.

48. HES to Barbie, July 9, 1944, box 184, HES Papers, CU.

49. For an extended analysis of this fear, see Davis and Trani, *Distorted Mirrors*.

50. HES, *Journey for Our Times*, quotes on 272, 275–76, 279–84, 292.

51. Ibid., 292–93; HES, *Russia on the Way*, ch. 1.

52. HES, *Russia on the Way*, 247–53, quotes on 247, 248, 253.

53. Ibid., 349.

54. Ibid., 350.

55. Ibid., quotes on 361, 369.

56. Ibid., 395.

57. HES, *Journey for Our Times*, 287–89.

58. Ibid., 293.

59. Ibid., 296–98.

60. Ibid., 301.

61. Ibid., 302. See also *NYT*, December 26, 1948, for the editorial and Salisbury's article in the magazine section. He accused the Soviet press of a "bombardment of censure" and of vilifying intellectuals at home and abroad. It was an effort to immasculate Soviets against bourgeois decadence. James pressed in his editorial the importance of both sides getting better acquainted with each other and pointed to the *Times* effort to present both sides. The *Times*, he insisted, "regretted exceedingly that it is unable to maintain a news bureau in Moscow as it does in London, Paris, Rome and other great capitals of the world. We think we could help toward that better understanding."

62. HES, "What I have left out of my Memoirs," May 3, 1982, box 256, HES Papers, CU.

63. Ibid.

64. HES to his mother, August 26, 1947, box 311, HES Papers, CU.

65. HES to his mother, September 3, 1947, box 311, HES Papers, CU.

66. HES to his mother, September 12, 1947, box 311, HES Papers, CU.

67. HES, "Voice of the Politburo," *NYT*, magazine section, October 4, 1947. Though typecast as the "relentless State Prosecutor" in the purge trials, Vishinsky is presented as a passionate advocate of Soviet law and diplomacy and a brilliant debater. Like his Politburo masters, as number two man in the Foreign Ministry, he was a realist.

68. HES to his mother, October 4, 1947, box 311, HES Papers, CU.

69. HES to [no addressee], February 21, 1948, box 311, HES Papers, CU.

70. HES to his mother, June 23, 1948, box 311, HES Papers, CU.

71. HES to his mother, June 24, 1948, box 311, HES Papers, CU.

72. HES to his mother and Jan, June 28, 1948, box 311, HES Papers, CU.

73. HES to his mother and Jan, June 29, 1948, box 311, HES Papers, CU.

74. HES to his mother and Jan, October 10, 1948, box 311, HES Papers, CU.

75. HES to his mother and Jan, December 27, 1948, box 311, HES Papers, CU.

76. HES to his mother and Jan, January 2, 1949, box 311, HES Papers, CU.

77. HES to his mother and Jan, January 10, 1949, box 311, HES Papers, CU.

78. See the announcement of his appointment in the *NYT*, January 23, 1949. It had been almost two years that the *NYT* had no representative in Moscow due to the inability of a correspondent to get a visa. "Now a visa has been granted to Harrison E. Salisbury, a journalist of high standing, who represented The United Press in Russia in 1944 and was for a time foreign news editor of that agency. Mr. Salisbury will reopen our Moscow Bureau."

79. HES to his mother and Jan, January 24, 1949, box 311, HES Papers, CU.

80. HES to his mother and Jan, January 27, 1949, box 311, HES Papers, CU.

3. MOSCOW BUREAU CHIEF

1. Harrison E. Salisbury (hereafter HES), *A Journey for Our Times: A Memoir* (New York: Harper & Row, 1983), 228, also see 312–19.

2. Ibid., 301; HES to "Dearest," March 12, 1949, box 3, HES Papers, Columbia University (hereafter CU).

3. HES to "Dearest," March 15, 1949, box 3, HES Papers, CU.

4. HES to "Dearest," March 25, 1949, box 3, HES Papers, CU.

5. HES to "Dearest," April 6, 1949; April 12, 1949; April 14, 1949, box 3, HES Papers, CU.

6. HES to "Dearest," April 20, 1949, box 3, HES Papers, CU.

7. HES to "Darling," July 19, 1949, box 3, HES Papers, CU.

8. HES to "Darling," October 3, 1949, box 3, HES Papers, CU.

9. HES to "Darling," October 3, 1949; November 5, 1949; November 6, 1949; and November 8, 1949, box 3, HES Papers, CU.

10. HES, *Journey for Our Times*, 323, 368.

11. HES to "Darling," November 19, 1949; November 26, 1949; December 7, 1949, box 3, HES Papers, CU.

12. Bernard Reswick to HES, March 8, 1950; March 29, 1950, including divorce agreement, box 311, HES Papers, CU.

13. HES to his mother and Jan, June 20, 1950, box 311, HES Papers, CU.

14. HES to his mother and Jan, March 8, 1950, box 190; HES to Jan, March 24, 1950; HES to his mother, April 11, 1950; and HES to Jan, April 24, 1950, box 311, HES Papers, CU.

15. HES to his mother and Jan, September 15, 1950, box 190, HES Papers, CU.

16. Harrison E. Salisbury, *Moscow Journal: The End of the Stalin Era* (Chicago: University of Chicago Press, 1961), 12, 16–18.

17. HES to Jacop Lomakin, April 9, 1949, box 187, HES Papers, CU; HES, *Moscow Journal*, 26. HES wanted Stalin's comments on Germany's future, the fate of Berlin, the economy, and so on; see HES to Stalin, April 20, 1949, box 187, HES Papers, CU. He also wrote to Andrei Vishinsky (March 29, 1949) and Boris Isakov (March 29, 1949), both in box 187, HES Papers, CU. For his letters to James and Sulzberger, check HES to James, March 28, 1949; HES to Sulzberger, March 28, 1949, both in box 187, HES Papers, CU.

18. HES to Sulzberger, April 4, 1949, box 187, HES Papers, CU.

19. Simon Sebag Montefiore, *Stalin: The Court of the Red Tsar* (New York: Alfred A. Knopf, 2003), 597, 609.

20. HES to Sulzberger, April 4 and 5, 1949; Manny Freedman to HES, April 5, 1949, box 187, HES Papers, CU.

21. HES, *Moscow Journal*, quote on 26; also see 27–28.

22. HES to Sulzberger, May 23, 1949, box 187, HES Papers, CU.

23. HES to Sulzberger, May 6, 1949, box 187, HES Papers, CU; quote from HES to Reswick, May 5, 1949, box 9, HES Papers, CU.

24. HES to Sulzberger, June 6, 1949, box 187, HES Papers, CU; HES to Reswick, June 6, 1949, HES Papers, CU; HES, *Moscow Journal*, 22, 38.

25. HES, *Moscow Journal*, 42; Turner Catledge to HES, August 4, 1949, box 2, HES Papers, CU.

26. HES to Stalin, June 21, 1949, box 187, HES Papers, CU; HES to Freedman, July 5, 1949, box 187, HES Papers, CU; *Moscow Journal*, 42–43.

27. Montefiore, *Stalin*, 585–91, quote on 587.

28. HES to Sulzberger, July 5, 1949, box 187, HES Papers, CU.

29. HES to Sulzberger, July 24, 1949, box 187, HES Papers, CU; HES to Freedman, August 4, 1949, box 187, HES Papers, CU.

30. HES, *Journey for Our Times*, 337.

31. HES to James, October 10, 1949; October 12, 1949, box 187, HES Papers, CU.

32. HES to Freedman, September 2, 1949, box 187, HES Papers, CU; quote from HES to Freedman, September 3, 1949, box 187, HES Papers, CU.

33. HES, *Moscow Journal*, 58.

34. HES to Andy Nolan, October 9, 1949, box 9, HES Papers, CU.

35. HES to Joe, September 8, 1949, box 9, HES Papers, CU.

36. HES, *Moscow Journal*, 61; first quote from HES to Freedman, September 19, 1949, box 187, HES Papers, CU; second quote from HES to James, September 22, 1949, box 187, HES Papers, CU. As to his questions to Stalin, see HES to Stalin, September 24, 1949; September 30, 1949, box 187, HES Papers, CU.

37. HES to Sulzberger, October 24, 1949, box 187, HES Papers, CU; HES to James, October 24, 1949, box 187, HES Papers, CU. See also Whitman Bassow, *The Moscow Correspondents: Reporting on Russia from the Revolution to Glasnost* (New York: Paragon House, 1989), 125.

38. HES, *Journey for Our Times*, 353–54.

39. HES to Lissner, November 30, 1949, box 187, HES Papers, CU.

40. HES, *Journey for Our Times*, 356.

41. HES to James, December 2, 1949, box 187, HES Papers, CU.

42. HES to Gromyko, November 19, 1949, box 187, HES Papers, CU.

43. Gay Talese, *The Kingdom and the Power* (New York: World Publishing, 1969), 439.

44. HES, *Journey for Our Times*, 358–59.

45. HES to a friend, December 6, 1949, box 9, HES Papers, CU; HES to Stalin, December 14, 1949, box 187, HES Papers, CU.

46. HES, *Moscow Journal*, 90, 92–93; Montefiore, *Stalin*, 604–6.

47. Montefiore, *Stalin*, 604; HES et al. to Mao, December 19, 1949, box 187, HES Papers, CU; HES, *Moscow Journal*, 98.

48. For quote, see HES, *Moscow Journal*, 106. Also see HES to Manny, January 8, 1949, box 187, HES Papers, CU.

49. HES, *Moscow Journal*, 104; HES to Vishinsky, January 21, 1950, box 187, HES Papers, CU.

50. HES, *Moscow Journal*, 109–11, quote on 109.

51. Montefiore, *Stalin*, 606–67.

52. HES to Sulzberger, January 27, 1950, box 10, HES Papers, CU.

53. HES to Sulzberger, February 21, 1950, box 187, HES Papers, CU.

54. Ibid.

55. HES to Sulzberger, April 7, 1950, box 187, HES Papers, CU.

56. HES to James, February 25, 1050, box 187, HES Papers, CU.

57. James to HES, March 10, 1950; April 4, 1950, box 187, HES Papers, CU.

58. Talese, *Kingdom and Power*, 437.

59. HES, *Journey for Our Times*, 369–73.

60. HES to Joe, September 8, 1950, box 9, HES Papers, CU.

61. HES, *Moscow Journal*, 146–49; quote in Catledge to HES, September 22, 1950, box 2, HES Papers, CU.

62. HES, *Journey for Our Times*, 374, for first quote; Catledge to Julius Adler, October 2, 1950, box 2, HES Papers, CU, for second quote; HES, *Journey for Our Times*, 375, for third quote.

63. HES to Catledge, October 5, 1950, box 2, HES Papers, CU, for first quote; HES, *Journey for Our Times*, 374, for second quote.

64. Catledge to HES, October 10, 1950, box 2, HES Papers, CU.

65. HES, "No 'Scare' Buying in Moscow Stores," *New York Times* (hereafter *NYT*), October 13, 1950.

66. HES, *Journey for Our Times*, 375.

67. HES, "No 'Scare' Buying in Moscow Stores," *NYT*, October 13, 1950.

68. HES to Bernie Reswick, October 30, 1950, box 9, HES Papers, CU.

69. HES, *Journey for Our Times*, 144.

70. Arthur Hayes Sulzberger to Cy Sulzberger, November 7, 1950, box 13, HES Papers, CU; Talese, *Kingdom and Power*, 439.

71. Arthur Hayes Sulzberger to Cy Sulzberger, November 7, 1950, box 13, HES Papers, CU.

72. Cy Sulzberger to Arthur Hayes Sulzberger, November 22, 1950, box 13, HES Papers, CU.

73. HES to Cy Sulzberger, January 12, 1951, box 187, HES Papers, CU.

74. HES, *Moscow Journal*, 157, 160, 164, 166.

75. Freedman to HES, January 4, 1950, box 187, HES Papers, CU.

76. HES to Freedman, January 17, 1951, box 187, HES Papers, CU.

77. HES, *Journey for Our Times*, 376.

78. HES to Schwartz, January 23, 1951, box 187, HES Papers, CU.

79. HES, *Moscow Journal*, 177, 178; HES to Sulzberger, February 19, 1951, box 12, HES Papers, CU.

80. HES to Sulzberger, February 21, 1951, box 187, HES Papers, CU.

81. HES, *Moscow Journal*, 184–85, 185n.

82. Atkinson to HES, March 2, 1951, box 1, HES Papers, CU.

83. Sulzberger to HES, March 6, 1951, box 14, HES Papers, CU.

84. HES to Sulzberger, March 25, 1951, box 211, HES Papers, CU.

85. HES to James, June 27, 1951, box 12, HES Papers, CU.

86. Sulzberger to HES, July 10, 1951, box 12, HES Papers, CU.

87. HES, *Journey for Our Times*, 377–91.

88. Talese, *Kingdom and Power*, quote on 439, also see 438–40.

89. HES to Sulzberger, July 13, 1951, box 211, HES Papers, CU; HES to Stalin, July 20, 1951, box 211, HES Papers, CU.

90. HES to James, July 22, 1951, box 211, HES Papers, CU.

91. HES to Freedman, July 29, 1951; HES to James, July 29, 1951; HES to Freedman, July 31, 1951, all in box 211, HES Papers, CU.

92. HES to Catledge, November 15, 1951, box 2, HES Papers, CU.

93. Talese, *Kingdom and Power*, 439.

94. For Salisbury's quote from Admiral Kirk, see *Moscow Journal*, 217; for the Kennan quote, see George F. Kennan, *Memoirs, 1950–1963* (New York: Pantheon, 1972), 106.

95. HES to Sulzberger, November 22, 1951, box 12, HES Papers, CU; HES to Catledge, December 4, 1951, box 211, HES Papers, CU.

96. HES to Reston, December 7, 1951, box 211, HES Papers, CU. See also James Reston, *Deadline: A Memoir* (New York: Times Books, 1992), 158. HES planned to publish that Kennan would not be approved. He was glad the censors blocked him. See John Lewis Gaddis, *George F. Kennan: An American Life* (New York: Penguin, 2011), 437–38, 732n53.

97. HES, *Moscow Journal*, 234.

98. Cy Sulzberger to HES, December 20, 1951, box 12, HES Papers, CU; HES, *Moscow Journal*, 235.

99. Kennan, *Memoirs*, 106–10, quotes on 107, 110.

100. Ibid., 111, 112. See also Gaddis, *Kennan*, 454–55.

101. HES, *Moscow Journal*, 245.

102. Catledge to HES, January 10, 1952, box 2, HES Papers, CU; HES to Arthur Hayes Sulzberger, January 13, 1952, box 211, HES Papers, CU; HES to Cy Sulzberger, January 23, 1952, box 10, HES Papers, CU.

103. HES to Cy Sulzberger, February 15, 1952, box 211, HES Papers, CU, for first quote; HES, *Moscow Journal*, 245 and 246 for second quote.

104. HES, *Moscow Journal*, 250–56, quote on 256.

105. Kennan, *Memoirs*, 116–26, quotes on 116, 126.
106. HES, *Journey for Our Times*, 410–17, quotes on 411, 417.
107. Ibid., 418–21.
108. HES, *Moscow Journal*, quote on 259, also see 261 for embassy's move.
109. HES to Sulzberger, August 11, 1952, box 211, HES Papers, CU. There was serious fuss over whether Stalin wanted to see Kennan and over forced entries into the U.S. embassy to embarrass Kennan, as well as Stalin's interview with an Italian journalist, Pietro Nenni, but nothing came of these. See Gaddis, *Kennan,* 456–58. HES believed Stalin was testing Kennan.

4. A DEATH IN MOSCOW

1. Harrison E. Salisbury (hereafter HES), *Moscow Journal: The End of Stalin* (Chicago: University of Chicago Press, 1961), 266–68.
2. HES, *A Journey for Our Times: A Memoir* (New York: Harper & Row, 1983), 416.
3. HES to Manny Freedman, July 31, 1952, box, 10, HES Papers, Columbia University (hereafter CU).
4. Nikita Khrushchev, *Khrushchev Remembers* (Boston: Little, Brown, 1970), 250.
5. George F. Kennan, *Memoirs, 1950–1963* (New York: Pantheon, 1972), 131.
6. HES, *Journey for Our Times*, 411.
7. HES to Cy Sulzberger, August 25, 1952, box 10, HES Papers, CU.
8. HES to Sulzberger, August 27, 1952, box 10, HES Papers, CU; HES, *Moscow Journal*, 277.
9. HES, *Moscow Journal*, 281–82.
10. Kennan, *Memoirs*, 148, 153–56.
11. Ibid., 158–59.
12. Ibid., 163–64; HES, *Moscow Journal*, 285–86, quote on 286.
13. HES, *Moscow Journal*, 287.
14. HES to Sulzberger, October 22, 1952, box 10, HES Papers, CU.
15. HES to Sulzberger, October 23, 1952, box 10, HES Papers, CU.
16. HES to Sulzberger, November 16, 1952; November 28, 1952, box 12, HES Papers, CU.
17. Simon Sebag Montefiore, *Stalin: The Court of the Red Tsar* (New York: Alfred A. Knopf, 2004), 624.
18. Ibid., 627–33, quote on 627; HES, *Moscow Journal*, 312.
19. HES, *Moscow Journal*, 313–14.
20. Ibid., 325, 327; Montefiore, *Stalin*, 629–36, quotes on 636.
21. Svetlana Alliluyeva, *Twenty Letters to a Friend* (New York: Harper & Row, 1967), 10.
22. HES, *Moscow Journal*, 334–39, quote on 334. See also HES, "Stalin Succumbs," *New York Times* (hereafter *NYT*), March 6, 1953. Harrison saved his "*propusk*" ticket to view Stalin's body, number 21-9354.
23. "Russia Re-Viewed," *Time*, October 4, 1954.
24. HES, *Journey for Our Times*, 468–70, quotes on 470, 469.
25. HES, memorandum, March 11, 1953, box 189, folder "Moscow Correspondence, 1952–54," HES Papers, CU.
26. On these matters, see HES to Cy Sulzberger, March 16, 1953, and form letters to Malenkov, Molotov, Voroshilov, Mikoyan, and others, beginning March 10, 1953, box 189, folder "Moscow Correspondence, 1952–54," HES Papers, CU.
27. HES, "Russia Re-Viewed: Under New Management, Soviet Tactics Change," *NYT*, September 19, 1954.
28. Ibid.
29. Ibid.
30. HES, "Was Stalin Put to Death to Avert a Blood Purge?," *NYT*, September 20, 1954.
31. Ibid.
32. Ibid.
33. Ibid.

34. Ibid.

35. Ibid.

36. HES, "Beria's Troops Held Moscow, but He Hesitated and Lost," *NYT*, September 21, 1954.

37. Ibid.

38. Ibid.

39. Ibid.

40. Ibid.

41. Ibid.

42. Ibid.

43. Ibid.

44. Montefiore, *Stalin*, 652.

45. HES, "Army Playing a Major Role, with Zhukov Key Figure," *NYT*, September 22, 1954.

46. Ibid.

47. Ibid.

48. HES, "Members of the Ruling Clique Are Depicted Close Up," *NYT*, September 23, 1954.

49. Ibid.

50. Ibid.

51. HES, "Life of Soviet Common Man Is a Constant Struggle," *NYT*, September 24, 1954.

52. HES, "Chou Talks Back in Moscow to Communist Sponsor," *NYT*, September 25, 1954.

53. Ibid.

54. Ibid.

55. Ibid.

56. HES, "Amnesty Too Late for Many; Mme. Molotov Was Saved," *NYT*, September 26, 1954.

57. HES, "The Prison Camps of Siberia," *NYT*, September 27, 1954.

58. Ibid.

59. HES, "The Spets' System of Exile," *NYT*, September 28, 1954.

60. Ibid.

61. Ibid.

62. Ibid.

63. Ibid.

64. HES, "Anti-Semitism and Religion," *NYT*, September 29, 1954.

65. HES, "Atomic Sites Are Deduced," *NYT*, September 30, 1954.

66. HES, "Crime Wave Goes Unchecked," *NYT*, October 1, 1954.

67. HES, "Censorship of News Is Erratic," *NYT*, October 2, 1954.

68. Ibid.

69. Ibid.

70. Ibid.

71. Kirk to HES, May 2, 1955, box 6, folder "Grayson Kirk," HES Papers, CU.

72. Kirk to HES, May 3, 1955, box 6, folder "Grayson Kirk," HES Papers, CU. The actual Pulitzer citation is in box 193, folder 1, HES Papers, CU.

73. As quoted in "1955 Pulitzer Prizes," *Wikipedia*, http://en.wikipedia.org/wiki/1955_Pulitzer_Prize (accessed July 9, 2009).

74. Adler to HES, May 3, 1955, box 1, folder 1, "Adler, J.O.," HES Papers, CU.

75. Canfield to HES, September 29, 1954, box 2, folder "Canfield," HES Papers, CU.

76. Krock to HES, telegram, May 2, 1955, box 6, folder "Krock," HES Papers, CU.

77. Middleton to HES, telegram, May 3, 1955, box 7, folder "Middleton," HES Papers, CU.

78. Clark to HES, telegram, October 6, 1954, box 14, folder 2, "Salisbury Correspondence 1954," HES Papers, CU.

79. Clark to HES, October 19, 1954, box 14, folder 2, "Salisbury Correspondence 1954," HES Papers, CU.

80. HES to Clark, October 28, 1954, box 14, folder 2, "Salisbury Correspondence 1954," HES Papers, CU.

81. Otto to HES, October 14, 1954, box 14, folder 2, "Salisbury Correspondence 1954," HES Papers, CU.

82. HES to Otto, October 28, 1954, box 14, folder 2, "Salisbury Correspondence 1954," HES Papers, CU.

83. Anson to HES, January 27, 1955, box 14, folder 2, "Salisbury Correspondence 1954," HES Papers, CU.

84. HES to Wallace, December 14, 1954, box 14, folder 2, "Salisbury Correspondence 1954," HES Papers, CU.

85. Wallace to HES, December 20, 1954, box 14, folder 2, "Salisbury Correspondence 1954," HES Papers, CU.

86. Wallace to HES, February 8, 1955, box 14, folder 2, "Salisbury Correspondence 1954," HES Papers, CU.

5. LIFE IN A SATELLITE

1. Harrison E. Salisbury (hereafter HES), *A Time of Change: A Reporter's Tale of Our Time* (New York: Harper & Row, 1988), 74–77.

2. Ibid., 78–81, quote on 78.

3. Ibid., 82–94, quotes on 93–94.

4. HES, "Americans Flock to East Europe," *New York Times* (hereafter *NYT*), July 28, 1957.

5. HES, "Political Gains by Tito Implied," *NYT*, August 4, 1957.

6. HES, "Bulganin's Role on Satellite Ties Believed Reduced," *NYT*, August 5, 1957.

7. HES, "Tito Stands Firm on Full Equality among Red Lands," *NYT*, August 6, 1957.

8. HES, "Big Soviet Shift Seen in Belgrade," *NYT*, August 7, 1957.

9. Ibid.

10. HES, "Yugoslavs Are Frank," *NYT*, August 10, 1957.

11. HES, "Yugoslavs Are Still Wary of All Soviet Advances," *NYT*, August 11, 1957.

12. HES, "Yugoslavs Appear Unworried over Djilas' Book on Red System," *NYT*, August 8, 1957.

13. Ibid.

14. HES, "Tito Paper Attacks Djilas," *NYT*, August 11, 1957.

15. HES, "Djilas Book Stirs Yugoslav Worry," *NYT*, August 17, 1957.

16. HES to his mother and Jan, August 14, 1957, box 571, HES Papers, Columbia University (hereafter CU).

17. HES, "Building Pattern Set by Belgrade," *NYT*, August 22, 1957.

18. HES, "Rift Expected to Continue," *NYT*, August 19, 1957.

19. HES, "U.S. Comics (Zowie!) Captivate Yugoslav Newspaper Readers," *NYT*, August 24, 1957.

20. HES, "Yugoslav Crops to Set a Record," *NYT*, August 20, 1957.

21. HES, "Purged Marshal Cleared in Soviet," *NYT*, August 14, 1957.

22. HES, "Role of Bulganin Found Diminished," *NYT*, August 18, 1957.

23. HES, "New Djilas Book Is Life of Bishop," *NYT*, September 1, 1957.

24. HES, "Fatal Flaw in the Soviet System," *NYT*, August 25, 1957.

25. Ibid.

26. Ibid.

27. HES, "Diversity in East Europe Replaces Stalinist Rigidity," *NYT*, October 21, 1957.

28. HES to his mother and Jan, August 10, 1957, box 571, HES Papers, CU.

29. HES, "Albanian Asks Tie to U.S. but Denounces Its Policy," *NYT*, August 29, 1957.

30. HES, "Albania Is Emerging from Isolation," *NYT*, September 9, 1957.

31. HES, "Albania Persists as Nation in Arms," *NYT*, September 10, 1957.

32. HES, "Albania Industry Still Far Behind," *NYT*, September 11, 1957.

33. HES, "Albanians Feast in Palace of Zog," *NYT*, September 12, 1957.

34. HES, "Chance for West Seen in Albania," *NYT*, September 13, 1957.

35. HES, "Diversity in East Europe Replaces Stalinist Rigidity," *NYT*, October 21, 1957.

36. HES to his mother and Jan, September 10, 1957, box 571, HES Papers, CU.

37. HES, "West's Ideas on Art Impress Rumanians," *NYT*, September 7, 1957.

38. Ibid.

39. HES, "Bucharest Cats Hep to U.S. Jive," *NYT*, September 8, 1957.

40. HES, "Diversity in Arts Found in Rumania," *NYT*, September 15, 1957.

41. HES, "Tito-Rumania Tie Close," *NYT*, September 19, 1957.

42. HES, "Iowa Corn Breeder Sows Seeds of Amity for U.S. in Rumania," *NYT*, September 26, 1957.

43. HES, "Radio, Rumanian-Style," *NYT*, October 6, 1957.

44. HES, "Diversity in East Europe Replaces Stalinist Rigidity," *NYT*, October 21, 1957.

45. HES, "Bulgarian Red Chief Urges Early Renewal of U.S. Ties," *NYT*, September 22, 1957.

46. Ibid.

47. HES, "Bulgaria Tempering Stalinist Outlook," *NYT*, September 23, 1957.

48. HES, "Rock 'n' Roll a Bulgarian Fad Despite Stern Ideological Edicts," *NYT*, September 24, 1957.

49. HES, "Bulgaria Builds Eastern Riviera," *NYT*, September 25, 1957.

50. HES, "'American' Wins Sofia's Plaudits," *NYT*, September 29, 1957.

51. HES, "Diversity in East Europe Replaces Stalinist Rigidity," *NYT*, October 21, 1957.

52. HES, "Young Refugees Long for America," *NYT*, August 8, 1957.

53. HES, "Siege of Cardinal Seems Near End," *NYT*, October 4, 1957.

54. HES, "Hungarian Leader Invites Offer on Mindszenty Exit," *NYT*, October 3, 1956.

55. HES, "Budapest Nervous at Approach of Anniversary of 1956 Revolt," *NYT*, October 5, 1957.

56. Ibid.

57. Ibid.

58. HES, "Kadar Battling Stalinist Group," *NYT*, October 6, 1957.

59. HES, "Hungarian Authors End Strike; Czechs Follow Own Literary Line," *NYT*, October 7, 1957.

60. HES, "Budapest Youths Found Apathetic," *NYT*, October 8, 1957.

61. HES, "Hungarian Prices Soar, Wages Fall," *NYT*, October 10, 1957.

62. HES, "Hungary Waits for Another October," *NYT*, October 20, 1957.

63. HES, "Diversity in East Europe Replaces Stalinist Rigidity," *NYT*, October 21, 1957.

64. HES, "Polish Premier Urges Step by Powers to Solve Issues," *NYT*, October 13, 1957.

65. HES, "Diversity in East Europe Replaces Stalinist Rigidity," *NYT*, October 21, 1957.

66. Ibid.

67. Ibid.

68. Ibid.

69. Ibid.

70. Quoted in Walter Russell Mead, *Special Providence: American Foreign Policy and How It Changed the World* (New York: Rutledge, 2002), vii.

71. HES, "Fount of Amity in East Europe Is Largely Untapped by the U.S.," *NYT*, October 22, 1957.

72. HES, "Eastern Europe Keeps Pay Down," *NYT*, October 23, 1957.

73. HES, "Eastern Europe Is Now Seeking More Democratic Communism," *NYT*, October 24, 1957.

74. HES, "East Europe Seen as a Third Force," *NYT*, October 25, 1957.

75. HES, ERF note, December 13, 1957, box 348, HES Papers, CU.

76. Ibid.

77. Ibid.

78. Ibid.

79. Ibid.

80. HES to Nuci Kotta, December 2, 1957, box 571, HES Papers, CU.

81. HES to Kotta, December 17, 1957, box 571, HES Papers, CU.

82. W. Colston Leigh, Inc., "Harrison Salisbury on Eastern Europe," box 15, HES Papers, CU.

83. Nelson Buhler to Lewis M. Marcy, January 6, 1958, box 15, HES Papers, CU.

84. Frank L. Dennis to HES, January 28, 1958, box 15, HES Papers, CU.

85. Comments by the U.S. Information Agency on Articles on Eastern Europe by Harrison Salisbury, box 15, HES Papers, CU.

86. HES to Washburn, January 31, 1958, box 15, HES Papers, CU.

87. HES to Vlado [Dedijer], March 13, 1980, box 307, HES Papers, CU.

6. "WITHOUT FEAR OR FAVOR"

1. Susan E. Tifft and Alex S. Jones, *The Trust: The Private and Powerful Family behind The New York Times* (Boston: Little, Brown, 1999), 629.

2. Harrison E. Salisbury (hereafter HES), "City Wages Constant Battle to Keep Street Litter-Free," *New York Times* (hereafter *NYT*), December 6, 1954; HES, "Litter Increased in Crowded Cities," *NYT*, December 7, 1954. See also Gay Talese's characterization of HES in *The Kingdom and the Power* (New York: World Publishing, 1969), 431, 442–43.

3. The seven HES articles are as follows: "Gangs That Plague the City Take Toll in Talents," *NYT*, March 24, 1958; "Youth Gang Members Tell of Lives, Hates and Fears," *NYT*, March 25, 1958; "'Shook' Youngsters Spring from the Housing Jungles," *NYT*, March 26, 1958; "Youth Outbreaks Traced to Turbulence in Family," *NYT*, March 27, 1958; "School Violence Reflects Instability in Adult World," *NYT*, March 28, 1958; "Well-Run Schools Solving Problems in City 'Jungles,'" *NYT*, March 29, 1958; "Lethargy of Public Found at Root of Youth Problem," *NYT*, March 30, 1958. For the book, see HES, *The Shook-Up Generation* (New York: Harper, 1958).

4. HES, *Shook-Up Generation*, 19.

5. Ibid., 163.

6. HES, "Youth, on the Streets, in the Schools," *NYT*, March 24, 1958.

7. HES, *Shook-Up Generation*, 23–38, quote on 46.

8. Ibid., 45, quote on 49.

9. Ibid., 53, quote on 61.

10. Ibid., 65, 67, 71, 79, 80, 84, quote on 77.

11. Ibid., 96, 117, 123, quote on 128.

12. Ibid., 167.

13. Ibid., 168, 171, 174, 180.

14. HES, *Without Fear or Favor:* The New York Times *and Its Times* (New York: Ballantine, 1980), 379–80.

15. Ibid.

16. HES, *A Time of Change: A Reporter's Tale of Our Time* (New York: Harper & Row, 1988), 42–51, quote on 51.

17. HES, *Without Fear*, 379; HES, *Time of Change*, 54–55.

18. HES, "Fear and Hatred Grip Birmingham," *New York Times*, April 12, 1960.

19. Ibid.

20. HES, *Time of Change*, 56–60, quotes on 58, 60; for quote on the malice standard, see "New York Times Co. v. Sullivan," *Wikipedia*, http://en.wikipedia.org/wiki/New_York_Times_Co._v._Sullivan (accessed July 13, 2012). HES discussed the Sullivan case in some detail in *Without Fear*, 388–90.

21. HES, *Time of Change*, 67.

22. Ibid., 71.

23. HES, "An Introduction to the Warren Commission Report," in *Report of the Warren Commission on the Assassination of President Kennedy* (New York: Bantam, 1964), xv–xix, quote on xix.

24. Ibid., xxv.

25. Ibid., xxix.

26. Ibid.

27. HES, *Without Fear*, 207–08, quotes on 207, 605.

28. Ibid., 209–10.

29. Ibid., 8–12, 213–15, quote on 7. Also see HES, *Time of Change*, 297, 316.

30. Neil Sheehan, introduction to *The Pentagon Papers*, edited by Neil Sheehan et al. (New York: Bantam, 1971), ix.

31. HES, *Without Fear*, 35, 121, 240, 246, quote on 187.

32. Ibid., 257.

33. Ibid., 259.

34. Ibid., 260, 282.

35. Ibid., 304–10.

36. Ibid., 312–13, 320–23, quotes on 313.

37. Ibid., 320, 329, 331, 333–36, quotes on 333, 334.

38. Ibid., 336, 339–41, quotes on 339–40, 341.

39. Ibid., 418.

40. Ibid., 423–24.

41. Ibid., 434–47.

42. Joseph C. Goulden, *Fit to Print: A.M. Rosenthal and His* Times (Secaucus, NJ: Lyle Stuart, 1988), 135–38, quotes on 138, 325.

43. Ibid., 324, 325.

44. Ibid., 139–41.

45. Ibid., quotes on 144, 145.

46. Ibid., 167. A photocopy of Daniel's letter is in Richard F. Shepard, *The Paper's Paper: A Reporter's Journey through the Archives of* The New York Times (New York: Times Books, 1996), 185. For more on Salisbury's Hanoi reporting, see chapter 7 below, and for his time as op-ed editor, see chapter 10.

47. HES to A. O. Sulzberger, September 2, 1966, box 641, HES Papers, Columbia University (hereafter CU).

48. HES to Abe Rosenthal, November 14, 1978, box 669, HES Papers, CU.

49. HES, *Time of Change*, 288, 289.

50. Ibid., 292.

51. See "Solzhenitsyn: Writer Caught Between," *NYT*, September 10, 1972.

52. HES to Heeb, March 7, 1974, box 240, HES Papers, CU.

53. Ibid. It should be noted that Solzhenitsyn's biographer D. M. Thomas points out Solzhenitsyn's "special rage" in the *NYT* "finessing a 'scoop.'" Michael Scammel, the "Open Letter's" translator, had offered the *NYT* his translation. That is when the *NYT* got the YMCA Press to give them a copy, claiming Scammel had authorized that. Scammel's friends in London translated it, but it was a toned-down version for Western readers, omitting the stronger anti-Western slant of the one sent to the Soviet leaders. See D. M. Thomas, *Alexander Solzhenitsyn: A Century in His Life* (New York: St. Martin's Press, 1998), 431.

54. Theodore Shabad, "Solzhenitsyn Asks Kremlin to Abandon Communism and Split Up Soviet Union," *NYT*, March 3, 1974.

55. Solzhenitsyn to HES, March 18, 1974, box 10, HES Papers, CU. There are sixteen signed letters from Solzhenitsyn to Salisbury, thirteen of them in Russian. Salisbury sent Solzhenitsyn forty letters. Solzhenitsyn discusses his "Open Letter" in *The Oak an the Calf: Sketches of Literary Life in the Soviet Union* (New York: Harper & Row, 1975), 350–51, 386–87. Olga Carlisle elaborates on the publication problems involved in its printing in her book *Solzhenitsyn and the Secret Circle* (London: Routledge and Kegan Paul, 1978), 176–80, 188–89.

56. HES to Sulzberger, November 5, 1985, box 348, HES Papers, CU.

57. HES, *Time of Change*, 293–96, quote on 298.

58. Ibid., 296–98, quotes on 296, 298.

59. Ibid., 299.

60. Ibid., 302.

61. HES, *Without Fear*, 589, 591, quote on 587.

62. William McGowan, *Gray Lady Down: What the Decline and Fall of the* New York Times *Means for America* (New York: Encounter Books, 2010), 1.

63. Ibid., 8–12, quote on 9.

64. HES, *Without Fear*, 230, 282, and chapter 28; Edwin Diamond, *Behind the Times: Inside the New* New York Times (Chicago: University of Chicago Press, 1995), 116.

65. Diamond, *Behind the Times*, 118.

66. Ibid., 181.

67. Ibid.,181, 219.

68. Ibid.

69. Ibid., 170.

70. Ibid., 177.

71. Ibid., 177–78.

72. Tifft and Jones, *The Trust*, 444.

73. Interview with Ross Terrill, October 27, 2010.

74. Talese, *Kingdom and Power*, 432.

75. Diamond, *Behind the Times*, 170.

76. Talese, *Kingdom and Power*, 432.

7. HANOI HARRY

1. Stanley Karnow, *Vietnam: A History* (New York: Penguin, 1983), 693–97.

2. Turner Catledge, *My Life and* The Times (New York: Harper & Row, 1971), 291.

3. Harrison E. Salisbury (hereafter HES), *A Time of Change: A Reporter's Tale of Our Time* (New York: Harper & Row, 1988), 125.

4. HES, *Behind the Lines—Hanoi December 23, 1966–January 7, 1967* (New York: Harper & Row, 1967), 10. See also HES, *Orbit of China* (New York: Harper & Row, 1967), especially 183–85.

5. HES, *Time of Change*, 119. Stanley Karnow believed it was a suggestion by the Australian journalist Wilfred Burchett to North Vietnamese officials that got him in. See Karnow, *Vietnam*, 503.

6. Zalin Grant, *Over the Beach: The Air War in Vietnam* (New York: W. W. Norton & Company, 2005), 119; for Seymour Topping's remark, see his *On the Front Lines of the Cold War: An American Correspondent's Journal from the Chinese Civil War to the Cuban Missile Crisis and Vietnam* (Baton Rouge: Louisiana State University Press, 2010), 312.

7. HES, *Behind the Lines*, 9, 11.

8. All these articles have been conveniently collected in *Harrison E. Salisbury's Trip to North Vietnam: Hearing Before the Committee on Foreign Relations, United States Senate, 19th Cong., 1st Sess., February 2, 1967* (Washington, DC: U.S. Government Printing Office, 1967), 86–144. (hereafter Fulbright Committee). The quotes are from HES, *Behind the Lines*, 39, 6.

9. Clifton Daniel to General M. C. Woodbury, January 25, 1967, noting Harrison's briefing to Rusk. See box 7, file "Harrison Salisbury, 1964–72," Clifton Daniel Papers, New York Public Library.

10. Neil Sheehan et al., ed., *The Pentagon Papers* (New York: Bantam, 1971), 542–55. The *Times* began publishing articles based on the Pentagon Papers on June 13, 1971. For the quote, see HES, "Visitor to Hanoi Inspects Damage Laid to U.S. Raids," *New York Times* (hereafter *NYT*), December 24/25, 1966 (here and below, first date indicates when the story was dispatched, the second when it was published).

11. "Draft Memorandum for President Lyndon B. Johnson, 'Actions Recommended for Vietnam,'" from Secretary of Defense Robert S. McNamara, October 14, 1966, in *Pentagon Papers*, 542–43 (hereafter Draft Memorandum, October 14, 1966).

12. CIA/DIA Report, "An Appraisal of the Bombing of North Vietnam through 12 September 1966," in *Pentagon Papers*, 551.

13. McNamara to LBJ, "Recommended FY67 Southeast Asia Supplemental Appropriation," November 17, 1966, in *Pentagon Papers*, 554.

14. CIA/DIA Report, "An Appraisal of the Bombing of North Vietnam through 12 September 1966," in *Pentagon Papers*, 551.

15. Draft Memorandum, October 14, 1966, 544.

16. Ibid.

17. McNamara to LBJ, "Recommended FY67 Southeast Asia Supplemental Appropriation," in *Pentagon Papers*, 554.

18. General Earle G. Wheeler, Chairman, to McNamara, October 14, 1966, in *Pentagon Papers*, 552–53.

19. Karnow, *Vietnam*, 504.

20. HES, *Time of Change*, 151.

21. Transcript of a panel discussion held at the Waldorf Astoria, January 5, 1967, box 454, file 1, HES Papers, Columbia University (hereafter CU). After a January 1, 1967, *CBS Face the Nation* program, Rusk got aggressive. "You should tell Mr. Salisbury to ask the North Vietnamese if they have any regiments in South Vietnam." Then Rusk said in jest but with considerable forcefulness, "Don't bother, I already talked to Punch Sulzberger and Clifton Daniel over the telephone about that." Rusk emphasized that if a bombing pause did not work, *NYT* editorials should support the administration. See "Memo on Rusk's Off-the-Record Comments," January 1, 1967, box 7, file "Harrison Salisbury, 1964–72," Clifton Daniel Papers, New York Public Library.

22. HES, "Visitor to Hanoi Inspects Damage Laid to U.S. Raids," *NYT*, December 24/25, 1966.

23. Ibid.; HES, *Behind the Lines*, 63, 67.

24. HES, "U.S. Raids Batter 2 Towns: Supply Route Is Little Hurt," *NYT*, December 25/27, 1966; HES, "Foes Transport Little Affected by Raids on Key Supply Route," *NYT*, December 26/27, 1966.

25. Ibid.

26. HES, "Hanoi During an Air Alert: Waitresses Take Up Rifles to Fire at Planes," *NYT*, December 27/28, 1966.

27. HES, "New Capital Planned by Hanoi," *NYT*, December 28/29, 1966.

28. HES, *Behind the Lines*, 94. Daniel called Harrison's dispatches a "journalistic coup" with no parallels of being behind the enemy lines, and Walter Lippmann told Sulzberger that Harrison's reports "will long be remembered as an example of the fact that the highest obligation of a newspaper is to put the search for truth in the first place, second to no other consideration." See Daniel to Turner Catledge, January 27, 1967; Lippmann to Sulzberger, January 7, 1967; and Sulzberger to Lippmann, January 16, 1967, box 7, file "Harrison Salisbury, 1964–72," Clifton Daniel Papers, New York Public Library.

29. HES, *Behind the Lines*, 95–96.

30. Ibid., 97, 97n.

31. Ibid., 100, quote on 103.

32. Ibid., 98, quotes on 99, 102–04. For Phil G. Goulding's remarks, see his book *Confirm or Deny: Informing the People on National Security* (New York: Harper & Row, 1970), 52–67. Karnow quotes him as later saying that Harrison's dispatches presented the administration with a "credibility disaster" and that Salisbury's reports were a "reasonably accurate picture" of the damage. Karnow, *Vietnam*, 504.

33. HES, "U.S. Raids Batter 2 Towns; Supply Route Is Little Hurt," *NYT*, December 25/27, 1966.

34. Ibid., and HES, *Behind the Lines*, 97.

35. For George C. Wilson's supposed revelation, see "Salisbury's 'Casualties' Tally with Viet Reds'," *Washington Post*, January 1, 1967; for a transcript of the report, see Fulbright Committee, 81–85. Another transcript is in John Gerassi, *North Vietnam: A Documentary* (Indianapolis: Bobbs-Merrill, 1968), 77–82. Gerassi toured Namdinh on January 1, 1967, and came to Salisbury's conclusions. For the controversial data, see page 79. Gerassi emphasized that Salisbury "had to be blasted" by the Department of Defense. Arthur Sylvester, assistant secretary of defense for public affairs, claimed Salisbury's reports were full of "mistaken fact."

In other words, Salisbury was a liar. See Gerassi, *North Vietnam*, 46. One of the air raid pilots, Dick Wyman, came to agree with Salisbury and challenged the other pilots. See Zalin Grant, *Over the Beach*, 125–26.

36. The careful historian Barbara Tuchman in her book *The March of Folly: From Troy to Vietnam* (New York: Ballantine, 1984), 340, notes that Salisbury's reports on hits to civilian areas—which were "first denied, then admitted by the Air Force—raised an uproar." LBJ's poll ratings slid to the negative, and he never regained popular support for the war. Grant in *Over the Beach*, 301, agrees, referring to Salisbury's *Behind the Lines*: "No work was more influential in forming opinions about the air war, and one finds it hard to remember—at least until one reads it a second time—that his book was based on a two-week stay in North Vietnam."

37. For the articles mentioned, see "Washington Wire," *Wall Street Journal*, January 6, 1967; Joseph Alsop, "Matter of Fact: Hanoi's Propaganda Offensive," *Washington Post*, January 9, 1967; Joseph Kraft, "The Salisbury Affair," *Washington Post*, January 9, 1967; John Chamberlain, "Control of Red Propaganda Urged," *Washington Post*, January 9, 1967. More could be said about the press rhubarb over Salisbury's Namdinh dispatches. For an outstanding and full review of press reaction, see Mark Atwood Lawrence, "Mission Intolerable: Harrison Salisbury's Trip to Hanoi and the Limits of Dissent against the Vietnam War," *Pacific Historical Review* 75, no. 3 (August 2006): 429–60. It should be noted that Salisbury kept a file of these newspaper articles in his archive: box 400, HES Papers, CU.

38. Walter Lippmann, "Harrison Salisbury in Hanoi," *Washington Post*, January 10, 1967. He would later support Harrison's Pulitzer Prize bid. See Walter Lippmann to Arthur Ochs Sulzberger, January 7, 1967, where he praises Salisbury's dispatches, box 400, HES Papers, CU; and Lippmann to Pulitzer Prize Advisory Board, January 30, 1967, box 454, HES Papers, CU. For Topping's criticism of Salisbury for "attribution," see his *On the Front Lines*, 317.

39. "Targets Military, Johnson Believes," *NYT*, December 29, 1966. See also the later Transcript of Johnson's actual news conference, December 31, 1966, in *Public Papers of the Presidents, Lyndon Baines Johnson, 1966* (Washington: GPO, 1967), 1461–62, or check http://www.presidency.ucsb.edu/ws/index.php?pid=28076 under the sections titled "Bombing Targets in North Vietnam" and "Peace Negotiations."

40. HES, *Time of Change*, 152, 153. (LBJ does not mention HES in his memoir, *The Vantage Point: Perspectives of the Presidency, 1963–1969* [New York: Holt, Rinehart and Winston, 1971].)

41. Walt Rostow to the president, December 31, 1966, box 252, file "Texas Libraries," HES Papers, CU.

42. Karnow, *Vietnam*, 504.

43. Joseph C. Goulden, *Fit to Print: A.M. Rosenthal and His* Times (Secaucus, NJ: Lyle Stuart, 1988), 142.

44. Neil Sheehan, "Raids' Precision Seen in Reports," *NYT*, December 29/30, 1966.

45. Hanson W. Baldwin, "Bombing of the North—U.S. Officers Assert It Has Proved Effective, Restrained and Essential," *NYT*, December 30, 1966. There was an article that appeared in *Look* magazine, November 29, 1966, p. 62, by Norman Barrymaine, "Memo from Haiphong, North Vietnam: Under American Bombs," which supposedly contradicted Salisbury, claiming the bombing was effective. It also gave no attributions and focused only on Haiphong.

46. "Hanoi Dispatches to the *Times* Criticized," *NYT*, January 1, 1967. Also, according to Turner Catledge, then executive editor at the *Times*, "The criticism was silly, but it had a certain effectiveness when put to people who had not thought through the situation." See Catledge, *My Life*, 292.

47. Editorial, *NYT*, January 2, 1967.

48. See, for instance, Ann B. Bilpusch to "gentlemen," January 24, 1967, in box 455, file 5-7, HES Papers, CU. She asked whether the *Times* was a communist paper. After all, she wrote, Salisbury copied his data from a North Vietnamese propaganda pamphlet. Harrison and the *Times* received many such letters. Harrison mentions receiving over three hundred letters with three-to-one favorable and the *Times* got another thousand letters in about the same ratio. See HES, *Time of Change*, 167.

49. "U.S. Pilot Says Enemy Missiles Fell Near Hanoi," *NYT*, January 3, 1967.

50. Drew Middleton, "Hanoi's Bomb Damage—Western Diplomats See in Reds' Protests Signs the U.S. Raids Hurt War Effort," *NYT*, January 10, 1967.

51. William P. Bundy interviewed by Paige E. Mulhollan, June 2, 1969, Lyndon B. Johnson Presidential Library (hereafter LBJ Library), http://webstorage4.mepa.virginia.edu/lbj/oralhistory/bundy_william_1969_0602.pdf (hereafter Bundy Interview), 21.

52. "Flack from Hanoi," *Time*, January 6, 1967; "Static of Distress," *Time*, January 13, 1967.

53. I. F. Stone, "Harrison Salisbury's Dastardly War Crime," *I.F. Stone's Weekly* 15, no. 1, (January 9, 1967): 1, 4. See Halberstam's take on the *Post*'s war stance and belated change in mid-1969 in his *The Powers That Be* (New York: Alfred A. Knopf, 1979), chapter 19; note especially his description of Roberts as the "very embodiment of an establishment reporter" (534). Kennedy wanted Halberstam out of Saigon in 1963 (445–46).

54. HES, "Hanoi's Propaganda Stresses Tradition: War against Odds," *NYT*, December 29/30, 1966.

55. HES, "No Military Targets, Hanoi Insists," *NYT*, December 30/31, 1966; HES, "Problems of Coverage," *NYT*, December 30/31, 1966. (Sometimes these two dispatches are confused as a single dispatch.)

56. HES, "Attacks on North Disrupt Economy," *NYT*, December 31, 1966/January 1, 1967; HES, "Villagers Tell of Raids in North," *NYT*, January 1/2, 1967.

57. HES, "North Vietnam Runs on Bicycles," *NYT*, January 5/7, 1967.

58. HES, "Catholic Charity Aide Visiting Hanoi," *NYT*, January 7/9, 1967. For a summary of the pope's message and Ho's full response, see George C. Herring, ed., *The Secret Diplomacy of the Vietnam War: The Negotiating Volumes of the Pentagon Papers* (Austin: University of Texas Press, 1983), 473–74.

59. Hanoi's four basic conditions were as follows: (1) withdrawal of all U.S. military personnel, equipment, and bases; (2) pending reunification, the North and South must not enter into any foreign military alliances and must not allow foreign troops, equipment, or bases in either; (3) internal affairs of the South must be settled according to the NLF's program; (4) peaceful reunification must be the work of the peoples of each and without foreign interference. For Pham Van Dong's sanitized interview with Salisbury and the four points, see Fulbright Committee, 145–50 and 150–51, respectively.

60. State 121586 to Amembassy, Warsaw, S/Nodis, January 19, 1967, in Herring, *Secret Diplomacy*, 335–36, italics ours.

61. For Salisbury's version of his interview with Premier Pham Van Dong, see HES, "Hanoi Premier Tells View; Some in U.S. Detect a Shift," *NYT*, January 3/4, 1967.

62. Herring, *Secret Diplomacy*, 211ff. See also James G. Hershberg, *Marigold: The Lost Chance for Peace in Vietnam* (Stanford: Stanford University Press, 2012).

63. As to the apparent contradictions between Salisbury's second dispatch and the Defense Department concerning the announcements of air raids on Namdinh, see the letter of Deputy Assistant Secretary for Public Affairs of the Defense Department Philip G. Goulding to Congressman Ogden Reid, reproduced in Fulbright Committee, 49–54, at 53. For quote, see Karnow, *Vietnam*, 504.

64. HES, "Aide Says Liberation Front Is Independent of the North," *NYT*, January 4/5, 1967.

65. "Ashmore reported to State Department officials that he and Baggs felt that 'Ho seemed prepared to consider a specific proposal based on a formula of mutual de-escalation' of the fighting" (Herring, *Secret Diplomacy*, 511).

66. Ibid., 511–16. See also Chalmers Roberts, "Chronology of the Viet Peace Efforts," *Washington Post*, September 18, 1967.

67. HES, "Hanoi Inviting Westerners to Inspect Bomb Damage," *NYT*, January 10/11, 1967.

68. HES, "North Vietnamese Roads Come to Life at Nightfall, *NYT*, January 11/12, 1967; HES, "Bomb Controversy: View from the Ground," *NYT*, January 11/13, 1967.

69. HES, "Hanoi's Industry Being Dispersed," *NYT*, January 11/14, 1967; HES, "North Vietnam Spirit Found High," *NYT*, January 11/15, 1967.

70. HES, "Hanoi Denies Aim Is to Annex the South," *NYT*, January 11/16, 1967.

71. HES, "Soviet-China Rift Hurting Hanoi Aid," *NYT*, January 11/17, 1967.

72. HES, "A Turning Point in War Is Seen by Hanoi Visitor," *NYT*, January 11/18, 1967.

73. HES, *Behind the Lines*, 203. (In reviewing this book, Lee Lockwood complained about it and the articles: "Salisbury was in a position to demolish the lie [LBJ's] singlehandedly. Instead, through carelessness, he gratuitously created a little credibility gap of his own, which inevitably dulled the impact of his on-the-scenes observations." (See Lee Lockwood, "Salisbury's Stake," *New York Review of Books*, August 3, 1967.)

74. HES, *Behind the Lines*, 217–18, 242, quote on 218.

75. HES, *Time of Change*, 154–55.

76. Harrison E. Salisbury interviewed by Paige E. Mulhollan, June 26, 1969, LBJ Library, http://millercenter.org/scripps/digitalarchive/oralhistories/detail/2963 (hereafter HES Interview), 15, 27.

77. David Halberstam, *The Best and the Brightest* (New York: Ballantine, 1992), 632.

78. Ibid., 644–45.

79. HES, *Time of Change*, 148.

80. Herring, *Secret Diplomacy*, 211–13.

81. Actually, Rusk had attempted to communicate with Salisbury through the *Times* publisher Punch Sulzberger in order to make sure Harrison asked the premier the "right questions." See HES Interview, 18.

82. HES, *Time of Change*, 164–65, quote on 165; Rostow to LBJ, January 3, 1967, 7:10 p.m., box 252, HES Papers, CU.

83. Memorandum of a talk with Rusk, January 13, 1967, box 591, file 8, "Conversations," HES Papers, CU.

84. HES Interview, 17.

85. Ibid.

86. "Memorandum for the President: Highlights of Harrison Salisbury's Private Report to Me," January 14, 1967, box 252, file "Texas Libraries," HES Papers, CU.

87. See the *New York Times*, January 8, 1967, or the *Washington Post*, January 9, 1967, or as reprinted by the Fulbright Committee, "Text of the Statement Made by Premier Pham in Hanoi," 145–51.

88. "Memorandum for the President: Highlights of Harrison Salisbury's Private Report to Me," January 14, 1967, box 252, file "Texas Libraries," HES Papers, CU.

89. Ibid.

90. HES, *Time of Change*, 166.

91. Bundy Interview, 18, 21.

92. Conversation with Arthur Goldberg, January 20, 1967, box 590, file 5, HES Papers, CU.

93. HES to Bundy, January 17, 1967, box 2, file "Bundy," HES Papers, CU.

94. Bundy to HES, January 25, 1967, box 2, file "Bundy," HES Papers, CU. In the HES archive there is an interesting research paper by David Barboza, "The Dispatches of Harrison E. Salisbury: A Study in Passionate Journalism," dated November 18, 1989. He also gave Harrison a "B" and agreed with denying Salisbury a Pulitzer Prize, mainly on the question of attribution. Barboza is now a well-known journalist himself. See box 294, file 1, HES Papers, CU.

95. HES to Bundy, June 5, 1967, box 2, file "Bundy," HES Papers, CU.

96. "Peter Jennings and the News," January 12, 1967, 6:30 p.m., box 400, file 12, HES Papers, CU.

97. Ibid.

98. See, for example, Atwood Lawrence, "Mission Intolerable," 456, where he calls Salisbury's series "journalistically sound." Lawrence further asserts, "At no point are readers ever in doubt that they are reading reports based on information available within North Vietnam, whether written information supplied by Hanoi authorities or eyewitness observations" (456).

99. "Commentary by ABC correspondent John Scali after network program *Scope—Eyewitness* interview with Harrison Salisbury of *New York Times* in Hong Kong. Program aired, full network, (135 stations) Saturday night," January 14, 1966, in box 400, file 12, HES Papers, CU.

100. HES to William Sheehan, January 17, 1967, box 400, file 12, HES Papers, CU.

101. Ibid.

102. See the exchange of letters, Scali to HES, January 16, 1967; HES to Scali, January 18, 1967, box 400, file 12, HES Papers, CU.

103. See J. W. Fulbright to HES, January 24, 1967, thanking Harrison for accepting an invitation to testify, and afterward his appreciation for Harrison's observations, J. W. Fulbright to HES, February 7, 1967, box 5, file "Fulbright," HES Papers, CU.

104. Fulbright Committee, 1–11.

105. Ibid., 13–15.

106. Ibid., 20.

107. Ibid., 21.

108. Ibid., 24–25.

109. Ibid., 26.

110. Ibid., quote on 28–29.

111. Ibid., 30–32, quote on 32.

112. Ibid., 33–34. (For the quote and an explanation of Sunflower, see Herring, *Secret Diplomacy*, 211; for the two letters, see 440–41, 476–77.)

113. Fulbright Committee, 36.

114. Ibid., 39–40.

115. Ibid., 40–41.

116. Ibid., 42.

117. Ibid., 49–51, quotes on 49, 50.

118. Ibid., 51–53, quotes on 51, 53.

119. Ibid., 61, quote on 62. (For the Alsop and Wicker articles, see 59–61. Alsop's appeared in the *Washington Post*, "The Biggest News," February 1, 1967; Wicker's ran in the *New York Times*, "Vietnam: If Astrologers Were Diplomats," February 2, 1967.)

120. Ibid., 63–64. (For the Sheehan article, see 65–75. It appeared in the *New York Times* as "Crisis in Vietnam: Antecedents of the Struggle," April 27, 1964 and "Not a Dove, but No Longer a Hawk," October 9, 1966.)

121. Ibid., 76.

122. Karnow, *Vietnam War*, 504.

123. Ibid.

124. Catledge, *My Life*, 293; interview with Charlotte Y. Salisbury, May 29, 2008, Salisbury, CT. Harrison had written that 1967 was especially bad for the *NYT* and Pulitzer Prizes. Tom Wicker's team had done a series of articles on the CIA but only came out a close contender. And then there was Topping's complaint that once the *Times* failed to get the Pulitzer for Harrison, Topping could not be considered. Check Topping, *On the Front Lines*, 317.

125. Maurice Carroll, "Rift Is Disclosed in Pulitzer Vote," *NYT*, May 2, 1967.

126. See John Hohenberg, *The Pulitzer Prize: A History of the Awards in Books, Drama, Music, and Journalism Based on the Private Files over Six Decades* (New York: Columbia University Press, 1974), quotes on 297, 298. See also his 392n3 and a listing of the names of the advisory board members, 359–60. For the composition of the jury and its votes and ranking, see "To: Advisory Committee, In Category 5—International Reporting, Jury Submits These Recommendations, March 9, 1967." For the quotes from the exchange of telegrams between Kirk and Pulitzer, check Kirk to Pulitzer, May 1, 1967 and Pulitzer to Kirk, May 1, 1967. The authors are indebted to Claudia Stone Weissberg, website manager, and Professor Sig Gissler, administrator, Pulitzer Prizes, Columbia University, for the archival materials. Also see the *Saint Louis Post-Dispatch* of May 1, 1967, for what transpired with the advisory board.

127. "Declining Honor," *Time*, May 12, 1967.

128. *NYT*, July 1, 1967.

129. Gay Talese, *The Kingdom and the Power* (New York: World Publishing, 1969), 449.

130. Carroll, "Rift Is Disclosed in Pulitzer Vote," *NYT*, May 2, 1967.

8. THE MIDDLE KINGDOM

1. Harrison E. Salisbury (hereafter HES), *A Time of Change: A Reporter's Tale of Our Time* (New York: Harper & Row, 1988), 234.

2. Ibid., 246.

3. Ibid., 200–209, quotes on 204, 208.

4. HES to Anna Louise Strong (hereafter ALS), July 30, 1956, box 10, HES Papers, Columbia University (hereafter CU); ALS to HES, August 4, 1956, box 10, HES Papers, CU.

5. HES to ALS, October 14, 1958, box 214, HES Papers, CU.

6. ALS to Zhou Enlai, November 4, 1958, box 214, HES Papers, CU.

7. ALS to HES, November 10, 1958, box 10, HES Papers, CU; ALS to HES, November 30, 1958, box 10, HES Papers, CU.

8. HES to ALS, December 21, 1958, box 214, HES Papers, CU.

9. HES to Zhou Enlai, January 2, 1959, box 214, HES Papers, CU; Frankel to HES, January 19, 1959, box 4, HES Papers, CU; HES to Zhou Enlai, February 3, 1959, box 214, HES Papers, CU; ALS to HES, May 13, 1959, box 10, HES Papers, CU. On July 19, 1959, Strong told Salisbury not this year, but maybe 1960; see ALS to HES, July 19, 1959, box 10, HES Papers, CU.

10. HES, "Haunting Enigma of Red China," *New York Times* (hereafter *NYT*), June 12, 1960.

11. HES to ALS, February 24, 1961, box 10, HES Papers, CU; ALS to HES, April 4, 1961, box 10, HES Papers, CU.

12. Snow to HES, April 4, 1961, box 10, HES Papers, CU. For further discussion of this issue, see Edgar Snow, *The Other Side of the River: Red China Today* (New York: Random House, 1961), 8–9. Dulles forbade Americans to go by threatening violators with loss of their passports, fines, and imprisonment. Eisenhower himself appealed to a few important publishers who were disinclined to defy him.

13. HES to Snow, June 27, 1961, box 10, HES Papers, CU.

14. HES to ALS, June 27, 1961, box 214, HES Papers, CU.

15. ALS to HES, July 15, 1961, box 10, HES Papers, CU.

16. HES to ALS, August 3, 1961, box 214, HES Papers, CU; HES to ALS, December 1, 1961, box 214, HES Papers, CU; HES to ALS, August 31, 1962, box 214, HES Papers, CU.

17. ALS to HES, November 11, 1963, box 10, HES Papers, CU.

18. Snow to HES, September 25, 1962, box 212, HES Papers, CU; HES to ALS, November 18, 1963, box 10, HES Papers, CU.

19. Gerald Long (Reuters), "Chou, in Interview, Scores U.S. on 'Aggression' toward China: Premier Says Threats Prevent Ties—Affirms Desire for India Accord and Calls Economy Improved," *NYT*, October 14, 1963; Edgar Snow (*Le Nouveau Candide*), "China Rejects 'Two China's,'" *NYT*, February 3, 1964.

20. HES to ALS, February 5, 1964, box 214, HES Papers, CU; HES to ALS, May 4, 1965, box 214, HES Papers, CU; HES to ALS, January 27, 1966, box 214, HES Papers, CU; HES to Snow, February 21, 1966, box 10, HES Papers, CU; HES to ALS, March 8, 1966, box 214, HES Papers, CU; HES to ALS, March 21, 1966, box 214, HES Papers, CU.

21. Catledge to Joseph Callahan, March 29, 1966, box 2, HES Papers, CU; HES to Eaton, April 8, 1966, box 3, HES Papers, CU; Eaton to HES, April 13, 1966, box 3, HES Papers, CU.

22. HES, *Orbit of China* (New York: Harper & Row, 1967).

23. HES, "China—Nuclear Gains Worry Asia: Advances in Peking More Rapid Than Was Expected," *NYT*, August 15, 1966.

24. HES, "Mao Effort to Steel Youth Seen behind Peking Purge," *NYT*, August 16, 1966.

25. HES, "Customs Check Strict—Soviet-Chinese Hostility Found along Frontier," *NYT*, August 17, 1966.

26. HES, "Indians Seek to Counter Power of Chinese in Asia," *NYT*, August 18, 1966.

27. HES, "Japan, Spurred on by China, Ponders Atomic Weapons," *NYT*, August 19, 1966.

28. "Literary Supplement," *London Times*, 1966.

29. HES, *Orbit of China*, 195–96.

30. Letters of HES to ALS, May 5, 1966; September 29, 1966; January 27, 1967; February 7, 1967; December 15, 1967, box 214, HES Papers, CU.

31. HES to Snow, January 19, 1967, box 10, HES Papers, CU.

32. HES to Eaton, November 14, 1967, box 3, HES Papers, CU.

33. HES to Snow, December 15, 1967, box 212, HES Papers, CU; HES to Snow, December 6, 1967, box 10, HES Papers, CU; HES to Snow, April 3, 1968, box 10, HES Papers, CU.

34. Myrdal to HES, January 24, 1969, box 8, HES Papers, CU.

35. HES to Snow, July 25, 1969, box 10, HES Papers, CU.

36. HES to Snow, March 31, 1971, box 212, HES Papers, CU; HES to Snow, June 18, 1971, box 212, HES Papers, CU.

37. HES to Zhou Enlai, April 21, 1971, box 215, HES Papers, CU; July 12, 1971, box 215, HES Papers, CU.

38. HES, *To Peking and Beyond: A Report on the New Asia* (New York: Capricorn Books, 1973), 10.

39. Ibid., 8.

40. Harrison, according to Ross Terrill, was astonished when after their 1972 visit to China Joseph Alsop told him, "Well, Harry, I guess you and I were the only ones that were right about China all along." Ross Terrill, Diary, April 26, 1974.

41. HES, *Peking and Beyond*, 13.

42. Ibid., 17, 18, 21, 31, 37, 40.

43. Ibid., 27–28.

44. Ibid., 31–40.

45. Ibid., 43–57.

46. Ibid., quotes on 61, 70.

47. Ibid., chapter 6.

48. Ibid., 86–92.

49. Ibid., 109, quote on 114.

50. Ibid., 117, 120.

51. Interview with Mrs. Charlotte Y. Salisbury, May 29, 2008. See HES's detailed notes of this encounter, "Dinner with Chou Enlai," June 16, 1972, box 365, HES Papers, CU.

52. HES, *Peking and Beyond*, 258–59.

53. Ibid., chapters 20–23.

54. HES to Zhou Enlai, August 1, 1972, box 215, HES Papers, CU; HES to Zhou Enlai, March 1, 1973, box 215, HES Papers, CU; HES to Zhou Enlai, January 3, 1974, box 215, HES Papers, CU.

55. HES, *Time of Change*, 196, 197.

56. Ibid., 198–99. See also Allen Brinkley, *The Publisher: Henry Luce and His American Century* (New York: Vintage, 2011).

57. HES, *Time of Change*, 204–10.

58. Ibid., 214, 215.

59. Ibid., 218, 219.

60. Ibid., 220, 221.

61. Ibid., 228.

62. Ibid., chapter 23.

63. Ibid., 258.

64. HES to Service, February 9, 1977, box 219, HES Papers, CU.

65. HES to Huang Hua, June 1, 1979, box 212, HES Papers, CU.

66. HES to Yao Wei, December 16, 1979, box 215, HES Papers, CU.

67. See dust jacket of HES, *China: 100 Years of Revolution* (New York: Holt, Rinehart and Winston, 1983).

68. HES interview with Vice Premier and Vice Party Chairman Li Xiannian, July 25, 1980, box 215, HES Papers, CU.

69. HES to Foreign Minister Huang Hua, December 26, 1980, box 212, HES Papers, CU.

70. HES to a friend, December 22, 1980, box 5, HES Papers, CU.

71. Charlotte Y. Salisbury, *Long March Diary: China Epic* (New York: Walker & Co., 1986), 101–9, quote on 109. See also John Paton Davies Jr., *China Hand: An Autobiography* (Philadelphia: University of Pennsylvania Press, 2012).

72. HES, *Tiananmen Square: Thirteen Days in June* (Boston: Little, Brown, 1989), 3, 5, 56, 68.

73. Ibid., 160.

74. Ibid., 150–70, quote on 171.

75. Ibid., 173.

76. Ibid., 20.

77. Ibid., 28–39.

78. Ibid., 67.

79. Ibid., 45.

80. Ibid., 77–79, 89, 90.

81. Ibid., 137.

82. Ibid., 147, 156, quote on 154.

83. HES to Jan, July 7, 1989, box 8, HES Papers, CU.

84. HES, "Notes, with Zhang Yuanyuan, Lui Yadong," October 30, 1989, box 232, HES Papers, CU.

85. HES to Yao Wei, November 27, 1989, box 232, HES Papers, CU.

86. HES to Lao Zhang, December 23, 1990, box 232, HES Papers, CU.

9. HISTORIAN AND NOVELIST

1. Harrison E. Salisbury (hereafter HES), *The 900 Days: The Siege of Leningrad* (Cambridge, MA: Da Capo Press, 2003), 28–29, 35–38.

2. Ibid., 45.

3. Ibid., 46–47.

4. Ibid., 51–52.

5. Ibid., 57–60, 64–65, quotes on 66.

6. Ibid., 81.

7. Ibid., 68–69, 75, 77, quotes on 73, 76, 80, 81.

8. Ibid., 119.

9. Ibid., 133–35, 138–40, quote on 141.

10. Ibid., 144–48, quote on 143.

11. Ibid., 181–91, quote on 188.

12. Ibid., 196–201, quote on 210.

13. Ibid., 217–20, quotes on 217–18, 220.

14. Ibid., 222–38, quote on 238n1.

15. Ibid., 243–45, 249.

16. Ibid., 251–59.

17. Ibid., 263, 268–69, quote on 260.

18. Ibid., 273.

19. Ibid., 273, 275, 279–80, 286, quote on 273.

20. Ibid., 291–94.

21. Ibid., 311–12, 314–15.

22. Ibid., 573, 575–77, quotes on 575, 576.

23. Ibid., 579–83, quotes on 581, 582; see especially 579n7–8.

24. A. J. P. Taylor, "The Hero City," *New York Review of Books*, April 10, 1969. For HES's response, see "Stalin's Bad Character," *New York Review of Books*, May 22, 1969.

25. HES, *Black Night, White Snow: Russia's Two Revolutions, 1905–1917* (Garden City, NJ: Doubleday & Company, 1977), Author's Note, and 488.

26. Ibid., 2–3, 608–9, quote on 612.

27. Ibid., 73.

28. Ibid., 48.

29. Ibid., 74, quote on 75. See also 94n and chapter 23, "The Starets."

30. Ibid., 243, 245.

31. Ibid., 268.

32. Ibid., 269–70, 314ff.

33. Ibid., chapters 30–32. Salisbury recounts the changeover of ministers by Rasputin through his domination of the Czarina.

34. Ibid., 314–486.

35. Ibid., 489.

36. Ibid., 494.

37. Ibid., 474.

38. Ibid., 424.

39. Ibid., 509–11, 534, 539, 548, 553.

40. Ibid., 559, 579–612.

41. Ibid., 609.

42. Robert Conquest, review of *Black Night, White Snow*, by HES, *New York Times*, January 29, 1978.

43. HES, *The Long March: The Untold Story* (New York: Harper & Row, 1985), 4.

44. HES, *A Time of Change: A Reporter's Tale of Our Time* (New York: Harper & Row, 1988), 251.

45. Charlotte Y. Salisbury, *Long March Diary: China Epic* (New York: Walker and Company, 1986), xi, 5.

46. Authors' conversation with Chinese scholars, May 2010, in Shanghai.

47. C. Salisbury, *Long March Diary*, 41.

48. Ibid., 15–16, 19, 20, 25, 29, 47–48, 67, quote on 41.

49. Ibid., 64.

50. HES, *Long March*, 5, 9, 29, 57, 59, 60–63.

51. Ibid., 69.

52. Ibid., 75.

53. Ibid., 76.

54. Ibid., 78.

55. Ibid., chapter 8 and page 69.

56. Ibid., 100, 104–5, 110, 113, quote on 126.

57. Ibid., 127, 146, 153, 155–56, quote on 164.

58. Ibid., 180, 182, 187, quote on 186.

59. Ibid., 194, 198, 227, 229–30, 232, 243–44, quotes on 224, 226.

60. Ibid., 250–51, 260, 261, 269, 271, quote on 263.

61. Ibid., 274–75, 279–85, 287–88, quotes on 281, 282, 296.

62. Ibid., 316–17, 319, 321, 323.

63. Ibid., 330, 339, quote on 348.

64. Steven C. Averill, review of *The Long March*, by HES, *Journal of Asian Studies* 46, no. 1 (February 1987): 118–21; authors' interview Ross Terrill, October 27, 2010.

65. HES, *The New Emperors: China in the Era of Mao and Deng* (Boston: Little, Brown, 1992), 9, 11, 12–15ff, quote on 47.

66. Ibid., 47–53, Mao quote on 55.

67. Ibid., 56ff.

68. Ibid., 84–85.

69. Ibid., 89–90, quote on 90.

70. Ibid., 91.

71. Ibid., quote on 97, 99.

72. Ibid., 103.

73. Ibid., 115, 121–23.

74. Ibid., 136, 138, quote on 139.

75. Ibid., 144–45, quote on 146.

76. Ibid., 149–50, quote on 151, 157–59.

77. Ibid., quotes on 176, 177.

78. Ibid., 181, 183, 185–86.

79. Ibid., 191–92, 196–97, quote on 207.
80. Ibid., 209, 212, 213.
81. Ibid., 222–23.
82. Ibid., 222–24, quote on 225.
83. Ibid., 236–37, 243, 247, 254, 270–71, 272.
84. Ibid., 288–89, 292–302, 305, quote on 306.
85. Ibid., 325–26, 330–31, 344, 346ff, 369, quotes on 332, 337, 340.
86. Ibid., 373–74, 383–84, 389–90, 392, 405, quotes on 385, 422.
87. Ibid., 430–31, 433–37, 439–45, 450–51, 457–58, quote on 457. This gloomy prediction followed Harrison's commentary in his book *Tiananmen Diary: Thirteen Days in June* (Boston: Little, Brown, 1989). His judgment there was that "The trend is down and it will not change" (173). The old guard of party elders had gained control, especially Yang Shangkun. In 2010 the authors visited a remarkably free and rapidly advancing China, contrary to Harrison's forecast. See Eugene P. Trani's op-ed piece, "China on the Move," *Richmond Times Dispatch*, Sunday, June 13, 2010: "Wherever we went, we saw the same signs of China clearly emerging as a major world power in the 21st century."
88. Ross Terrill, Diary, November 14, 1989, New York.
89. Interview with Ross Terrill, October 27, 2010. See also Anne Stevenson-Yang, "The New Emperors," *China Business Review* (May–June 1992): 40; John Pomfret, "Two Men, One Dynasty," *Far Eastern Economic Review*, October 8, 1992, 40; Michael Fathers, "China Whisperers," *Independent*, August 23, 1992; Frederick C. Teiwes, "The New Emperors," *China Quarterly*, no. 137 (March 1994): 248–50; and R. James Ferguson, "The Dangers of Dramatic Biography," *Culture Mandala* 1, no. 1 (1994): 69–73.
90. See Anthony Astrachan's review of *The Gates of Hell*, where he complains about the novel's historical veracity (*New York Times*, November 2, 1975).
91. HES, *The Northern Palmyra Affair* (New York: Harper & Brothers, 1962).
92. See David Dempsey's review of *The Northern Palmyra Affair* (*New York Times*, April 15, 1962).
93. HES, *The Gates of Hell* (New York: Random House, 1975).

10. THE GREAT GADFLY

1. Harrison E. Salisbury (hereafter HES), telex No. 011-342, box 55, HES Papers, Columbia University (hereafter CU).
2. "Social Gadfly," *Wikipedia*, http://en.wikipedia.org/wiki/Social_gadfly (accessed July 14, 2012).
3. For his marriage to Charlotte Young, see the *New York Times* (hereafter *NYT*), April 19, 1964; for changes at the *NYT*, see HES, *A Time of Change: A Reporter's Tale of Our Time* (New York: Harper & Row, 1988), 98–99; as for his advice, see HES, memorandum for Catledge, October 10, 1968, box 571, HES Papers, CU.
4. HES, *Time of Change*, 316. Actually, Bayard Swope of the *New York Evening World* started the first modern op-ed (opposite the editorial page) in 1921. HES was referring to an opinion-editorial as a first in the *NYT*, or what he would call an "alternate opinion" to the one expressed in the *Times*. See "Op-ed," *Wikipedia*, http://en.wikipedia.org/wiki/op-ed (accessed July 14, 2012).
5. HES, *Time of Change*, quote on 316–17, and see 318–19.
6. HES, "Memorandum for the Files," March 25, 1970, box 144, HES Papers, CU.
7. HES, *Time of Change*, 316.
8. HES with David Schneiderman, ed., *The Indignant Years: Art and Articles from* The New York Times *Op-Ed Page* (New York: Crown / Arno Press, 1973), 5.
9. Ibid., 6; and see HES, "Introduction Part II: 'Face to Face,'" box 143, HES Papers, CU.
10. HES, "China and the World Crisis," box 534, HES Papers, CU.
11. HES, "Image and Reality in Indochina," *Foreign Affairs* 49, no. 3 (April 1971): 383–94, quotes on 386, 387.

12. Ibid., 387–88.
13. Ibid., 387–90, quote on 389.
14. Ibid., 392–94, quotes on 391, 392, 394.
15. HES, "America and the Triple Revolution," box 535, HES Papers, CU.
16. HES, "Failure of the Press," *Penthouse*, June 1974, 43, quote on 44.
17. Ibid., quotes on 104, 106, 107.
18. HES, "American Society after 20 Years of Radical Change," box 469, HES Papers, CU.
19. Ibid.
20. HES, "The Russia Nobody Knows," *Penthouse*, July 1983, 104.
21. Ibid., quotes on 104, 175.
22. Harrison E. Salisbury, *Without Fear or Favor:* The New York Times *and Its Times* (New York: Ballantine, 1980), 463.
23. William F. Buckley Jr., "Firing Line Special Edition: Harvest of Despair," *Firing Line*, September 4, 1986.
24. HES, "Roll Over Lenin . . . Tell Gorbachev the News," *Penthouse*, December 1990, 59.
25. Ibid., 59, 60.
26. Ibid., 60, 64.
27. Ibid., 168; also see HES, "Trip to Moscow," May 11, 1990, box 627, HES Papers, CU, where he quotes his friend the poet Andrei Voznesensky as saying, "Everything was flying apart."
28. HES, "America and Russia: Peace and Troubles," November 12, 1990, box 305, HES Papers, CU.
29. HES, "China Reporting: Red Star to Long March—Romance vs. Reality," March 1990, box 212, HES Papers, CU.
30. "Tiananmen Diary: Thirteen Days in June," *Booknotes*, October 15, 1989, video and transcript available at http://booknotes.org/Watch/9545-1/Harrison+Salisbury.aspx (accessed July 14, 2012).
31. Ibid.
32. HES, *Heroes of My Time* (New York: Walker and Company, 1993), ix.
33. Ibid., viii, x.
34. Ibid., 88, 92.
35. Ibid., 88, 92, quotes on 36, 42.
36. "A World Split Apart," http://www.columbia.edu/cu/augustine/arch/solzhenitsyn/harvard1978.html, (accessed July 14, 2012).
37. HES, "6/10/78 Solzhenitsyn," box 240, HES Papers, CU.
38. Ibid.
39. Israel Shanker, "Solzhenitsyn, in Harvard Speech, Terms West Weak and Cowardly," *NYT*, June 9, 1978.
40. HES, "6/10/78 Solzhenitsyn," box 240, HES Papers, CU.
41. Ibid.
42. HES, *Heroes of My Time*, 45–46.
43. Ibid., 49, 53.
44. Ibid., 100.
45. Ibid., 158, 162, quotes on 137, 157.
46. Ibid., 57–60, quote on 56.
47. Ibid., 25–27.
48. Ibid., 82.
49. Ibid., 115.
50. Ibid., 176–80, quotes on 175, 178, 180.
51. Ibid., 198, quote on 201.
52. Ibid., 3.
53. Ibid., 69.
54. Ibid., 21.
55. Ibid., 105.
56. Ibid., 132.
57. Ibid., 184.

58. HES, *Time of Change*, 330.

59. Ibid., 334–42, quotes on 334, 342.

60. Telephone conversation with Harrison's stepson Curtis Rand, August 31, 2010; American Academy of Arts and Letters, Tributes, Rome Dedication, November 4, 1993, box 648, HES Papers, CU.

CONCLUSION

1. William McGowan, *Gray Lady Down: What the Decline and Fall of the* New York Times *Means for America* (New York: Encounter Books, 2010).

2. Alex S. Jones, *Losing the News: The Future of the News That Feeds Democracy* (Oxford: Oxford University Press, 2009).

3. William Butler Yeats, "The Second Coming," in *The Norton Anthology of English Literature*. 3rd ed. (New York: W. W. Norton & Company, 1975), 2361.

Bibliography

ARCHIVAL SOURCES

Harrison E. Salisbury Papers, Columbia University: 677 ms boxes, 13 ms boxes at Rare Book and Manuscript Library, remainder at ReCAP (Research Collections and Preservation Consortium, Inc., Princeton, New Jersey). A survey of the collection is available at http://findingaids.cul.columbia.edu/ead/nnc-rb/ldpd_5685745/summary#using_collection (accessed July 14, 2012).

Clifton Daniel Papers, New York Public Library.

Pulitzer Prize Papers (private collection), Columbia University.

Ross Terrill, Diary, April 26, 1974, November 14, 1989, July 6, 1993.

Public Papers of the Presidents, *Lyndon Baines Johnson, 1966* (Washington, DC: U.S. Government Printing Office, 1967).

INTERVIEWS

Charlotte Y. Salisbury, May 29, 2008.

Curtis Rand, telephone interview, August 31, 2010.

Ross Terrill, telephone interview, October 27, 2010.

Jean Halberstam, December 2, 2011.

NEWSPAPERS

London Times
Washington Post
New York Times
Saint Louis Post-Dispatch

Note: Two digital newspaper sources failed to reveal anything else on Harrison Salisbury: Readex's *American Newspaper Archives* and *America's Historical Newspapers*, and the Library of Congress's *Chronicling America*.

ANNUALS

North High, *The Polaris*, 1924.
University of Minnesota, *The Gopher Yearbook*, 1927, 1928.
Note: Both can be accessed through http://www.ancestry.com.

SELECTED BOOKS BY HARRISON SALISBURY

Russia on the Way. New York: Macmillan, 1946.
American in Russia. New York: Harper, 1955.
Stalin's Russia and After. London: Macmillan, 1955.
The Shook-Up Generation. New York: Harper, 1958.
To Moscow and Beyond: A Reporter's Narrative. New York: Harper, 1960.
Moscow Journal: The End of Stalin. Chicago: University of Chicago Press, 1961.
A New Russia? New York: Harper & Row, 1962.
The Northern Palmyra Affair. New York: Harper, 1962.
The Key to Moscow. Philadelphia: Lippincott, 1963.
Russia: An Introduction to Russia, from Czars to Commissars, with Emphasis on the Factors That Suggest the Future. New York: Athenaeum, 1965.
Anatomy of the Soviet Union. London: Nelson, 1967.
Behind the Lines: Hanoi, December 23, 1966–January 7, 1967. New York: Harper & Row, 1967.
Children of Russia. London: Oak Tree Press, 1967.
Orbit of China. New York: Harper & Row, 1967.
Editor. *The Soviet Union: The Fifty Years*. New York: Harcourt, Brace & World, 1967.
The 900 Days: The Siege of Leningrad. New York: Harper & Row, 1969.
The Coming War between Russia and China. New York: Norton, 1969.
The Many Americas Shall Be One. New York: W. W. Norton, 1971.
Editor. *The Eloquence of Protest: Voices of the 70's*. Boston: Houghton Mifflin, 1972.
Editor, with David Schneiderman. *The Indignant Years: Art and Articles from* The New York Times *Op-Ed Page*. New York: Crown / Arno Press, 1973.
To Peking and Beyond: A Report on the New Asia. New York: Capricorn Books, 1973.
The Gates of Hell. New York: Random House, 1975.
Travels around America. New York: Walker, 1976.
Black Night, White Snow: Russia's Revolutions, 1905–1917. Garden City, NJ: Doubleday and Company, 1977.
Russia in Revolution, 1900–1930. New York: Holt, Rinehart & Winston, 1978.
The Unknown War. New York: Bantam Books, 1978.
Advisory editor. *Soviet Society since the Revolution*. New York: Arno Press, 1979.
Without Fear or Favor: The New York Times *and Its Times*. New York: Ballantine, 1980.
China: 100 Years of Revolution. New York: Holt, Rinehart & Winston, 1983.
A Journey for Our Times: A Memoir. New York: Harper & Row, 1983.
The Book Enchained. Washington, DC: Library of Congress, 1984.
Editor. *Vietnam Reconsidered: Lessons from a War*. New York: Harper & Row, 1984.
The Long March: The Untold Story. New York: Harper & Row, 1985.
A Time of Change: A Reporter's Tale of Our Time. New York: Harper & Row, 1988.
The Great Black Dragon Fire: A Chinese Inferno. Boston: Little, Brown, 1989.

Tiananmen Diary: Thirteen Days in June. Boston: Little, Brown, 1989.
The New Emperors: China in the Era of Mao and Deng. Boston: Little, Brown, 1992.
Heroes of My Time. New York: Walker, 1993.

SELECTED ARTICLES BY HARRISON SALISBURY

"The Failure of the Press." *Penthouse*, June 1974, 42–44, 102–7.
"The Gentlemen Killers of the CIA." *Penthouse*, May 1975, 46–53, 144–56.
"The Russia Nobody Knows." *Penthouse*, July 1983, 104–5, 175.
"Roll Over Lenin . . . Tell Gorbachev the News." *Penthouse*, December 1990, 58–66, 168.

SELECTED WORKS CONTRIBUTED TO BY HARRISON SALISBURY

The Eighth Day of the Week by Marek Hlasko. Translated by Norbert Guterman. Introduction by Harrison E. Salisbury. New York: Dutton, 1958.
Chekhov, Stendhal, and other Essays. Selected and with an introduction by Harrison E. Salisbury. Translated by Anna Bostock, Yvonne Kapp, and Tatiana Shebunina. New York: Alfred A. Knopf, 1963.
Black Man in Red Russia: A Memoir. Introduction by Harrison Salisbury. Chicago: Johnson Publishing, 1964.
Moscow by William Klein. Preface by Harrison E. Salisbury. New York: Crown, 1964.
Report of the Warren Commission on the Assassination of President Kennedy. Introduction by Harrison E. Salisbury. With additional material prepared by the *New York Times*. New York: McGraw-Hill, 1964.
Leningrad 1941: The Blockade by Dmitri V. Pavlov. Translated by John Clinton Adams. Foreword by Harrison E. Salisbury. Chicago: University of Chicago Press, 1965.
Progress, Coexistence, and Intellectual Freedom by Andrei D. Sakharov. Translated by the *New York Times*. Introduction, afterword, and notes by Harrison E. Salisbury. New York: W. W. Norton, 1968.
Bleeding Earth: A Doctor Looks at Vietnam by Alistair Brass. Foreword by Harrison E. Salisbury. Sydney: Alpha Books, 1969.
Marshal Zhukov's Greatest Battles by Georgii K. Zhukov. Edited and with an introduction and explanatory notes by Harrison E. Salisbury. Translated by Theodore Shabad. New York: Harper & Row, 1969.
Assassination and Political Violence: A Report to the National Commission on the Causes and Prevention of Violence by James F. Kirkham, Sheldon G. Levy, and William J. Crotty. Introduction by Harrison E. Salisbury. Washington, DC: U.S. Government Printing Office, 1970.
Mountaintop Kingdom: Sikkim by Charlotte Y. Salisbury. Photography by Alice S. Kandell. Introduction by Harrison E. Salisbury. New York: W. W. Norton, 1971.
Russia: The Post-war Years by Alexander Werth. Epilogue by Harrison E. Salisbury. London: Hale, 1971.
Siege and Survival: The Odyssey of a Leningrader by Elena Skrjabina. Foreword by Harrison E. Salisbury. Translated, edited, and with an afterword by Norman Luxemburg. Carbondale: Southern Illinois University Press, 1971.
Solzhenitsyn: A Documentary Record. Edited and with an introduction by Leopold Labedz. Foreword by Harrison E. Salisbury. New York: Harper & Row, 1971.
Red Square at Noon by Natalia Gorbanevskaya. Translated by Alexander Lieven. Introduction by Harrison E. Salisbury. New York: Holt, Rinehart & Winston, 1972.

Face to Face: A Collection of Drawings & Political Cartoons by Fons Van Woerkom. Introduction by Harrison E. Salisbury. New York: Alfred A. Knopf, 1973.

Sakharov Speaks by Andrei D. Sakharov. Edited and with a foreword by Harrison E. Salisbury. New York: Alfred A. Knopf, 1974.

The Silver Dove by Andrey Biely [B. N. Bugaev]. Translated and with an introduction by George Reavey. Preface by Harrison E. Salisbury. New York: Grove Press, 1974.

The Russian War, 1941–1945 edited by Daniela Mrázková and Vladimír Remeš. Preface and notes by A. J. P. Taylor. Introduction by Harrison Salisbury. New York: Dutton, 1975.

The World Today edited by Phineas J. Sparer. Memphis: Memphis State University Press, 1975.

Mischling, Second Degree: My Childhood in Nazi Germany by Ilse Koehn. Foreword by Harrison E. Salisbury. New York: Greenwillow Books, 1977.

Imperial China: Photographs, 1850–1912 by Clark Worswick and Jonathan Spence. Foreword by Harrison Salisbury. New York: Pennwick Publishing, 1978.

I Don't Want to Be Brave Anymore by Ruth Turkow Kaminska. Introduction by Harrison E. Salisbury. Washington, DC: New Republic Books, 1978.

The Coming Decline of the Chinese Empire by Victor Louis. Introduction by Harrison E. Salisbury. New York: Times Books, 1979.

Inside Red China by Helen Foster Snow [Nym Wales]. Introduction by Harrison Salisbury. New York: Da Capo Press, 1979.

The October Revolution by Roy A. Medvedev. Translated by George Saunders. Foreword by Harrison E. Salisbury. New York: Columbia University Press, 1979.

The Allies on the Rhine, 1945–1950 by Elena Skrjabina. Translated, edited, and with a preface by Norman Luxenburg. Foreword by Harrison E. Salisbury. Carbondale: Southern Illinois University Press; London: Feffer & Simons, 1980.

The Kennedys: A New York Times *Profile* edited by Gene Brown. Introduction by Harrison E. Salisbury. New York: Arno Press, 1980.

The Russians by Nathan Farb. Foreword by Harrison E. Salisbury. Woodbury, NY: Barron's, 1980.

The Superstar Show of Government by Roger-Gérard Schwartzenberg. Translated by Joseph A. Harriss. Foreword by Harrison Salisbury. Woodbury, NY: Barron's, 1980.

Thunder out of China by Theodore H. White and Annalee Jacoby. Foreword by Harrison Salisbury. New York: Da Capo Press, 1980.

At the Barricades: Forty Years on the Cutting Edge of History by Wilfred Burchett. Introduction by Harrison E. Salisbury. New York: Times Books, 1981.

Tibet by Ngapo Ngawang Jigmei et al. Preface by Harrison Salisbury. New York: McGraw-Hill, 1981.

The Bells of the Kremlin: An Experience in Communism by Arvo Tuominen. Edited by Piltti Heiskanen. Translated by Lily Leino. Introduction by Harrison E. Salisbury. Hanover, NH: University Press of New England, 1983.

Cold War, Cold Peace: The United States and Russia since 1945 by Bernard A. Weisberger. Introduction by Harrison E. Salisbury. New York: American Heritage, 1984.

Return to a Chinese Village by Jan Myrdal. Translated by Alan Bernstein. Photographs by Gun Kessle. Foreword by Harrison E. Salisbury. New York: Pantheon Books, 1984.

Coming of Age in the Russian Revolution: The Soviet Union at War by Elena Skrjabina. Volume 4. Translated, edited, and with an introduction by Norman Luxenburg. Foreword by Harrison E. Salisbury. New Brunswick, NJ: Transaction Books, 1985.

Almost at the End by Yevgeny Yevtushenko. Translated by Antonina W. Bouis, Albert C. Todd, and Yevgeny Yevtushenko. Foreword by Harrison E. Salisbury. New York: Henry Holt, 1987.

Iphigene: My Life and The New York Times; *the Memoirs of Iphigene Ochs Sulzberger* by Susan W. Dryfoos. Foreword by Barbara W. Tuchman. Introduction by Harrison E. Salisbury. New York: Times Books, 1987.

Russia at War, 1941–45 by Vladimir Karpov. Translated by Lydia Kmetyuk. Edited by Carey Schofield. With text by Georgii Drozdov and Evgenii Ryabko. Preface by Harrison E. Salisbury. New York: Vendome Press, 1987.

Memoirs of Anastas Mikoyan. Translated by Katherine T. O'Connor and Diane L. Burgin. Edited by Sergo Mikoyan. Foreword by W. Averell Harriman. Preface and notes by Harrison E. Salisbury. Madison, CT: Sphinx Press, 1988.

Over China by Kevin Sinclair. Photographs by Dan Budnik et al. Foreword by Harrison Salisbury. Los Angeles: Knapp Press, 1988.

Connecticut by Roger Eddy. Photography by William Hubbell. Foreword by Harrison E. Salisbury. Portland: Graphic Arts Center, 1989.

World War II: A 50th Anniversary History by the writers and photographers of the Associated Press. Foreword by Harrison Salisbury. New York: Holt, 1989.

China: From the Long March to Tiananmen Square by the writers and photographers of the Associated Press. Foreword by Harrison Salisbury. New York: Holt, 1990.

China Journal, 1889–1900: An American Missionary Family during the Boxer Rebellion. Notes by Robert H. Felsing. Foreword by Harrison E. Salisbury. New York: Collier Books, 1990.

Coming Home Crazy: An Alphabet of China Essays by Bill Holm. Introduction by Harrison E. Salisbury. Minneapolis: Milkweed Editions, 1990.

This Is War: A Photo-narrative of the Korean War by David Douglas Duncan. Foreword by Harrison E. Salisbury. Boston: Little, Brown, 1990.

Essential Liberty: First Amendment Battles for a Free Press. Essays by Francis Wilkinson. Preface by Joan Konner. Introduction by Harrison E. Salisbury. Afterword by Floyd Abrams. New York: Columbia University Graduate School of Journalism, 1992.

Forward Positions: The War Correspondence of Homer Bigart. Compiled and edited by Betsy Wade. Foreword by Harrison E. Salisbury: Fayetteville: University of Arkansas Press, 1992.

Shurik: A Story of the Siege of Leningrad by Kyra Petrovskaya Wayne. Introduction by Harrison E. Salisbury. New York: Lyons & Burford, 1992.

Fifty Russian Winters: An American Woman's Life in the Soviet Union by Margaret Wettlin. Introduction by Harrison Salisbury. New York: John Wiley & Sons, 1994.

OTHER BOOKS

Alliluyeva, Svetlana. *Twenty Letters to a Friend.* New York: Harper & Row, 1967.

Bassow, Whitman. *The Moscow Correspondents: Reporting on Russia from the Revolution to Glasnost.* New York: Paragon House, 1989.

Brinkley, Allen. *The Publisher: Henry Luce and His American Century.* New York: Vintage, 2011.

Carlisle, Olga. *Solzhenitsyn and the Secret Circle.* London: Routledge & Kegan Paul, 1978.

Catledge, Turner. *My Life and* The Times. New York: Harper & Row, 1971.

Clark, Joseph. *The Real Russia: A Former Moscow Correspondent, Who Saw Harrison Salisbury See Russia, Tells Why the* New York Times *Correspondent Forgot His Own Eyewitness Reports from the U.S.S.R.* New York: New Century Publishers, 1954.

Cronkite, Walter. *A Reporter's Life.* New York: Ballantine, 1996.

Davies, John Paton, Jr. *China Hand: An Autobiography.* Philadelphia: University of Pennsylvania Press, 2012.

Davis, Donald E., and Eugene P. Trani. *Distorted Mirrors: Americans and Their Relations with Russia and China in the Twentieth Century.* Columbia: University of Missouri Press, 2009.

Dean, John. *The Strange Alliance: The Story of Our Efforts at Wartime Cooperation with Russia.* New York: Viking, 1947.

Diamond, Edwin. *Behind the Times: Inside the New* New York Times. Chicago: University of Chicago Press, 1995.

Frankel, Max. *The Times of My Life and My Life with* The Times. New York: Random House, 1999.

Gaddis, John Lewis. *George F. Kennan: An American Life.* New York: Penguin, 2011.

Gerassi, John. *North Vietnam: A Documentary.* Indianapolis: Bobbs-Merrill, 1968.

Goulden, Joseph C. *Fit to Print: A.M. Rosenthal and His* Times. Secaucus, NJ: Lyle Stuart, 1988.

Goulding, Phil G. *Confirm or Deny: Informing the People on National Security.* New York: Harper & Row, 1970.

Grant, Zalin. *Over the Beach: The Air War in Vietnam.* New York: W. W. Norton & Company, 1986.

Green, Felix. *Awakened China: The Country Americans Don't Know.* Westport, CT: Greenwood Press, 1973.

Halberstam, David. *The Best and the Brightest.* New York: Ballantine, 1992.

———. *The Next Century.* New York: William Morrow and Company, 1991.

———. *The Powers That Be.* New York: Alfred A. Knopf, 1975.

Harriman, W. Averell, and Elie Abel. *Special Envoy to Churchill and Stalin, 1941 to 1946.* New York: Random House, 1975.

Harrison E. Salisbury's Trip to North Vietnam. Hearing, Ninetieth Congress, First Session, with Harrison E. Salisbury, Assistant Managing Editor of the New York Times. February 2, 1967. Washington, DC: U.S. Government Printing Office, 1967.

Herring, George C., ed. *The Secret Diplomacy of the Vietnam War: The Negotiating Volumes of the Pentagon Papers.* Austin: University of Texas Press, 1983.

Hershberg, James G. *Marigold: The Lost Chance for Peace in Vietnam.* Stanford: Stanford University Press, 2012.

Hohenberg, John. *The Pulitzer Prizes: A History of the Awards in Books, Drama, Music, and Journalism, Based on the Private Files over Six Decades.* New York: Columbia University Press, 1974.

Johnson, Lyndon B. *The Vantage Point: Perspectives of the Presidency, 1963–1969.* New York: Holt, Rinehart & Winston, 1971.

Jones, Alex S. *Losing the News: The Future of the News That Feeds Democracy.* Oxford: Oxford University Press, 2009.

Karnow, Stanley. *Vietnam: A History.* New York: Penguin, 1983.

Kennan, George F. *Memoirs, 1950–1963.* New York: Pantheon, 1972.

Kennedy, David M. *Freedom from Fear: The American People in Depression and War, 1929–1945.* New York: Oxford University Press, 1999.

Khrushchev, Nikita. *Khrushchev Remembers.* Boston: Little, Brown, 1970.

Krock, Arthur. *Memoirs: Sixty Years on the Firing Line.* New York: Funk & Wagnalls, 1968.

Maisky, Ivan. *Memoirs of a Soviet Ambassador: The War, 1939–1943.* New York: Charles Scribner's Sons, 1968.

McGowan, William. *Gray Lady Down: What the Decline and Fall of the* New York Times *Means for America.* New York: Encounter Books, 2010.

Mead, Walter Russell. *Special Providence: American Foreign Policy and How It Changed the World.* New York: Rutledge, 2002.

Montefiore, Simon Sebag. *Stalin: The Court of the Red Tsar.* New York: Alfred A. Knopf, 2003.

Olson, Lynne. *Citizens of London: The Americans Who Stood by Britain in Its Darkest, Finest Hour.* New York: Random House, 2010.

Reston, James. *Deadline: A Memoir.* New York: Times Books, 1991.

Salisbury, Charlotte Y. *Long March Diary: China Epic.* New York: Walker and Company, 1986.

Sheehan, Neil, ed. *The Pentagon Papers.* New York: Bantam Books, 1971.

Shepard, Richard, F. *The Paper's Papers: A Reporter's Journey through the Archives of* The New York Times. New York: Times Books, 1996.

Snow, Edgar. *The Other Side of the River: Red China Today.* New York: Random House, 1961.

Solzhenitsyn, Alexander. *The Oak and the Calf: Sketches on Literary Life in the Soviet Union.* New York: Harper & Row, 1975.

Talese, Gay. *The Kingdom and the Power.* New York: World Publishing, 1969.

Thomas, D. M. *Alexander Solzhenitsyn: A Century in His Life.* New York: St. Martin Press, 1998.

Tifft, Susan E., and Alex S. Jones. *The Trust: The Private and Powerful Family Behind* The New York Times. Boston: Little, Brown, 1999.

Topping, Seymour. *On the Front Lines of the Cold War: An American Correspondent's Journal from the Chinese Civil War to the Cuban Missile Crisis and Vietnam.* Baton Rouge: Louisiana State University Press, 2010.

Tuchman, Barbara. *The March of Folly.* New York: Ballantine, 1984.

White, Theodore. *Thunder Out of China.* New York: William Sloane Associates, 1946.

Williams, T. Harry. *Huey Long.* New York: Alfred A. Knopf, 1969.

SELECTED ARTICLES

Alsop, Joseph. "Matter of Fact: Hanoi's Propaganda Offensive." *Washington Post*, January 9, 1967.

Atwood Lawrence, Mark. "Mission Intolerable: Harrison Salisbury's Trip to Hanoi and the Limits of Dissent against the Vietnam War." *Pacific Historical Review* 75, no. 3 (August 2006): 429–60.

Averill, Steven C. "The Long March." *Journal of Asian Studies* 46, no. 1 (February 1987): 118–21.

Baldwin, Hanson W. "Bombing of the North—U.S. Officers Assert It Has Proved Effective, Restrained and Essential." *New York Times*, December 30, 1966.

Barrymaine, Norman. "Memo from Haiphong, North Vietnam: Under American Bombs." *Look*, November 29, 1966, 62.

Chamberlain, John. "Control of Red Propaganda Urged." *Washington Post*, January 9, 1967.

Conquest, Robert. "*Black Night, White Snow.*" *New York Times*, January 29, 1978.

Editorial. *New York Times*, January 2, 1967.

Fathers, Michael. "China Whisperers." *Independent*, August 23, 1992.

Ferguson, R. James. "The Dangers of Dramatic Biography." *Culture Mandala* 1, no. 1 (1994): 69–73.

"Hanoi Dispatches to the *Times* Criticized." *New York Times*, January 1, 1967.

Kraft, Joseph. "The Salisbury Affair." *Washington Post*, January 9, 1967.

Lippmann, Walter. "Harrison Salisbury in Hanoi." *Washington Post*, January 10, 1967.

"Literary Supplement." *London Times*, 1966.

Lockwood, Lee. "Salisbury's Stake." *New York Review of Books*, August 3, 1967.

Long, Gerald (Reuters). "Chou, in Interview, Scores U.S. On 'Aggression Toward China': Premier Says Threats Prevent Ties—Affirms Desire for India Accord and Calls Economy Improved." *New York Times*, October 14, 1963.

Oakes, John B. "Harrison E. Salisbury (13 November 1908–5 July 1993)." *Proceedings of the American Philosophical Society* 139, no. 2 (1995): 193–95.

Pace, Eric. "Harrison E. Salisbury, 84, Author and Reporter, Dies." *New York Times*, July 7, 1993.

Pomfret, John. "Two Men, One Dynasty." *Far Eastern Economic Review*, October 8, 1992, 40.

"Remembering Harrison." Pieces by David Halberstam, Clifton Daniel, Thomas Whitney, Gloria Emerson, Arthur Miller, Roger Wilkins, Vladimir Pozner, Betsy Ward (quoting Solzhenitsyn), and David Schneiderman. *Nieman Reports*, fall 1993, 4–12.

Sheehan, Neil. "Raids' Precision Seen in Reports." *New York Times*, December 30, 1966.

Snow, Edgar (*Le Nouveau Candide*). "China Rejects 'Two China's.'" *New York Times*, February 3, 1964.

Stevenson-Yang, Anne. "The New Emperors." *China Business Review* (May–June 1992): 40.

Stone, I. F. "Harrison Salisbury's Dastardly War Crime." *I.F. Stone Weekly* 15, no. 1 (January 9, 1967): 1, 4.

Taylor, A. J. P. "The Hero City." *New York Review of Books*, April 10, 1969.

Teiwes, Frederick C. "The New Emperors." *China Quarterly*, no. 137 (March 1994): 248–50.

"Washington Wire." *Wall Street Journal*, January 6, 1967.

Index

in death of, 41, 43

Malik, Andrei, 58, 60

Mao Zedong: Bolsheviks, pushed aside by, 198; Cultural Revolution, 161, 171, 177, 178, 197, 201, 217; death, 207; Deng Xiaoping and, 201; domestic revisionism, fear of, 168; Gang of Four, 206; Great Leap Forward, 204, 205; Great Wuhan Bridge, 224; as ignorant and cruel, 209; independence from Russia, 49; Lin Biao, attempted coup, 161, 174, 207; Long March and, 173, 177, 183, 197–201, 202, 225; May Seventh schools, founding, 172; as new Genghis Khan, 170; 1949 success, 215–216; on nuclear war, 164; Red Guards, support for, 171–172, 206, 230; Russia showing little interest in, 30; Salisbury criticism of last years, 161; Sino-Soviet treaty negotiations, 47; Edgar Snow and, 199, 206; Soong Chingling and, 230; Joseph Stalin and, 46–47, 163, 175–176, 203–204, 216; Anna Louise Strong and, 162, 167; Zhou Enlai and, 172, 177, 199, 203, 204–205, 207, 230; Zhu-Mao base, 198

Marigold, secret negotiation, 140, 145, 147, 154

Markel, Lester, 32, 50, 51, 163, 215

Matthews, Herbert, 116, 126, 155

McCarthy, Joseph, 84, 137, 170, 175, 176

McCloskey, John J., 146

McNamara, Robert S., 111, 112, 125, 127–128, 133, 142, 144, 145, 148

Middleton, Drew, 32, 37, 42, 52, 80, 136

Mikoyan, Anastas, 43, 46, 48, 66, 70, 71, 73, 75, 88, 163

Miller, Arthur, 3, 4, 227

Mindszenty, Joseph, 94

Ministry of Internal Affairs (MVD), 44, 45, 46, 49, 63, 67, 70, 71–72, 73, 76–77

Minneapolis Journal, 7, 8, 11

Mitchell, John N., 113

Molotov, Vyacheslav: Vasily Bluecher rehabilitation, against, 87; Committee of State Defense membership, 187; Doctor's Plot affecting, 71; junta membership, 73, 74; Leningrad, defense of, 190; loss of power, 43, 85;

Georgii Malenkov rivalry, 49, 54; Mao Zedong, treaty discussions with, 46, 47; Nazi attacks and, 185, 186; Stanislaus Orlemanski and, 27; political slights, 43, 64, 66, 70; Poltava bombing mission, 27; Joseph Stalin and, 29, 31, 48, 65; Timoshenko scandal, 23, 24, 25, 26; Yugoslavia and, 101

Molotova, Polina, 43, 44, 66, 75, 76

Morrison, Anne and Norman, 126

Morse, Wayne, 153–154, 157

Munnich, Ferenc, 94, 99

Myrdal, Jan, 169, 173

Namdinh: American communiqués, 132, 138, 156; announcement of raids, 140, 151; bombing attacks, 131, 134, 141; civilian casualties, 116, 130, 144, 151; criticism of dispatches, 132, 134, 135, 144; lack of military targets, 130, 132, 134, 149, 150, 151; *Report on U.S. War Crimes in Nam-Dinh City*, 132, 134, 144; Senate Committee on Foreign Relations testimony, 150, 153; as textile center, 131, 156

National Liberation Front (NLF), 125, 139, 140, 142, 145, 154, 255n59

Nenni, Pietro, 64, 246n109

The New Class: An Analysis of the Communist System (Djilas), 83, 86, 87, 88

Newman, Edwin, 129

Ngo Dinh Diem, 125

Nguyen Van Tien, 139, 140, 142

Niemöller, Martin, 139, 141

Nixon, Richard: China and, 161, 169, 170, 174, 176, 177, 204, 207; condolences for Salisbury, 2; cynicism in America, as cause of, 218; Hu Yaobang, friendship with, 224; Tricia Nixon's wedding day, 111, 112; Pentagon Papers, 113, 115; Watergate, 115–116

Nosenko, Yuri, 46

Oakes, John B., 2–3, 118, 126, 214, 215

Orlemanski, Stanislaus, 26–27, 242n44

Oswald, Lee Harvey, 109–110

Pace, Eric, 2

About the Authors

Donald E. Davis is professor emeritus of history at Illinois State University and editor of *No East or West: The Memoirs of Paul B. Anderson*. He served as professor of Russian history at Illinois State University from 1964 to 2004 and has authored numerous articles, reviews, papers and opinion pieces.

Eugene P. Trani is president emeritus and university distinguished professor at Virginia Commonwealth University. He has authored, coauthored, annotated, and edited eight books and published more than one hundred articles and opinion pieces. An historian of American diplomatic history, Trani is the author of *The Presidency of Warren G. Harding*. He has also written on the role universities play as key drivers of economic development in their communities.

Friends from graduate school at Indiana University, Bloomington, Davis and Trani have coauthored three books: *The First Cold War: The Legacy of Woodrow Wilson in U.S.-Soviet Relations* (University of Missouri Press), published first in English, then translated and published in Russian and Chinese; *Distorted Mirrors: Americans and Their Relations with Russia and China in the Twentieth-Century* (University of Missouri Press), also published in Russian and Spanish; and now this significant contribution to the understanding of a major figure in the history of journalism, Harrison E. Salisbury.